Human Rights Constitutionalism in Japan and Asia

The Writings of Lawrence W. Beer

Lawrence Ward Beer was born in Portland, Oregon on May 11, 1932. In 1966 he received the Ph.D. degree from the University of Washington, Seattle. In over fifty years of studying the constitutional law and politics of Japan and other Asian countries, he has written and lectured extensively on human rights law (e.g., *Freedom of Expression in Japan*, 1984). He taught at the University of Colorado, Boulder, 1966–1982, and was F.M. Kirby Professor of Civil Rights, Lafayette College, 1982–1997.

Lawrence W. Beer has chaired the Committee on Asian Law of the Association for Asian Studies and the World Association of Law Professors of the World Peace through Law Center. He received the Distinguished Asianist Award of the Mid-Atlantic Association for Asian Studies in 2003.

In retirement, he lives with his wife Keiko in Boulder, Colorado, USA.

⌘

Less noticed in the West than wars, terrorism and economic trends has been the historic development since World War II of constitutional government and law in Asia. Lawrence W. Beer has been a close observer of Asian linkages among law, politics, culture, and national security issues for over fifty years. His perspectives have been refined during long residence in Asia, especially Japan, by substantial friendly interactions with Asian legal scholars, judges and attorneys involved in the world of human rights constitutional law.

This volume, which will be widely welcomed by students and researchers, brings together a selection of Lawrence W. Beer's many works previously published in diverse venues, but no longer easily accessible.

The collection opens with a review of constitutionalism in Asia and the United States and concludes with a recent examination of Japan's rejection of war: 'Japan's Constitutional Discourse and Performance'. By way of Afterword, the author offers an in-depth review of 'Globalization of Human Rights in the 21st Century'.

Lawrence W. Beer

THE WRITINGS OF
Volume 1

Human Rights Constitutionalism in Japan and Asia

THE WRITINGS OF LAWRENCE W. BEER

⌘

GLOBAL
ORIENTAL

Series: THE WRITINGS OF

Volume 1
HUMAN RIGHTS CONSTITUTIONALISM IN JAPAN AND ASIA
The Writings of Lawrence W. Beer

First published 2009 by
GLOBAL ORIENTAL LTD
PO Box 219
Folkestone
Kent CT20 2WP
UK

www.globaloriental.co.uk

ISBN 978-1-905246-71-7

British Library Cataloguing in Publication Data
A CIP catalogue entry for this book is available from the British Library

Set in Plantin 10 on 11pt by RefineCatch, Bungay, Suffolk
Printed and bound in England by Antony Rowe Ltd., Chippenham, Wilts

Contents

⌘

Preface

⌘

In the second half of the twentieth century the colonial powers—the United Kingdom, the United States, Holland, Japan, Portugal, and France—yielded to Asian demands for independence and went home. Each Asian country, drawing on indigenous and Western sources, adopted a single-document national constitution with some provision for human rights. This book brings together a selection from many writings on human rights constitutionalism in Asia published over the past fifty years but not now easily accessible to students of Asia.

During long residence in Asia, especially Japan, I have learned much from indigenous constitutional lawyers while introducing the non-Asian world to the legal, political and cultural dimensions of human rights in Asia. A byproduct of this work has been to join in the dialog among Asian scholars unfamiliar with each other's constitutional systems. The geographical, legal, and cultural distances between Asian countries, for example, between Pakistan and Korea, are formidable.

The occasion for producing the first of two panoramic books on constitutionalism in Asia was the 1976 bicentennial of the United States Declaration of Independence. The Committee on Asian Law of the Association for Asian Studies co-sponsored with many public agencies and private organizations a month-long program of presentations by some of Asia's most distinguished jurists. As they traveled the country, they shared their perspectives on the American influence, if any, on constitutionalism in their respective countries. This resulted in *Constitutionalism in Asia: Asian Views of the American Influence* (University of California Press, 1979); this and a subsequent second edition are out of print. Years later, as the bicentennials of the Constitution of the United States of America (1987) and the Bill of Rights (1991) approached, professional colleagues, most persistently Professor Albert P. Blaustein, urged on the publication of a second volume, containing thirteen country studies, *Constitutional Systems in Late Twentieth Century Asia* (University of Washington Press, 1992), from which comes the first chapter of the present book.

The other items were chosen for inclusion based on favorable comment by colleagues in the field, earlier republication, or a belief that they lent helpful perspective on the status of human rights constitutional law in the country discussed.

PREFACE

Comparative constitutional studies seem best served by a methodological approach which gives attention to constitutional and statutory texts, policies, judicial decisions, institutions, and elements of legal culture peculiar to the country and issue under study.

This book is suffused with the conviction that a country's performance with respect to constitutionalism is a more valid measure of "advanced" or "high civilization" than its prowess in economic, technological, military or legal terms, because modern barbarism is compatible with all those standards. And among the various alternative foundations for a nation's constitutionalism a preoccupation with defense and promotion of human rights sets the bar highest.

For fifty years of generous sharing of their perspectives on human rights in constitutional law, I should thank many legal scholars, judges and lawyers of Asia, especially Japan. For their support of this republication project, I am most grateful to Arthur Stockwin, Kendall Whitney, Larry Repeta, Hidenori Tomatsu, and Paul Norbury.

Lawrence W. Beer
Boulder, Colorado USA

PART I

ASIA

■ First published in Lawrence W. Beer (ed.), *Constitutional Systems in Late Twentieth Century Asia*, Seattle, University of Washington Press, 1992, pp. 1-52.

1

Constitutionalism in Asia and the United States

⌘

INTRODUCTION

The latter decades of the twentieth century will be remembered, as many times past, for wars, leaders and economic changes, and as no time past, for human entry into space, computers, and genetic codes. It may also be noticed a hundred years hence that this was an era of unprecedented experimentation in forms of government and law under written constitutions, as colonialism ended and each newly independent state sought its constitutional identity while other countries responded to challenge by revising or amending their basic laws. The trend was global, but most dramatic in 1989 and 1990 when Mikhail Gorbachev's government allowed the waves of independence and constitutionalist creativity to sweep through Mongolia, Eastern Europe, and the Soviet Union.

Three phenomena attended these historic decades of frenetic constitution-making activity: (1) a convergence in the world towards relatively few living traditions of modern law, and the beginnings of mutual comprehension among legal scholars and practitioners of these different traditions; (2) the achievement of at least formal global political consensus on the centrality—once national independence and stability are achieved—of human rights to sound and moral government and law (though with differences among nations on which rights to emphasize); and (3) at the deepest level, like the sliding together of suboceanic continental plates, convulsive interactions among profoundly different cultures, all reciprocally accepted for the first time as authentically human by educated international elites. That sometimes contradictory emphases characterize world discourse on human rights is less surprising than the level of mutual comprehension achieved (the basis for all genuine disagreements) across all seas, and the virtually universal compulsion felt by national leaders to act on the world stage as if they were responsive advocates of human rights. While the primordial observer could not see the overlapping plates change the seas and continents, we can view the wrenching clash of cultural forces in wars internal and external, in Asia's trade relations with the West, and in contrasts between religious and sociopolitical systems. But in the late twentieth century it is hard to even imagine where and with what aspect the new peaks of world civilization, law, and constitutional government will arise in the next century.

The difficulty of cross-cultural communication about constitutionalism is daunting, because constitutionalism is where national history, custom, religion, social values and assumptions about government meet positive law, economic force, and power politics, because few authors blend knowledge of such elements to render a country's constitutional life easily comprehensible to the uninitiated foreign reader, and because few legal scholars are committed to such interdisciplinary writing for a foreign audience. This book attempts to further understanding of constitutionalism in many radically diverse Asian nations while taking note of instances where United States constitutional experience has been influential or relevant. Although each writer was asked to explain his country's constitutional structure, principles, and operation in historical and sociopolitical context, care was taken not to impose a foreign analytical approach (such as the editor's) on accomplished Asian scholars, in the belief that such editorial imposition would presumptuously tamper with academic freedom and cross-cultural tolerance. Rather, for most chapters, one or two distinguished indigenous constitutional lawyers were asked to introduce their country's constitutional system as they deemed appropriate, stressing features they considered most important for the foreign reader to understand, and adopting a mode of exposition and analysis preferred in their own tradition of constitutional scholarship. The styles of thought and language in some chapters may be alien to some readers and may test their intellectual tolerance and openness. A number of chapters may administer a jolting legal culture shock, rather than a sense of flowing easily along with other chapters or in the mainstream of some American approach to law and social science writing. Such intellectual discomfiture seems inevitable now in mature dialogue on constitutionalism with colleagues in Asia and other non-Western regions. They have studied us; let us study them. After mutually chastening intercultural exchanges on how best to write about law and constitution for foreigners without culture-specific intolerance, some mix of legal and interdisciplinary discourse may become very widely accepted for comparative constitutional studies (for example, the stress on the "living constitution" suggested later). But that development awaits a later stage in scholarly history. At the bicentennial, this book offers a partial remedy for the widespread Western unfamiliarity with Asia's constitutional systems.

In the late 1980s, the bicentennial of the Constitution of the United States of America, the world's oldest single-document constitution, was an occasion for justifiable celebration of achievement. The bicentennial years commemorated a series of events, from the signing of the Constitution on September 17, 1787 to the ratification of the Bill or Rights on December 15, 1791. Unfortunately, American cups raised in toast of the Constitution and Bill of Rights sometimes ran over with unreflective self-congratulation. The 200-year record of American progress towards compliance with constitutional rights principles has been quite mixed; still, the quest for the dream of equality and freedom under a government of laws and limited power continues, and the republic stands.

The United States is one of the few countries whose basic ideas about government institutions, approach to law, and national experience commonly are taken into account when constitutionalism is debated around the world. Among America's contributions to the discourse of making and interpreting constitutions are the following: a single-document national constitution with a preamble setting forth the basic institutions of government, their interrelationships, and the relations between government and citizenry; a list of constitutional rights to be defended in laws, government administration, and independent courts;[1] the notion of a constitution as "the supreme law of the land"; the institution of a constituent or constitutional assembly representing all the people of a country which has the authority to adopt the nation's basic law; the implementation of the view that the branches of government should be separated so that the power of each is limited and counterbalanced by the power of another; a federalism uniting autonomous democracies in a sovereign union[2] with legislators representing both member states and the union; and finally, the conviction that government should be inspired and constrained "by the people and for the people" in recognition that "all men are created equal" and have inherent inviolable rights as individual humans.

The sheer present power of the United States in the planet's politics, military affairs, economics, and mass media diffusion of facts and views regarding America has drawn disproportionate attention to U.S. constitutionalism, especially since the end of the Second World War in 1945. That admitted, scholars and leaders in some Asian countries have adapted one or more elements of American constitutionalism based on freely conducted study of many alternatives. Other knowledgeable Asians have rejected either some foundation principle of U.S. constitutionalism, or its cultural particularization in American life, or both. This chapter presents a reformulation of some meanings of "constitutionalism," some instances in Asia of American influence on or relevance to local constitutionalism, and some patterns and preferences in Asia revealed by the studies in this book and elsewhere.

Constitutions in Asia

For perspective on the constitutions of the United States, Asia and the world, consider that of 167 single-document constitutions in effect as of 1991, only about twenty dated earlier than 1950 (see Figure 1.1).[3] Very few countries, such as Norway (1814) and Columbia (1886), continue with constitutions of the nineteenth century, and only the U.S. basic law has been in force since the eighteenth century. Most thought-provoking, well over 100 of today's constitutions trace their origins only as far back as 1970. In every continent, constitutional experimentation and change continue, but in pursuit of stable order.

In Asia's constitutional chronology, only four nations have basic laws written as early as the 1940s: Japan, whose 1947 constitution has yet to be amended; the Republic of China, 1947, written for China but only in force on Taiwan and in the process of major change in 1991; Indonesia, 1945, but two other constitutions were in effect between 1949 and 1959; and India, whose constitution has been amended sixty-two times.[4] Other current constitutions were adopted as follows: Afghanistan, 1987; Bangladesh, 1972; Bhutan, 1953; Brunei, 1984; Myanmar (Burma), 1974; Cambodia, 1989; China (PRC), 1982; Laos, 1975; Malaysia, 1963; Mongolia, 1960; Nepal, 1990; North Korea, 1972; Pakistan, 1973; Papua-New Guinea, 1975; the Philippines, 1987; Singapore, 1963; South Korea, 1987; Sri Lanka (Ceylon), 1978; Thailand, 1991; and Vietnam, 1980.

1788 U.S.A.
1814 Norway
1831 Belgium
1853 Argentina
1868 Luxembourg
1874 Switzerland
1901 Australia
1917 Mexico
1919 Finland
1920 Austria
1921 Liechtenstein
1937 Ireland
1944 Iceland
1945 Indonesia
1947 China (Rep.)
Italy
Japan
1949 Costa Rica
Germany
India
1952 Jordan
Poland
1953 Bhutan
Denmark
1958 France
1960 Côte d'Ivoire
Cyprus
Czechoslovakia
Mongolia
West Samoa
1961 Malta
Venezuela
1962 El Salvador
Jamaica
Kuwait
Monaco
1963 Malaysia
Senegal
Singapore
1966 Barbados
Botswana
Dominican Rep.
Malawi
1967 Bolivia
Paraguay
Tonga
Uganda
Uruguay
1968 Maldives
Mauritius
Nauru
1969 Kenya
1970 Gambia
Iraq
Qatar
1971 Bulgaria
Egypt
U.A.E.
1972 Bangladesh
Cameroon
Hungary
Korea (PDR)
Morocco
1973 Bahamas
Bahrain
Pakistan
Swaziland
Syria
Zambia
1974 Grenada
Mali
Myanmar
Niger
Romania
Turkey
Yugoslavia
1975 Gabon
Greece
Laos
Madagascar
Mozambique
Papua New Guinea
Sweden
1976 Albania
Cuba
Dem. Kampuchea
Trinidad & Tobago
1977 Djibouti
U.S.S.R.
1978 Comores
Dominica
Mauritania
Panama
Rwanda
Sierra Leone
Solomon Islands
Spain
Sri Lanka
Zaire
1979 Congo
Ecuador
Iran
Kiribati
Nigeria
Peru
St. Lucia
St. Vincent
Seychelles
Somalia
Togo
Zimbabwe
1980 Angola
Chile
Guyana
Vanuatu
Vietnam
1981 Antigua & Barbuda
Belize
Cape Verde
1982 Canada
China (PRC)
Equatorial Guinea
Ghana
Guinea
Honduras
Turkey
1983 El Salvador
Lesotho
Netherlands
St. Chris.-Nevis
1984 Brunei
Guinea-Bissau
Liberia
South Africa
Vatican City State
1985 Guatemala
Mauritania
Sudan
1986 U. Rep. Tanzania
Central African Rep.
Nicaragua
Tuvala
1987 Afghanistan
Burundi
Ethiopia
Haiti
Korea (Rep.)
Philippines
Surinam
1988 Brazil
1989 Algeria
Cambodia
Chad
Iran
Lebanon
Portugal
Tunisia
1990 Benin
Burkina Faso
Fiji
Mozambique
Namibia
Nepal
Sao-Tome Principe
Yemen
1991 Thailand
Cambodia
NO ONE DOC. CON.
Israel
Libya
New Zealand
Oman
Saudi Arabia
United Kingdom
NOT INCLUDED
Andorra
San Marino

Figure 1.1 The 167 National Constitutions—Latest Revision Dates

WESTERN "CONSTITUTIONALISM" AND COLONIALISM IN ASIA

What is "constitutionalism"? What is "a constitution"? Are all Asian countries, by virtue of having a single-document basic law, "constitutionalist"? How is "democratic" theory and practice related to "constitutionalism"? The terms "constitutionalism" and "a constitution" in the Western world have a rich and sometimes confusing content. How the words have been understood has depended in fair measure on the academic specialty, nationality, or profession of the writer. For example, many American historians have taken "constitutionalism" to be shorthand for the constitutional ideas of the founding period. Legal realists and positivists among lawyers in the United States have had trouble relating the descriptive and prescriptive elements implied by "constitutionalism." British scholars, such as Albert V. Dicey, without a one-document constitution and with "conventions of the constitution" to live with, have focused on the rule of law under an "unwritten constitution" (or a constitution in part unwritten and in part expressed in key statutes and other documents). In the same common law tradition, Edward S. Corwin analyzed the "higher law background" of American constitutional law which also contains much that is theoretical, cultural and unwritten. Continental European authors have worked within the quite different but historically parallel Western tradition of "civil law," with its coherent comprehensive "Codes," closer ties with Roman Law, and magisterial theories. More specifically, along with the pivotal French Revolution, students of French constitutionalism see before them fifteen constitutions since 1791, not all democratic. Each Western country has had its own story and slant on the meaning of constitutionalism; and each colonial power brought its own distinctive heritage to its Asian region of paramountcy between the sixteenth and twentieth centuries.

Thus, British constitutionalism and legalism found roots in the varied soils of India, Sri Lanka, Bangladesh, Myanmar, Malaysia, Singapore, Hong Kong, Pakistan, and other lands, while Dutch thought and law have left a legacy in Sri Lanka and Indonesia. France influenced its "Indochina" of Cambodia, Laos and Vietnam, while the United States began around 1900 to supplant Spanish legalism with its own in the Philippines. Japan was forcefully persuaded to adopt Western constitutional thought and legalism as a step toward regaining full independence from imposed unequal treaties, and chose European (especially German) models rather than common law approaches to modern law. In turn, Japan gained sovereignty over Taiwan in 1895 after defeating China in war. She annexed Korea in 1910 after the Russo-Japanese War (1904–05), making Japan's law Korea's. From 1842 until 1945, China was exploited and, in varying degrees, influenced by colonialists from Great Britain, France, Germany, Italy, Japan, Russia, the United States, and smaller European countries. Since 1945, almost all Asian countries have gained the independence necessary to pursue their own constitutional destinies; as they have done so, the colonialist and pre-colonialist past has cast shadows of different length and shape in each nation.

In the multi-cultural and contemporary context of the present book, it seems best to leave behind the past and to attempt to reformulate theoretical guidelines for comparing and evaluating present and future constitutional systems. Here, the goal is to sketch out a theory bridging perennial Western and modern Asian understandings of constitutionalism in a way that is transculturally persuasive and "omnidirectional."

"East" and "West," like "North" and "South" or "First," "Second," "Third" and "Fourth Worlds," have had a limited utility for identifying and analyzing clusters of nations with some shared political or economic characteristics. However, these words are inadequate pointers to the diverse geographical and cultural roots of contemporary constitutional systems and may even discourage the kind of constitutional theory that is now needed. Constitutional development does not depend on some specific type of economic development. Nor can law and constitution be adequately analyzed solely in political terms. Humans are to some degree "rational actors," but there is much more complexity, depth, diversity, and community in human motivations than suggested by economistic theories and the drive for power. Use of the term "omnidirectional" is an attempt to shatter the prism of West-dominated perspectives through which the immense variety of national constitutional systems is often viewed in the United States, implicitly or explicitly. Any theoretical account of what "constitutionalism" means is rooted historically in the particular cultural matrix of its author and usually responds most directly to the concerns and experience of that nation with a style of argumentation comfortable to indigenous colleagues. However, for a theoretical account of constitutionalism to be most useful at this stage in history, it needs to be "transculturally persuasive."

By "transcultural," I mean that the basic principles of the theory proposed—those of a very general nature which are not inherently limited in relevance by their particularity to the country of origin—must be applicable and relevant to many or all cultures, at least prescriptively, and in some cases descriptively. If the principle is nowhere concretized in a state's performance, few other nations are likely to be persuaded of its salience. On the other hand, a country's manner of formulating or implementing a sound principle may bias other people against the principle itself. For example, some American conceptions of "individualism" are neither transculturally valid nor philosophically convincing,[5] but must be taken into account to understand the strong and weak points of American constitutionalism. (This assertion in no way implies dismissal of general theories asserting the importance of human dignity and individual rights.) We do not yet have a terminology which adequately reflects awareness of and sensitivity to the multiplicity of current nation-state experiences and constitutional cultures.

Western constitutionalism developed slowly and often painfully over millennia *within* the parameters of the Greco-Roman, Judaeo-Christian, and Enlightenment traditions; it was latterly affected by such phenomena as scientific, industrial, and political revolutions and war. None of that is true of the non-Western world. Western powers superimposed principles and practices derived from their own governmental experience and reflection about law on the Asian constitutional cultures they dominated. Under colonial regimes, no time was given the Asians by history for gradual, organic, indigenous development, or for autonomous and selective adaptation of foreign ideas. With the exceptions of Japan and Thailand, Asian countries had limited options or no choice about their own law and constitution until independence was conferred some time after the Second World War. Thus, it is only in the latter half of this century that most countries of Asia have begun, at an accelerated pace, the autonomous development of a constitutional system which appropriately mingles the past and the present, the indigenous and the foreign, the traditional and the new, to meet the needs of the future. Modern constitutional traditions in Asia have just begun.

Some Meanings of "Constitutionalism" Today

Europeans and Americans still tend towards a residual chauvinism in their views of constitutionalism in Asia, while many Asian systems strain as their new traditions evolve. How in this context should one explain "constitutionalism" in a transculturally persuasive manner?

How we frame questions and discourse about constitutionalism predetermines the type and range of answers that may emerge. What do our ways of talking about constitutionalism and law include and exclude, implicitly or with firm explicitness? What questions do we tend to think most meaningful, useful, and worthy of exploration as we grope toward understandings for the future? What do we tend to assume?

American constitutional lawyers and social scientists assume a lot, and those assumptions may seriously impede the world's dialogue on constitutionalism, because they sometimes confuse the essential with the unessential, principle with culture-specific particularity, and this breeds insensitivity to contrasting cultural emphases in Asia that are compatible with principle. Many American lawyers and legal scholars exaggerate, for example, the importance of American (not Western) liberalism, capitalism, and judicial review. At best, in the midst of exaggerated claims, the American constitutional lawyer shows awareness of shortcomings in U.S. human rights performance.

> [W]hile there is probably no society, certainly no complex and pluralistic one, which has recognized a greater range of individual rights entitled to protection or fulfillment than the United States, there is also a substantial gap between rights in the abstract and their reality in practice.[6]

Many countries of great complexity in Asia and elsewhere recognize a greater range of human rights than the U.S. and arguably do a better job of rights protection and governance than America. More telling in the long run, by the standards of Asia and Europe, American "grand theory" in constitutional law, however refined within its own court-centered world, offers little grand analysis of many dimensions of "constitutionalism."[7] Some American constitutional theorists are also hamstrung by a unicultural framework while the subject area requires responsiveness to both cultural diversity and crucial principle.

Less influential in constitutional studies and the constitutional affairs of Asia than law, social science and its assumptions affect American and Asian thinking about constitutionalism:

> The social sciences are primarily products of Western civilization, and Africans, Asians, and other non-Westerners who work in the social sciences generally use the theory and methods of the Western social sciences as their framework.[8]

The field of Asian Studies mixes to unusual smoothness the disciplines of history, social sciences, and the humanities, and most of the relatively few American specialists in Asian law and constitutionalism are in this mold. Critical to the development of cross-cultural coherence in understandings of constitutionalisms, Asian Studies may be settling into a balanced middle ground between the old extremes of cultural relativism and culture-blind universalism, a third intellectual way, a result of decades of explicating the fully human within the diverse particularities of many Asian cultures. As Andrew Nathan suggests, "It is the view that holds one culture's values are not relevant to another that turns out to be insular."[9] By what standards should the quality of governance be judged? A distinction is often made in the United States, though not always with clarity, between "constitutionalism" and "democracy."[10] Useful additional distinctions can be made between these two terms and "documentary constitutionalism," "non-constitutionalism," and "human rights constitutionalism."

I would submit that human rights constitutionalism provides the most persuasive set of normative standards by which to assess the quality of a constitutional system and its day-to-day operation—the human rights of each individual in the community. Of the theories discussed below, only "human rights constitutionalism" is grounded in recognition of the equal inherent dignity and nobility of each individual and a comprehensive notion of human rights.

Human rights provide the omnidirectional, transcultural axis around which the gyroscope of constitutional government, law and politics should spin. Respect for human rights is now the best test of humane civilization, if not of great art and gentility. Human rights are not vague, abstract or culture-specific. Many of the concrete requirements of service and protection of the individual that are implied by respect for each person's dignity are spelled out in United Nations human rights documents; others regarding government structure and process are explicated below.

Article 55 of the United Nations Charter (1945) gave treaty law very general language on human rights, such as the following:

> [B]ased on respect for the principle of equal rights and self-determination of peoples, the United Nations shall promote. . . . (c) universal respect for, and observance of, human rights and fundamental freedoms for all without distinction as to race, sex, language, or religion.[11]

Clarification and refinement of the meaning of human rights have been provided by the thirty articles of the Universal Declaration of Human Rights—approved without dissent by the United Nations General Assembly on December 10, 1948[12]—and by the other elements in the so-called "International Bill of Human Rights," namely the 1966 "International Covenant on Economic, Social and Cultural Rights," the "International Covenant on Civil and Political Rights," and the "Optional Protocol to the International Covenant on Civil and Political Rights" which came into effect for ratifying countries in 1976.[13] Additional specificity has come in other instruments, such as the "Convention on the Elimination of All Forms of Discrimination against Women" (1979)[14] and the "Convention against Torture and Other Cruel, Inhuman, or Degrading Treatment" (1984).[15] Among the regional human rights formulations developed on all continents are the "Basic Principles of Human Rights" issued by the Human Rights Committee of the nongovernmental Law Association for Asia and the Pacific (LAWASIA).[16] What is remarkable in the late twentieth century is not the continuing failure of governments to adhere to some or most international human rights standards, but the worldwide diffusion of these standards, their transcultural acceptance, and their gradually increasing effect in the international law and constitutional law of nations (see Figure 1.2).

A government of human rights constitutionalism would include the following:

1 a constitutional division of governmental power among two or more basic organs or "branches";
2 some form of independent judicial system, with jurisdiction including cases on civil rights and liberties;
3 regularized limits on the amount of governmental power possessed by anyone and, generally, on the length of time power may be legitimately possessed. (A few Asian constitutional monarchies present partial exceptions.) Democratic elections using the secret ballot assure peaceful, routine passage from one national leader or group of leaders to the next, and encourage public agreement on the legitimacy and composition of the leadership;
4 government authority and means of coercion under law sufficient to maintain public peace, security of person, and national security, within limits defined by the human rights of citizens and those of other countries. Rigorous restraints on military power and military involvement in government politics.
5 government involvement in socioeconomic problem-solving in order to meet citizens' subsistence needs (e.g. food, clothing, shelter) and a life compatible with human dignity, insofar as the private sector fails to meet these needs. Property rights and economic freedom are protected insofar as they do not result in such inequitable distribution as to deny the socioeconomic rights of other citizens, particularly the least fortunate;
6 legally protected and encouraged freedom of peaceful expression and a right to silence;
7 legal tolerance and government support for expression of personal and group beliefs about the meaning of human life and the universe, insofar as such expression is compatible with respectful treatment of other people in the circumstances of the specific society;
8 a system of local autonomy showing the maximum respect for regional desires for self-governance that is compatible with human rights claims in other affected territories;
9 procedural rights in criminal and civil justice for each citizen equal to those of all others within the national community; the standard for treatment of the most privileged members of society is applied to the least fortunate;
10 acceptance of the constitution and human rights as the supreme law of the land, by the government and by the general public.

The unequivocal commitment to human rights implied here is not characteristic of documentary constitutionalism, democracy, or constitutionalism. *Documentary constitutionalism* reflects the rare level of worldwide agreement achieved that a modern nation state needs a single document of basic law setting forth constitutional arrangements. "Documentary constitutionalism" refers only to the adoption by a nation state (and, by analogy in federal systems, by States or Provinces, as in Australia and Canada) of a single document to state its fundamental formal law on the major divisions, structures, principles and powers of government, and the rights and duties of citizens. The term does not touch on the question of whether or how a government implements that constitution in whole or part. (In parallel, the formal acceptance by almost all governments of the ideals in the Universal Declaration and

States	1	2	3	4	5	6	7	8	9	10	11	12	13	14	15	16	17	18	19	20	21	22
Afghanistan	x	x		x	x		s	x	x	x	x	x	x	x						x		x
Australia	x	x		x			x	x		x	x	x	x		x	x	x	x	x	x		
Bangladesh				x	x		x			x	x	x	x	x								
Bhutan				s			x															
Burma								x		x	x	x		s						s		
China				x	x		x	x		x	x				x	x						s
Dem. Kampuchea	s	s		x	x		s	x					x									
North Korea	x	x						x	x													
Fiji				x				x		x	x	x	x		x	x		x	x	x	x	
India	x	x		x	x	x	s	x	x	x	x	x	x	x					s	x		
Indonesia						s	x													x		s
Iran	x	x		x	x	s		x		x			x	s	x	x						
Japan	x	x					x							x	x	x				x		
Kiribati																	x	x				
Laos				x	x		x	x	x				x	x						x		
Malaysia						x							x						x			
Maldives				x	x	s	s	x														
Mongolia	x	x	x	x	x	s	x	x	x		x	x	x							x		
Nauru																						
Nepal				x	x	s	x	x				x	x							x		
New Zealand	x	xa		x			x	x		x	x	x	x		x	x			x	x	x	s
Pakistan				x	x			x				x	x	x					s	x		
Papua New Guinea				x				x				x			x	x				x		
Philippines	x	xa	s	x	x	x	x	x	x			x	x	x	x	x		s		x	x	x
Republic of Korea	x	xa	x	x		x	x	x						x				x		x		
Samoa																					x	
Singapore													x	x					x			
Solomon Islands	x			x						x	x	x	x							x		

Sri Lanka	x	xa		x	x		x	x				x	x	x					x		s	
Thailand							x													x		
Tonga				x				x														
Tuvalu															x	x						
Vanuatu																						
Vietnam	x	x		x	x		x	x	x													

x Ratification, accession, notification of succession, acceptance or definitive signature
s Signature not yet followed by ratification
a Declaration recognizing the competence of the Human Rights Committee under article 41 of the International Covenant on Civil and Political Rights
b Declaration recognizing the competence of the Committee on the Elimination of Racial Discrimination under article 14 of the International Convention on the Elimination All Forms of Racial Discrimination

1. International Covenant on Economic, Social, and Cultural Rights
2. International Covenant on Civil and Political Rights
3. Optional Protocol to the International Covenant on Civil and Political Rights
4. International Covenant on the Elimination of all forms of Racial Discrimination
5. International Covenant on the Suppression and Punishment of the Crime of *Apartheid*
6. International Covention Against Apartheid in Sports
7. Convention on the Elimination of All Forms of Discrimination Against Women
8. Convention on the Prevention and Punishment of the Crime of Genocide
9. Convention on the Non-Applicability of Statutory Limitations to War Crimes and Crimes Against Humanity
10. Slavery Convention of 1926
11. 1953 Protocol amending the 1926 Convention
12. Slavery Convention of 1926 as amended
13. Supplementary Convention on the Abolition of Slavery, the Slave Trade, and Institutions and Practices Similar to Slavery
14. Convention for the Suppression of the Traffic in Persons and of the Exploitation of the Prostitution of Others
15. Convention relating to the Status of Refugees
16. Protocol Relating to the Status of Refugees
17. Convention on the Reduction of Statelessness
18. Convention relating to the Status of Stateless Persons
19. Convention on the Nationality of Married Women
20. Convention on the Political Rights of Women
21. Convention on the Consent to Marriage, Minimum Age for Marriage and Registration of Marriages
22. Convention Against Torture and other Cruel, Inhuman, or Degrading Treatment or Punishment

Figure 1.2 Human Rights International Instruments: Signatures, Ratifications, Accessions, etc. June, 1991

Sources: *The LAWASIA Human Rights Bulletin*, Vol. 6, Nos. 1 & 2, Jan., 1988, 137; *Multilateral Treaties Deposited with the Secretary-General: Status as at December 1989, New York United Nations, 1990; and Ann Reichel, Treaty Section, United Nations, May, 1991.*

international Covenants on human rights may be taken as illustrating, at the very least, "international documentary constitutionalism.")

The single-document constitution may not be equated with "the constitution" of a nation, which may also include other fundamental documents, judicial decisions, speeches by a key leader (for example, Abraham Lincoln in the U.S.), theories, public values, customs, and laws. The "laws" may be statutes, administrative rules or, as in some one-party states (for example, China), the basic party rules. Nevertheless, it is not a trivial advance in civilization that after millennia of reflection and political experience, statements of basic law and some structures of modern government have become a shared part of discourse and world legal culture for the first time. In the face of human imperfection and contemporary barbarism, the substantive human accomplishment represented by worldwide documentary constitutions, a sign of and a basis for cross-cultural comprehension and communication, often goes unnoticed.

Relationships are often complex between printed provisions, government policies, and social practices. The constitutional document may be near sacred writ in one country and an object of little interest to the government or the public in another. (For the general public in the U.S., it is a rarely studied but sacred document.) A constitutional provision may accurately reflect the *serious intent* of a government and a people on a problem of governance or rights, but history, economy, and/or sociopolitics may make achievement of that goal in the short run improbable or impossible. In other cases, no linkage may exist between written constitutional principle and government intent, as in what I later refer to as "non-constitutionalist" regimes or actions. A government's intent may be obvious upon cursory investigation, or discernible only with detailed knowledge of the incident or the country. The contours of a country's ruling agencies may reflect a distinctive history or the politics of a recent coup, and may endow with more or less formal authority a legislature, an elected executive, a court system, a bureaucracy, a monarch, a general, or a local government office. National *priorities* regarding citizen rights and duties vary of course, both in documentary language and in operative policy. It is in terms of the different degrees of seriousness and comprehensiveness of a system's commitment to human rights that I distinguish between "human rights constitutionalism," other meanings of "constitutionalism," and "democracy."

In both Asia and the West, definitions of "*democracy*" often rest on a recognition of human dignity, but without insisting upon comprehensive protection of human rights. Unlike much American constitutional thought, "democracy" implies an optimistic view of political life and human nature. Democracy denotes government grounded in popular sovereignty, the right of final determination as actualized in majoritarian decision-making processes. Democracy makes *the expressed will of the majority* of voting adults the determinative political value. A human is defined in terms of individual autonomy and free will; no clear account is given of community, reason, or the satisfaction of minority needs at variance with the majority will. A "want" is accorded primacy; the "need" of another may be downplayed in political and legal processes, and in theory. Thus understood, democracy is not the antithesis of authoritarian government or repression of rights, because the majority may prefer very strong government, inequalities, and the repression of rights, and because democratic processes do not by themselves imply protection of human rights other than those of political participation; nor do they imply some other public value demanding restraints on public and private power, such as a stress on or a deemphasis of private property rights. Indeed, majoritarian politics did not inspire America along her tortuous path toward universal suffrage and equal voting rights, theoretically the all-important rights in this understanding of democracy. Democracy may be less preoccupied with substance than with a particular type of *process* for legitimizing acts of government and the accession of particular citizens to positions of *public authority*.

Democracy's ultimate demand seems to be that each vote be equal in weight and be cast freely for or against a policy proposition or a candidate for public office. Acts of the political community or its government are legitimate and authoritative only insofar as freely approved by the majority of sovereign voters. The "clear and distinct idea" of the mathematically precise and decisive majority vote is compelling. The sanguine implicit assumptions are that adults in appropriate numbers will vote and that they will have a reasonably equal opportunity to participate, and will be reasonably well informed, concerned, fair, and responsible. However, funds, organization and media access, rather than quality of citizen participation, seem decisive to garnering majority approval in some democratic systems (for example, the U.S.).

Neither of the following constitutes a manifestation of democracy: passive acceptance of a government or its actions—as often in authoritarian systems and sometimes in democracies—or mass participation in discussing and implementing government-made policies without a legitimizing process of direct voting or the election of leaders who vote on policy. Freedom and equality of participation in majority decision-making processes are the crucial ideals of democracy, so freedom of expression about alternatives, egalitarian election laws, and the secrecy of the ballot are essential. But most other issues of human rights (for example, in criminal and social justice) are irrelevant to democratic legitimacy. The relative wisdom or morality of a majoritarian decision or law does not affect its legitimacy.

Matters undecided by majoritarian government are left to personal choice and private competition for power. Some rights, responsibilities, and relations between the public and private sectors are left unaccounted for by such democratic theory. In some democracies, these empty spots have not been filled in by cultural sensitivity toward minorities and the poor. In the U.S. the fusion of legal positivism with democracy has strengthened theoretical underpinnings for authoritarian democracy and relativist indifference to human rights values. Stated thus, in broad theory democracy is not transculturally persuasive. In sum, democracy is an optimistic faith; democratic processes are essential but insufficient means for protecting the liberty and promoting the other human rights of the individual.

"*Constitutionalism*" as here defined connotes organization, division, and limitation of governmental power under law more unequivocally than does democracy. Democracy clearly limits power only with respect to majoritarian politics and decision making, and is silent on many issues regarding human rights and restraint of power. Constitutionalism mirrors less trust in democratic processes and human nature, and more reliance on laws and institutions which set the parameters of legitimate government action. Like a democracy, a constitutionalist system may become authoritarian, with or without a change in the written constitution or avowed public ideology. The configuration of laws, structures, social culture, economy, politics and public values making up each nation's "constitutional culture" is its own. In all nations, some cultural elements support while others hinder constitutionalism. Western writers sometimes refer to tolerance, to British restraint, to French or American individualism, or to some attitude towards law or authority as buttressing constitutionalism. Most other constitutional cultures also have elements on which constitutionalism is or can be built. For example, the groupism of Japanese society generally assures the limitation of government power through competitive factionalism in the political parties, bureaucracy, and society.

As used here in a transcultural setting, constitutionalism does not imply a comprehensive or overriding commitment to individual rights (as does human rights constitutionalism), or to a particular way of distributing powers and functions among government structures. It does not, for example, denote preference for a republic or a monarchy, a parliamentary prime minister or a president, a federal or a unitary system, civil law or common law, or two rather than three branches of government. "Constitutionalism" *does* assume commitment to and institutionalization of *some* basic principle(s) requiring restraint of the governmental power of all agencies and individuals. Insofar as it implies some regularized restraint of power under law, democracy is a form of constitutionalism, but some forms of constitutionalism do not include majoritarian democracy. Authority in a constitutionalist government, past or present, is defined and limited by written and/or unwritten basic rules in a way generally recognized among the populace (promulgated), and these restraints are mandated by national constitutional values and legitimized by compatible political processes.

However complex the local law and politics of voting may be, majoritarian democratic theory is remarkable for the simplicity of its appeal to all nations to adopt a mathematically clear idea: honor the majority vote. The understanding of constitutionalism suggested here offers no such simple guideline for determining whether and how a state is constitutionalist. Such determinations may prove easy or may presuppose investigation of a country's constitutional culture on its own terms, in order to learn how power is understood, organized, used, abused and restrained there, and why. (Asian examples are discussed later.) What fundamental values (i.e. state, religious, economic, familial), what decision-making processes (i.e. authoritarian, consultative, consensual, magical, or democratic), what patterns of public attitude and behavior affect the flow of power and the style of government, legal processes, and politics? What assumptions and rules govern the distribution of resources and the restraint of power? How power is exercised and limited in everyday community life and why are keys to comprehending the status of constitutionalism in a nation, because official power-holders are of their country's constitutional culture.

Although in some contexts, the state is separate from or even in opposition to society or the individual—as when rights related to eminent domain, criminal justice or free speech are at issue—Western constitutional theory may overemphasize the distinctions (and separations) between the public and the private, the state and society, the written statutory and/or judicial law and customary law, and law and the patterned manner in which a given people orders authority and propriety in community life.[17] Where constitutionalism is present, the country's "living constitution" suffuses government, society and the legal system. Government power may be limited by "checks and balances" among an executive, a legislature, a council, a court system, a military, an ombudsman, a monarch, or some other official agency.

Private power centers may or may not be critically important in properly or wrongly restraining the use of government power in service of avowed constitutional values. Examples of such powerful private forces in some Asian countries include: Buddhist, Christian or Islamic religious leaders; criminal organizations; people of immense wealth; civic movements; opposition political parties; unions; a foreign government or business.

Ideally, a constitution reflects both a people's shared ideals and their weak points. A constitution should exalt public virtues emerging from a nation's history and society, but also attempt with remedial provisions to grapple with serious, even intractable problems arising from the same cultural sources. For example, slavery and its aftereffects have confronted America since the inception of U.S. constitutionalism. Cogent analysis of socially systemic anti-constitutionalist tendencies can serve as the basis for enhancing the quality of a country's constitution or at least for sharply focused constitutional debate. A few Asian examples will clarify the problem.

In some Asian political cultures, there is no old or modern national tradition of a leader relinquishing power after a set term of office. (The lack of an orderly succession system at the national level may contrast with well-established processes of leadership change and communitarian democracy in villages.) For instance, from South Korea's independence in 1948 until 1988, no President gave up office at the end of the term(s) specified by South Korea's Constitution at the time he took office. In recognition of this problem, the 1988 Korean Constitution of the Sixth Republic limited the President to one five-year term. Analogously, in response to the repeatedly extended years in office of ousted President Ferdinand Marcos, the 1987 Philippine Constitution limited the President to one six-year term. A similar provision and a restriction on the total allowable years in elective office at each level of government (to, say, twelve years) might well improve the quality of American politics and governance.

A second Asian problem has been the tendency of high officials in some countries to show extreme favoritism for members of their immediate or extended families. In admirable response, the 1987 Constitution of the Republic of the Philippines (Article 7, Section 13) prohibits presidential appointment of "spouse and relatives . . . within the fourth civil degree" to public office; and a 1987 law bans the election candidacy of "relatives of high-ranking government officials within the second degree of consanguinity."[18]

Another example of remedial constitutionalism is the antimilitarist, quasi-pacifist 1947 Constitution of Japan (Article 9), which excludes the military from Cabinet posts and denies Japan the usual sovereign rights to arm at will and to resort to force to settle international disputes. In part, these popular provisions are a reaction to the aggressive and repressive military regime of the 1930s and early 1940s.[19]

As elsewhere, challenges for constitutionalism in Asia arise from social culture. The serious private obligation of a civil servant or politician to exchange favors and manifest particularistic loyalty in patron-client relations may clash with impartial performance of public duty. Striking differences of ethnic culture (for example, between the Malays, Indians, and Chinese of Malaysia, between the Tamils and Sinhalese of Sri Lanka), or religion (for example, between Sikhs, Christians, Hindus and Muslims in India) may result in deeply embedded mutual distrust and contempt inimical to stable government under law. On the other hand, diverse community identities may lend power to free speech rights and constitutionalist restraint of official power, and religious faith may provide the primary motivation for tolerance.

It seems essential to the viability of human rights as a transculturally proposed set of constitutional standards that they be secular rather than inherently religious in nature, because such standards must provide empirical tests in public law needing no reference to any specific system of ideas, or beliefs (for example, a proscription on ripping out fingernails and other torture bans only behavior), and because primary linkage with any one religion, even with one of the few great universalist religions, would invite *prima facie* rejection in too many cases by adherents of other universalist religions or local belief systems, and would add to the difficulty of precise intercultural communication. Here "secular" does not imply opposition to any or all religions but the absence of linkage to any one religion.

On the other hand, we must ask: Where do the underlying public values come from that can motivate development of "a living human rights constitution" in official and popular attitudes, institutions and actions? Of all the available ideas in any culture, those which are most essential to legitimizing, justifying human rights (or alternative public standards) can be termed that culture's "religious" ideas.[20] "Religion" here denotes the most important, most binding ideas at the heart of a culture, those which in the minds and daily lives of the people give ultimate meaning to the state community (or to a subnational portion in a weakly integrated multi-national state), with attendant institutions and customs which embody that community's way of expressing and honoring what it sees as most important. The core of a constitutional culture is a religion in that sense, the coherent (as sociopolitical force if not as concept) set of public values underlying and legitimizing government and law. Human rights standards must deal effectively with such "constitutional religion"; they must be linked with what is already seen as most important in a community, or fail.

In challenging the tendency in American law schools to isolate legal discourse from religion and moral values (which are part of "religion" in the above, broader sense), Mary Ann Glendon captures the ethos well:

> The most commonly *stated* reasons for drawing a *cordon sanitaire* around legal political discourse . . . . are not that moral and religious beliefs are essentially arbitrary or foolish, or that ordinary men and women are unfit to rule. They are, rather, that religion has often been a source of civil strife, and that particularistic groups are often intolerant and "illiberal." All too frequently, what is implied is that religion and particular communities are *presumptively* intolerant and socially divisive.[21]

Besides Western ideas of secular democracy, constitution, legalism, Christianity, capitalism, and socialism, diverse Asian traditions influence current understandings of state purposes to some extent; for example:

There is no reason to *presume* today anything positive or negative *a priori* about the impact of a particular religious idea on social or governmental behavior affecting a specific human right of an individual in a given time and place; that is an empirical question. One must discover what really happened and why in each case of right protection and right violation. There is, however, good reason to assume that maximizing positive linkage between indigenous religion and human rights is an indispensable approach to mobilizing a community in favor of tolerance and a strong human rights performance.[22] *The goal is to make behavior respectful of human rights an integral part of the religious ethos in every nation's constitutional culture.* Besides Western ideas, diverse Asian traditions influence current understandings of state purposes to some extent:

1 State harmony by adherence to Confucian ethics and obedience to a virtuous monarch with an extremely broad mandate from Heaven to govern (for example, the traditional kings of China, Korea, and Vietnam; recent leaders there and in Sinic Singapore);[23]
2 The just service of Allah (for example, the heavily Islamic states of Pakistan, Bangladesh, Malaysia, and Indonesia);[24]
3 Prosperity in state and society based on kingship in tune with the cosmos, at times by observance of astrologically legitimizing rituals (for example, the Brahmanic and Buddhist monarchies of Nepal and Thailand);[25]
4 Sacrificial dedication to the nation as a uniquely sacred collectivity under a quasi-divine monarch (for example, Japan under the Emperor from around 1870 to 1945).[26]

These alternative state foundations seem to have in common four tendencies: (1) to relate, not separate, religion and state; (2) to conceptually and institutionally integrate, not divide, the public and the private, the economic, the social and the political, in short, to view community life organically; (3) to see the individual person as achieving fulfillment within a dense network of family and community relationships, rather than as an autonomous individual; and (4) to give the state great formal power, not without restraining responsibilities, but with vagueness about how rulers are to be held accountable. Theories of democracy and constitutionalism, indigenous traditions, religion and social culture interact in late twentieth-century Asian law and constitutional politics.

"*Human rights constitutionalism*" combines the features of majoritarian democracy and constitutionalist restraint on power. However, as here used, it goes beyond both in two respects, asserting: (1) that government is required to engage in *remedial discrimination* to promote equal treatment of all citizens under the law, and to assure all the satisfaction of such basic needs as food, clothing, shelter and personal security; and (2) that, pursuant to a constitutional attribution to each person of equal, inherent and politically transcendent value, the state's appropriate *preoccupation* is with public policies which protect and promote *all* the human rights, as comprehensively understood in the International Bill of Human Rights and some modern constitutions, not, for example, with protection of free enterprise to the neglect of worker rights or with press freedom more than criminal justice rights. Human rights constitutionalism insists upon a broader conception of rights and government responsibility than democracy, with its focus on majority rule and political liberties, or American constitutionalism, with its restraints on state power, stress on property rights and unequal assurance of criminal justice rights.

Finally, the clumsy term "*nonconstitutionalism*" is employed: (1) to refer to that substantial number of nation-state *regimes* which do not support democracy, constitutionalism, or human rights constitutionalism; and (2) to categorize *official actions in all* the world's systems which are incompatible with any reasonably constitutionalist theory. A nonconstitutionalist state is one which does not clearly limit the power of government under law and principle. It is a state where official power is absolute or vague in scope and unpredictable in its exercise, where human rights are subject to capricious violation and neglect. Insofar as the quality of government and law is an indicator of civilization, the extent of any state's nonconstitutionalism is a reliable measure of its barbarism.

Whether a country's laws, institutions and normative political attitudes, or its recent behavior in a specific issue area, manifest democracy, constitutionalism, human rights constitutionalism, or nonconstitutionalism is an *empirical question.* Precisely how and with what understandings and purposes do government personnel act with respect to affected citizens? Compliance is a matter of degrees even where constitutionalism is apparently deep-rooted. In Asia, in the United States, the relationships between law and constitution, theory and popular myth, fact and boastful political rhetoric, ideals and practice, are inconsistent and sometimes bafflingly complex. For example, although American democratic theory places great emphasis on voting, the United States ranks very low among democracies in its voting rates.[27] Similarly contrary to myth, compared to many systems in Asia and Europe, the American constitutional order seems intolerant of free expression of diverse political ideas, witness the narrow range of ideological views institutionalized in political parties and the internal authoritarianism of private corporations. How strong is free speech in a country where employees may be fired "at will," even for revealing the criminal activities of employers (as in the United States)?

Documentary constitutionalism, democracy, constitutionalism, human rights constitutionalism, and nonconstitutionalism have been distinguished as guidelines for assessing the systems and behavior of countries in Asia and elsewhere. Applying the standards discussed to the *apparent general intent* of national leaders, as shown by recent operative policies, laws, and institutions, how might one characterize specific Asian systems? Brunei, Cambodia, China, Myanmar, North Korea and Vietnam seem among the nonconstitutionalist regimes of Asia, due in part to their systemic opposition to restraints on government power and (in most cases) their failure to establish predictable processes of leadership succession under law. Indonesia and Singapore embody limited democracy and two of many contrasting indigenous constitutionalisms, Indonesia is slowly building a theistic modern military state with limited government resources over a vast archipelago with staggering subcultural diversity. Singapore is a tiny, prosperous Confucian state where socioeconomic rights and somewhat restrictive laws and policies are effectively implemented. While the operative systems of the Philippines, South Korea, Taiwan and Thailand have lent nonconstitutionalist power for substantial periods to the military and a relatively few wealthy families, the general thrust of government intent since 1978 in Thailand, and since the late 1980s in the others, was toward human rights constitutionalism. With radically different cultures and with continuing problems and exceptions, India (e.g. the caste system)and Japan, along with Sri Lanka (for Sinhalese more than Tamils), have generally pursued the ideals of human rights constitutionalism since the late 1940s.

Theory, culture and guidelines of intermediate abstraction such as the above can be brought to bear on performance. However, broad characterizations of regime are prone to chauvinism and imprecision, investigation, analysis, and reporting of specific cases of human rights violation and promotion are far more useful not only in politics but also at the intellectual foundations. Human Rights constitutionalism involves the fusing of a radical empiricism with humanistic universalism. Monitoring and measuring both general and highly specific regime behavior in terms of democracy and human rights has become the work of scholars and public and private agencies around the world.[28] Dedicated official and private activism now meshes with increased though damnably spasmodic coverage of problems by the world media, careful scholarship, and ever-more-precise debate on the meaning and observance of human rights.[29]

CONSTITUTIONALISM IN ASIA AND THE UNITED STATES

Among elite and populist constitutionalists in many Asian countries, the appeal and influence of United States constitutionalism lies not so much in American democracy or constitutionalism per se, or in economic or military prowess, as in America insofar as it can be perceived as a symbol and/or supporter of a full panoply of human rights and respect for each person's dignity.[30] This symbolism does not fit very well with American reality today. More common among American constitutional lawyers and other custodians of the system is commitment to democracy, constitutionalism, legal positivism, some variant of economic liberalism, and "individualism."[31] Where human rights are analyzed, the question is often: Which human rights can/should be made legal rights under positive law? The answer usually limits legal rights to civil liberties, property rights, and procedural safeguards. Sadly, relatively few seem ready for the incorporation into constitutional law of social and economic rights.

The record and prospects for human rights in the United States do not seem very bright—especially for the socioeconomic rights of the less fortunate 40% of American families and for equal treatment under the law of those with modest means.[32] In the 1980s the gap in living standards between those in the upper and lower thirds on the income scale widened, and not, as in some Asian countries, due to a shortage in aggregate national resources.[33] David Apter argues that a low level of enjoyment of socioeconomic rights in economically developed nations will negatively affect rights stressed by democracy and constitutionalism.[34] Other sober voices point out serious deficiencies in America's constitutional system with respect to mass media freedom, educational opportunity, election campaign law, criminal justice, economic justice, discrimination problems, and national purpose.[35] Granted, the constitutional accomplishments of the past 200 years give grounds for pride, but humility seems especially healthy to counter an American tendency to exaggerate the positive and neglect the negative when comparing the United States favorably with foreign constitutional systems, not least those in Asia.

Relativism, Individualism, and Mutualism

Two other characteristics of American constitutional culture bear brief consideration: value relativism and "individualism." If a human rights theory is not somehow grounded in an intellectual conviction that each human being does indeed have inherent and great value, the question legitimately rises: Why bother with the human rights of others? (How pursuit of human rights constitutionalism may be *motivated* in response to personal and national experience, feelings, faith and/or convictions is a separate set of critically important issues.) If all humans are accorded equal value in constitutional theory, how much value? Are all equal in near meaninglessness, or are all to be treated "as if" each is an end in him/herself, rather than a means to be used by other individuals or the state? Or does the public value inherent in each person transcend all human categories for differentiation, based on God's alleged attribution to each of value and cosmic destiny? Or must the state and its law calibrate carefully rewards and punishments to favor the allegedly best and brightest, those with useful skills, intelligence, and/or moral quality? Or with wealth? Does hereditary position or higher education confer special public value on an individual which law and constitution should take into account? Since social hierarchy is virtually universal, why fuss with equality issues in constitutional life?

Here, the position taken is that, whatever its source in the cosmos—the most widely relied upon source is God, following the Judaeo-Christian-Islamic tradition—each person has equal and great intrinsic dignity justifying its formal recognition in state law and constitution, and that compatibility with respect for that dignity is the ultimate standard for testing the constitutionality of a law or other official act covered in a nation's constitution. That is, an intersubjectively (not subjectively or objectively) persuasive nexus must be demonstrated between the official treatment of an individual within a given community and *respect* for that individual and others affected. In reconciling this attribution of value to humans with obvious cultural diversity in symbols of respect and other matters of community standard, "*relationalism*" may be a better term than "relativism." Relativism honors diversity, but does not claim certainty about the great inherent value of each person.[36] The "relationalist" position here suggested sees humans everywhere as interrelated within communities and respects the cultural standards affecting governance and human rights performance in any given polity, with one transcultural proviso: that the indigenous standard is intersubjectively compatible with human rights as understood by the generality of local leaders committed to human rights constitutionalism. Each country needs its own autonomous existence, has its own story to tell, and develops from within its own constitutional culture affecting human rights.

When comparing constitutionalism in the United States and in Asian countries, perhaps the most distinctive American constitutional conviction that emerges is "individualism." The individualism espoused in the United States and urged upon the world as "Western" is more American than typically Western in some respects, and is often a barrier to American communication in Asia, Europe, and elsewhere. "Individualism" is an element in the collective psyche which often affects the cross-cultural constitutional analysis of individualist constitutional lawyers. Alasdair MacIntyre, Robert Bellah and others have criticized and tried to clarify the varieties of American individualism.[37] Every year, Fulbright professors in American Studies go abroad to explain the United States to puzzled foreign university students. One of these, David Kolb, wrote insightfully as follows for group-oriented Japanese:[38]

> What is crucial for understanding American individualism as many Americans think about it is the belief in the priority of the individual and desirability in principle of having all the content of a person's life stem from his or her decision. . . . What is required is that we be able to think about a core person

> who consists of a naked chooser. I use the word "naked" to indicate that this chooser must be thought of as separated from all the content which the person's choices give to his or her life. Such a core person is not an individual member of a group, but an individual first and then a member of a group. . . . But if we want to describe "what" a person is we must say that first and foremost he is a free deciding person, a core naked individuality, plus the results of past decisions and commitments. Yet the priority of freedom does mean that past commitments never can completely define a person. There is always the possibility of change. . . . [I]f a person is first of all a core free decider, then no choices can be final, and commitments are sustained by continual renewal. I am not merely the sum of my commitments; I must be defined as the core freedom that has made those commitments and accepted those roles. *I must be respected as such a freedom* (emphasis added). . . .
>
> (American beliefs regarding the universality of individualism) are not simple; they represent an alternative to cultural relativism based on a theory of man which makes room for diversity but also asks for certain basic realities to be respected, realities which are the foundation of the variety that does exist. Such assertions seem more strong than those of other nations based on cultural or religious grounds or on specific cultural achievements. The notion of naked core individuality may more plausibly be widely applied than other social notions such as the Japanese [or other Asian] family system, precisely because the core individual is so purified and naked. Americans may be narrowing their conceptions of what kinds of *institutions can express core individuality* (emphasis added), but their basic ideas are not naive.
>
> If human beings are indeed such core freedoms, if all content of one's life should be created or ratified by free decision, then the universality of individualism is well established, since all cultural and national differences will be subsequent to free individuality.
>
> Americans therefore are willing to reject the idea that another nation's culture should be left the way it is. They must repudiate such a view, if they are to be true to their own beliefs about individuality. If humans are, beyond and behind culture, pure individual choosers, then it would be wrong to connive at the avoidance of this truth and the suppression of individual freedom even among people who do not realize that they are being imposed upon.

With all due allowance made for the diversity among Americans and the difficulty of capturing in cross-culturally intelligible words a nation's core constitutional conceptions, Kolb's formulation is helpful. He states a major component of America's "constitutional religion" as that term was discussed earlier.[39] Each Asian nation and many Asian subcultures rest on core concepts of the individual, community, loyalty, authority, duty, power, law, and human destiny which affect their systems of government and law. Many allow ample room for respecting human dignity and achieving mature individuality and self-realization, while others do not. In any case, the American understanding of individualism is not a theory or cultural norm which would ever occur to most Asians as a way of comprehending social reality, or which would seem a useful way of formulating the ideal as one worked for human rights and limited government within an Asian constitutional culture.

A tyranny of terms seems to impede transcultural discourse on constitutionalism. "Individualism" is often a verbal barrier to communication. Like "collectivism," "liberalism," "conservatism," "socialism" and a few other key terms, it is brittle and burdened with overtones peculiar to a particular country, world region, time, theory, or ideology, not a transculturally suggestive way of integrating conceptions of human rights, law, government, the individual and community.

Better than "individualism," the term "*mutualism*" expresses a theoretically and transculturally valid perspective on human rights and human rights constitutionalism. In general, humans are community beings, not "naked choosers" standing alone with a high degree of autonomy. In Asia, as elsewhere, governmental power is limited and abused, human rights are enjoyed, violated and fought for, generally within the dense interpersonal relationships of a coherent, established social culture. Normally, change towards greater regard for human rights constitutionalism comes by modification over time of the value and behavior content of those relations, or not at all. Without supportive change in social foundations, governmental changes of principle, structure or process in a constitution do not take hold.

"Mutualism" is intended to reflect recognition of the non-individualist (not anti-individual) nature and the social and historical embeddedness of rights and constitutional government. Mutualism implies two people's awareness within an interpersonal relationship of the interplay, the inherent interdependence, and the equality of each other's rights; it includes acknowledgment of the mutual responsibility and rights reciprocity essential to democratic citizenship, vigorous pluralism, and responsible limited government. The term calls for more appreciation of interdependence, community and cooperation and less emphasis on competition, while fully honoring the integrity and rights of the individual. "Mutualists" seems to reflect well the high civilizational ideal of human rights constitutionalism: a people with a strong and disciplined sense of responsibility for the human rights of others as a correlative of recognizing their own individual dignity and rights.

Principle, culture, institutional structure and legal forms meet best in moderate systems, open to humane transcultural challenge but protective and proud of national tradition. As Fritz Gaenslen suggests: "[P]urely cultural accounts of human behavior portray man as *less* malleable than we suspect he really is . . . [while] purely structural accounts of human behavior portray man as *more* malleable than we suspect he really is."[40] With respect to ideology, though extremes may sharpen comprehension of fundamental problems and may for a time inspire to needed revolution—a shift in basic direction—in the long run, extremes generally do not work and are transculturally repugnant. In Asian tendencies, *pragmatic democratic socialism*, for example, has been stronger than the extremes of unbridled capitalism and repressive communism. Western dominance was not a result of cultural superiority, but of severe Asian disorientation and military weakness at a time of forced confrontation with radically different peoples. Khan Marut's concluding words hint at Asia's agony and resentment: "[T]he scourge and bane of most Asian principalities [was] the takeover of the nation by a colonial power, in the name of 'progress' or 'civilization.' "[41]

Since liberation, elements of Japanese, European and American popular culture, technology, and constitutional thought have become part of daily Asian life;

but pride of nation has grown, not diminished in the latter half of the century. Each polity has its distinctive view of what "progress" in "civilization" means. Constitutionalists in Asia are less inclined than American counterparts to regard their own constitutional faith as applicable in other lands; and they are conscious of the deep tensions everywhere between a moderate human rights constitutionalism and cultural, democratic or non-constitutionalist preferences. In general, notions of "natural justice" and "natural law," both indigenous and Western in origin, are accorded far more respect by law professionals and intellectuals than in the United States.

Comparisons among Asian and American constitutional features will illustrate such tensions and serve as background for discussing instances of U.S. constitutional influence in Asia.[42] Among topics touched on are legal development, preambles and policy principles, executive, legislative and judicial systems, the military, monarchy, religion and the state, individual rights, and ways of changing constitutions.

One caveat: Level of *legal and institutional development* may affect constitutional practice. Here I refer to the development of national state law, not customary, religious or traditional local law. Some Asian systems have fully elaborated statutory law and highly articulated administrative and judicial systems to implement law and constitution throughout the country; others do not, and cannot be accurately assessed on an assumption that they do. In criminal justice, for example, a reformist national government may need many trained professionals serving as police, prosecutors, judges, defense attorneys, and prison officials in many locales, or its performance—regardless of policy—may not measure up to constitutionalist standards due to entrenched practices. On the other hand, if Japan or Singapore—states highly developed in law—violates the rights of an accused person or censors the press, in most cases that may be taken fairly to reflect policy. Vietnam, China and Indonesia, on the other hand, have put in place relatively few criminal law professionals due to both policy and lack of resources. The less developed the system of law and legal services, the less predictable and the more difficult to interpret may be the reasons for a government act. Ironically, as in parts of the United States, a lawyer must be ready at hand to tell one what highly developed local and national law allows or requires. America may well have the world's most complex legal system; perhaps most Asians never or rarely use an attorney.

Preambles proclaim a mix of national values, history, accomplishments, ideology and aspirations. At best, they accurately reflect the country's "constitutional religion."[43] In addition, some Asian constitutional systems establish a source of law intermediate between the general provisions and preamble of a constitution and a statute. (These statements differ from the great Codes of the world's civil law systems, which comprehensively state the basic law pertaining to private relationships, crime and commerce.) They are variously referred to as a "Declaration of Principles and State Policies" (the Philippines) or "Directive Principles of State Policy" (for example, Thailand and India).[44] Analogously, every five years Indonesia's People's Consultative Assembly (*Madjelis Permusjawaratan Rakjat* or MPR) of 1,000 elects the President and passes "Resolutions" regarding "the basic outlines of state policy" (Article 3) to guide law making by presidential decree or action of Parliament (DPR).[45] This is similar to, but more general than, multi-year economic plans used by governments worldwide. In Communist states such as China,

North Korea and Vietnam, speeches and party rules and policies promulgated after meetings of a Central Committee or Party Congress tell what the constitution has come to mean at a given stage in revolutionary processes. In effect, basic party policy is "the supreme law" of the constitution.

The United States Constitution is missing an adequate formal statement of what the country stands for. The Preamble of the U.S. Constitution might well be reformulated to incorporate some of the inspiring language of the Declaration of Independence, the Gettysburg Address, and other expressions of the ideal American consensus. Periodic general outlines of a few national policies—not in the mode of a plank in a party election platform but on the Indonesian model—might add coherence and focus to national legislative debate.

Asian executive systems display one or more of five institutions in various combinations: *presidents, prime ministers* with cabinets, *monarchs, party* chiefs, *military* leaders. In the Philippines, South Korea, Taiwan, and Indonesia, a strong president also serves as ceremonial head of state, as in the United States. More commonly, parliamentary prime ministers rule, with cabinets or councils and with a president (for example, India, Singapore, China) or monarch (for example, Malaysia, Japan) fulfilling the role of head of state. Though Pakistan's President is generally only a head of state, his authority to ask someone to form a government on the basis of election results is substantial, particularly as in 1988 when no party had a parliamentary majority, and Benazir Bhutto became Prime Minister.[46]

The rich Asian tradition of kingships continues in Japan, Brunei, Malaysia, Nepal, Thailand, the Himalayan principalities (Sikkim, Bhutan), and in the influence of Prince Sihanouk in war-ravaged Cambodia. Japan's powerless imperial institution (not Emperor Akihito as a person) is occasionally caught in the swirl of controversy pitting the mainstream against minority Shinto nationalist calls for "restoring" state power to the Emperor.[47] In Nepal, the directives of King Birendra carry much more than ceremonial weight, as in his sweeping restoration of the right to form political parties and the establishment of a new democratic constitution in 1990.[48] King Bhumibol Adulyadej has ably added to stability and democratic inclinations as Thailand's constitutional monarch.[49] The Sultan of Brunei (or *Brunei Darussalam*) is virtually an absolute monarch, though English common law and the country's judges—who are brought from Hong Kong—temper his exceptional prerogatives as law-giver and executive.[50] In Malaysia, a king (*Yang di Pertuan Agong*) is elected every five years from among the nine hereditary sultans on the thirteen-member Conference of Rulers.[51]

In Asian Communist states, government is generally controlled by a small party elite. In most instances, these leaders are influenced by Confucian constitutionalist tradition under which the authoritarian king-figure (for example, Mao Zedong, Deng Xiaoping) and ruling group are accepted as legitimate as long as they manifest benevolent paternalism, the power to maintain order, and administrative ability. However, as in China intermittently since the 1950s, government, party and military positions may be juggled unpredictably in internal struggles over leadership or policy. The "pro-democracy" movement of May and June, 1989 in Beijing and elsewhere, like the 1988 student demonstrations against the twenty-six year rule of U Ne Win and his Socialist Program Party in Myanmar, resulted in draconian use of military force and illustrates the tragic tensions between democratic political aspirations and authoritarian establishments in a few Asian systems.[52]

The ruling Nationalist Party (*Kuomintang*, KMT) on Taiwan, while culturally and organizationally similar to the Chinese Communist Party, presides over a prosperous and increasingly democratic Confucian state. Its leader, Lee Teng-hui, like his predecessors Chiang K'ai-shek and Chiang Ching-kuo, is also President in the government. In power, the government has been subordinate to the party-military tandem since the 1920s: but major constitutional reform was in process in 1991.[53]

Although the military-industrial-financial complex has shaped much about America since the Cold War began in the 1940s, the armed forces themselves have remained subordinate to civilian leaders and have not engaged in administering the country. In many Asian nations, the *military* has had a deep impact on constitutional governance, for many reasons: some military men found themselves in a privileged position after international war and were loath to relinquish power. Some refused to abide by a constitution requiring political neutrality or forbidding involvement in government. In other cases, they had once filled a vacuum as the government's main source of professionalized administrators and had grown accustomed to power. Others were seen as legitimate leaders of government because of the military's role in gaining liberation from colonialism. The military may have controlled the ruling party and the means of coercion, with or without popular support. And in some instances the military assumed governmental power to cleanse a country of corruption or to end instability.

For a mix of reasons, at one time or another in recent decades, generals or retired generals have ruled Bangladesh, Burma, Indonesia, Pakistan, South Korea, and Thailand, and their roles have deeply affected government in China, the Philippines, and Taiwan. In Thailand, "The King holds the position of Head of the Thai Armed Forces" (Chapter 1, Section 8), but from 1932 onward generals have generally ruled Thailand.[54] Under Indonesia's constitution, "The President holds the highest authority over the Army, Navy, and Air Forces" (Article 10),[55] but President Soeharto is himself a general and the extra-constitutional "ABRI," a politico-military group of immense influence in government, has a "dual function":

> This key theoretical and doctrinal construct, which spells out a "sociopolitical" as well as defense and security role for the armed forces, was strongly reaffirmed in the February 22 [1988] law on military affairs. This dual role, moreover, is seen as a permanent one . . . Indeed, given . . . [its] legacy in the founding and the preservation of the Indonesian state, its self-perception [is] as the institutional embodiment of Indonesian nationalism . . .[56]

Elsewhere, martial law or emergencies (for example, Malaysia) have put constitutionalism on hold or at best in an ambiguous position, but demilitarized government may well be more common by the turn of the century. Taiwan was under martial law longer than any other nation, from 1949 until July 15, 1987. The rigors of control varied over time; civilian law and democratic tendencies grew in uneasy parallel with martial law. With the end of martial law, some restraints continued, but the constitution functioned more autonomously and the KMT showed increasing tolerance of political diversity and opposition.[57] South Korea's politics have often been turbulent, with government under six constitutions since 1948, and under generals since 1961. In 1988 for the first time, the party of an incumbent President (Roh Tae-woo, a retired general) failed to win a majority in the National Assembly; three civilian-controlled parties held a parliamentary majority until two joined in a coalition with the President's party in 1990.[58] The question asked by the Koreans, as by other Asians, was: Will the military permit the democratic constitutional system to function and develop? As the military is an irregular center of public power, its primacy in a government generally indicates constitutionalist weakness, as does a "military-industrial complex." It is not that military officials tend more to corruption or abuse of power than civilians, but that the skills and mental set, the criteria and processes of leader selection in a military are not those appropriate for modern governance and human rights development.

Civilian rule is preferable to military rule. On the other hand, it affects not human rights constitutionalism whether a state is federal or unitary, and whether a national *legislature* has one, two, or three houses. Asian legislative traditions owe more to British and continental European institutions than to American traditions. Most parliaments are bicameral, but those of South Korea and Singapore have one chamber. Only Malaysia and India have *federal* systems analogous to America's, but Indonesia experimented with "the United States of Indonesia" in 1950.[59] Tun Mohamed Suffian compared the U.S., India, and Malaysia:

> [I]n the United States the Constitution spells out what powers "are delegated" to the center "nor prohibited" to states and provides that anything not so delegated to the center nor prohibited to the states is reserved to the states respectively or to the people. The Malaysian Constitution . . . follows the Indian Constitution in providing for a federal list, a state list, and a concurrent list, which spell out in great detail federal subjects, state subjects, and concurrent subjects with respect to which the federation, the states, and both . . ., respectively, have legislative and executive power, and further in providing in Article 77 that residual power on subjects not in the lists shall be vested in states. (Malaysia is a small country, and needs a strong central government; thus subjects like the police and education . . . are federal. . . .)[60]

India looked to several precedents when developing its federal structure: experience under the British Government of India Act (1935) and the systems of Australia, Canada and the United States.[61] The central government can dissolve a state government and rule directly in time of crisis. Parliament may legislate on a *state* matter (Article 249), if the upper house has first passed by a two-thirds majority a resolution declaring it "necessary or expedient in the national interest."[62]

Of more critical importance to constitutionalism in Asia than the federal-unitary question have been myriad intractable problems in balancing the interests of central government with local territorial, religious, and ethnic needs, and in pursuing acceptable forms of confederation or integration of territories. A few examples. "Reunification" has been a persistent constitutional demand in both the communist North and the democratic South of the Korean peninsula, where one government ruled one people from 668 until 1945.[63] Normalcy in either sector seems unlikely until some form of confederation has ended this most tragic of national divisions; yet, radical differences between the constitutional systems of North and South make prospects vague. In the late 1990s, China will absorb Hong Kong and Macao, but with what measure of autonomy? The degree of local self-rule allowed in these territories and in Tibet (controlled as an area of China since 1950) may well determine whether some form of constitutional confederation between China and Taiwan is developed, or Taiwan formally declares "independence" from China (its *de facto* status since the late 1940s).

In Indonesia, tensions continue between the central government and some of the many distinctive peoples on islands across its vast archipelago. For example, tiny East Timor was forcibly incorporated into Indonesia in 1976 when Portugal suddenly ended its colonialism; it continues to desire its measure of autonomy. In Sri Lanka, a constitutional democracy, endemic conflict between the majority Sinhalese and the Tamils exploded into large-scale violence in the 1980s. With the help of India under the Indo-Lankan Accord of July, 1987, Sri Lanka's government has kept the unitary state intact, but has also sought ethno-territorial reconciliation by creating a "federal-style" devolution of functions to elected "Provincial Councils."[64] Perhaps only in the Civil War and in relations with Native Americans has the United States faced challenges analogous to some of the Asian problems touched on above.

The *judiciaries* of Asia have not been co-equal with the executive or legislative branches of government except where the United States tradition of judicial review has been at work, directly or indirectly. In general, English and European legalisms are the key foreign influences. Soviet law has provided a partial model for China, North Korea, Mongolia and Vietnam. Courts are commonly located under a justice ministry. In the non-communist Asian systems, many courts enjoy a high degree of independence, others do not. The legacy of British law in some South and Southeast Asian nations is profound. German, Swiss and French approaches to judicial thinking have affected Japan, Taiwan, Thailand, and South Korea, while Dutch law has contributed to jurisprudence in Indonesia and Sri Lanka.

English common law parliamentarism and/or civil law deference to statutes passed by democratically elected legislatures have in some countries added to the local political factors restraining judges from applying constitutional provisions to court cases. Yet, America's most appreciated contribution to constitutional cultures in Asia may be the example of a fully independent judicial system with the power to determine the constitutionality of laws and other official acts. Judicial review powers are constitutionally conferred on the courts of India, Japan, and the Philippines, and on South Korea's "Constitution Court."[65] Elsewhere, they are viewed as a respected possibility or as undemocratic. The Philippine Supreme Court—especially before the 1972 imposition of martial law and after the 1986 "People's Revolution"—has been the most prestigious organ of that country's government. In Japan as well, the Supreme Court and the 1947 Constitution are by far the most trusted and respected national political institutions. In India, and through India's influence in Malaysia, Singapore, Sri Lanka, and other countries, judicial review generally reinforces limited, responsible government and human rights.[66] The general logic of human rights constitutionalism suggests judicial review in some form as a necessary check on executive, legislative, and private violations of human rights.

To compare *individual rights* in one country (here, the United States) with rights in an immense multi-national region containing about 60% of humankind and hundreds of cultures is admittedly presumptuous and a daunting task. One needs to clarify who one is talking about; one must differentiate within a given country, for example, between the economically powerful and the poor, the highly educated and the illiterate, the urban and the remote rural, the authoritarian and the democratic.

That admitted, even the briefest of comparisons must touch on basic differences of emphasis as much as upon specific rights issues.

In Asia, *freedom* has been valued highly by many governments and peoples. To a meaningful degree, *voting rights* have been institutionalized in most non-communist countries and have been discussed seriously with respect to China, Vietnam, and Cambodia. However, the freedom of the individual is commonly seen as inextricably linked with and even dependent upon the freedom of one's family (nuclear or extended) or work unit, ethnic and/or religious group, local or regional subculture, or even one's country. But *equality* has been stressed even more strongly than freedom, both as an individual and as a nationalist matter. This is based on general principle among the educated, and because many citizens have suffered severely from poverty, maldistribution of wealth, lack of opportunity, and national and international economic exploitation. Generally, economic justice and national development have had higher priority than individual property rights among Asian friends of human rights constitutionalism. In Singapore press freedom is limited; more unusual, no right to real property is constitutionally recognized.[67] While business prospers, as in some other Asian states, stronger concern for socioeconomic rights is manifest in Singapore than in the United States.

What Asians ask is respect for their civilizations, and a fair measure of national benefit from economic activity carried on by domestic and international business interests in the country. Elites in and out of government find weak evidence of a linkage between free enterprise and individual rights and freedoms generally, and so disagree with a common American assumption. Anti-communist Asians inclined toward human rights constitutionalism separate clearly economic liberty from political and social freedoms, giving the latter more vigilant attention. Like democracy, capitalism can co-exist with both strong and weak protection of key human rights, such as *freedom of expression, religious liberty*, and *criminal justice rights*.

Freedom of the press and other forms of expression in Asia generally became more vigorous during the 1980s, in its exercise if not in its legal protection.[68] The freedom of the mass media is more often restricted in some Asian countries than in the United States; but the range of views in the free Asian press is much broader than in the United States. Advertising is generally a less dominant factor in Asian than in American serial publication; political advertisements are less crucial to Asian than to U.S. democratic processes. Occasionally, repressive governments which claim commitment to press freedom allege that controls are necessary for public peace, security and/or national development. Some such appeals manifest nonconstitutionalist authoritarianism; others do not, as when communal violence would surely result from insensitive media coverage (for example, in India or Malaysia).

Legal technicalities abound in the area of criminal justice, from the moment of contact with a policeman until sentencing and incarceration or release. Differential treatment based on economic means as in the United States, or torture or prolonged detention without trial for peaceable political dissent as in a number of Asian countries, are always contrary to human rights constitutionalism. Discrimination on the basis of ethnic group, race, religion, and sex vary less with constitutional system than with local culture, but problems are endemic as in America.

Full *religious liberty* presupposes official and societal tolerance for the public existence of diverse belief systems, not simply for the private and silent adherence of an individual to a faith or idea system. With a public, institutionalized, officially protected existence, a religion first enjoys freedom to speak to issues and to influence society, law and policy. How to protect and moderate by law the free individual and institutional expression of belief systems in a pluralist society or a secularist state so that the rights of all are honored? In a country where one persuasion (whether religious, secular, or anti-religious) is dominant? The answers proffered by Asian constitutional systems and the United States differ.

America would protect religious liberty by strictly maintaining distance between the state and all religion (in theory), by prohibiting laws which either establish one religion or interfere with the free public exercise of any religion. Yet, American public life abounds with "in God we trust" and other signs of "civil religion." Many Asians, like many Europeans and others, have found the American understanding of the "separation of church and state," as concretized in judicial decisions and commentary, sometimes strained, convoluted, inconsistent and more compatible at times with rigid secularism than with a neutral or friendly attitude toward religion in general. Be that as it may, United States doctrine does express movement towards tolerance in a distinctive history of religious politics and deep intolerance; great progress has been made, especially since the presidential election of a Catholic, John F. Kennedy, in 1960.

A multitude of ethnic and religious divisions and harsh history have made enforcement of tolerance a higher priority of constitutionalism in many South and Southeast Asian nations than in America. However, religion, taken seriously, can generally be a powerful motivational force for, rather than an obstacle to, "modernization."[69] A great majority of the world's Muslims and Buddhists live in Asia. The Islamic countries, the Philippines, and Christian minorities in almost all Asian countries adhere to monotheism. Hinduism, Buddhism, Taoism, Confucianism, nation-specific belief systems, and animism add to this broadest of the world's continental arrays of religions. In South and Southeast Asia, the Islamic revolution has sharpened religio-political debate among Muslims, and has led to efforts to establish Islam more firmly in constitution and/or law. For example, Islam became the state religion of Bangladesh under the 1988 Constitution (8th Amendment) Act, but without restricting other religions.[70]

Some Muslim countries establish Islam, others, like Indonesia, do not. Indonesia instead makes belief in God one of its five constitutional pillars (*Pancasila*).[71] A large majority of Asia's Muslims are moderates (generally Sunni) rather than "Fundamentalists." In a few countries people continue to die over their religious differences. Examples include the recurrent communal violence in India involving Hindus, Muslims, and Sikhs, and in Malaysia between Muslim Malays and Chinese-Malaysians. Buddhism is the major religion, in a few cases established, in countries such as Sri Lanka, Burma, Thailand, Kampuchea, Laos, Vietnam and Japan.[72] In Japan's constitutional thinking, the quasi-pacifist human rights constitutionalism embodied in the basic law, rather than Buddhism or Shinto, has become virtually the national faith.[73] India is a secular multi-religious state. Singapore, Taiwan and South Korea have become secular Confucianist democratic states, but the large Christian minority in the latter has continued a leadership role in democratic nationalism since the 1919 "March First (independence) Movement."[74] Thailand's Constitution provides: "The King is a Buddhist and Upholder of religions."[75] In general, religious liberty is honored in practice by Asian constitutional systems. The consensus, apart from the Communist states, may be: The wisdom or danger of establishing a religion depends on local factors. Law and constitution should assure tolerance, prevent religious discrimination, and foster respect for all religions.

All Asian states have *changed their constitutions* by amendment or replacement since the Second World War, but all except the Communist countries have aspired to a constitutional document that is relatively stable and permanent in its substance,[76] like the United States. A few examples. Since readopting its short 1945 Constitution in 1959, Indonesia has passed no amendments. Japan did not once amend its 1889 constitution and has yet to amend the 1947 constitution, but that displeases only a small minority. On the other hand, Thailand's fourth constitution since 1932 came into effect in 1978 and a fifth was being written in 1991; South Korea's sixth came in 1988.[77] India's constitution, the world's longest, is of book length and had been expanded by sixty-two amendments as of 1991. Amendment requires only a simple majority with "a majority of not less than two-thirds of the members" of each house "present and voting."[78] Malaysia's amendment processes, used twenty times, are modeled on India's, but establish different levels of difficulty for amending provisions of different subject matter.

Such are some of the similarities and differences between constitutionalism in the United States and Asia with respect to executive, legislative, judicial, military and party powers, individual rights, and the place of religion. With exceptions, Asians, like Americans, support freedom of expression, elections, and limited government. Among American systemic characteristics that seem to contrast with Asian patterns are: clarity about military subordination to civilian leaders; incomprehension of long-term government planning; little apprehension about government stability; an extraordinarily elaborate system of written law; courts which are not only independent but have a decisive power of judicial review; overemphasis on economic freedom and underemphasis on basic socioeconomic rights; muddled and rigid law on religion and the state; and a consensual belief that the Constitution is really "*supreme*" over all laws and leaders. How equality and hierarchy mesh and contend in both regions defies simple formulation.

American Influence on Constitutionalism in Asia

Since 1945, the United States has affected constitutionalism in many countries of East, Southeast and South Asia. Subsequent chapters indicate the nature and limits of American influence and its absence in some cases. Here the contexts of influence and some instances not cited in the country studies are presented.

American constitutionalism has influenced many Asian countries during U.S. occupations and by their free consultation of America's constitutional experience. America occupied the Philippines (1898–1946, except 1942–1945), Japan (1945–1952), and South Korea (1945–1948) and encouraged democratic revolution there, with quite different policies and results. The more common context of U.S. influence has been free consultation by Asian constitution-makers, politicians and scholars, of seminal American documents, constitutional law scholarship, and judicial decisions. Many Asian constitutional lawyers, judges, and leaders have been for decades *au courant* with major developments in American case law, by reading case reporters, professional journals, newspapers, or American news weeklies.

In some cases reading has been supplemented by ongoing associations with American colleagues. At the origins of some constitutions, consultations with American scholars and public figures have taken place in Asia and in the United States. In addition, judges in some Asian countries have used and sometimes cited in their decision-making the doctrines of American courts, particularly the U.S. Supreme Court. Numerous Asian scholars and students, and some judges, have spent short or long periods in the United States, studying and experiencing American constitutionalism, and American counterparts have studied in Asia. (Relatively few Asian professors have taught about their countries' law in America.) In some cases, impact has depended on the intensity of the exposure, not on the length of a stay. More weighty than any particular documents, books, or judicial decisions, has been the degree to which the United States has been perceived by the Asian as deeply committed to human rights constitutionalism in law and policy.

The United States Constitution has been less relevant to American influence in Asia than other documents such as the 1776 "Declaration of Independence" and Abraham Lincoln's "Gettysburg Address." Before 1945, American ideas might inspire, but to subjugated Asian leaders as to most Europeans, simply as part of the Western political heritage, not as a model for possible imitation. For example, the Indonesian Nationalist Party (PNI) was proclaimed on July 4, 1927, in conscious commemoration of the U.S. Declaration of Independence. In the decades that followed before independence, Indonesian speeches and political posters abounded with phrases from the Declaration and the Gettysburg Address. They were seen as appropriate for people everywhere who supported the cause of anticolonialist democracy.[79] Later, framers of the 1945 Constitution of Indonesia, such as Mohamed Yamin, consulted American documents:[80]

> Before me is the structure of the Republic of the United States of America, which time and again has been used as an example for several constitutions in the world, for this is the oldest constitution existing in the world, and contains three elements: (1) the Declaration of Rights in the city of Philadelphia (1774); (2) the Declaration of Independence of July 4, 1776; (3) and finally, the Constitution of the United States of America (1787).

At the end of the last century, the United States reimposed colonial control on the Filipinos just as they were gaining freedom from Spain. By the time independence came on July 4, 1946, America had institutionalized its own ideas of law and constitution in the island nation. Public health and education were also promoted, but wealth was left in the hands of an exploitive few families. The constitution approved by both the United States government and the Filipinos in 1935 became the "supreme law" of the land from 1946 until martial law was declared in 1972 by President Ferdinand Marcos.[81] The 1987 Constitution of the Philippines, explained by Professors Fernando in this book, goes beyond the American tradition in its emphasis on socioeconomic rights and other features.[82]

At times, America's constitutional wisdom has been explicitly rejected, as by Sir Ivor Jennings when drafting Sri Lanka's "Soulbury Constitution" in the 1940s. He opposed an American-style Bill of Rights as superfluous, noting that Britain has "no Bill of Rights: we merely have liberty according to law, and we think—truly, I believe—that we do the job better than any country."[83] After independence, in the absence of rights provisions, Sri Lankan judges relied on law and on judicial precedents to affirm individual rights. They drew some precedents from India and the United States.[84] However, the later Constitutions of 1972 and 1978 contain declarations of rights which represent "a radical break from the British tradition . . . [They are] reminiscent of the Constitutions of the United States, Ireland and India and of certain countries of Europe."[85]

Asian constitution-makers have on occasion solicited the views of American constitution scholars and judges. For example, leaders such as A.S. Chowdhury and Kamal Hossein consulted with Professor Albert P. Blaustein of Rutgers University and other Americans as they drafted a constitution for Bangladesh in the early 1970s.[86] By bloody rebellion, Bangladesh, the former East Pakistan, had detached itself from federation with West Pakistan. Abu Sayeed Chowdhury, the first President, said of individual rights in the Bangladesh Constitution:

> A study of these rights would at once make it clear that in their formulation, Magna Carta (1215), the Petition of Right (1628), the Bill of Rights (1689), and the Constitution of the United States of America, together with its amendments, were kept in mind. It is in this part of the Constitution that the full benefit of the written Constitution of the United States was taken as a model, and in fact, in dealing with these provisions the courts of Bangladesh freely refer to the judicial pronouncements of the Superior Courts of Britain, America, and the Commonwealth countries.[87]

American influence on judicial review, federalism and rights in Indian constitutionalism has been substantial, and through the Indian filter it has extended to other former British possessions such as Bangladesh, Sri Lanka, Malaysia and Singapore.[88] During the long drafting process, "Sir B.N. Rau, the Constitutional Adviser to the Constituent Assembly, and Sir Alladi Krishnaswamy Ayyar, one of the . . . most respected lawyer members of the [Assembly committees] . . ., frequently relied on the Constitution of the United States."[89] Rau also consulted President Harry Truman, American constitutional lawyers, and judges Felix Frankfurter and Learned Hand, and cited such documents as the Articles of Confederation and John Marshall's opinion in *McCulloch v. Maryland.*[90] Since India's Constitution came into force in 1950, American judicial precedents have been cited in over 1,000 Indian court cases.[91]

Although China's search for stable modern statehood has taken her down quite different paths, Nationalist leaders in the 1920s seriously proposed the establishment of "united autonomous provinces" of China with a federal government analogous to the United States.[92] Moreover, the ideology of KMT leader Dr. Sun Yat-sen, still prevailing on Taiwan, has been compared to Lincoln's view on "government of the people, by the people and for the people."[93] Those words were heard again in the student democracy movements of Myanmar (Burma) and China in 1988 and 1989.

The influence of the United States during and since the occupations of South Korea and Japan are covered by our authors, below.[94] A few comparisons may be added. The "USAMGIK" (U.S.A. Military Government in Korea) directly governed southern Korea from its liberation in 1945 until independence began under the 1948 Constitution. USAMGIK had little preparation or expertise for the task. In 1948, Americans did not participate in drafting the Constitution; but USAMGIK gave its essential backing to the autonomy of Korea's constitution-making progress. In Japan, on the other hand, General MacArthur's offices ruled indirectly through Japan's government apparatus, wartime planning had yielded useful guidance for the Occupation, and Americans drafted a good deal of Japan's Constitution. MacArthur, Charles Kades and a few others are among the principal pioneers of Japan's human rights constitutionalism. Except for the many years of colonial rule in the Philippines, this constitution-writing may be the most significant extension of United States governance into a foreign land in American history.

CONCLUSION

Asia's post-colonial constitutional history is brief, but, with exceptions, impressive. Besides unexcelled competence, many of Asia's constitutional lawyers display great learning about foreign systems and creative openness to adapting constitutional and legal devices of others to their own nations' needs. By emulating them, more American counterparts can learn to think in a transculturally comparative manner, and freshen perspective on U.S. constitutional problems. Harold Berman contends that for about 1,000 years, revolutionary challenges from within the West have recurrently revitalized its legal tradition, but that now this legal tradition is in crisis:

> A social theory of law must move beyond the study of Western legal systems, and the Western legal tradition, to a study of non-Western legal systems and traditions, and of the development of a common legal language for mankind. For only in that direction lies the way out of the crisis of the Western legal tradition in the late twentieth century.[95]

The authors here manifest a common language of constitutional discourse. Consideration of Asian experiences of government and law can revitalize and broaden the West's understanding of its own transcultural principles and may serve as a corrective to ossified thinking about constitutional issues. One would hope that if the United States celebrates a tercentenary, it will be joined by many Asian countries fêting their constitutional centennials, and that Americans may have enriched their own heritage by learning of other traditions of human rights constitutionalism, where community lives with individuality and equality with freedom.

NOTES

1 Klaus Stern, "The Genesis and Evolution of European-American Constitutionalism," Berlin Conference on the Law of the World, World Peace Through Law Center, July, 1985, 8. The American theory and list of rights is more an indigenous product than a derivation from English common law. The U.S. Bill of Rights can be traced to early state constitutions and very early colonial documents such as the Massachusetts Body of Liberties (1641). Donald S. Lutz, "U.S. Bill of Rights in Historical Perspective," presented at the American Political Science Association meeting, Atlanta, September, 1989.

2 Thomas Fleiner-Gerster, "Federalism, Decentralization and Rights," in Louis Henkin and Albert Rosenthal, eds., *Constitutionalism and Rights: The Influence of the United States Constitution Abroad*, New York, Columbia University Press, 1990, 19.

3 Albert P. Blaustein provided the latest revision dates of constitutions. See his *Constitutions of the Countries of the World*, 17 volumes, Dobbs Ferry, NY, Oceana Publications, 1988. The first constitution to establish a sovereign entity was the Fundamental Orders of Connecticut, 1638. Albert P. Blaustein and Jay A. Sigler eds. and comps., *Constitutions That Made History*, New York, Paragon House Publishers, 1988, 1.

4 On India's Constitution, *see infra* note 69 and ch. 5.

5 See, for example, Robert N. Bellah et al., *Habits of the Heart: Individualism and Commitment in American Life*, Berkeley, University of California Press, 1985.

6 Joel B. Grossman, "Teaching Civil Liberties in the Bicentennial Year," *Focus on Law Studies*, Vol. 6, No.2, spring, 1991, 9. see also American Society of Learned Societies, *The ACLS Comparative Constitutionalism Project*, ALCS Occasional Paper No.13, 1990, especially 5–16.

7 Mark Tushnet, *Red, White, and Blue: Critical Analysis of Constitutional Law*, Cambridge: Harvard University Press, 1988, the "Introduction".

8 David L. Sills and Robert K. Merton, "Social Science Quotations: Who Said What, When and Where," *Items: Social Science Research Council*, Vol.45, No. 1, March, 1991, 3.

9 As quoted in David D. Buck, "Forum on Universalism and Relativism in Asian Studies: Editor's Introduction, "*The Journal of Asian Studies*, Vol.50, No.1, February, 1991, 32.

10 The best analysis of democracy and constitutionalism as found in U.S. constitutional law may be Walter F. Murphy, James E. Fleming, and William F. Harris, II, *American Constitutional Interpretation*, Mineola, NY, Foundation Press, 1986.

11 United Nations, *United Nations Actions in the Field of Human Rights*, New York, United Nations, 1980, 5–6 [hereinafter *UN*]; David R. Forsythe, *Human Rights and World Politics*, Lincoln, University of Nebraska Press, 1981, 8.

12 Resolution 217 A(III) of the General Assembly, December 10, 1948, in UNIFO ed., *International Human Rights Instruments of the United Nations, 1948–1982*, Pleasantville, NY, UNIFO Publishers, 1983, 5–7 [hereinafter, *UNIFO*].

13 *UNIFO*, 86–100; *UN*, 8–10, 12–14. For a thoughtful analysis of the comparative context of current democratic theorizing, see John E. Lent, "Thoughts on Political Thought: An Introduction," *International Political Science Review*, Vol. 11, No. 1, 1990, 5. A second Optional Protocol to the International Covenant on Civil and Political Rights to abolish the death penalty, was adopted by the General Assembly in 1990. G.A. Res. 44/128, U.N. Press Release GA/7977, at 406, 1990. For a concise account of the historical and regional development of international human rights instruments, and a summary of the content of human rights of the three "generations," see Burns H. Weston, "Human Rights," in R.P. Claude and B.H. Weston eds., *Human Rights in the World Community: Issues and Action*, Philadelphia, University of Pennsylvania Press, 1989, 17–28.

14 Resolution 34/180 of the General Assembly, December 18, 1979, in effect on September 3, 1981; *UNIFO*, 150–154.

15 Resolution 39/46 of the General Assembly, December 10, 1984; *Amnesty International Report 1985*, 10–11, 353–357. United States policy is *not* to ratify international human rights agreements.

16 This 1985 LAWASIA statement deals only with civil rights and liberties, the preoccupation of democratic law elites in a number of Asian countries.

"Basic Principles of Human Rights"

(LAWASIA Human Rights Committee, 1985)

Principle 1

(a) Everyone has the inherent right to life, and shall not be arbitrarily deprived of his life.

(b) The death penalty may be imposed only for the most serious crimes and after fair public trial on evidence presented to a legally competent, independent and impartial tribunal.

Principle 2

(a) Everyone has the inherent right to liberty and security of person and shall not be subjected to arbitrary arrest or detention.

(b) Anyone who is arrested or detained shall be informed of the reasons therefore at the time of his arrest and shall be entitled to communicate the fact of his arrest to a person of his choice.

(c) Anyone arrested shall be entitled to access to counsel of his choice.

(d) Anyone charged with an offence is entitled to a fair and public trial within a reasonable time by a legally competent, independent and impartial tribunal.

Principle 3
Everyone is equal before the law and is entitled without any discrimination to the equal protection of the law.

Principle 4
No one shall be held guilty of any criminal offence for any act or omission which did not constitute a criminal offence when it was committed.

Principle 5
(a) Anyone deprived of his liberty shall be treated with respect for his inherent dignity as a human person.
(b) No one shall be subjected to torture, or to cruel, inhuman or degrading punishment or treatment.

Principle 6
No one should be subject to preventive detention but in those countries where preventive detention exists, everyone so detained shall be entitled to prompt periodic review of his detention by a legally competent, independent and impartial tribunal.

Principle 7
(a) No one shall be arbitrarily deprived of the right to enter his own country.
(b) Anyone who is an alien, lawfully in a country, shall not be expelled except pursuant to a decision reached in accordance with the law in force at the time he entered the country.

Principle 8
No one shall be subject to coercion which would restrict his choice of religion or belief. Freedom to manifest one's religion or beliefs may be subject only to such limitations as are prescribed by law and are necessary to protect public safety, order, health or morals or the fundamental rights and freedoms of others.

Principle 9
To ensure the enjoyment of these minimum standards everyone is entitled to have legal assistance available to him.

Principle 10
These principles have been formulated on the basis that they are the minimum standards to be observed at all times after allowing for the fact that emergencies threatening the life of a nation may occur from time to time.

For further information on the Human Rights Committee and its Human Rights Bulletin, contact: LAWASIA Human Rights Committee, Law School, Ateneo de Manila University, Salcedo Village, Makati, Metro Manila 3116, Philippines. A broader conception of human rights applying only to ASEAN countries, is contained in the "Declaration of the Basic Duties of ASEAN Peoples and Governments," adopted on December 9, 1983, Jakarta, Indonesia. A.P. Blaustein, R.S. Clark, and J.A. Sigler, eds., *Human Rights Sourcebook*, New York: Paragon House Publishers, 1987, 646.

17 Although "cultural fluidity" and change may well be more noteworthy in Asia than in most Western countries since 1945, perennial understandings of social obligations, religion, public authority and power continue to influence government and politics. See Lucian Pye, *Asian Power and Politics*, Cambridge, Harvard University Press, 1985; John T. Noonan, *Bribes*, Berkeley, University of California Press, 1987; Crawford Young, *The Politics of Cultural Pluralism*, Madison, University of Wisconsin Press, 1974; S.N. Eisenstadt, M. Abitol, and H. Chazan, "Cultural Premises, Political Structures and Dynamics," *International Political Science Review*, Vol. 8, No. 4, 1987, 291; Larry Diamond, Juan J. Linz, and S.M. Lipset eds., *Democracy in Developing Countries: Volume 3, Asia*, Boulder, Westview Press, 1988; and John R. Bowen, "On the Political Construction of Tradition: *Gotong Royong* in Indonesia," *Journal of Asian Studies*, Vol. 45, No. 3, May, 1988, 545.

18 *The Constitution of the Republic of the Philippines*, Quezon City, 1987.

19 *The Constitution of Japan*, Tokyo, 1947. For a translation, see Hiroshi Itoh and Lawrence W. Beer, *The Constitutional Case Law of Japan: Selected Supreme Court Decisions, 1961–70*, Seattle, University of Washington Press, 1978, 258.

20 This perspective borrows from Richard John Neuhaus, Editor of *First Things*, Institute on Religion and Public Life, New York.

21 Mary Ann Glendon, "Notes on the Culture Struggle: Dr. King in the Law Schools," *First Things*, No. 7, November, 1990, 9.

22 On the salience of religion to Asian development, see David E. Apter, *Rethinking Development: Modernization, Dependency, and Postmodern Politics*, Beverly Hills, Sage Publications, 1987.

23 I.W. Mabbett, ed., *Patterns of Kingship and Authority in Traditional Asia*, London, Croon Helm, 1985; James C. Hsiung ed., *Human Rights in East Asia*, New York, Paragon House Publishers, 1986.

24 John L. Esposito, ed., *Islam in Asia: Religion, Politics and Society*, New York, Oxford University Press, 1987; Majid Khadduri, *The Islamic Conception of Justice*, Baltimore, Johns Hopkins University Press, 1985; M.B. Hooker, *Islamic Law in Southeast Asia*, Singapore, Oxford University Press, 1984; and R. Israeli and A.H. Johns, eds., *Islam in Asia: Vol. II, Southeast and East Asia*, Boulder, Westview Press, 1984.

25 I.W. Mabbett, *Patterns of Kingship*; Robert Heine-Geldern, *Conceptions of State and Kingship in Southeast Asia*, Data Paper No. 18, Southeast Asia Program, Cornell University, Ithaca, April, 1976.

26 Lawrence Ward Beer, *Freedom of Expression in Japan: A Study in Comparative Law, Politics and Society*, Tokyo, Kodansha International, 1984, chapter 2.

27 Bingham Powell, Jr., "American Voter Turnout in Comparative Perspective," *American Political Science Review*, Vol. 80, No. 1, March, 1986, 35.

28 Among the periodic surveys of human rights performance are: *The Lawasia Human Rights Bulletin*, Human Rights Committee, *supra* note 16; U.S. Department of State, *Country Reports on Human Rights Practices* (annual), Washington, D.C., U.S. Government Printing Office; Raymond D. Gastil, ed., *Freedom in the World: Political Rights and Civil Liberties* (annual), New York, Freedom House; *Amnesty International Report* (annual), London, Amnesty International; *World Survey of Press Freedom* (annual), Columbia, Journalism School, University of Missouri; *Report on Science and Human Rights* (newsletter), Washington, D.C., American Association for the Advancement of Science.

In addition, some of the above and other agencies issue reports on individual countries and problems; for example: the United Nations Human Rights Committee, the International Commission of Jurists, *Article 19* (freedom of expression), and Asiawatch.

On problems of assessment and measurement, see Jack Donnelly and Rhoda E. Howard, "Assessing National Human Rights Performance: A Theoretical Framework," *Human Rights Quarterly*, Vol. 10, No. 2, May 1987, 214, and their edited work *International Handbook of Human Rights*, Westport, CT, Greenwood Press, 1987; and David Hollenbach, *Claims in Conflict*, New York, Paulist Press, 1979. Donnelly's earlier analysis of human rights conceptions in the non-Western world is valuable but not very well grounded in precise understanding of Asia; see "Human Rights and Human Dignity: An Analytic Critique of Non-Western Conception of Human Rights," *American Political Science Review*, Vol. 76, No. 2, June, 1982, 303.

29 Milestones were the 1979 founding by Richard Pierre Claude of *Universal Human Rights*, now *Human Rights Quarterly*, Johns Hopkins University Press, and the 1981 establishment of the International Association of Constitutional Law (IACL); see *Years of IACL, 1981–1986*, IACL, Beograd, Yugoslavia, 1987, 3–11.

30 C.G. Weeramantry, *Equality and Freedom: Some Third World Perspectives*, Colombo, Hansa Publishers, 1976.

31 Bellah, *Habits of the Heart*; Walter F. Murphy, "Constitutions, Constitutionalism, and Democracy," a paper for the American Council of Learned Societies, September, 1988.

32 A Congressional Budget Office Report, 1989, indicates the following trends in after-tax family income, adjusted for inflation in constant 1987 dollars, and including food and housing benefits:

Families		***1979***	***1987***	***Difference***
Lowest	20%	$ 6,692	$ 6,178	−7.7%
Second	20%	$14,742	$13,986	−5.1%
Middle	20%	$21,742	$22,035	+1.3%
Fourth	20%	$29,293	$30,997	+5.8%
Top	20%	$45,404	$52,584	+15.8%

See David Ellwood, *Poor Support: Poverty in the American Family*, New York, Basic Books, 1988; and Michael B. Katz, *The Underserving Poor: From the War on Poverty to the War on Welfare*, New York, Pantheon Books, 1989.

33 See *The Forgotten Half: Non-College Youth in America*, Washington, D.C., William T. Grant Foundation Commission on Work, Family and Citizenship, January, 1988. The proportion of jobs that are low paying will continue to increase rapidly in the years ahead. *See also* the U.S. Census Bureau

report to the House Committee on Children, Youth, and Families, Washington, D.C., March, 1990. For detail on socioeconomic conditions in Asia, see "Regional Performance Figures," *Asia Yearbook 1991*, Hong Kong, Far Eastern Economic Review, 1991, 6–9.

34 David E. Apter, *Rethinking Development: Modernization, Dependency, and Postmodern Politics*, Beverly Hills, Sage Publications, 1987.

35 For example, Gary J. Jacobson, *The Supreme Court and the Decline of Constitutional Aspiration*, Totowa, N.J., Rowman & Littlefield, 1986; Michael Harrington, *The New American Poverty*, New York, Holt, Reinhart & Winston, 1984; Jerold Auerbach, *Unequal Justice: Lawyers and Social Change in Modern America*, New York, Oxford University Press, 1976; Norman E. Isaacs, *Untended Gates: The Mismanaged Press*, New York, Columbia University Press, 1986; Nathan Glazer, *Affirmative Discrimination: Ethnic Inequality and Public Policy*, Cambridge, Harvard University Press, 1987; and U.S. Bishops, *Economic Justice for All: Catholic Social Teaching and the U.S. Economy*, Washington, D.C., U.S. Catholic Conference, 1985.

36 See Buck, *supra*, n. 9; Alison Dundee Renteln, "The Unanswered Challenge of Relativism and the Consequences for Human Rights," *Human Rights Quarterly*, Vol. 7, No. 4, November, 1985, 514; and James H. Mittelman, "Opening the American Mind: International Political Science," *PS: Political Science and Politics*, March, 1989, 52.

37 Bellah, *Habits of the Heart*; Alasdair MacIntyre, *After Virtue: A Study in Moral Theory*, Notre Dame, University of Notre Dame Press, 1981, especially 233–237; Amatai Etzioni, "The 'Me First' Model in Social Sciences Is Too Narrow," *Chronicle of Higher Education*, February 1, 1989; "Crisis in Political Thought: In Search of New Directions," *Participation*, International Political Science Association, fall, 1986, 6; and James A. Bill, "Area Studies and Theory-Building in Comparative Politics: A Stocktaking," *PS*, fall, 1985, 810.

38 David Kolb, "American Individualism: Does It Exist?" *Nanzan Review of American Studies*, Vol. 6, 1984, Nanzan University, Nagoya, Japan, 25–26, 30–31. The quite different perspectives of Europe, and their scholarly effects, are succinctly stated in David McKay, "Why Is There a European Political Science?," *PS: Political Science and Politics*, fall, 1988, 1051. U.S. individualism does not seem to translate into excessive use of law for rights protection; see Marc Galanter, "Reading the Landscape of Disputes: What We Know and Don't Know (and Think We Know) about Our Allegedly Contentious and Litigious Society," *UCLA Law Review*, Vol. 31, No. 1, October, 1983, 4.

39 See *supra*, text at n. 20.

40 Fritz Gaenslen, "Culture and Decision-making in China, Japan, Russia and the United States," *World Politics*, October, 1986, 78.

41 See *infra* chapter 13, last sentence.

42 Besides the country studies here, see my *Constitutionalism in Asia: Asian Views of the American Influence*, 1988 edition, Baltimore, OP/Reprint Series in Contemporary Asian Studies, University of Maryland Law School, 1988; Vernon Bogdanor, ed., *Constitutions in Democratic Politics*, Aldershot, U.K., Gower Publishing Co., 1988; Jack Donnelly and Rhoda Howard, eds., *International Handbook of Human Rights*, Henkin and Rosenthal, *Constitutionalism and Rights*.

43 See *supra* text at n. 20.

44 See Article 2, The Constitution of the Republic of the Philippines, 1987; Chapter 5, Constitution of the Kingdom of Thailand, 1978.

45 Article 3, the Indonesian Constitution of 1945; *see infra* "Appendix" to chapter 6.

46 Rasul B. Rais, "Pakistan in 1988: From Command to Conciliation Politics," *Asian Survey*, February, 1989, 199; P.M. Bhutto was removed by coup in 1990 in a regression to military government. See Lawrence Ziring, "Pakistan in 1990: The Fall of Benazir Bhutto, "*Asian Survey*, February, 1991, 113.

47 *See infra* chapter 7, and Lawrence Beer, *Freedom of Expression in Japan*, chapter 7.

48 Dor Bahadur Bista, "Nepal in 1988: Many Losses, Some Gains," *Asian Survey*, February, 1989, 223; B.N. Aziz, "Nepal's Monarch Is Teetering," *Christian Science Monitor*, March 21, 1990; *New York Times*, April 7–10, 1990; and Hiranjan Koirala, "Nepal in 1990: End of an Era, "*Asian Survey*, February, 1991, 134.

49 *See infra* chapter 13.

50 *See infra* chapter 8, and K.U. Menon, "Brunei Darussalam in 1988: Aging in the Wood," *Asian Survey*, February, 1989, 140.

51 *See infra*, chapter 10, and K.S. Nathan, "Malaysia in 1988: The Politics of Survival," *Asian Survey*, February, 1989, 129; Fred R. von der Mehden, "Malaysia in 1990: Another Electorial Victory," *Asian Survey*, February, 1991, 164.

52 Lowell Dittmer, "China in 1988: the Continuing Dilemma of Socialist Reform," *Asian Survey*, January, 1989, 12, and "China in 1989: The Crisis of Incomplete Reform," *Asian Survey*, January,

1990, 25; *New York Times* and *Far Eastern Economic Review*, July and August, 1988, May and June, 1989; Burma Watcher, "Burma in 1988: There Came a Whirlwind," *Asian Survey*, February, 1989, 174. When the democratic opposition in 1990 swept to easy election victory, the Burmese military disregarded the results and continued its regime. See James F. Guyot, "Myanmar in 1990: The Unconsummated Election," *Asian Survey*, February, 1991, 205.

53 See *infra*, chapter 3; James D. Seymour, "Taiwan in 1988: No More Bandits," *Asian Survey*, January, 1989, especially 56–60; June T. Dreyer, "Taiwan in 1989: Democratization and Economic Growth," *Asian Survey*, January, 1990, 52, and "Taiwan in 1990: Finetuning the System," *Asian Survey*, January, 1991, 57.

54 *Infra*, chapter 13, "Appendix 4." See Larry A. Niksch, "Thailand in 1988: The Economic Surge," *Asian Survey*, February, 1989, 165; Scott Christensen, "Thailand in 1990: Political Tangles," *Asian Survey*, February, 1991, 196; and David Morell and Chai-anan Samudvanija, *Political Conflict in Thailand*, Cambridge, Oelgeschlager, Gunn, and Hain, 1982. More generally, see Clark D. Neher, *Politics in Southeast Asia*, Cambridge, Schenkman Publishing Co., 1981.

55 *Infra*, chapter 10, "Appendix."

56 Gordon R. Hein, "Indonesia in 1988: Another Five Years for Soeharto, *Asian Survey*, February, 1989, 119; and Hans Thoolen, ed., *Indonesia and the Rule of Law: Twenty Years of New Order Government*, London, Frances Pinter, Publishers, 1987.

57 James Seymour, "Taiwan in 1988;" June T. Dreyer, "Taiwan in 1990."

58 William Shaw, ed., *Human Rights in Korea: History and Policy Perspectives*, Cambridge, Harvard Council on East Asian Studies Publications, 1991; Donald Macdonald, *The Koreans*, Boulder, Westview Press, 2d ed. 1990; and Young Whan Kihl, "South Korea in 1989: Slow Progress Toward Democracy," *Asian Survey*, January, 1990, 67.

59 Oemar Seno Adji, "An Indonesian Perspective on the American Constitutional Influence," in Lawrence Beer, *Constitutionalism in Asia*, 102. See generally Chung-5: Ahn, ed., *The Local Political System in Asia*, Seoul: Seoul National University Press, 1987.

60 Tun Mohamed Suffian, "The Malaysian Constitution and the United States Constitution," in *id.*, 136; *infra*, chapter 10; and Tun Mohamed Suffian, H.R. Lee & F.A. Tindale, eds., *The Constitution of Malaysia, 1957–1977*, Kuala Lumpur, Oxford University Press, 1978, 101–122.

61 P.K. Tripathi, "Perspectives on the American Constitutional Influence on the Constitution of India," in Lawrence Beer, *Constitutionalism in Asia*, 62–63.

62 *Id.* 57–71.

63 Donald Macdonald, *The Koreans*.

64 Bruce Matthew, "Sri Lanka in 1988: Seeds of the Accord," *Asian Survey*, February, 1989, 229; and annual articles on Sri Lanka in February issues of *Asian Survey*.

65 *Infra* chapters 2 and 7.

66 *Infra*, chapters 10 and 12.

67 *Infra*, chapter 12. As John Lent contends:

> "[T]he definition of values must go beyond property or *raison d'Etat*. Humans are a moral force, not just an economic one. We think as well as produce and consume. We desire, we are moral creatures. For its part, if the state is to receive our allegiance, if it is to be legitimate, it must also serve basic human needs, including those of the impoverished. Nor is it sufficient for leadership to be by technique—by opinion polls, imagery, thought control and manipulation."

Lent, *supra* note 13, at 17.

68 For example, consider the periods of more open political expression during the years 1986–1989 in Bangladesh, Myanmar, China, the Philippines, Pakistan, and Taiwan. See *Asian Survey*, January and February, 1985–1990.

69 Fred von der Mehden, *Religion and Modernization in Southeast Asia*, Syracuse, Syracuse University Press, 1986; and Leroy Rouner, ed., *Human Rights and World Religions*, Vol. 9, Boston University Studies in Philosophy and Religion Series, Notre Dame, Notre Dame University Press, 1988.

70 Syedur Rahman, "Bangladesh in 1988: Precarious Institution Building Amid Crisis Management," *Asian Survey*, February, 1989, 218; Craig Baxter, "Bangladesh in 1990: Another New Beginning?" *Asian Survey*, February, 1991, 146.

71 *Infra* chapter 10.

72 Fred von der Mehden, *Religion and Modernization in Southeast Asia*.

73 Lawrence W. Beer, "Japan (1947): Forty Years of the Post-War Constitution," in Vernon Bogdanor, *Constitutions in Democratic Politics Politics*, 174–183.

74 William Shaw, *Human Rights in Korea.*
75 Constitution of the Kingdom of Thailand, 1978, Chapter 1, Section 7, *infra*, chapter 13, Appendix 4.
76 On current constitutions and their ratification dates, see *supra*, Figure 1.1.
77 *Infra* chapters 9 and 13.
78 Jagdish Lal, *The Constitution of India as Amended* . . . Delhi, Delhi Law House, 1977, 173. W.D. Morris-Jones explains: "The Constitution has been amended 55 times [62 as of 1991] . . . It is doubtful, however, that this has had any ill effect on the extent of respect for the Constitution. The relevant public understands quite well the reasons for change. The very length (22 Parts, comprising nearly 400 Articles plus 10 Schedules) and detail of the documents invites 'adjustment' amendments. An examination of the first 42 amendments reveals . . . 15 were occasioned simply by changes in the status or boundaries of the States or other constituent units and . . . 14 were concerned with minor and virtually routine adjustments. 11 can be identified as significant responses to interpretations of the document made in Supreme Court Judgments." In "The Politics of the Indian Constitution (1950)," in Bogdanor, *Constitutions in Democratic Politics*, 149–150.
79 Adam Malik, *In the Service of the Republic*, Jakarta, Gunung Agung, 1980, 8–9, 129.
80 M. Yamin, as quoted in Lawrence Beer, *Constitutionalism in Asia*, 104. The Preamble of the 1945 "Constitution of the Proclamation State," as it is called by Indonesians, is reminiscent of the Declaration of Independence; *see infra* chapter 6, Appendix.
81 James L. Magavern and Enrique M. Fernando in Lawrence Beer, *Constitutionalism in Asia*, 141–148. *See also* Robert Pringle, *Indonesia and the Philippines*, New York, Columbia University Press, 1980; and Harry M. Scoble and Laurie S. Wiseberg, eds., *Access to Justice*, London, Zed Books, 1985, 101–105.
82 *Infra* chapter 11.
83 Joseph A.L. Cooray, *Constitutional and Administrative Law of Sri Lanka*, Colombo, Hansa Publishers, 1973, 509–511.
84 Discussion in March, 1985, with past Justice C.G. Weeramantry, Supreme Court of Sri Lanka.
85 Joseph Cooray, *Law of Sri Lanka*, 510–511.
86 Albert P. Blaustein, "The United States Constitution: A Model in Nation Building," *National Forum*, fall, 1984, 17.
87 Abu Sayeed Chowdhury, "The Bangladesh Constitution in American Perspective," in Lawrence Beer, *Constitutionalism in Asia*, 30.
88 Even where a British or indigenous precedent has been of primary importance, as in Malaysia, legal scholars have been aware of American commentary and alternative views on an issue. For relevant references, see Tun Mohamed Suffian et al., *The Constitution of Malaysia*, 10, 31, 34, 37, 126, 136, 177, 181.
89 P.K. Tripathi in Lawrence Beer, *Constitutionalism in Asia*, 64.
90 *Id.* 64–71.
91 Communication from George Gadbois, University of Kentucky, 1984.
92 Herbert H.P. Ma in Lawrence Beer, *Constitutionalism in Asia*, 39–55.
93 *Id.* 42–50.
94 *Infra*, chapters 7 and 9. *See also* Lawrence W. Beer, "Constitutionalism and Rights in Japan and Korea," in L. Henkin and A. Rosenthal, *Constitutionalism and Rights*.
95 Harold J. Berman, *Law and Revolution: The Formation of the Western Legal Tradition*, Cambridge, Harvard University Press, 1983, 1–4.

■ First published in *Occasional Paper No. 1*, Center for Democracy and Social Change, Lehigh University, 1996, 17 pp.

2

Current Human Rights Issues in Asia

⌘

What aspects of the human rights situation in Asia are most deserving of attention in a brief summary assessment? How best to convey the extremely complex reality with some semblance of fairness and accuracy? How to avoid painting too dark or too bright a picture of the status of human rights in general or in a given country? Over 60% of humankind live between Japan and Afghanistan. The diversity of Asian civilizations is mind-boggling, especially in Southern Asia. The task is daunting. That said, I hope the reader will be inclined toward compassion rather than outrage if at some point the assessment seems far off the mark.

I will first give a bit of context relevant to understanding human rights practices in Asia. I will then outline a few patterns of human rights problems recurring in a number of Asian countries. I will also mention recent human rights success stories in Asia.

We have all tended to be transfixed since 1985 with the tumultuous developments leading up to and following the end of the Cold War and the dissolution of the Soviet Union. Of course Asia has been affected by all this and by its own continuing rapid economic growth during this period; but I would invite you to shift your attention to long-term developments of arguably greater import for Asia. The half-century since the end of the Second World War has brought a virtual end to colonialism and the emergence of many independent nation-states throughout Asia. During the Second World War Japan was the only fully independent nation in Asia; now, almost all are independent. Admittedly, diverse related problems remain in such places as French Polynesia, Kashmir, Tibet, Sri Lanka, Burma, and East Timor, and the excessive American military presence on Okinawa is a thorn in the side of U.S.-Japan relations. Since independence, wars or other upheavals have come and gone and sadly come again in some Asian countries; but in Asia as elsewhere independence has ushered in an era of unprecedented national experimentation with institutions of law, government and politics. In fact, we live at the time in world history of the most exciting and creative developments of constitutional systems.

The most important element in this modern revolutionary process may be the unprecedented *worldwide diffusion and legitimation of human rights standards.* The concrete content and goals of the human rights movement are spelled out in the United Nations Universal Declaration of Human Rights (1948), numerous U.N. Covenants and Protocols (especially those passed in 1966), regional instruments,[1] and in most national constitutions and much pursuant law.[2] The Human Rights Standing Committee of the broadly representative Law Association for Asia and the Pacific (commonly referred to as "Lawasia") established in 1985 the "Basic Principles of Human Rights" in Asia.[3] Citizen rights and responsibilities are set forth in single-document national constitutions.

It is worth noting that only twenty of the 181 current national constitutions date back before 1950, and that 130 have been ratified since 1970.[4] There is now a virtual consensus in the world that a single-document constitution is an essential of modern statecraft.[5] Asia has many ancient and accomplished cultures, and is now variously affected by Buddhist, Islamist, Christian, Hindu, Confucian, Marxist, capitalist and other sociolegal foundations; but it has, with the exceptions of Japan and Thailand, only very brief experience with independence and with the government and law relevant to human rights protection and promotion. However, by 1996 many formerly subject Asian nations have regained their sense of national pride and identity after enduring long and humiliating cultural agonies under colonialism and imperialism.

Part of their present indigenous constitutional thought derives from the West, but they no longer defer to foreigners, particularly Western foreigners. Their able legal professionals work at the fusion of perennial national values and modern ideologies with transcultural principles of human rights law. Typically, Asian jurists bring a much richer comparative perspective to their tasks than is common with their counterparts in the United States. The leaders of these countries insist on respectful treatment because it is due them under human rights principles, not just because of their nations' great commercial successes in recent times. On the other hand, human rights principles and other world developments have weakened the power of state sovereignty to justify or explain away domestic human rights violations. Along with independence and constitutional development has come a new wave of world interdependence and attention to transcultural human rights principles. This has been unnerving for authoritarian leaders. Nationalist sensitivities, not a clash between human rights and cultures, are often behind the ruffled responses of a few Asian governments—such as those of Burma, China and Indonesia—to foreign, including Asian criticism of their human rights violations. Of course, some leaders oppose certain human rights, some openly, others more indirectly.

As in the United States, serious problems exist in Asia. But regional human rights dialogue is characterized less by despair than by the view expressed by a Chinese intellectual to an American friend who wondered at his calm in the face of the killings at Tiananmen Square in Beijing in 1989 and subsequent crackdowns: "Anything worth doing takes at least 500 years. In China, things are just beginning. Do not lose heart." The human rights tradition began only short decades ago in many Asian countries. Along with rage at injustice and sadness at the suffering of fellow human beings, realism and good humor are typically behind the widespread Asian efforts to firmly establish human rights in their respective countries.

A final contextual factor complicating American perceptions of Asian human rights realities—and US relations with Asia as well as other continents—is the common but inadequate American conception of human rights.[6] Americans tend to stress majoritarian democracy, rights as legal and as absolute, minimally regulated property rights in a mythical "free market," competition, and individualistic liberty. But Asians more often than not emphasize a communitarian view of rights, a developmental cooperative notion of capitalist economics, and clarity about responsibilities attendant to freedom as outlined in the UN Covenant on Economic, Social and Cultural Rights and in most national constitutions. For example, Asians more commonly than Americans recognize as human rights education, health care, and working conditions and compensation necessary for a decent life. Freedoms are important in Asia, but equality, survival rights and stability seem of more concern to many. Not too many Asians friendly towards human rights tend to think that private businessmen and a free market economy are more likely to yield economic justice than their government. When they complain about a human rights problem, their perception is often not that the government is intruding too much—unless it is with torture—but that it is interfering too little on behalf of the ordinary citizen, or that it is in league with corrupt or rapacious businessmen. In US political discourse, many characterize those who support government measures to assure the survival rights of children and the poor as "bleeding heart liberals." This epithet strikes Asians, and many elsewhere, as strong evidence of a deranged national mentality.

In sum, many Asian countries emphasize socioeconomic rights and are still in the process of making the laws and infrastructure—schools, courts, government organs, legal professionals, rigorously trained police—necessary for the protection and promotion of these and other human rights spelled out in international and national documents. Whatever the human rights situation in their respective systems, they bring to dialog understandings of national dignity, the past, law, present priorities and principles that at some points differ significantly from those common in the United States.

PATTERNS OF HUMAN RIGHTS PROBLEMS IN ASIA

I will next try to identify a few problems in the human rights failures of some Asian countries, focusing more on problems based primarily on government policy preferences than on scarcity of national resources. Too much human rights commentary by economically comfortable critics seems to assume all nations have all the resources necessary to honor comprehensively and immediately all human rights if only they had the will to do so. That is unfair. For example, while education is a human right, it would be unfair to criticize a low literacy rate, if the country is systematically increasing literacy within limits allowed by its resources, if the rate of female literacy is roughly equal to that of males, or, in India for example, if the proportion of lower caste students is increasing.

With respect to the human right to health care, it would be appropriate to criticize a government for failing to assure vaccinations to all infants if that country has the resources for such preventive medicine but has a low vaccination rate. An example of this is the United States, with the second lowest vaccination rate in the Western Hemisphere. But such criticism is not appropriate if a nation's vaccination rate is steadily rising and reasonable in light of its limited resources.

I would draw attention more to the following four patterns of human rights violations common in Asia which are significantly due to official policies rather than inadequate resources:

1. *Restrictions on freedom of expression*

Specifically, this includes restraints on press freedom and media independence, free speech, freedom of peaceable assembly (in the absence of any demonstrable danger to public order), and freedom of association. Most Asian nations guarantee at least limited democratic voting rights and a good measure of religious liberty to all. In the mass media and specialized commentary, well institutionalized repression in a country of all citizens sometimes receives less attention than restraints on one well known public figure, such as Aung San Su Kyi in Burma or Taslima Nassin in Bangladesh (attacked for a novel *Lajja* [*Shame*] which allegedly defames Islam). The more repressive Asian regimes are those of North Korea, China, Vietnam, Indonesia, Brunei, Malaysia, Singapore and Burma. Many other Asian systems show a pattern of well-established or increasing freedom (e.g. Japan, Taiwan, South Korea, Mongolia, Nepal). And freedom has had its ups and downs in other nations, such as Sri Lanka, India and the Philippines.

2. *Violations of worker rights*

These rights concern just compensation and healthy working conditions compatible with a decent life. There is as yet no "new world economic order," but a new order should include transcultural *guidelines for minimum compensation levels* in light of human rights law and principles, as well as varied economic realities. The flip side of burgeoning free trade in Asia is the wide-spread phenomenon of unreasonably low wages and inhumane working conditions. On the other hand, even countries not allowing political dissent may allow worker rights to organize and to strike. For example, both China and Vietnam now recognize a limited right to strike.

Among worker issues in Asia, the plight of many millions of boys and girls contracted or sold from villages to work in the sweatshops of Asia, especially South Asia, may call out loudest for reform. The Anti-Slavery Society estimates their numbers at well over 100 million in India, Nepal, Bangladesh, Pakistan, Indonesia, China, Thailand, the Philippines and Sri Lanka. They make for Western consumers clothing, car parts, toys and fireworks. Many in India, Nepal and Pakistan tie knots for high-quality carpets.[7] The living and working conditions of these children are appalling; their compensation is extremely low. Typically, they suffer from serious health deterioration within a few years. Some remarkable youngsters have tried to organize a union, and national and international bodies have shown interest in their cause. However, the plight of child labor receives little world media attention, and too little powerful response from local society or government. The Indian government hopes to remove two million children "from hazardous occupations" by the year 2000, and requires that children be paid at the same rate as adults in order to remove the profit incentive for child exploitation. Children are the least able of all to insist effectively on their rights.

3. *Treatment of women in a subhuman manner*

Although opportunities for women are expanding and a number of Asian women have risen to eminence, most notably in South Asia (for example, as prime ministers of Pakistan, Bangladesh, India, and Sri Lanka), women are subject to discriminatory treatment or worse in these and other Asian countries. This seems to be one of the two most serious and pervasive human rights problems in Asia. The recognition of the equal human dignity of women and men in human rights law is admittedly in revolutionary conflict with certain social ideas and practices in some Asian nations.

I would focus on only two of many problems: *the killing of female fetuses and female infants* due to son-preference and population controls; and *trafficking in prostitutes.* Asia's prostitute traffic is heavy, involving hundreds of thousands of women. This does not reflect cultural attitudes more permissive than those of the West. Some are young girls; market demand for such virgins has grown with the fear of AIDS. Thailand has long been a world hub for the traffic. Thai and Burmese women in vast numbers service the international market. Filipina and other Southeast Asian women are also moved around East Asia. Thousands of Nepalese women have been shipped to India for brothel duty. Prostitution may be common; it is also tragic. The scale, organization and slave-like conditions of women in the Asian traffic may be unmatched anywhere, and serve non-Asians as well as Asian men.

Modern ultrasound technology has combined with son-preference to the detriment of women in the world's two most populated states, India and China. As in some other countries, both mothers and fathers prefer to have a son rather than a daughter, and the Chinese and Indian governments encourage small families. Among other problems in India, in-law demand for dowry as a road to economic betterment has led to the "dowry death" killing of brides with insufficient dowries (officially, 6,200 such deaths in 1994), and to avoidance of such daughter problems by aborting females. China imposes painful sanctions on those who have more than one child, should a woman not receive special permission to have a second child or should a woman not be sociopolitically or legally coerced into aborting a second child. Although not officially approved for the purpose, ultrasound is used increasingly to detect the sex of a fetus in China and India. If the unborn infant is female in China, the parents may choose an abortion with the hope of having a son later. This is not an ethically justifiable choice by human rights standards, but it is not uncommon. Although opposed by the government, female infanticide remains a noteworthy problem in China. As in the US, violence against women is also a serious problem in some Asian countries. In September, 1995 the U.N. Fourth World Conference on Women in Beijing admirably raised international consciousness of these and other problems (e.g. economic discrimination, female genital mutilation). I wish well to all who seek reforms respectful of women's dignity.

4. *Violations of human rights in criminal justice processes*

Women have been at a special disadvantage in the criminal justice context as well, because sometimes police rape them, and usually with impunity. A considerable number of violations can be involved in criminal justice procedures from the time of initial apprehension by police until the end of official processing of a case. A few examples are: apprehension, interrogation, and beating without official "arrest" and thus without a warrant; confessions coerced by long interrogation and sleep deprivation; use of torture to gain information or just for the fun of it. Incidentally, although it is illegal, there is now more and more painful torture in the world than ever before, thanks to modern technology.[8] Other problems include denial to a detainee of access to family, friends or an attorney; prolonged incarceration without charges (e.g. "administrative detention" in China and elsewhere), or with charges but without a credible trial before an independent court; torture-like prison conditions or punishments; the death penalty, which does not have a deterrent effect; denial of state compensation should a convicted prisoner turn out to have been innocent.

In part at least, violation of the human rights of people in custody are due to government policy, and not just to capricious *ad hoc* local police behavior; but to some extent, it may also be due to inadequate government resources for training, or the difficulty of breaking down a sick tradition of rights abuse (e.g. by private armies in the Philippines). Only empirical research on a criminal justice system can give one a sense of the balance between policy, community ethos, and resources as determinative factors. Extreme police harshness may be supported more strongly by a community than by its government. There is need to go beyond the treatment of "prisoners of conscience," the admirable emphasis of Amnesty International, to ask attention to criminal justice processes which affect *all* citizens. In many Asian countries, such processes are fraught with a variety of human rights abuses, for which perpetrators are rarely held accountable by anyone.[9]

If one assumes that a government seriously intends to end violation of criminal justice rights, what resources might it need to solve the problem once it has unequivocally communicated its will to all relevant officials, the police and the public? Punishments for such violations must be seen as clear, simple and unavoidable. Authorities primarily responsible for the abuses must be purged. Extensive and rigorous police training (preferably over a year, not just two or three months) should be instituted, insofar as it is affordable. Finally, the government should establish a comprehensive system of human rights education, like the compulsory program for all police and other appointive officials in the Philippines. Recurrent police violations of minority rights in American cities illustrate the centrality of ethos education in human rights in a meaningful long-term reform program.

In both authoritarian and democratic, highly developed and underdeveloped systems of criminal law, one may find small rules which violate rights in painful ways. Japan may have Asia's best human rights record and one of the world's most lenient criminal justice systems; but those few who do go to prison are generally not allowed to talk or even to look at fellow inmates while working.[10] Japan's other criminal justice rights problems stem for the most part from inadequate access to legal counsel from the time of police apprehension.

To summarize, the two most critical areas of human rights violation in Asia seem to be the treatment of the officially detained and the treatment of women. Women's problems begin before they are born. Workers' problems may begin when they are children and lead to premature death or debility. Authoritarian regimes show particular alacrity in suppressing domestic criticism of their own human rights records.

Academic human rights studies have burgeoned since the late 1970s (e.g. the development of *Human Rights Quarterly* and *Human Rights Internet*). Principles and culturally sensitive understandings of the implications of human dignity for rights law are developing. Vigorous international criticism of human rights violations by the mass media, NGOs (e.g. Human Rights Watch, Amnesty International, Article 19, the International Center against Censorship), and individuals is not only appropriate, but respectful of what is most humane in all cultures. Criticism of repression can excite the shame and embarrassment necessary to induce some oppressors to desist, but if it is done by people who deny the importance and binding force of socioeconomic rights, it lacks moral force in Asia. *Both* civil liberties *and* socioeconomic rights are *human* rights; the property right is but one of many rights, and the right to engage in business is not deserving of the pride of place it is accorded in the U.S. Economic interest should not be allowed to override concern about a pattern of torture. Governments need not wag righteous fingers at violative actions to be effective in many cases. They can respectfully disagree on priorities and occasionally show just outrage at barbarism. But they can also methodically discover what an inhumane government wants and quietly deprive it; they can quietly punish barbaric regimes by carefully designed economic, cultural and diplomatic actions that hurt, quietly. Given time, sophisticated sanctions work. It is irresponsible, but admittedly compatible with free market economics, to place concern about severe human rights violations below economic considerations in dealing with another country.

Recent Human Rights Successes

I will conclude on a positive note, recognizing successes and efforts. I go back to the statement quoted earlier: “Do not lose heart.” The human rights situation *can* improve. Indeed, it *has* improved in Asia over the past twenty years. In observing many Asian human rights advocates over the years—scholars, lawyers, judges, housewives, students, business people and workers, men and women—I have come to admire immensely their courage and persistence, their good humor in impossible situations, and their patient conviction that human rights in recognition of human dignity will out in the end. (Only in the American civil rights movement of the 1950s and 1960s have I met so many of similar inspiring character outside Asia.) They did not lose heart. And the status of human rights has improved markedly since 1985; for example, in South Korea, Taiwan, Mongolia, the Philippines, Nepal, Thailand, and even in ravaged Cambodia and Vietnam. Human rights constitutionalism, an understanding which makes the human rights of citizens the top priority of official acts, is now a major part of government and law in East, Southeast and South Asia. However ambiguous in long-term implications, the flare-ups of democracy between 1988 and 1990 in Burma and China were preferable to the dull silence of earlier times. The economy and the infrastructure of laws and institutions necessary for effective human rights protection and promotion are being gradually developed or already exist in most countries of Asia. Barbarism does not go unchallenged. New national human rights commissions are being formed in Asia, and the United Nations and NGOs are increasingly active around the continent. There is good reason not to lose heart about human rights in Asia.

NOTES

1 The major documents can be conveniently found in the Center for the Study of Human Rights, *Twenty-Five Human Rights Documents* (New York: Center for the Study of Human Rights, Columbia University, 2nd ed., 1994). Regional instruments include the African (Banju) Charter on Human and Peoples' Rights (1986); American Convention on Human Rights (1969); European Convention for the Protection of Human Rights and Fundamental Freedoms (1953; and Nine Protocols); European Social Charter (1961); The Cairo Declaration on Human Rights in Islam (1990); American Declaration of the Rights and Duties of Man (1948); Conference on Security and Cooperation in Europe: Final Act 1975. 1(a), European Convention on the Prevention of Torture (1987); and the Charter of Paris for a New Europe: A New Era of Democracy, Peace and Unity (1990).

2 On constitutional developments in Asia, see Lawrence W. Beer (ed.), *Constitutional Systems in Late Twentieth Century Asia* (Seattle: University of Washington Press, 1992).

3 Asia's Basic Principles of Human Rights are:

Principle 1

(a) Everyone has the inherent right to life, and shall not be arbitrarily deprived of his life.

(b) The death penalty may be imposed only for the most serious crimes and after fair public trial on evidence presented to a legally competent, independent and impartial tribunal.

Principle 2

(a) Everyone has the inherent right to liberty and security of person and shall not be subjected to arbitrary arrest or detention.

(b) Anyone who is arrested or detained shall be informed of the reasons therefore at the time of his arrest and shall be entitled to communicate the fact of his arrest to a person of his choice.

(c) Anyone arrested shall be entitled to access to counsel of his choice.

(d) Anyone charged with an offence is entitled to a fair and public trial within a reasonable time by a legally competent, independent and impartial tribunal.

Principle 3

(a) Everyone is equal before the law and is entitled without any discrimination to the equal protection of the law.

Principle 4

(a) No one shall be held guilty of any criminal offence for any act or omission which did not constitute a criminal offence when it was committed.

Principle 5

(a) Anyone deprived of his liberty shall be treated with respect for his inherent dignity as a human person.

(b) No one shall be subjected to torture, or to cruel, inhuman or degrading punishment or treatment.

Principle 6

(a) No one should be subject to preventive detention, but in those countries where preventive detention exists, everyone so detained shall be entitled to prompt periodic review of his detention by a legally competent, independent and impartial tribunal.

Principle 7

(a) No one shall be arbitrarily deprived of the right to enter his own country.

(b) Anyone who is an alien, lawfully in a country, shall not be expelled except pursuant to a decision reached in accordance with the law in force at the time he entered the country.

Principle 8

(a) No one shall be subject to coercion which would restrict his choice of religion or beliefs. Freedom to manifest one's religion or beliefs may be subject only to such limitations as are prescribed by law and are necessary to protect public safety, order, health or morals or the fundamental rights and freedoms of others.

Principle 9

(a) To ensure the enjoyment of these minimum standards everyone is entitled to have legal assistance available to him.

Principle 10

(a) These principles have been formulated on the basis that they are the minimum standards to be observed at all times after allowing for the fact that emergencies threatening the life of a nation may occur from time to time.

In addition, Lawasia's Human Rights Standing Committee has developed, in consultation with Pacific island nation leaders, a "Pacific Human Rights Charter." *Lawasia Human Rights Newsletter*, March, 1993, p.27.

4 Albert P. Blaustein, *The Blaustein Register of Latest Constitutional Revisions*, June 23, 1994.

5 The exceptions to the rule are: Libya, Oman and Saudi Arabia which count the Qran as their constitution; Israel; the United Kingdom, where the need for a written charter of rights is widely recognized (Charter '88 Movement); and New Zealand, where debate on the issue of a written constitution with a bill of rights continues to be very lively.

6 On this U.S. problem, see Mary Ann Glendon, *Rights Talk: The Impoverishment of Political Discourse* (New York: The Free Press, 1991), and the communitarian journal, *The Responsive Community*.

7 Peter James Spielmann, Associated Press article, Sept. 19, 1995.

8 Edward Peters, *Torture* (New York: Basil Blackwell, 1985); and R.D. Crelinsten and A.P. Schmid (eds.), *The Politics of Pain* (Leiden: The Center for the Study of Social Conflicts, 1993).

9 Among the most useful issue, country and regional reports are those of Amnesty International; Human Rights Watch: Asia; Article 19, the Freedom House annual, *Freedom in the World*; and the U.S. State Department, Office of Human Rights and Humanitarian Affairs, annual *Country Reports on Human Rights Practices*.

10 On Japan's criminal justice system, see Daniel H. Foote, "The Benevolent Paternalism of Japanese Criminal Justice," 80 *California Law Review*, No. 2, March, 1992, 317; 23 *Law in Japan: an Annual*, 1990.

■ First published in L. Henken & A. Rosenthal (eds.), *Constitutionalism and Rights: The Influence of the United States Constitution Abroad*, New York, Columbia University Press, 1990, pp. 225-259.

3

Constitutionalism and Rights in Japan and Korea

⌘

Western notions of constitutional rights entered the isolated countries of Northeast Asia in the latter half of the nineteenth century, as European and American imperialists forced trade, diplomatic relations, and new ideas upon East Asia. Japan had been closed to most contacts with the West for centuries pursuant to the foreign policy of the ruling family, the Tokugawa (1603–1868); the ancient kingdom of Korea, unified under a peninsular government since A.D. 668, was rightly termed "the Hermit Kingdom." China had fallen under the sway of a series of imposed unequal treaties with the West beginning in 1842. Commodore Matthew Perry had initiated a similar system of treaty subservience for Japan when his ominous American "black ships" arrived in 1853 and 1854; but by 1876 Japan had progressed sufficiently on the road back to legal independence and into the exploitive company of Western powers to be able to lead the way in forcing Korea open to commerce and diplomacy. Japan achieved treaty equality by around 1900. Unfortunately, Korea was annexed by Japan soon after, and was not liberated until 1945.[1]

The modern constitutional histories, political cultures, and recent human rights records of Japan and South Korea differ profoundly, yet indigenous understandings of individual rights common today in both countries are generally similar to those expressed in United Nations human rights documents; both nations have been influenced by American constitutionalism, particularly since World War II, the period of primary focus for this paper. Two major modern breaks in legal tradition have taken place:[2] when under foreign pressure, Japan reshaped traditional law into a civil law system on the continental European model in the nineteenth and early twentieth centuries, and Korea did the same by virtue of its occupation by Japan; and when, under military occupations beginning in September 1945, American understandings of constitutionalism and rights joined, even took precedence over, European conceptions. Pre-Western, European, and American understandings of law have gradually achieved dynamic integration into the Japanese and Korean legal systems; but in East Asia there is no continuity of constitutional development parallel to the long historical processes of the United States and Europe.[3] Its present ideas and institutions did not emerge as refinements or as adaptive responses from indigenous or regional premodern thought and practice; no domestic tradition of philosophical, religious, legal, or literary reflection informed a constitutional politics leading, for example, to such institutions as independent courts, the rights of an accused, civil liberties, or elected legislatures.

Words for "rights" did not exist, but it should be asked: did some forms of functional equivalents of individual rights perhaps pervade the mature civilizations of East Asia? Early in any discussion of American influence on rights abroad we need to consider, at least in passing, what it is that has been influenced. The accomplished cultures of East Asia were not a *tabula rasa* with respect to conceptions and practices relevant to current understandings of individual rights. Along with Western state theories, indigenously developed traditions of natural law continue to affect understandings of the individual, the family, government, the group, and community.[4]

Buddhism and neo-Confucianism from China have been sources of understanding government, morality, and the cosmos for Japan and Korea. But many centuries ago each country developed its own distinctive system for an unusually homogeneous population.[5] Korea's king governed a centralized state from Seoul through a small ruling class. From the seventeenth to the mid-nineteenth century, the Tokugawa Shogun's feudal federalism allowed hundreds of domain lords limited local rule, and generally ignored the powerless emperor except to require him to formalize the legitimacy of each successive shogunal ruler. Neither tradition recognized constitutional rights as in the United States or any *a priori* reason for minimizing government power and functions, and both valued hereditary position and a clearly defined sociolegal hierarchy. Although feudal house rules were important in Japan, one was a good subject or ruler more by virtuous adherence to the requirements of natural justice than by attention to written law, which was not comprehensive but generally penal in nature. Both legal cultures also saw an element of reciprocity as a reasonable part of understanding duties. Everyone had duties appropriate to his/her social position; the Japanese thought in terms of highly personalized duties rather than impersonal legal rights. Fulfillment of duty brought self-satisfaction, security, a respected place in the family and community.

Consciousness of the reciprocal element in duty—an authentic form of rights consciousness—has been a perennial aspect of East Asian natural law and justice. In theory and often in practice, irresponsibility was not acceptable in law or government; the good ruler or member of the elite class (the feudal lord of *samurai* in Japan, the *yangban* in Korea) was expected to be dutiful and loyal to superiors, but also to show benevolent condescension toward those of lower station. The latter could reasonably ask that. Of course the laws and institutions for rights protection were not adequate by today's Japanese, Korean, and American standards, but to overemphasize this would be anachronistic. Summing the matter up in a way foreign to past East Asian perspectives, the subordinate had "a rightful claim" to benevolent treatment by a superior in response to dutiful behavior and respectful demeanor because the superior had a duty to reciprocate and hierarchy did not legitimate disrespect for subordinates.

Reciprocal duty consciousness still permeates Japanese and Korean society. A principal problem for rights consciousness in Northeast Asia today seems to lie in expanding the individual's strong sense of reciprocal duty beyond particularistic human relations, as in one's family, so as to include respect for the rights of all fellow citizens. The Japanese commonly view individual rights in terms of a rightful expectation that the other (whether an equal, a superior, or a subordinate in the hierarchy within the organic community) will voluntarily fulfill his/her duty to self within a relationship of reciprocity, rather than in terms of one individual's right *vis-à-vis* another individual or state power without reference to any inherent mutuality or reciprocity, community, or, in some cases, hierarchy. The integration of new understandings of legal equality with sociolegal hierarchy has been a major theme in the development of rights thought and practice in modern East Asia. In broader terms, it would add significantly to the cross-cultural cogency of human rights theory to ground it in "mutualism" rather than in one of the array of Western notions of "individualism," and to work at a synthesis of cross-cultural understandings of right and duty, equality and hierarchy, under constitutional democracy. Constitutional rights pertain to individuals, but as "persons-in-community," not as isolated "individuals-in-nature."[6] As a remedy for the excessive abstractness and cultural chauvinism of much "individualist" discussion of rights, it is necessary to emphasize how individuals within different cultural communities prefer different sorts of behavior as manifestations of respect for their human and legal rights. No one enjoys torture, of course, but the degree, for example, to which emphasis is placed on freedom of verbal expression or a presumption of innocence varies greatly among equally democratic cultures.

American constitutional ideas were a known but not very influential element in academic discourse on law in Japan and Korea in the nineteenth century. The Declaration of Independence, Abraham Lincoln's speeches, and a few other classics inspired many, then as now, but the great repository of European legal experience and constitutional thought weighed much more heavily in practical affairs. As Justice Masami Ito, Japan's leading student of Anglo-American constitutional law, cautions, the attention given by some Japanese to English and American constitutional ideas from the early Meiji period does not mean that such ideas influenced the Meiji Constitution or its interpretation. The Western European legal influence was dominant in Japan and thus in Korea.[7] American ideas gained authoritative currency only in the late summer of 1945, when the United States began military occupations of Japan and South Korea.

In a cruel irony, the defeat of Japan, which meant "liberation" for Korea, ushered in for Korea a most tragic time of division, political violence, and turmoil, exacerbated by American unfamiliarity with Korean affairs and the lack of a coherent plan for the future.[8] A "temporary" military division of Northern and Southern sectors of the Korean peninsula between the United States and the USSR was agreed to in the last days of the war, for purposes of administering the Japanese surrender and the eventual return of sovereignty to the Korean people. Although the division still seemed permanent as of this writing, so did the Korean belief in eventual reunification of some type. The Korean conflict of 1950–53 left vast numbers dead and ten million relatives rigidly separated from each other between North and South with no contacts permitted; the first small groups of relatives were allowed exchange visits between Seoul and Pyongyang only in September 1985.[9] For decades that division has profoundly affected not only U.S.–Korean relations generally and the influence of U.S. constitutional ideas in particular, but also, as will be explained later, the unstable status of individual rights and freedoms in Korea.

Emerging from unprecedented defeat in World War II, the Japanese were expelled from Korea and other Asian possessions and lay devastated at home. But defeat brought success, as they entered their longest period of uninterrupted peace in modern history. Like the citizens of their former possessions, they were liberated from an oppressive government; a relatively well-prepared American Occupation (1945–1952) helped the enemy democratize in keeping with the dictates of the Potsdam Declaration (July 26, 1945). Japan's economic achievements are commonly overstressed, in a one-sided manner, as the basis for its democracy; one can argue instead that unmilitarized peace and constitutional democracy have been the foundations for this era of unmatched economic improvement for the country and its general citizenry.

Since 1945, academic, cultural, and political interactions relevant to constitutional rights between the United States and its allies in Northeast Asia have become institutionalized within a context of interdependence. The fact that superior military force was initially a decisive condition for the nineteenth-century induction of Western concepts of law and constitution, and for the considerable American impact during the Occupation period, does not diminish for most Japanese today the legitimacy of individual rights ideas that are both indigenous and compatible with American constitutionalism. A look at a few aspects of the United States' influence on rights in Japan and Korea may further the understanding of American strengths and limitations while providing a clarified perspective on two of America's close non-Western friends.

JAPAN

The 1947 Constitution of Japan[10] embodies a very good statement of the rights of an American, as envisioned by some American occupationnaires in the authentically idealistic months following World War II. Nevertheless, for most Japanese the Constitution has also become the most authoritative statement of the vastly expanded rights of the Japanese under postwar law, and arguably the most sacred writ of the country's current civilization.

When Japan's door was wedged open by the West in the mid-1800s, no words had existed in Japanese for "right" *(kenri)* or "human rights" *(jinken)*,[11] although there were generally understood and enforceable legal standards. There was nothing resembling the distinctive American understandings of rights enumerated in a single-document constitution and defensible in courts with the power of judicial review.

The growth of constitutional repression

However, within a few decades, large numbers of the curious and literate Japanese had familiarized themselves with the corpus of Western legal and political thought. Moreover, in one of history's remarkable technical linguistic achievements, a few official scholars had invented legal terminology in East Asian ideographs which further indigenized Anglo-American and various European understandings of law, constitutional rights, and civil liberties. After long investigations and debates, Japan's leaders and scholars found the civil law tradition in general more suited to their needs, on balance, than the common law heritage and American constitutionalism.[12]

In formulating the Constitution of the Empire of Japan (1889, the Meiji Constitution),[13] Japan adapted particularly ideas and institutions found in the Prussian Constitution of 1850.[14] The Tokugawa class hierarchy of *samurai* nobility, farmers, craftsmen, merchants, and outcastes was abolished; a strong state was established, but so was equal subordination to the law of almost everyone but members of the imperial house. The basic law provided for dynastic monarchy, a strong modern bureaucracy, limited parliamentarianism with a two-house Diet, and limited rights and liberties for the emperor's subjects. Leading Western constitutional lawyers of the day lauded the wisdom of this structure, perhaps too readily.

The emperor, often neglected and virtually powerless for many centuries, was made over into a charismatic sovereign of a Westernized constitutional state after the "Meiji Restoration" (1868). In theory, the emperor was thus "restored" to his allegedly ancient and proper place in governmental communion with his subjects;[15] but able oligarchs actually ruled Japan in the emperor's name. They used modern means of political education and control to overcome traditional popular apathy and to make devotion to the emperor coincident with modern nationalism. The rights of individual subjects provided for in the Meiji Constitution were not based on either East Asian or Western notions of natural law, but were conceived of as the gifts of a sovereign who was by definition sacred, kindly, and paternal. Civil liberties, for example, were subject to easy restraint by law, administrative rules, police authority, and coercive sociolegal means. Western legalism did sink social roots over the decades, but until after World War II no effective means of legal redress existed when officials violated such rights. Conformity of thought with State Shinto and selfless service became each subject's duty to the quasi-divine land and monarch; the emperor was seen as the latest in an everlasting royal line originating in mythical prehistoric times with the Sun Goddess, Amaterasu Omikami. The warmth of spiritual closeness to the emperor as a member of the close-knit "national family" (a literal rendering of *kokka*, the Japanese term for the national state), not egocentric concern for individual rights, became the increasingly dominant preoccupation.

From 1868 to 1912, a dense system of official controls was gradually put in place. And yet democratic thought found some vigor, particularly perhaps in the early Meiji period and in the heady years after World War I, in which Japan was aligned against Germany. Symbolic of opposing currents in 1925 were the expansion of suffrage to all men twenty-five or older[16] and the passage of the notorious Peace Preservation Law[17] which provided the legal rationale for highly refined restraints during the "wartime period," of 1930–1945. Militarism and emperor-centered ultranationalism, then as now, implied disregard of all individual rights and liberties.

The postwar constitutional revolution

Relatively few twentieth-century Japanese scholars and officials took seriously as a possible model for Japan the American approach to constitutionalism and rights until that decisive time in the fall of 1945 when Japan's current constitutional revolution began.[18]

How did it begin? In one of history's extraordinary cross-cultural conjunctions, some Americans and Japanese worked together for a relatively short period and remade Japan's system and its place in Asia. Before describing America's influence on rights at that time, it bears emphasizing that we are dealing here with one of the few seminal changes in the history of an ancient nation.

The Japanese experienced a stark juxtaposition of opposites after repressive government and a war catastrophe when it moved suddenly toward constitutional democracy in late 1945 and 1946. The catalytic influence of the United States at the outset seems to have been essential for Japan's metamorphosis; it seems improbable that Japan would have evolved peacefully into a democracy on its own.

In 1987, the Constitution of Japan (1947) was one of only 22 out of 164 single-document constitutions in the world dating back as far as the 1940s; over 100 constitutions trace their beginnings only to 1970 or later in this era of unprecedented creative search for appropriate constitutional forms and stability.[19] In Japan, rights have never been suspended or otherwise limited by exceptional means since the Occupation. Problems of malapportionment and exorbitant election campaign costs continue; but all transfers of national leadership have been peaceful and according to democratic law. This peace and democratic predictability have themselves bolstered the status of individual rights.

Civil rights and liberties came to the Japanese people in a rush. The Potsdam Declaration (July 26, 1945) insisted on democracy, rights, and freedoms (para. 10) in its terms of surrender; so did President Harry Truman's "United States Initial Post-Surrender Policy for Japan," received by General Douglas A. MacArthur, Supreme Commander for the Allied Powers (SCAP) on August 19, 1945.[20] This Policy also provided that Japan was to be governed indirectly by SCAP directives, called "SCAPIN," rather than by occupation organs, as in the Korean and German occupations. SCAPIN would be translated into Japanese law and carried out. Imperial Ordinance 542 (September 20, 1945) empowered the Japanese government to convert the intent of SCAPINs into Japanese law through ordinances, in compliance with the Potsdam Declaration. In all, some 520 ordinances, referred to as "Potsdam Ordinances," were established by the end of the occupation, but a few in the fall of 1945 altered to this day the status of individual rights in Japan.

The beginning of Japan's constitutional revolution came in September 1945, in a confrontation with the Japanese government, when SCAP ended restrictions on freedom of expression about the emperor and expanded individual rights generally. For example, when the government tried to prevent Tokyo newspapers from publishing a photo of Emperor Hirohito standing humbly beside the commanding figure of General MacArthur at SCAP offices on September 27, SCAPIN 66 was issued to forbid any media restrictions not specifically approved by SCAP, and to order the repeal of any laws to the contrary.[21] When Japan's government persisted in telling writers to honor the spirit of the repressive Peace Preservation Law in reverence for emperor-centered ideology, another occupation directive, SCAPIN 93 (October 4, 1945), ordered the government in sweeping terms to release and restore civil rights to all political prisoners, to "abrogate and immediately suspend . . . all [undemocratic] laws, decrees, orders, ordinances and regulations," and to eliminate all antidemocratic agencies. Within a few months, the edifice of antirights law and administration came tumbling down. These "freedom orders" *(jiyu no shirei)* and other SCAPINs, and consequent ordinances issued by the Japanese government, marked a critical first phase in the establishment of individual rights. Along with the Emperor's public denial of his divinity and the clarification of his ordinary humanness on January 1, 1946, they set the stage for the constitution-making of 1946.

These early instances of forceful and comprehensive American support for the constitutional revolution deserve much attention from students of the occupation origins of constitutional rights in Japan.

An unavoidable ambiguity attended the occupation's expansion of rights and freedoms under Japanese law: 1) Although the overwhelming majority of Japanese citizens from then until now has supported and expected extensive individual rights, a small but influential political minority has been opposed and has called for constitutional revision. However, neither leaders nor other Japanese really had the option to refuse freedom early in the occupation. 2) On the other hand, SCAP imposed limited censorship on the mass media and other *ad hoc* or systemic restraints.[22] Where a temporarily ruling democratic conqueror bypasses privileged power to force open and free an authoritarian system, initial official backing is not necessary for the long-term legitimacy of constitutional rights (in Japan or in general), as long as there is ample evidence of support by the sovereign people. The burden of proof to the contrary would seem to lie with those opposed to individual rights.

Writing the rights provisions

SCAP encouraged discussion of the emperor institution, but limited media reporting and criticism of occupation activities.[23] High on the list of taboo topics was the American role in writing the Constitution of Japan, the greatest accomplishment of the Occupation period. The background and history of the Occupation have been detailed elsewhere;[24] here I would only recount a few points in the process of drafting the rights provisions in the Constitution, a critical instance of United States influence.

MacArthur looked to Washington for guidance on basics, but of necessity had broad discretion.[25] Like earlier directives from Washington in 1945, the State Department's fourteen-page paper, "Reform of the Japanese Governmental System," which was sent to MacArthur on January 9, 1946, insisted on the firm establishment of human rights in Japanese law, among other features of constitutional democracy.[26]

Under SCAP prodding, Prime Minister Kijuro Shidehara's government had established the Matsumoto Commission under Joji Matsumoto in October 1945 to consider possible modifications of the Meiji Constitution along democratic lines. Its final report, submitted on February 1, 1946, recommended little change and was found unacceptable by MacArthur and his associates.[27] Besides its decisive SCAPINs and private urgings on the Japanese government, on October 11, 1945, SCAP had called for "Five Great Reforms": the liberation of women, the encouragement of labor unions, more democratic education, the end of all repression, and democratization of the economy. The Matsumoto report was seen as unresponsive to these concerns, and General Douglas MacArthur despaired of the government's reform initiative.[28] He decided to entrust the task of drafting a model constitution for Japan to the Government Section of SCAP headquarters, headed by his confidant, General Courtney Whitney. Whitney was given a free hand, except for three requirements: that he retain the emperor system but make it subject to the will of the people; that he include a renunciation of the nation's right of belligerency; and that he eliminate all forms of feudalism and aristocracy.[29]

On February 3, 1946, Charles L. Kades,[30] deputy chief of SCAP's Government Section, formed a steering committee with two other lawyers, Alfred R. Hussey and Milo E. Rowell, to set the ground rules for drafting the model constitution which he presented to Japan's government on February 13.[31] "They, individually and collectively, wrote many of the provisions of the draft and rewrote, revised, or vetoed most of the provisions drawn up by their colleagues on the legislative, executive, judiciary, civil rights, local government, and finance committees into which the staff were divided."[32] Neither they nor the staff on committees drafting different sections of the basic law were specialists in the law of American constitutional rights, let alone Japanese public law.

Generals MacArthur and Whitney were supportive in the background, and affected certain provisions; a sizable group contributed, but the steering committee, especially Kades, stands out among the principal authors. Kades himself maintains that the drafting process "was a group project with group thinking and group ideas."[33]

Although initially taken aback, the Shidehara government ordered the Cabinet Legal Bureau to prepare a new draft constitution on the basis of the SCAP document;[34] the feared alternative presented orally by Whitney and the Steering Committee was the early submission to voters of a choice between the Meiji Constitution and SCAP's democratic constitution. At critical junctures in the process, such as on February 22 and March 5, the Emperor was consulted and indicated his support for far-reaching changes. The draft was completed by March 4, and further modifications were negotiated with SCAP by March 6; then the text was made public in both Japanese and English, along with a supportive imperial rescript.[35] Then and later in deliberations, translations from one language to the other continued; but the revolutionary thrust of the emerging constitution was apparent, and the public's response was positive.

The amendment procedures of the Meiji Constitution were followed;[36] but the House of Representatives that amended the draft and approved the Constitution of Japan was elected on April 10, 1946, in the first postwar general election. Eighty-one percent of the victors were new to Diet politics, and women voted and held Diet offices for the first time. The House of Representatives Election Law of December 17, 1945, had initiated female suffrage and extended the vote to all twenty-year-old men and women. In summer debates, the House of Representatives added two articles, deleted one, and amended twenty-two, and finally approved the constitution of Japan by a vote of 421 to 8 on August 24, 1946, as the first amendment to the Meiji Constitution. The document was later approved by the House of Peers and promulgated on November 3, 1946; it went into effect on the next May 3, a date honored by a national holiday.[37]

The Constitution of Japan has succeeded because of Japanese support and efforts since 1946; but in 1946, before and after the pivotal dates of February 13 and March 6, many Japanese and Americans in Tokyo offices contributed to the process of writing and refining its provisions. The Constitution is, in important respects, a binational product. Of the Americans contributing to provisions affecting human rights since 1946, at least the following seem to deserve special identification. Hussey and Kades wrote the Preamble, with its eloquent advocacy of liberty and peace; General Whitney authored Article 97: "The fundamental human rights by this Constitution guaranteed to the people of Japan are fruits of the age-old struggle of man to be free; they have survived the many exacting tests for durability and are conferred upon this and future generations in trust, to be held for all time inviolate."

Rowell and Hussey, with critical Japanese input, worked on the chapter establishing for the first time a judiciary as a separate branch of government with the power to decide whether laws and official acts are constitutional. Beate Sirota, Pieter K. Roest, and Harry Emerson Wildes constituted the Government Section's Committee on Civil Rights. Kades provided dynamic support throughout for progressive human rights ideas, but with the important assistance of Beate Sirota. Sirota, an American of European background with long residence in Japan and fluency in Japanese, insisted that equal rights for women and other human rights should be inserted into the constitution. Women's rights figured little in the various reform proposals emanating from public and private Japanese sources, but thanks in good measure to Beate Sirota's lobbying of Kades and other American and Japanese drafters, a revolution was begun in women's status under law. Sirota, along with Joseph Gordon, also played a major role in reconciling the language of Japanese and English texts at the critical meetings of March 4 and 5, 1946, and in finding reference material on other nations' constitutions.[38]

In their deliberations, none of the Americans had available a library of the world's wisdom on constitutions; but they did have a 1939 compendium of constitutions borrowed from the Tokyo Imperial University Library.[39] Far more important as sources in the act of drafting were the convictions and memories of Western, especially American, politics, law, and thought.

Individual rights in Japan's Constitution

In places the phraseology of the Constitution of Japan echoes American constitutional documents, not Japanese writings. For example, the Preamble proclaims that "we shall secure for ourselves and our posterity the fruits of peaceful cooperation with all nations and the blessings of liberty throughout the land," and Article 13 recognizes the individual's "right to life, liberty, and the pursuit of happiness."[40] But of greater practical moment to Japan's civil rights and liberties was the constitution's denial of governmental power to the military and to the emperor—that is, to those who might well have sought to rule Japan, as before, in the manipulable mystic name of the emperor[41]—and its establishment for the first time of a constitutionally independent judicial branch of government with comprehensive jurisdiction and the power of judicial review. The courts and how well they have functioned are an important part of the story of human rights in Japan since 1947; but that part can be exaggerated and other agencies and factors neglected by a too-narrow focus.[42]

The Diet is "the highest organ of state power and . . . the sole lawmaking organ of the State" (Art. 41); had it been hostile over the years to democracy and constitutional rights, prospects would indeed be dim. Although the Diet's actions on progressive legislation in some rights areas, like that of the U.S. Congress, have been exceedingly slow and not always admirable because civil rights and liberties have rarely been their preoccupation, the two houses of Japan's parliament (the House of Representatives and the House of Councillors) have not often figured prominently in Japanese discourse on rights and on the American influence. The 512-member House of Representatives is the core area of political power in Japan, and the inner segment of the core has been the Cabinet, where "executive power shall be vested"

(Art. 65), and the Prime Minister's Office. The Liberal Democratic party has controlled the Diet since late 1955; opposition parties have been unable to coalesce and mount an effective challenge.

Over the decades some in the ruling party have wanted to revise the Constitution in ways that most constitutional lawyers and a very strong popular majority see as detrimental to the constitutional principles of individual rights and pacifism. For example, they would change Article 9, which commits Japan—uniquely—to non-military solutions to international disputes. Recent American pressures on Japan to play a major military role in East Asia's security are at variance with Japan's internal constitutional principles, and of questionable propriety. Article 9 has buttressed individual rights indirectly by explicitly excluding antidemocratic militarism from national politics and governmental power. Besides the opposition of all but a few constitutional lawyers to any constitutional change, the consistent support for the Constitution of most opinion makers, the general public, the organized union movement, and the vast mass media system have effectively blocked revision efforts.

The range of human rights in Chapter 3, Articles 11 to 40, and elsewhere, is quite wide. Here I will briefly describe the major categories of rights as they are commonly clustered by representative Japanese constitutional lawyers, and then give examples of how they have been implemented during and since the Occupation. First, in general terms, Articles 11 to 13 and 97 speak of the Constitution's guarantee of "fundamental human rights," "eternal and inviolate," which "shall be maintained by the constant endeavor of the people," and "to the extent that it does not interfere with the public welfare, be the supreme consideration in legislation and in other governmental affairs." Citizens are given an explicit duty not to abuse rights and to use them "for the public welfare" (Art. 12).[43] The public welfare has been judicially defined as "the maintenance of public order and respect for the fundamental human rights of the individual";[44] but the phrase has been given both abstract jurisprudential and specific meanings by the courts over the decades in setting forth both restrictive and liberal decisions. For the past twenty years, judges have moved away from the abstract and conceptual jurisprudence found in the prewar tradition influenced by Europe toward concreteness of standards, sometimes with an eye to past and recent American judicial decisions. The major groupings of specific rights include:[45]

EQUALITY OF RIGHTS UNDER THE LAW

Article 14 bans "discrimination in political, economic, or social relations because of race, creed, sex, social status, or family origin," and, except for the imperial family, eliminates aristocracy and the inheritance of honors. In a similar prohibition with respect to qualifications for voting and candidacy for the Diet, Article 44 adds "education, property or income" to the list of invalid considerations. Article 24 recognizes "the equal rights of husband and wife" in all matters, and requires that all law adopt "the standpoint of individual dignity and the essential equality of the sexes." This latter wording is made the governing principle in interpreting private law by Article 1–2 of the civil code.[46]

Japan suffers from no pattern of socioeconomic discrimination as widespread and deep as America's treatment of blacks and, especially in the past, minority religions and ethnic groups; but its record relevant to Article 14 equality requirements is stained here and there. From a human rights perspective, the position of women has radically improved since 1945. Women's enjoyment of rights with respect to marriage, property, inheritance, education, voting and candidacy for office, freedom of expression, and employment opportunities have been substantially enhanced. A 1985 Equal Employment Opportunity Law has been improving opportunities for career-oriented women. Starting salaries for women are approaching parity with those of men with similar educational attainments (approximately 94 percent); but, as in the United States, sex discrimination remains in opportunities for advancement. However, Japanese women enjoy prestige and social power in their functions as wives, mothers, and managers of the family budget. Relatively few have been encouraged to seek public office or managerial positions.

Although there are relatively few loci in Japanese law that legitimate unequal treatment, social discrimination problems of varying severity are still faced at times by relatively small minorities: the *dowa* or *burakumin* (between 1.5 and 3 million, depending on one's source), ethnic Japanese descended from premodern occupational outcasts; Koreans in Japan as a result of colonial and wartime politics (670,000); Chinese (50,000); Okinawans (about 1 million); the Ainu, a few thousand proto-Caucasians found primarily in the northern large island of Hokkaido; atom bomb victims *(hibakusha)* and their children, whose feared genetic contamination makes them undesirable marriage partners; the illegitimate offspring, left fatherless, of Japanese women and foreigners, primarily American servicemen; the few thousand Vietnamese refugees; and, to a minor degree, the small resident alien population.

ECONOMIC FREEDOMS AND PROPERTY RIGHTS

These are contained in Articles 22 and 29. Japanese enjoy the freedom to choose their occupations and the right to hold and use property under law, in conformity with "the public welfare." Article 30 establishes a duty to pay taxes. Japan seems, in law and fact, a pragmatically capitalist welfare state which recognizes but does not exaggerate property rights.[47]

RIGHTS RELATED TO THE QUALITY OF SOCIOECONOMIC LIFE

Under Article 25, all have a right—in some cases justiciable—"to maintain the minimum standards of wholesome and cultured living," and the state is obliged to provide "social welfare and security"; low-cost medical care is also assured by the state.[48] A right to free compulsory education is buttressed with the duty of parents or guardians to see that the right is exercised (Art. 26). All "have the right and the obligation to work" under laws setting reasonable standards for "wages, hours, rest and other working conditions," and the exploitation of children is prohibited (Art. 27). Unions are given an unprecedented stamp of approval with the workers' rights "to organize and to bargain and act collectively" (Art. 28); a new Ministry of Labor was established to provide supportive oversight. (ibid., pp. 23–27).

THE RIGHT TO PARTICIPATE IN ELECTION POLITICS

Article 15 is central in recognizing the people's "inalienable right to choose public officials and to dismiss them" and the nature of officials as the people's servants, not their masters as in prewar Japan; it also establishes universal adult suffrage and the secrecy of the ballot, and makes it a constitutional matter that a voter "not be answerable, publicly or privately, for the choice he has made." Article 44 prohibits discrimination in matters of Diet candidacy and voting, as noted above. These rights have been exercised and respected with comparative honesty and efficiency; but malapportionment, a ban on door-to-door canvassing, and severe limits on the related rights of all public employees remain notable constitutional problems.

PROCEDURAL RIGHTS

A full panoply of such rights is provided in Articles 31 to 40, with Article 31 setting the tone: "No person shall be deprived of life or liberty, nor shall any other criminal penalty be imposed, except according to procedure established by law."[49] "Involuntary servitude, except as punishment for crime, is prohibited" (Art. 18). A Japanese has rights of access to the courts, counsel, speedy and public trial, and "compulsory process to obtain witnesses" at public expense. Torture and other cruel punishment are "absolutely forbidden"; serious debate about capital punishment, which is imposed a few times a year, did not begin until mid-1985. Arrests, searches, and seizures must be justified by duly issued warrants. In cases of acquittal after detention, a person may sue the state for redress under law (Art. 40), as one may for damages against an illegal act of any public official (Art. 17). No one may be compelled to testify against oneself; confession under duress is not admissible as evidence, and a confession alone is not adequate grounds for conviction. With relatively few exceptions, Japan's record of procedural justice and relatively lenient penology has been very good, thanks to a highly professionalized triad of judges, prosecutors, and police.[50] The key remaining issues revolve around the degree of attorney access to suspects in the period after arrest when prolonged interrogation usually yields a confession, and the quasi-judicial discretion of prosecutors to dispose of most cases with little interaction with courts or attorneys.

RIGHTS AND FREEDOMS OF THE SPIRIT *(SEISHINTEKI JUYŪKEN)*

These rights are delineated in Articles 16, and 19 to 23. To a closed, repressed, ultranationalist and militarist society just devastated by war, these provisions, and attendant reforms of law and institution, ushered in a dramatic increase of freedom, openness, and tolerance; the constructive consequences altered the context of all human rights in Japan, and began the long process of opening a closed society. It is this category that has received the most scholarly attention in Japan, along with procedural rights. Unfortunately, Japanese scholars have generally neglected other categories of "human rights." However, I would argue that constitutionally protected freedom of expression is the most demanding test of a healthy constitutional democracy in any nation.[51] In Japan, "freedom of assembly and association as well as speech, press and all other forms of expression are guaranteed. . . . No censorship shall be maintained" (Art. 21). Chapter 3 also enumerates a right of peaceful petition (Art. 16), freedoms of thought and conscience (Art. 19), religion (Art. 20), and professional academic activity (Art. 23, the first such provision). Also guaranteed are the rights to choose one's occupation and place of residence as long as it does not "interfere with the public welfare," and the right to go abroad and to give up citizenship (Art. 22).

In reaction against earlier intolerance under State Shinto, Article 20 stresses freedom from state coercion to engage in religious activity and prohibits a "religious organization" from receiving "privileges" or exercising "any political authority." Article 89 may reflect more America's distinctive perspectives on "church and state" than Japanese or European traditions in withholding public moneys and property from "any religious institution or association, or for any charitable, educational or benevolent enterprises not under the control of public authority." A more liberal interpretation is widely supported by the Japanese; and their government supports private religion-related, educational institutions. More unusual to Western conceptions, in prewar Japan as today, many who have favored establishing State Shinto as the compulsory orthodoxy have simply denied that Shinto is a "religion" in the meaning of the Constitution;[52] religion about which one has freedom refers only to belief systems other than State Shinto.

The role of the judiciary

Along with Chapter 3 of the Constitution, perhaps Chapter 6 on the judiciary is the critical locus for constitutional rights.[53] Judicial independence in deciding individual cases was an honored tradition of the Japanese bench from the late 1800s, but only in 1947 was this fused with broad authority. In the give-and-take of the constitutional drafting process, it was the Japanese, not the Americans, who insisted the more on giving the bench full powers of judicial review,[54] as in American constitutional law. The Supreme Court also makes rules for and administers Japan's entire court system. It is composed of fifteen justices who sit, except for relatively few cases, as three petty benches *(shōhōtei)* of five members each.[55] Justices are chosen by the cabinet from lists submitted by the chief justice, and for the most part his preference is honored. The retirement age is seventy for justices and sixty-five for other judges.

At present there are 8 high courts with 6 branches, 50 district courts with 242 branches, as many family courts, and 575 summary courts for handling minor offenses. The actual number of judges deciding cases for over 120 million citizens is around 1,600, many with excessively heavy case loads. Since the late 1940s, virtually all new judges, prosecutors, and lawyers have received common training with the Supreme Court's Legal Training and Research Institute, which is modeled on the German system for educating *Referendar* and is Japan's nearest postgraduate analogue to an American law school.[56] Annually, about 500 of approximately 30,000 who take the National Law Examination are admitted. Most legal education in Japan is carried on at the undergraduate level in the many university "faculties of law," where all become familiar with codes and major statutes, and even more familiar with the constitutional rights they have learned about in their earlier schooling. Legal professionals are familiar with the techniques of case analysis which derive from American influence, but their use is mixed with civil law, common law, and Japanese traditions. Some of the major holdings of Japan's Supreme Court are available in English translation, and comment on numerous additional cases in the human rights area has crossed the formidable linguistic barrier between Japanese and English.[57] The lower courts, which also have judicial review powers, are considered by many Japanese and foreign observers to be generally more liberal than the Supreme Court on constitutional rights issues. In the 1980s, although problems attendant to the unusually closed nature of Japanese society remain, the general status of individual rights and freedom under law in Japan ranks high among the world's political systems. Japan's judiciary must now be reckoned among the most competent and sociopolitically significant.

The occupation work of implementing the constitution

Once the Constitution became law, many Americans contributed to the implementation of its intent by Japanese laws and other means; of these perhaps Alfred Oppler was most important. Oppler arrived at the SCAP offices from the United States on February 23, 1946, bringing with him an expertise in continental German law needed and largely lacking until then in the SCAP. A 1939 refugee from Nazism, this former judge also brought a deep commitment to individual rights which facilitated his work as a bridge between SCAP common lawyers and Japanese civil lawyers in creating and revising laws to conform with the new Constitution.

The sheer quantity and complexity of the law that had to be made then by the Japanese government and its American overseers is mind-boggling.[58] Oppler, who became chief of the Courts and Law Division of the Government Section, was ably assisted by Thomas Blakemore from Oklahoma, now America's senior specialist in Japanese law, and Kurt Steiner, now professor emeritus of political science at Stanford University. Oppler and his colleagues clearly understood their special mission:[59] "The changes we brought about in close cooperation with the Japanese legal world were not blindly copied from Anglo-Saxon jurisprudence, but were the fruit of an endeavor to combine the best features of both the continental and the Anglo-Saxon systems."

A project buttressing the new constitutional rights was the founding of the Japan Civil Liberties Union. In 1947, General MacArthur invited Roger Baldwin of the American Civil Liberties Union to Japan, and joined Oppler, Blakemore, Steiner, and committed Japanese lawyers, such as Shinkichi Unno, in inaugurating the Union on November 23, 1947.[60]

Later in the Occupation the American impact was noteworthy in other contexts. For example, in 1950, Oppler, with the help of Charles Kades (then of New York), brought five Japanese Supreme Court justices, including Chief Justice Kotaro Tanaka, to the United States for seven weeks to introduce them to American judicial ways. Subsequent interactions with American counterparts have continued to affect the perspectives of judges and other legal professionals on rights issues; less often but increasingly, one would hope, Americans have found Japan's experience relevant to their own understanding of human rights issues.

The contexts within which American constitutionalism has influenced individual rights in Japan are varied. Counterbalancing the Occupation instances of massive intervention (sketched above) were cases of cooperative interaction between Japanese and Americans in revising laws pursuant to the constitution. In the act, sometimes neither party could foresee the directions in which a new law or institution would develop. A symbolic illustration is found in the evolution of the Civil Liberties Bureau and the Civil Liberties Commissioner system. In 1947, Alfred Oppler mentioned in conversation with Yoshio Suzuki, the new justice minister, that the Office of the Attorney General in the United States had rather recently established a civil liberties unit; Suzuki "enthusiastically adopted the idea and established such a bureau in his ministry."[61] The inspiration at the time for the Civil Liberties Bureau of Japan came from the Civil Rights Section, Criminal Division, U.S. Department of Justice, which was to become the Civil Rights Division of today. In Japan, the bureau commenced operations in February 1948, but its leaders soon saw that its resources were inadequate for the defense and promotion of human rights; therefore, a system of lay civil liberties commissioners (*Jinken yogo iin*, literally "human rights protectors") was established, first by cabinet order in 1948 and then by the important 1949 Civil Liberties Commissioner Law.[62]

Neither the bureau nor the commissioners have any police powers or authority to prosecute; but, as of 1985, some 11,500 carefully selected and unpaid lay commissioners were dealing annually at the grass-roots level with thousands of citizen complaints and hundreds of thousands of human rights inquiries; they have also worked hand in hand with schools and communities in human rights educational projects.[63] Problems are handled quickly, cheaply, and respectfully with an emphasis on conciliatory methods, referrals, and the provision of needed information. In good part, the effective procedures still used today for choosing these volunteer community servants were developed in close consultation with Kurt Steiner during the Occupation period.

The continuing American influence

The Occupation period brought much greater legitimacy in Japan to American, Japanese, and European ideas and institutions affecting constitutional rights. The Communist victory in China (1949), the cold war, and the Korean War diminished democratic fervor in its latter years. Japan is now a non-Western, urbanized industrial democracy which continues its dynamic mix of indigenous, Anglo-American, and continental European ingredients in a distinctive constitutional culture. Over the decades since independence came in 1952, an American influence may be detected. Japanese scholars, judges, prosecutors, lawyers, and students have thought it interesting and at times useful to look at American perspectives on issues of civil rights and liberties when developing their own views on how best to deal with a Japanese problem. Japanese legal scholarship is replete with references to American judicial and scholarly work; the United States remains the primary foreign source of thought on constitutional law. Besides such contexts of influence *within* Japan, many Japanese professionals have come to the United States for a semester or more of legal study. Others come only for a matter of days or weeks, but influence is not proportionate to length of stay. For example, many years after a few discussions with Justice Felix Frankfurter, Justice Toshio Irie, whose tenure on the Supreme Court was the longest ever, remarked in 1970 how materially that brief occasion had affected his understanding of the importance of procedural rights to democracy.[64]

The influence of Japan's learned specialists in constitutional law and American law have assured the institutionalization of U.S.-derived ideas on rights in other contexts. The deliberations between 1957 and 1964 of the Commission on the Constitution *(Kempō Chosaki)* were headed by an eminent scholar of Anglo-American law, Kenzo Takayanagi.[65] Professor Takayanagi presided over a comprehensive six-year examination of each feature of the Constitution in committees both scholarly and politically minded, in public hearings around the country, and in consultations abroad. The ruling party's motivation in establishing the commission was to prepare the political ground for revising the Constitution, with possible negative implications for citizens' rights under the law;[66] but for many reasons, the final report of the divided commission recommended no amendments. The communal affirmation of consensual democracy in the unprecedented demonstrations of the security treaty crisis of 1960 was one reason. Demonstrators were protesting "undemocratic" reliance on a Diet majority vote to approve a treaty on so fundamental an issue as national security before sufficiently prolonged discussions in pursuit of a popular consensus. Another reason was the astute management of commission affairs by Takayanagi, his staff, and his supporters, who argued that there was no urgent need for revision, that the public seemed quite content with the Constitution, and that, in any event, judicial interpretation was a good and natural route to the refinement of constitutional doctrine. As of this writing, the first amendment was not in prospect, and the rising leadership of the Liberal Democratic party seemed less interested than their elders in revision.

For over twenty years, the Japanese American Society for Legal Studies has been a remarkable binational, bicultural, and bilegal vehicle for the reciprocal study of each other's law among Japanese and American legal scholars, lawyers, judges, and prosecutors. (The academic offices for this learned society have been the Faculty of Law, Tokyo University, and the Asian Law Program at the University of Washington in Seattle.) Among many influential Japanese members are a good number of Supreme Court justices (e.g. Masami Ito and Takaaki Hattori). The Japanese branch of the society publishes *Amerika Ho* (American Law), and the American branch *Law in Japan*.[67] In addition, established specialists on American constitutional law have been called upon to present expert testimony in court. A constitutional right of privacy with respect to information about one's private life was first established in Japanese law by a 1964 Tokyo district court decision against Yukio Mishima's novel *After the Banquet*; the expert testimony of Professor Masami Ito, now a Supreme Court justice, played a noteworthy role.[68] Again, the respected testimony by Professor Nobuyoshi Ashibe on behalf of a "less restrictive alternative" doctrine buttressed significantly the lower court cases for the freedom of expression of off-duty public employees.[69] The end result may or may not reveal that an American mode of legal reasoning has been taken into account by the Japanese bench; there is no reason why it should. The Japanese practice of consulting the constitutional law and human rights experience of other countries when trying to develop its own position on a domestic issue recommends itself to judges of all enlightened democratic nations.

Finally, some American and Japanese legal scholars have done major collaborative research, and a few of us—while doing our single-author scholarship—have relied regularly on each other for information, criticisms, and new and more precise perspectives on our respective systems.

With respect to the continued fruitful interplay, since the Occupation, of American and Japanese ideas on constitutional rights, the substratum of respect and friendship among Japanese and American law professors has perhaps been more important than formal collaborations or judicial use of American legal formulations. The expected continuation of dialogue bodes well for effective binational legal understanding in the midst of negotiations and controversies. One may hope that in time American scholars and judges will look to Japan for suggestive insights when grappling with problems in advancing the rights of an American.

KOREA

As noted earlier, the late nineteenth century brought the domination of Korea by American, Japanese, and European imperialists, but also new ideas about law and constitutional rights. The *Tonghak* Rebellion, which occasioned the Sino-Japanese War of 1894–95, was symbolic of early modern tensions in Korea, calling not only for the king's tolerance of the syncretic *Tonghak* religious movement, but also for the expulsion of foreigners and their ideas.[70] But with its own Asian colony, the Philippines, the United States acquiesced when Korea became a protectorate of Japan in 1905 following the Russo-Japanese War, and an annexed territory in 1910.[71] The direct influence of other governments disappeared, and Korea's law, economy, and educational system were developed for Japan's exploitive purposes. Most deeply offensive to this ancient people were Japan's attempts to suppress Korean civilization and remold the Korean people into reverently loyal subjects of the Japanese emperor under the Meiji Constitution. Japan's own creative adaptations of continental European law and state theory were oppressively stamped on the Korean legal mind until 1945.[72]

The independence movement and the United States

The Korean independence movement sometimes combined nationalist preoccupations with American ideas of constitutionalism and Christianity. For example, Christian political leaders such as Philip Jaisohn and Syngman Rhee were educated in the United States, while within Korea, from the late 1800s, Americans founded churches, public health facilities, and schools. Korean students came to the United States to study as they do today. Many of these Koreans and Americans were major conduits for democratic thought as well as for Western religious and educational ideas.[73]

Woodrow Wilson's call for national self-determination for all peoples after World War I found eager listeners in Korea, as elsewhere in the subjugated non-West. The Korean response was the dramatic March First Movement of 1919, on the occasion of the funeral of the last Korean king. Only Korea's religions had the noncolonialist, nationwide organizational network needed; so this first broadly based modern political movement relied upon an alliance of the *Chondogyo* (the *Tonghak* movement in modified form), Buddhist communities, and the Christian churches, many of the latter influenced by Americans, especially Presbyterians and Methodists.[74] The March First Movement remains for Koreans, with annual commemoration, "the cornerstone of their national politics, one of the few events of their history in which pride is shared and closely felt. For the first time they were united behind an idea, not fragmented by competition for the same power."[75] Carefully planned unarmed demonstrations for independence took place all over Korea. A declaration of independence, with a call for freedom and equality reminiscent of the American Declaration of Independence, was signed by thirty-three nationalists of varied social background and first read out in a Seoul public park. In eloquent Korean, it reads, in partial translation:

> We herewith proclaim the independence of Korea and the liberty of the Korean people. We tell it to the world in witness of the equality of all nations and we pass it on to our posterity as their inherent right. . . .
>
> A new era wakes before our eyes, the old world of force is gone, and the new world of righteousness and truth is here. . . .
>
> It is the day of the restoration of all things, on the full tide of which we set forth, without delay or fear. We desire a full measure of satisfaction in the way of liberty and the pursuit of happiness, and an opportunity to develop what is in us for the glory of the people.[76]

Multitudes marched peacefully through town and city streets in hundreds of demonstrations, shouting "*Tongnip Manse!*" (Long Live Independence!). It is important to dwell thus on the place of American democratic religious thought in the March First Movement, because it explains the special legitimacy in democratic opposition politics today of Korea's Christian churches, both Protestant and Catholic. Human rights, Christianity, and authentic nationalism are long-standing allies.

In 1919, national dignity, pride, and desire could not be accompanied by an expectation that independence would soon be achieved. A provisional government headed by Syngman Rhee was formed in Shanghai and it lasted in exile—first there and then elsewhere—until after Korea's liberation in 1945. However, the efficient Japanese easily crushed opposition within Korea; the nationalist cause drew little foreign attention and support and was bedeviled by frustration and factionalism. The Korean yearning for independence remained unsatisfied until a sympathetic United States defeated Japan in August 1945. On December 1, 1943, the United States, China, and the United Kingdom had issued the Cairo Declaration expressing their determination that "in due course Korea shall become free and independent";[77] this policy position was reaffirmed by the Potsdam Declaration of July 1945. However, the future of Korea was set on a tragic course later that summer when, on American initiative, the United States and the Soviet Union divided Korea "temporarily" at the thirty-eighth parallel for purposes of administering Japan's surrender, and the Americans arrived in the South unprepared.[78] In ignorance of Korean history and political culture and to the dismay of Koreans, the Americans and their allies had assumed a need for years of tutelage before Korean independence.

The American occupation, 1945–48

The relatively few Americans who had seriously supported self-determination for Korea also tended to assume that, once liberated, Korea would adopt democracy, freedom, and equality as constitutional foundations; but Korea's primary focus was freedom and equality for the nation, not for the individual Korean under law. American and European democratic ideas have indeed become an important element in South Korean constitutional thought and politics since 1945. However, the chaotic early postwar period saw a plethora of groups and ideologies in the political arena, violence for political advantage or revenge, heightened tensions as the shock of national division sank in, and a vacuum in government as the Japanese went home. Japanese colonial rule had left many Koreans sensitive to democratic values and individual rights; but the independence movement united people against *foreign* violation of individual rights, not Korean violations. Korea had no history of democratic government. Other Koreans had participated in Japan's police repression and authoritarian administration; *their* style became predominant although they enjoyed the least indigenous trust. As we briefly look at the U.S. military occupation and the slow and painful road toward a more stable Korean government, it should be kept in mind that internal disorders resulted in about 100,000 Korean deaths *before* the Korean Conflict began in mid-1950.[79]

For reasons both Korean and American in origin, the cause of constitutional rights fared much worse under the American occupation in a liberated Korea than in a conquered Japan. Lieutenant General John R. Hodge was given the following mission on September 8, 1945, after his arrival in southern Korea:

1 Take the Japanese surrender, disarm the Japanese armed forces, enforce the terms of the surrender, and remove Japanese imperialism from Korea;
2 maintain order, establish an effective government along democratic lines and rebuild a sound economy as a basis for Korean independence;
3 train Koreans in handling their own affairs and prepare Korea to govern itself as a free and independent nation.[80]

In a general sense, this support for effective democratic Korean government has remained a key element in American policy ever since, but it must be emphasized that American influence has been limited.[81]

General Hodge and his associates were not prepared by training or experience for the baffling complexity of the postliberation Korean situation. Korea was viewed as a very undesirable assignment, and military officers rotated in and out of Korea for career advantage as quickly as possible, thus denying the Occupation the internal continuity of key authorities. As with MacArthur in Japan, it is important not to exaggerate the importance of one man, General Hodge, in the situation. The American Occupation of 1945–48 lacked much of what its counterpart had in Japan: the knowledge; the prior planning; the accepted authority; the informed and able personnel and other resources; the preexisting indigenous government with the capacity to carry out democratic directives; the compliant populace; the well-developed indigenous legal system; and the political stability necessary for great democratic reforms in law and government.[82] In addition, seriously erroneous judgments were made about which Korean political groups and leaders were upstarts and which had legitimacy and broad support.

The USAMGIK (U.S. Military Government in Korea) ruled Korea directly through ordinances, but most law and most administrative and enforcement personnel were carryovers from the Japanese regime. For decades the people in authority had been Japanese. In the last years of Japanese rule, Korean police increased in proportion to Japanese, but constituted only one-fifth of patrolmen and one-tenth of officers. In 1945, the largest group of trained Korean functionaries in any government agency consisted of some 10,000 civilian and military police, men who were identified in Korean eyes more with the hated Japanese than with nationalist democratic interests. Yet USAMGIK relied heavily on these police for political information and action.

The legal system was also beset with a paucity of indigenous professionals, which is one reason why it has been difficult to develop a coherent tradition of rights protection, judicial independence, or judicial review. "In 1945, only 8 out of 120 prosecutors, 46 out of 235 judges and an estimated 195 qualified lawyers in the South were Korean. Only one of the lawyers had non-Japanese training."[83] Not one Western expert on Korean law existed at the time and, in contrast to the situation within Japan, USAMGIK never had the services of an American specialist on Japanese law.

USAMGIK *was* South Korea's government for three years, and issued some 211 legislative ordinances and some authoritative opinions; but it operated on the supposition that the freedom and onus for democratic legal reforms rested on the Koreans. (After all, Korea was a liberated ally, not a conquered enemy like Japan.) USAMGIK Ordinance 20 of November 2, 1945, continued in force the corpus of modern Japanese law in Korea "until repealed by competent authority."[84] Although some repressive Japanese law was repealed (as by Ordinance 11 of October 9, 1945), at the inception of the Republic of Korea in August 1948 an estimated 95 percent or more of its written law was that left by the Japanese.[85] Efforts to establish habeas corpus and other rights "were far too slight and too scantily administered" to be effective,[86] but as noted later, the Ordinance on the Rights of the Korean People, issued on April 4, 1948, influenced constitutional thought and provisions. Moreover, the revised Code of Criminal Procedure (March 20, 1948) introduced American concepts of procedural justice. USAMGIK's efforts for sexual equality included the establishment of women's suffrage before the national election of May 1948.[87]

In 1947, the United States–USSR Joint Trusteeship, which had been designed to prepare a unified Korea for independence, failed as the cold war commenced.[88] America took the Korea issue to the United Nations, and a UN Temporary Commission supervised National Assembly elections in the South on May 10, 1948, preliminary to independence.[89] A rather liberal democratic constitution took effect on July 17, 1948. In the North, the Democratic People's Republic of Korea also began its life in 1948, under the durable Premier Kim Il-sung. American and Soviet troops had withdrawn by 1949. USAMGIK's influence and accomplishments with respect to human rights were limited but important. The 1945 "liberation" of Korea had begun an era of unprecedented official and private American involvement in Korean affairs which hardened into long-term commitment with the three-year Korean War (1950–53).

Binational dependency and human rights

The influence of the United States on human rights in Korea has existed within an unusual network of public and private relationships of mutual dependency that may have more in common with America's relations with the Philippines than with Japan or Europe. This special relationship must be touched on before focusing on the U.S. impact on Korea's six constitutions. In contrast to the previous forty years of official unconcern and very limited public interest in Korean human rights, the past forty years have seen fitful official and private American pressures on successive Korean governments to honor human rights. The pattern in both American and Korean behavior, if not in declared policy, has been inconsistency.

When human rights and democratic processes have been disregarded by South Korean leaders, their explanations have been based on alleged exigencies of national security, development strains, and/or dissonance between constitutional democracy and Korean political culture. When American governments have quietly acquiesced in or only privately protested Korean rights violations, they have commonly stood on the same ground, explicitly or implicitly relying on official Korean judgments about what national security requires. The dilemmas have sometimes been quite genuine for American defenders of Korea's democratic independence. On the other hand, Korean and other critics of the U.S. and Korean governments have argued, sometimes persuasively, that South Korean stability and security are as inextricably dependent upon respect for human rights as upon military adequacy, and that survey data and other evidence indicate not popular passivity but sharp political awareness, assertiveness, and democratic value preferences among the Korean people.

Korean law and policy since 1953 have not very effectively protected and promoted human rights.[90] To some extent, law has continued to serve its colonial period role of maintaining a somewhat authoritarian order, allowing some freedom of discourse but not much comment on reunification or communism or much criticism of the government (the Anti-Communist Law). While unionism and wages have been held down, the general level of socioeconomic life for Koreans and attendant rights have improved dramatically since the 1960s.

American policy on human rights in South Korea has fluctuated between apparent indifference or hesitancy about criticizing the most egregious rights violations (e.g. torture) and making aid conditional upon respectful treatment of rights and democratic procedure. Since 1945, the religious element has fused with academic and other American activist forces for Korean democracy and human rights. Wisely and fairly or not, private sector American critics have allied with Korean opposition politicians, intellectuals, religious and literary leaders, and students in rather forcefully demanding government adherence to reasonable standards of human rights. Over the decades, the more common response of Korean citizens to public and private American pressures on behalf of human rights has not been nationalist resentment but rather a call for even heavier U.S. government leaning on Korea's leaders to desist from rights violations.[91] Korean government reactions to American pressures have generally been muted.

America's influence on constitutional rights in South Korea has often been indirect, passive, and based on economic relations and *ad hoc* political or governmental action. For Korean statute and constitution makers, America's style of draftsmanship has been less relevant than those of Japan and the European civil law democracies.[92] In 1953, for example, four Korean labor laws (never fully enforced) borrowed heavily from Japanese laws that had been formulated under American Occupation guidance.[93]

Education in the United States and Korea affects Korean perceptions of American constitutionalism. In Korean education the young learn about democratic rights, whatever the current government may be doing to or for rights. In the many interactions of Americans and Koreans through social and economic aid missions,[94] shared democratic values have been part of the binational currency.[95] The Asia Foundation of the United States has contributed to education, research, and service by assisting in the formation of the Korean Legal Center (Seoul) and the Asiatic Research Center of Korea University.[96] Many Korean professors and administrative personnel have received some of their higher education in the United States. (Korea has more personnel with economics doctorates from U.S. institutions than does the American government.) However, America-trained Korean businessmen and technocrats—in contrast to law professionals—do not seem identifiable as a force for human rights, although there is no necessary conflict between the reasonable pursuit of stable prosperity, on the one hand, and opposition to torture and press controls, or support for a living wage, on the other. Korean scholars, in noteworthy numbers, reside in the United States while retaining influential connections in Korea and vocally appealing from abroad for U.S. support of Korean human rights. Activist Korean and American religious leaders in the United States, today as in the 1919 March First Movement, illustrate the special human rights role of Christian democratic nationalists.[97]

Along with their admirable and humane concern some Americans show arrogance and inconsistency in comment and policy with respect to human rights in smaller countries with different ideologies than that of the United States and less cultural proximity or importance to U.S. ethnic politics. Sometimes in some countries overt and forceful U.S. action would exacerbate rather than alleviate human suffering. American influence on rights abroad seems best pursued by a policy of consistent and manifest intolerance for torture and other blatant rights violations and proportional public opposition to less flagrant failures and abuses, with careful attention to details of case and context and purposeful avoidance of differential standards for different countries. There should be rigorous indifference to whether a democratic country adopts a presidential or a parliamentary system, a federal or a unitary government, the common law or civil law tradition. The American influence on human rights in Korea has not been in making institutions and laws during a military occupation, as in Japan, but in standing for universalist constitutional ideals, a separation of powers, and judicial review.

Human rights, the presidency, and judicial review

In its turbulent postliberation history, the Republic of Korea has had six constitutions, promulgated in 1948, 1960, 1962, 1972, 1980, and 1987.[98] Tragic systemic flaws—an atrophied capacity for compromise in both ruling and opposition circles; a military's refusal to yield governance to democratic civilians; and a Confucian resistance to sharing or relinquishing political power—have coexisted with an inspiring widespread commitment among influential Koreans to constitutional democracy and recurrent organized opposition to authoritarianism.

The American influence on Korea's six constitutions has varied in degree, nature, and clarity; sources available on the drafting processes are limited in both Korea and the United States.[99] However, three strains in Korean constitutional thought bear an American stamp: the stress on civil rights and liberties; a directly elected president; and independent courts with the power of judicial review. I will briefly examine the past forty years in terms of these three themes.

Before 1945 Korea had had no experience of democratic self-government and individual rights under law. Insofar as the Korean drafters of the 1948 Constitution were versed at all in law and constitution, they were likely to know about those of prewar Japan and Europe, not the United States.[100] The principal author of that Constitution was the leading scholar Professor Yu Chin-O; he brought the socio-economic rights of the 1919 Weimar Constitution into Korea, but he was also influenced by American human rights concepts through an USAMGIK ordinance of long-term significance:

> Probably the most significant measure taken by the U.S. Military Administration for Korean civil rights was "The Ordinances on the Rights of the Korean People" issued by General Hodge on April 7, 1948. The Ordinance consisted of twelve articles guaranteeing the freedoms of religion, assembly and association, expression and publication, and the rights to legal counsel, to speedy and fair trial, and to equal protection under law. It also prohibited torture, and deprivation of freedom or property without due process of law. These precious principles were obviously derived from the basic doctrine of the Constitution of the United States.[101]

This and other ordinances gave legal authority to American human rights ideas for the first time; but American policy during the actual drafting process was not to proffer advice unless asked. Apparently, neither USAMGIK's "Woodall draft" nor its legal experts familiar with European constitutional law, such as Ernst Fraenkel, were consulted.[102] In 1948, Dr. Syngman Rhee, Korea's first president, was responsible for the choice of a strong presidency in preference to the parliamentary system and supreme court with judicial review powers that were recommended by the drafting committee. The 1948 Constitution of the Republic of Korea provided for election of the president by a two-thirds majority of the unicameral legislature, a presidentially appointed supreme court with limited jurisdiction, state controls on major enterprises and resources, and a wide range of individual rights.

Unfortunately Dr. Rhee's administration slipped into authoritarianism and, after corrupt elections in 1960, he was driven into exile by student demonstrations with the military's acquiescence.[103] Only during the short-lived Second Republic (1960–61) that followed has Korea been led by a parliamentary prime minister, Chang Myon. Following the 1961 military coup, Park Chung-hi, first as general then as civilian leader of the Democratic Republican party, ruled Korea until his assassination in October 1979. Like Rhee, he amended the Constitution to increase and prolong his power; nevertheless the period of the Third Republic (1962–1972) was pivotal for the development of judicial review in Korea.[104]

Korean "professors of constitutional law, administrative law, and political science played a dominant role" in the authorship of the 1962 Constitution.[105] The framers agreed on the adoption of a presidential system, but were divided on how best to institutionalize constitutional review. Some favored a special tribunal like the Federal Constitutional Court of West Germany. In the end, the power of judicial review was vested in ordinary courts. As under the U.S. Constitution, the Supreme Court was a constitutional branch of government, while the establishment of lower courts was left to law. Article 102 provided that "in case a question arises about whether or not a statute violates the constitution in a pending case, the Supreme Court shall make the final determination."[106]

Trial and appellate courts held several statutes unconstitutional in the late 1960s; but the Supreme Court turned away challenges such as that to Article 4(1) of the Anti-Communist Law, which allowed up to seven years imprisonment for expressions of comment, encouragement, or sympathy regarding any antistate group.[107] Only once (June 22, 1971)[108] has the Korean Supreme Court held statutes unconstitutional, but that landmark precedent remains a high point for the many who support the protection of human rights by judicial review. The provisions of two statutes were struck down: a July 1970 revision of Article 59(1) of the Judiciary Organization Law, by an eleven to five majority, and Article 2(1) of the Government Tort Liability Law (1967), by a nine to seven vote. Article 59(1) was designed by the government and ruling party to assure reversal on appeal of a Seoul High Court decision[109] against the liability law: "For the Supreme Court to hold a statute unconstitutional, more than two-thirds of the Justices must be present and more than two-thirds of the Justices present must concur."[110] The Supreme Court held that such an exception to the majority rule violated the separation of powers principle and could be established only by the Constitution itself. Article 2(1), which limited government liability for injury or death to one armed forces employee due to the negligent or willful act of another, was held contrary to equal protection clauses of the Constitution. The bar and the academic community praised the decisions as beginning an era of vigorous judicial protection of human rights against government abuses, while the government denounced the judiciary.

The 1971 Supreme Court actions, combined with the near-victory of Kim Dae Jung of the New Democratic party in the 1971 presidential election, were a major factor behind the 1972 constitutional revision. Under the *Yushin* (Revitalization) Constitution, Park was granted dictatorial powers and the possibility of many six-year terms in office; constitutional review power was taken from the courts and an ineffectual Constitution Committee established. Reflecting the ups and downs of human rights and democracy in Korea, the charismatic Kim Dae Jung was in and out of confinement on questionable charges from 1971 until July 1987.[111]

After Park's death, and a brief period of high hopes, another coup occurred, and General Chun Doo Hwan supervised the preparation of the Constitution of the Fifth Republic, which went into effect on October 27, 1980. As under the *Yushin* Constitution, the president was chosen by an electoral college of some 5,000 electors, but only for a single seven-year term. Concern about human rights and a widespread desire for direct election of the president under a new constitution generated large-scale student demonstrations as Korea prepared for the 1988 Olympics in June 1987.[112] On July 10, President Chun resigned as chairperson of the ruling Democratic Justice party; his successor, Roh Tae Woo, with the concurrence of the president and the party, agreed to cooperation with the opposition Reunification Democratic party of Kim Dae Jung and Kim Young Sam to restore civil liberties, release political prisoners, and establish a new constitution providing for direct popular election of the president. As it has been so often since 1948, the relevance of U.S., rather than purely Korean, considerations to the democratic resurgence was unclear.

CONCLUSION

Differences in the American influence on human rights in Japan and South Korea reflect distinctive differences in their respective national histories.

South Korea's present dependence on the United States for its security continues an historic pattern. The special prerogatives of China in Korea's traditional foreign relations yielded to the late nineteenth-century competition for "paramountcy" in Korea among exploitive Western powers and Japan, which in turn issued in Japan's

1910 annexation of Korea. The United States and the USSR became the post-1945 centers around which moved the Southern and Northern fragments of Korea. North Korea has followed the way of its lord, Kim Il-sung, in pursuit of a good measure of independence between Communist giants, national identity, and a Confucian-Communist understanding of human rights as limited to socioeconomic rights. South Korea, encouraged by other democracies, has sought realization of a more comprehensive view of human rights law as including both socioeconomic rights and civil liberties. Both Koreas suffer from a schizophrenic sense of identity: each wants both internal political firmness and reunification with the other and independence from intrusive foreign powers, but also depends for survival upon external support. America, with its influence on human rights in South Korea, has helped to keep alive the dream of political democracy while trying to avoid the extremes of entrapment in manipulative Korean politics and the abandonment of an important ally in ways detrimental to U.S. national interest.[113]

Japan's historical pattern contrasts sharply with Korea's in that full legal and political independence had been regained from Western imperialists by the turn of the century. In 1987, socioeconomic and technical equality with all foreign competitors was a dream realized. In pride of culture, Japan and Korea have at least equaled the United States within their triangular relationships; but the flow of cultural influence relevant to human rights has thus far been from America to Northeast Asia. War, war preparation, and imperialism have harmed modern U.S. relations with East Asia; yet, emerging from it all, the indigenization within Japan and Korea of American and other Western ideas of law, constitution, and human rights—along with supportive religious values, especially in South Korea—seems the West's most significant civilizational contribution to the region.

The catalyst of the American Occupation period in Japan gave lasting legitimacy and institutionalization to human rights ideas that until then had been perennially subordinate to statist authoritarianism; the Constitution of Japan fit in with the politico-legal culture and national needs and desires at a unique historical instance of catastrophic defeat. Constitutional pacifism has blocked a resurgence of repressive militarism. In post-1945 South Korea, human rights ideas gradually took hold in many sectors of society before, during, and after the horrors of the Korean War. However, human rights awaited stable legitimacy under law as Seoul prepared for the 1988 Olympics. While the Japanese have felt unthreatened by foreign powers—to a degree that exasperates many American observers—Korean human rights face easily identifiable threats from both North Korea and their own military, the decisive force in South Korean politics. Since the notion of human rights dominant in American politics has insisted unequivocally upon neither equality of treatment to all races nor socioeconomic survival rights, the United States has presented a mixed image to the world with a contrary clear consensus. Myopic preoccupation with economic, military, and geopolitical perspectives in the region has at times diverted the American mind from the rights of humans, which must justify the rest. However, America's democratic constitutionalism, power, and concern for freedom under law have on balance buttressed human rights in East Asia, a region that may be pivotal in the world of the twenty-first century.

NOTES

1 John K. Fairbank, Edwin O. Reischauer, and Albert M. Craig, *East Asia: Tradition and Transformation* (Boston: Houghton Mifflin, 1973).

2 Lawrence W. Beer, *Freedom of Expression in Japan: A Study in Comparative Law, Politics, and Society* (Tokyo and New York: Kodansha International, 1984), pp. 37–99; Lawrence W. Beer, "Constitutional Revolution in Japanese Law, Society, and Politics," *Modern Asian Studies* (1982), 16 (1):33; Edward Baker and William Shaw, eds., *Human Rights in Korea: Historical and Policy Perspectives*, forthcoming; Pyong-ho Pak et al., *Modernization and Its Impact Upon Korean Law* (Berkeley: Institute of East Asian Studies, University of California, 1981); Chongko Choi, "On the Reception of Western Law in Korea," *Korean Journal of Comparative Law* (December 1981), 9: 141.

3 Edward S. Corwin, *The "Higher Law" Background of American Constitutional Law* (Ithaca: Cornell University Press, 1959); Harold J. Berman, *Law and Revolution: The Formation of the Western Legal Tradition* (Cambridge: Harvard University Press, 1983).

4 Beer, *Freedom*, ch. 3; Baker and Shaw, *Human Rights in Korea*, ch. 1.

5 Ibid.; William Shaw, *Legal Norms in a Confucian State* (Berkeley: Institute of East Asian Studies, University of California, 1981); Dan Fenno Henderson, *Conciliation and Japanese Law: Tokugawa and Modern*, 2 vols. (Seattle: University of Washington Press, 1965); Dan Fenno Henderson, *Village "Contracts" in Tokugawa Japan* (Seattle: University of Washington Press, 1975).

6 For a personalist theoretical approach, see Beer, *Freedom*, pp. 30–37; L. J. Macfarlane, *The Theory and Practice of Human Rights* (London: Maurice Temple Smith, 1985); Terrence S. Shea, *Human Rights as an Instrument in the Humanist Reconstruction of Post-Modern Political Theory*, Ph.D. dissertation, University of Maryland, 1985.

7 Masami Ito, "*Nihonkoku Kempo to eibei Kempo*," *Nihonho to Eibeiho no 30nen*, symposium issue of *Jurisuto* (November 15, 1975), no. 600, p. 150; Ryosuke Ishii, *Japanese Culture in the Meiji Era: Legislation*, tr. W. J. Chambliss (Tokyo: Toyo Bunko, 1958); Kenzo Takayanagi, "Reception and Influence of Occidental Legal Ideas in Japan," in I. Nitobe, ed., *Western Influences in Modern Japan* (Chicago: University of Chicago Press, 1931); Dan Fenno Henderson, "Law and Political Modernization," in Robert E. Ward, ed., *Political Modernization in Japan* (Princeton: Princeton University Press, 1968); Kenzao Takayanagi, "A Century of Innovation: The Development of Japanese Law, 1868–1961," in Arthur von Mehren, ed., *Law in Japan: The Legal Order in a Changing Society* (Cambridge: Harvard University Press, 1963); Pyong-ho Pak et al., *Modernization*; Bong-Duck Chun et al., *Traditional Korean Legal Attitudes* (Berkeley: Institute of East Asian Studies, University of California, 1980); Harry Wray and Hilary Conroy, eds., *Japan Examined: Perspectives on Modern Japanese History* (Honolulu: University of Hawaii Press, 1983.)

8 Bruce Cumings, *The Origins of the Korean War: Liberation and Emergence of Separate Regimes* (Princeton: Princeton University Press, 1981); Bruce Cumings, ed., *Child of Conflict: The Korean-American Relationship* (Seattle: University of Washington Press, 1983).

9 *Mainichi Daily News*, May 29 and August 23, 1985.

10 For the text of the 1947 Constitution of Japan, see Hiroshi Itoh and Lawrence W. Beer, *The Constitutional Case Law of Japan: Selected Supreme Court Decisions, 1961–1970* (Seattle: University of Washington Press, 1978), pp. 256–269.

11 Beer, *Freedom*, pp. 110–111; Yosiyuki Noda, *The Character of the Japanese People and Their Conception of Law*, in Hideo Tanaka and M. D. H. Smith, eds., *The Japanese Legal System* (Tokyo: Tokyo University Press, 1976), pp. 304–305.

12 Beer, *Freedom*, pp. 45–49; see also the sources listed in note 7, above.

13 The English text of the Meiji constitution is in Tanaka and Smith, *The Japanese Legal System*, p. 107.

14 Alfred Oppler, *Legal Reform in Occupied Japan: A Participant Looks Back* (Princeton: Princeton University Press, 1976), p. 55; Beer, *Freedom*, pp. 45–53, 85–89.

15 Beer, *Freedom*, ch. 3.

16 The Universal Manhood Suffrage Law, Law 47 of March 29, 1925.

17 The Peace Preservation Law, Law 46 of April 22, 1925. On the law and politics of this period, see Beer, *Freedom*, pp. 59–70.

18 Beer, "Constitutional Revolution."

19 The data on constitutions was kindly provided by Professor Albert P. Blaustein, School of Law, Rutgers University, January 1987.

20 For documents and analysis of the Occupation period in Japan, see SCAP, *Political Reorientation of Japan* (Washington, D.C.: GPO, n.d. [1949]), hereafter cited as *Reorientation*; Beer, *Freedom*, pp. 71–82, and sources cited therein; Wray and Conroy, eds., *Japan Examined*, pp. 331–363;

D. Clayton James, *The Years of MacArthur*, vol. 3: *Triumph and Disaster, 1945–1954* (Boston: Houghton Mifflin, 1985); Jay Rubin, "From Wholesomeness to Decadence: The Censorship of Literature Under the Allied Occupation," *Journal of Japanese Studies* (1985), 17 (1): 17; Peter Frost, "Occupation," in *Kodansha Encyclopedia of Japan* (New York: Kodansha International, 1983), 6:51; Robert E. Ward and Yoshikazu Sakamoto, eds., *Democratizing Japan: The Allied Occupation* (Honolulu: University of Hawaii Press, 1987).

21 This famous photograph of General MacArthur and Emperor Hirohito is reproduced in Justin Williams, *Japan's Political Revolution Under MacArthur* (Athens: University of Georgia Press, 1978), opposite p. 82.

22 Beer, *Freedom*, pp. 77–79 and ch. 6.

23 Ibid., pp. 79–81.

24 Ibid.; Ward and Sakamoto, *Democratizing Japan*; James, *The Years of MacArthur*; Williams, *Japan's Political Revolution*; Oppler, *Legal Reform*; John M. Maki, *Japan's Commission on the Constitution: Its Final Report* (Seattle: University of Washington Press, 1980), pp. 49, 62, 220; Toshio Nishi, *Unconditional Democracy: Education and Politics in Occupied Japan, 1945–52* (Stanford: Hoover Institution, 1982); Theodore H. McNelly, *Domestic and International Influences on Constitutional Revision in Japan, 1945–1946*, Ph.D. dissertation, Columbia University, 1952. For a bibliography, see Robert E. Ward and Frank J. Shulman, *The Allied Occupation of Japan, 1945–1952* (Chicago: American Library Association, 1974). Many of the official records are now available on microfilm in *Confidential U.S. State Department Files—Japan: Internal Affairs, 1945–1954* (Frederick, Md.: University Publications of America, 1985).

25 Williams, *Japan's Political Revolution*, pp. 104–107.

26 Ibid., p. 101; SCAP, *Reorientation*, pp. 423–439; Theodore H. McNelly, ed., *Sources in Modern East Asian History and Politics* (New York: Appleton-Century-Crofts, 1967), p. 177. The document was State-War-Navy Coordinating Committee (SWNCC) 228. The principal author was Hugh Borton, now professor emeritus of Columbia University.

27 SCAP, *Reorientation*, pp. 603–631.

28 Williams, *Japan's Political Revolution*, pp. 104–105; Oppler, *Legal Reform*, ch. 5. No discussion of Japan's Constitution should omit mention of its most distinctive feature, the quasi-pacifism of Article 9. Many incomplete discussions of the constitutional renunciation of the right to belligerency exist in Japanese and English. The most reliable guide in Japan or the United States to the complex origins of the Article 9 pacifist provision of the constitution is Theodore H. McNelly; see his chapter in Ward and Sakamoto, *Democratizing Japan*, and in *Proceedings of the Asiatic Society of Japan* (1983). On the current role of Article 9 in Japanese constitutional politics see Lawrence W. Beer, "The Domestic Constraints on Japanese Security Policies," in Ronald A. Morse, ed., *Option 2000* (Washington, D.C.: Smithsonian Institution, Woodrow Wilson International Center for Scholars, 1987), p. 5. For public opinion data and case law on this sensitive issue, see Lawrence W. Beer, "Japan's Constitution and Its Judicial Interpretation," *Law in Japan* (1984), 17:11–13, 22–23.

29 Nishi, *Unconditional Democracy*, pp. 119–120.

30 On Charles Kades and his role, see Williams, *Japan's Political Revolution*, ch. 3 and passim. "How Kades escaped the notice of contemporary writers and observers is hard to understand. . . . American newspapermen by and large ignored him. They failed to sense that he was the second most important SCAP official, ranking just below Courtney Whitney. They were three disparate characters all working in near perfect harmony: MacArthur, the worldly-wise conservative; Whitney, his shrewd alter ego; and Kades, the brainy New Dealer" (p. 35). On another pragmatic linking of unlikes, see Forrest McDonald, *Novus Ordo Seclorum: The Intellectual Origins of the Constitution* (Lawrence: University of Kansas Press, 1985).

31 On Whitney, Rowell, Hussey, Oppler, and other key SCAP officials involved in the processes of making law and rights, see Williams, *Japan's Political Revolution*, chs. 4, 5.

32 Ibid., pp. 39–42.

33 Ibid., p. 52; and my correspondence with Charles L. Kades, January and February 1986 (hereafter cited as Kades).

34 Williams, *Japan's Political Revolution*, pp. 115–117; Kades. The bureau's chief, Toshio Irie, went on to serve well and long on the Supreme Court of Japan, 1952–1970. Tatsuo Sato, the deputy chief, and later head of the National Personnel Authority, interacted the most with the Americans on the constitution issue in the fateful months of 1946.

35 Nishi, *Unconditional Democracy*, p. 122.

36 Article 73 of the Meiji constitution provided: "When it becomes necessary in future to amend the provisions of the present Constitution, a project to the effect shall be submitted to the Imperial Diet by Imperial Order. In the above case, neither House can open the debate unless not less than two-thirds of Members are present, and no amendment can be passed unless a majority of not less than two-thirds of the Members present is obtained." Tanaka and Smith, *The Japanese Legal System*, p. 23.

37 Williams, *Japan's Political Revolution*, pp. 118–121.

38 For the composition of the constitutional committees of the Government Section, see SCAP, *Reorientation*, p. 813; Oppler, *Legal Reform*, p. 157; Kades; and discussions with other occupationnaires.

39 Williams, *Japan's Political Revolution*, p. 108; Dale Hellegers, panelist in *The Occupation of Japan: The Proceedings of a Seminar on the Occupation of Japan and Its Legacy to the Postwar World* (Norfolk, Va.: MacArthur Memorial, 1976), pp. 11–15.

40 Itoh and Beer, *Constitutional Case Law*, pp. 256–258.

41 Beer, "Constitutional Revolution," pp. 33–43.

42 For a fuller discussion, see ibid., and Lawrence W. Beer, "Japan's Constitution and Its Judicial Interpretation," *Law in Japan* (1984), 17:7.

43 Itoh and Beer, *Constitutional Case Law*, pp. 258, 268.

44 *Japan v. Sugino, 4 Keishu* 2012, 3014 (Sup. Ct., Grand Bench, 1950).

45 Itoh and Beer, *Constitutional Case Law*, pp. 258–261.

46 Law No. 89 of 1898, as amended. Concerning this code, see Kurt Steiner, "Postwar Changes in the Japanese Civil Code," in *Legal Reforms in Japan During the Allied Occupation*, special reprint volume of the *Washington Law Review* (Seattle, 1977), p. 97; and Taime Bryant, "Marital Dissolution in Japan: Legal Obstacles and Their Impact," *Law in Japan* (1984), 17:73. For further discussion of human rights issues in Japan, see Beer, *Freedom*; his "Japan's Constitution"; and his "Group Rights and Individual Rights in Japan," *Asian Survey* (April 1981), p. 437. For statistics on male-female compensation differentials, see "Wages," *Look Japan*, December 10, 1985, p. 27.

47 On voter opinion survey data, see Beer, "Constitutional Revolution," pp. 44–46.

48 There is a serious debate in Japan on the degree to which the provisions of Articles 25 and 27 are merely hortatory or legally binding. On a related case, see Beer, "Japan's Constitution," pp. 39–40. On Article 28, see Beer, "Japan's Constitution," pp. 23–27.

49 This language, which has appeared in other postwar constitutions (e.g. India's), affords protections equal to those provided by the vague American legal formulation "due process of law." In practice, the different phraseologies have not implied different degrees of legal protection of procedural rights. See, for example, P. K. Tripathi, "Perspectives on the American Constitutional Influence on the Constitution of India," in Lawrence W. Beer, ed., *Constitutionalism in Asia: Asian Views of the American Influence* (Berkeley: University of California Press, 1979), pp. 59–99.

50 See, for example, Beer, *Freedom*, passim; David H. Bayley, *Forces of Order: Police Behavior in Japan and the United States* (Berkeley: University of California Press, 1976); B. J. George, Jr., "Discretionary Authority of Public Prosecutors in Japan," *Law in Japan* (1984), 17:42.

51 Beer, *Freedom*, p. 21.

52 Ibid., ch. 7.

53 Itoh and Beer, *Constitutional Case Law*, pp. 265–266.

54 David J. Danelski, "Judicial Review and Democracy in Japan," paper presented at the International Political Science Association meeting, Paris, July 1985, pp. 1–6; Nobushige Ukai, "The Significance of the Reception of American Constitutional Institutions and Ideas in Japan," in Beer, *Constitutionalism in Asia*, pp. 114–127; Oppler, *Legal Reform*, especially chs. 6–8.

55 Beer, *Freedom*, p. 135.

56 Oppler, *Legal Reform*, p. 99; Beer, *Freedom*, pp. 131–133, 147, and 155, n. 16.

57 For translations of judicial decisions into English, see John M. Maki, ed., *Court and Constitution in Japan: Selected Supreme Court Decisions, 1948–1960* (Seattle: University of Washington Press, 1964); Itoh and Beer, *Constitutional Case Law*. Hiroshi Itoh and I, with help from other translators, are preparing a volume of case translations covering the years 1970 to 1990. For extended analysis of Japanese judicial decisions on human rights issues, see Beer, *Freedom*, and his "Japan's Constitution"; in Japanese, see the journals *Hanrei Jiho, Jurisuto, Horitsu Jiho*, and *Jiyu to Seigi*, all published in Tokyo.

58 Williams, *Japan's Political Revolution*, pp. 64–65.

59 Oppler, *Legal Reform*, p. 71.

60 Ibid., pp. 178–182.

61 Ibid., p. 172; Law for the Establishment of the Attorney General's Office, Law No. 193, December 17, 1947, (text in SCAP, *Reorientation*, p. 1059).
62 Law No. 139 of May 31, 1949.
63 Lawrence W. Beer, "Human Rights Commissioners (*Jinken Yogo lin*) and Lay Protection of Human Rights in Japan," Occasional Paper No. 31, October 1985, International Ombudsman Institute, Alberta, Canada.
64 Discussion with the author, Tokyo, 1970.
65 Kenzo Takayanagi, "Appendix: Opinion on Some Constitutional Problems: The Rule of Law," in Dan Fenno Henderson, ed., *The Constitution of Japan: Its First Twenty Years, 1947–1967* (Seattle: University of Washington Press, 1968), p. 89.
66 On the revision controversy, see Beer, "Constitutional Revolution," pp. 37–42, and works cited therein; Maki, *Japan's Commission on the Constitution*, pp. 15–31, 372–393.
67 The office of *Law in Japan* is: Asian Law Program, School of Law, JB–20, University of Washington, Seattle, Washington 98105.
68 Beer, *Freedom*, pp. 325–326.
69 The *Sarufutsu* case, *Japan v. Osawa*, 28 *Keishu* (No. 9) 393 (Sup. Ct., Grand Bench, November 6, 1974). See Beer, *Freedom*, pp. 236–237, and Ukai, "The Significance of the Reception of American Constitutional Institutions and Ideas in Japan," in Beer, *Constitutionalism in Asia*, pp. 124–125. Note that Japanese judges usually prefer not to mention specific U.S. precedents, even where they have had direct relevance in their decision making.
70 Chong-sik Lee, *The Politics of Korean Nationalism* (Berkeley: University of California Press, 1965), p. 19.
71 Wray and Conroy, *Japan Examined*, pp. 154, 136–140.
72 Edward J. Baker, "The Role of Legal Reforms in the Japanese Annexation and Rule of Korea, 1905–1919," and Wonmo Dong, "Imperial Japan's Colonial Legal System in Korea," both in Baker and Shaw, *Human Rights in Korea*.
73 Lee, *Korean Nationalism*, pp. 167, 277–278, and passim.
74 Ibid.; Gregory Henderson, *Korea: The Politics of the Vortex* (Cambridge, Mass.: Harvard University Press, 1968), pp. 80–86.
75 Henderson, *Korea*, pp. 82–83.
76 The Korean declaration of independence of 1919 can be found in Kyung Cho Chung, *Korea Tomorrow: Land of the Morning Calm* (New York: Macmillan, 1961), pp. 301–303.
77 Ibid., p. 303; McNelly, *Sources in Modern East Asian History and Politics*, p. 154. See also Han-Kyo Kim, "Japanese Colonialism in Korea," in Wray and Conroy, *Japan Examined*, p. 223.
78 Henderson, *Korea*, pp. 113–136.
79 Chung, *Korea Tomorrow*, p. 187; John P. Merrill, "The Impact of Civil Conflict," in Baker and Shaw, *Human Rights in Korea*; Cumings, *The Origins of the Korean War*, and his *Child of Conflict*.
80 Chung, *Korea Tomorrow*, p. 187.
81 Donald Macdonald, "Human Rights: Ideals and Reality," in Baker and Shaw, *Human Rights in Korea*; Donald Macdonald, *Korea and the Ballot: The International Dimension in Korean Political Development as Seen in Elections*, Ph.D. dissertation, George Washington University, 1977. See also Soon-sung Cho, *Korea in World Politics, 1940–1950* (Berkeley: University of California Press, 1967).
82 Gregory Henderson, "Human Rights in South Korea, 1945–1953," in Baker and Shaw, *Human Rights in Korea*; Macdonald, "Human Rights" and *Korea and the Ballot*; Cho, *Korea in World Politics*.
83 Henderson, "Human Rights," p. 17.
84 Ibid., p. 24.
85 Ibid., p. 31.
86 Ibid., p. 28.
87 Tscholsu Kim and Sang Don Lee, "The Influence of U.S. Constitutional Law Doctrine in Korea," in Lawrence W. Beer, ed., *Constitutional Systems in Late Twentieth-Century Asia*, forthcoming.
88 Cho, *Korea in World Politics*, pp. 61–158; Henderson, *Korea*, pp. 131–136; Bruce Cumings, *The Two Koreas* (New York: Foreign Policy Association, 1984), pp. 26–38.
89 Henderson, "Human Rights," pp. 25–26. USAMGIK had established a South Korean Interim Government on May 17, 1947, but in its short life its Interim Legislative Assembly (KILA) passed only twelve bills, mostly routine.
90 Macdonald, "Human Rights"; Jerome Alan Cohen and Edward J. Baker, "Foreign Policy and Human Rights: The Case of South Korea," in Baker and Shaw, *Human Rights in Korea*.
91 Macdonald, "Human Rights," pp. 111–113.

92 John Henry Merryman, *The Civil Law Tradition*, 2nd ed. (Stanford, Calif.: Stanford University Press, 1986), explains the differences between civil law and common law systems.

93 Hyong-bae Kim, "Labor Law in Korea," in Pyong-ho Pak et al., *Modernization*, p. 65; Ki Yop Lim, "Development of Korean Labor Law and Practice," *Journal of Korean Affairs* (January 1976), p. 25. Korean-Japanese constitutional studies are now institutionalized by a center at Korea University, Seoul, headed by Professor Byung-Sak Koo, president of the Korean Public Law Association (1987).

94 David C. Cole and Princeton N. Lyman, *Korean Development: The Interplay of Politics and Economics* (Cambridge: Harvard University Press, 1977), pp. 59–62; W. D. Reeve, *The Republic of Korea: A Political and Economic Study* (New York: Oxford University Press, 1963).

95 Sugwon Kang, "Thoughts on the 'Korean Style of Democracy,'" *Journal of Korean Affairs* (April 1974), p. 26; Jan-hae Yoo and Larry L. Wade, "A Study of Current Korean Political Culture: An Interpretive Perspective," *Journal of East Asian Affairs* (1981), pp. 118–172; Larry L. Wade, "South Korean Political Culture: An Interpretation of Survey Data," *Journal of Korean Studies* (1980), 2:1.

96 Macdonald, *Korea and the Ballot*, pp. 140–141.

97 For the tone of comment within the United States, see the *Monthly Review of Korean Affairs*, published by the Friends of the Korean People, P.O. Box 3506, Arlington, Virginia 22203; Chong-sik Lee, "Human Rights in South Korean and United States Policy," *Journal of Korean Affairs* (October 1975), p. 26; Baker and Shaw, *Human Rights in Korea*; John Sullivan and Roberta Foss, eds., *Two Koreas: One Future* (Lanham, Md.: University Press of America, 1987).

98 Henderson, "Human Rights," pp. 38–40; Macdonald, *Korea and the Ballot*, pp. 225–228. For texts of Republic of Korea constitutions as amended through 1969, see Sejin Kim and Chang-hyun Cho, *Government and Politics in Korea* (Silver Springs, Md.: Institute of Korean Affairs, 1972), p. 295; *Journal of Korean Affairs* (April 1973), p. 39 (on the Yushin constitution); and *The Korea Times* (Seoul), September 30, 1980, p. 4 (on the Fifth Republic constitution).

99 Kim and Lee, "Influence"; Yu Chin-O, *Memoirs on Drafting the Constitution* (Seoul: Ilchokak, 1980) (in Korean).

100 Kim and Lee, "Influence"; Kim Hyo-jun, "Korean Constitution and American Constitution," *The Dong-A Herald* (Pusan), June 1, 1987.

101 Kim and Lee, "Influence," p. 4.

102 Ibid.

103 Ibid., pp. 10–12; Robert Oliver, *Syngman Rhee and American Involvement in Korea, 1942–1960* (Westport, Conn.: Greenwood Press, 1978).

104 Kim and Lee, "Influence," pp. 13–16.

105 Ibid., p. 14. The Kennedy administration and interested private parties called for a return to civilian rule, but with what actual influence on events is not clear.

106 As translated in ibid., p. 16.

107 Ibid., pp. 17–23; Supreme Court, October 23, 1969, Case No. 66–Do–1337 (1969).

108 Supreme Court, June 22, 1971, Case No. 70–Da–1010 (1971).

109 Seoul High Court, March 11, 1970, Case No. 69–Na–1631 (1970).

110 As translated in Kim and Lee, "Influence," p. 19; the revision was passed by the National Assembly in July 1970.

111 Ibid., pp. 25–30; "Interview: Kim Dae Jung—Democracy and Dissidence in South Korea," *Journal of International Affairs* (Winter 1985), p. 181.

112 Author's communications with Korean legal professionals in Korea and Japan, May–July 1987; *Japan Times* and *Asian Wall Street Journal*, May–July 1987.

The 1987 Constitution that was ratified by referendum on October 25, 1987, provided for expanded rights and direct election of the president for no more than one five-year term. Elected over a divided opposition by a 36.6% plurality on December 16, 1987, Roh Tae-Woo took office on February 25, 1988. Thus, Chun Doo-Hwan became the first incumbent Korean leader to pass on the presidency under law to an elected successor. On April 26, 1988, the opposition parties won a majority of the seats in the National Assembly for the first time.

113 On entrapment and abandonment, see James W. Morley, "Presidential Address: Japan and America—The Dynamics of Partnership," *Journal of Asian Studies* (November 1985), p. 19.

■ First published in W. Shaw (ed.), *Human Rights in Korea: Historical and Policy Perspectives*, Cambridge, Harvard University Press, 1995, pp. 265-282, 333-335.

4

Comparative Perspectives on Human Rights in Korea

⌘

I would like to go beyond comment on the modern Korean human-rights experience and to locate that East Asian case within a broader historical, comparative, and theoretical framework. However interesting and significant a nation's story may be in its own right, it is no longer an intellectually adequate approach to fix attention solely on the human-rights behavior of a given country with myopic disregard for its comparative context and theoretical implications. This is particularly so with *human* rights, which attach not to people of a particular category or nation but universally to each person.

PARADOX AND TRAGEDY

The modern history of law and politics of human rights in Korea is replete with paradox and tragedy. Unified in A.D. 668, Korea was one of the world's most ancient and homogeneous territorial states until divided in 1945. In premodern times, the Kingdom of Korea enjoyed considerable autonomy in its internal affairs, while on occasion deferring to China in its external relations, as its model Confucian tributary state. While dynasties and foreign masters came and went in China (Mongols, Manchus, Europeans, and Americans), Korea's Chosŏn dynasty continued from 1392 until replaced by Japan early in the twentieth century. Particularly from the 1870s, Western nations and Japan brought notions of individual rights along with colonialist intrusion into Korean political and economic life. As in later times, competing Korean political interests seemed to cluster around different foreign powers (for example, China, Japan, Russia, the United States), and rival foreign and indigenous ideas contended for domestic ascendancy as the foundation for the Korean modern state.

A few of the paradoxical ironies for human rights in modern Korea are:

1. That in the decades from the late 1800s, as human rights ideas began entry into Korean society, Koreans came under ever more systematic governmental and foreign controls.

2 That the first sustained efforts at modern legal development took place as part of Japan's effort ultimately to absorb Korea into its own political culture.
3 That relatively straightforward human rights movements like the Equalization Society of the 1920s could not be easily accommodated by nationalists pre-occupied with rival visions for achieving independence.
4 That concerns for human rights and democracy, which were part of the political thought behind the March First Movement (1919) and other pre-Liberation politics, gave way to division, poverty, war, and repression after Liberation in 1945.
5 That long and savage civil conflicts between 1945 and 1953 only hardened the north-south division and heightened tensions so much in the south as to weaken inclinations to honor democratic rights and liberties.
6 That no constitution in independent South Korea has outlasted the ruler who presided at its inception.
7 That widespread support for democratic law and politics among the Korean people has co-existed with torture and repression by successive governments and with uncompromising rigidity on the part of some elements in the opposition.

Culture as well as history affects human rights today. The idea of "human rights" inhering in each person as a human was not part of pre-modern Korean legal culture; but one had duties according to one's place in the sociopolitical hierarchy, and within that context one's sense of duty might well carry with it, even in relations with superiors, a modest expectation that the other recognized a duty to reciprocate, if not in equal kind, at least with humane condescension. Thus, within the Confucian hierarchy of carefully differentiated stations in society, there existed to some degree a "reciprocal-duty consciousness" which in effect, and perhaps in perspective, functioned as a type of qualified individual-rights consciousness.[1] Irresponsibility was not an accepted principle of government or social rule, however often manifested by some elites. However, the notion of human rights established under government policy and formal law, with protective institutions, as developed in parts of the West, was new and alien when Korea was forced to open its ports for intercourse with Japan and the West. Now, more than a century later, human rights ideas may well be more powerfully integrated into the popular political consciousness than competing Confucian conceptions. As in all world regions, popular preference for human rights does not imply consistent governmental or societal support for a given right in a concrete context. Americans, for example, support free speech in principle, but not for those whose views differ too much from their own.[2]

THE HUMAN-RIGHTS REVOLUTION

Although universalist ideas of individual rights were institutionalized in such eighteenth-century national documents as the American Declaration of Independence and the French Declaration of the Rights of Man and Citizens, the history of human rights law under international standards is brief.[3] The worldwide diffusion of the human rights revolution may well be the most important development in twentieth-century law and politics. Human rights ideas were molded slowly in a cultural matrix of Western law, religion, government, and economics.[4] Human rights became an element in the indigenous government and law of most non-Western countries only with the demise of colonialism and independence after 1945.[5] International and comparative human rights studies are primarily a post-World War II phenomenon and did not burgeon as a coherent academic field until the 1970s.[6]

In the early 1860s, as slavery was abolished during the American Civil War, multilateral human rights treaty law began with the first Geneva Convention (1864) regarding victims of armed conflict as a result of the Swiss Red Cross movement. By 1949, this reaction against the horrors of war had evolved into four treaties dealing with prisoners of war, wounded and sick combatants, civilians, and civil wars.[7] Between the end of World War I and 1939, treaty law was developed to cover the rights of minorities, workers (by the efforts of the International Labor Organization), and individuals in League of Nations Mandated Territories. In 1926, the long campaign of non-governmental organizations in the Anti-Slavery League issued a treaty outlawing slavery at last.[8] Although Japan represented the non-Western, non-Caucasian world in some international contexts, such as development of the Kellogg-Briand Treaty of Paris (1928) against war, Korea continued in political slavery to Japan.

As turmoil followed liberation in Korea after 1945, collective revulsion at Nazi atrocities—with somewhat peripheral attention to the less-publicized Japanese atrocities in East and Southeast Asia—brought human rights to the center of the world stage for the first time.[9] The current human rights movement and international law may be dated from acceptance by nations of Article 55 of the United Nations Charter (1945), which reads in part:

> (B)ased on respect for the principle of equal rights and self-determination of peoples, the United Nations shall promote:
> a higher standards of living, full employment, and conditions of economic and social progress and development;
> b solutions of international economic, social, health, and related problems; and international cultural and educational cooperation; and
> c universal respect for, and observance of, human rights and fundamental freedoms for all without distinction as to race, sex, language, or religion.[10]

This complex norm of treaty law has served as the basis for later refinements and clarifications of the meaning of human rights, in the 30 articles of the Universal Declaration of Human Rights approved without dissent by the U.N. General Assembly on 10 December 1948,[11] and in agreements more precisely defining various human rights such as the 1966 United Nations International Covenant on Economic, Social, and Cultural Rights and International Covenant on Civil and Political Rights, which came into force for ratifying nations in 1976.[12]

The Declaration, these two covenants, and the 1966 Optional Protocol to the International Covenant on Civil and Political Rights, which provides for implementation machinery, are referred to as The International Bill of Human Rights.[13] Numerous other human rights instruments have appeared over the years, such as the international Convention on the Elimination of All Forms of Discrimination against Women (1979)[14] and the Convention against Torture and Other Cruel, Inhuman, or Degrading Treatment (1984).[15] In addition, regional efforts continue to develop under the European Convention on Human Rights (1950), the European Social Charter (1961), the Inter-American Convention on Human Rights (1969; in force since 1978), as well as in Arab League, African, and Asian organizations.[16] Since 1979, the most important regional body in Asia has been the Human Rights Committee of the nongovernmental Law Association for Asia and the Pacific (LAWASIA). Among its accomplishments have been the formulation of human rights principles for Asia, encouragement of the development of sub-regional human rights commissions, and publication of Asia-wide reports in its *Human Rights Bulletin* and newsletter.[17]

As of 1 January 1985, about 84 countries had become parties to the two major United Nations Covenants, which some had not yet ratified; 34 had signed the Optional Protocol on Civil and Political Rights, which a minority had ratified.[18] The Democratic People's Republic of Korea has acceded to both covenants, but not to any other of the 22 major human rights agreements; the more democratic Republic of Korea has ratified conventions against racial discrimination, genocide, and prostitution, and for the rights of stateless persons and the political rights of women, but not the covenants.[19]

THE STUDY OF LAW AND HUMAN RIGHTS IN FOREIGN COUNTRIES

The field of human rights studies, which pursues knowledge and understanding based on impartial scholarly investigation and analysis, labors under a peculiarly heavy burden of complexity, because of the nature of its subject matter, and because of encroachments by human rights advocates and opponents, governmental and private, domestic and foreign, on dispassionate academic inquiry. While their resources, levels of commitment, priorities, and degrees of effectiveness are wildly diverse, in the late twentieth century governments and national and international organizations almost universally espouse human rights. The United Nations and certain regional bodies take a broad view of such rights, while Amnesty International, for example, focuses on the plight of non-violent "prisoners of conscience." President Jimmy Carter injected a new concern for human rights into American foreign policy in the 1970s, and the Helsinki Accords have advanced pan-European dialogue on related issues. Few who care would have much time or patience with scholars so ungracious and wrongheaded as to ask: Why bother? How can one intellectually justify attribution of such importance to each person as is assumed by human rights advocates? A fundamental issue to a human-rights theorist, but a suspect distraction to the mass media, the policymaker, and the activist.

As citizens, human rights scholars are generally proponents of humane treatment of their fellows; but as scholars, their interests may focus on law, social science, history, or theory. Human rights studies are also a mixture of national, international, and comparative scholarship. One branch of human rights studies looks at the status of rights within a country, as of civil rights or free speech within the United States. Another cluster of scholars is preoccupied with international law and foreign policy affecting human rights, usually with an eye on the international bill of human rights. And a third group looks at the law and sociopolitics affecting one or more human rights in other countries for the purpose of comparative understanding of different national systems and problems. (Precise knowledge of the internal context of a country's human rights problems is often hard to come by, but is often a necessary precondition for reliable comment on issues.) Perhaps to a degree unsurpassed by human-rights studies of any other country, such studies of Korea combine all three distinctive dimensions of scholarship, and also carry with them an unusual sense of immediacy and public urgency in the United States and South Korea.

More broadly speaking, human rights scholars now need to integrate the implications of Asian, African, and other non-Western experience at the very time when those peoples are themselves in the process of selectively blending perennial national understandings of justice with universal human rights conceptions, Westernized legal institutions, and competing ideologies, and when all nations are grappling with the human rights implications of revolutions in science, technology, and communications. In fact, it is time that we cast aside the use of terms like "East and West" or "North and South" in favor of a more omni-directional perspective on issues. In one problem area or another, human rights ideals conflict with the politics of value and power in all legal cultures. (The United States, for example, deals reluctantly with problems in the treatment of Blacks and in the assurance of civilized subsistence to the less fortunate.)[20] More precise knowledge of a system on its own terms, as provided in this book, does not justify or excuse abuses, or give boasting privileges to some countries in relation to others; rather, by clarifying the locus of specific problems in law, society, and politics, studies can mitigate foreign misinterpretation of events and guide the use of limited resources to combat the most severe human-rights violations.

To gain accurate perspective on a foreign human rights issue, one needs to take into account at least five problems of contemporary American legal studies:[21]

1 Legal abstractionism, a tendency to restrict attention to formal legal rules or judicial reasoning on a human rights issue
2 Legal chauvinism, an inclination to exaggerate the relevance of American law and democratic institutions as a model for other legal cultures
3 Cultural insularism, treating the norms of the country studied as so unique and self-enclosed that general human rights principles and the experience of other legal systems are simply disregarded
4 Evolutionary thinking about human rights law, assuming that systems do not simply change over time, but also "develop" along certain lines (for example, American; ideological) and become "better"[22]
5 The difficulty of even bicultural communication about law and human rights in a world that requires multi-cultural discourse in terms of universal standards.

Although inroads have been made by some Asianists, other area specialists, and some law-social science scholars, a mind-set that is rigidly Western (even American) dominates discourse on national, international, and comparative human rights concerns in our legal, intellectual, and political communities.

To facilitate multi-cultural communication, human rights studies of a country might well include:

1 The author's theoretical presuppositions, with which the foreign reader cannot be assumed to agree. Too often an author's principles go unstated, on the assumption they are too obvious and acceptable to all to warrant mention.

Starting points matter much to the reader who wishes to discern whether he disagrees with the author on practical judgmental grounds or in basic principle.

2 The modern legal history of the issue in the country.
3 Patterns and rules of indigenous social thought, structure, value, and behavior which affect the context of the issue.
4 Officialdom as it bears on the human right studied (for example, police and judges; an administrative agency overseeing an area of concern, such as worker rights or health care).
5 The nature of the legal system (for example, civil law, common law, Islamic law, socialist law) and relevant provisions in the country's constitution, statutes, and administrative rules.
6 Where the courts are reasonably independent and have jurisdiction over human-rights questions, the facts and reasoning of relevant judicial decisions.
7 Indigenous views of the issue (for example, legal scholars, the mass media, victims, churches, local rights organizations).
8 Law and social-science findings with respect to the issue as it exists in other countries.

As Korea's future unfolds, scholars of whatever nationality need a richly interdisciplinary approach to human rights studies in order to convey reality in a precise, fair, and balanced way to the non-specialist, multi-cultural audience. Although not explicitly designed to illustrate a model, the present volume links human rights with policy, culture, and political history in a manner helpful to those who visit Korea. Few analyses of human rights in Asia provide such breadth of context.

Constitutions and Rights in Asia

Brief consideration of constitutional developments in other Asian countries and in the world will add perspective on Korea. Only about 20 of the 167 single-document constitutions in the world today date back as far as the 1940s or earlier.[23] The idea of such national legal documents, now the valued property of humankind, derives from the United States Constitution, which alone dates from the eighteenth century; very few countries (for example, Norway, 1814) have constitutions dating from the nineteenth century. More thought-provoking yet, over 100 constitutions in force today, such as those of North Korea (1972) and South Korea (1987), were established in 1970 or later. Only New Zealand, Israel, the United Kingdom, and 3 Islamic states employing the Koran as a constitutional document (Saudi Arabia, Oman, Libya) lack a formal modern constitutional document; and in some of these there is talk of a constitution or a bill of rights analogous to the 1982 Canadian Charter of Human Rights.

In Asia, only the following constitutions date from the 1940s: Japan (1947); Taiwan (Republic of China, 1947, but the territory was under martial law until 15 July 1987); Indonesia (1945, but two other constitutions were used between independence in 1949 and 1959, and a major upheaval occurred in 1965); and India (which has been amended 59 times since 1949).[24] Other Asian constitutions, with their adoption dates, include: Afghanistan (1980), Bangladesh (1972), Brunei (1984), Myanmar (Burma) (1974), China (1982), Cambodia (Kampuchea) (1989), Laos (1975), Malaysia (1963), Nepal (1962), Pakistan (1973), Papua-New Guinea

(1975), the Philippines (1987), Singapore (1963), Sri Lanka (1978), Thailand (1978), and Vietnam (1980).

The post-World War II era has seen an unprecedented burst of constitutional creativity and experimentation on all continents. Many documents have been short-lived, and the gap between provisions and human rights practices is wide in some states; but most nations continue to associate modernity, political stability, and legal predictability with maintenance of the same fundamental law over as long a period as possible. Constitutions are usually meant to be "permanent" rather than interim legal statements about a country's principles and government. When they work reasonably well over a considerable time, constitutions tend to take on an almost sacred communal symbolism which itself further reinforces stability. Within a few decades, most countries that became independent between 1945 and 1965 may achieve documentary stability. In some, this will reflect a firmer sense of corporate identity, as well as cultural preferences as to constitutional form and substance; but all are likely to include detailed human rights provisions echoing United Nations principles.

With national stability, the concerns of leaders about their own legitimacy, about leadership succession, and about internal security and order may diminish in intensity and become less frequently the cause of or excuse for human rights violations. Such current preoccupations may be especially strong in those countries capriciously carved out in Asia and Africa by colonialists, with boundaries unnaturally combining antagonistic peoples or dividing large ethnic groups between two territorial states or both. In this respect, Korea is a tragic oddity, because its peninsular territory has not been ambiguous or changing over the past 1,200 years and because there is no natural basis for division in colonial history or differences between north and south in language, ethnic group, or religion. Arguably, no other separation in the world has been so complete yet unnatural as that on the Korean peninsula.

More confident rulers and a stronger sense of constitutional identity in the recently defined states may also reduce, rather than increase, tolerance for unorthodoxy and may thus bring more unabashed violations of the human rights of minorities, the press, women, or workers.[25] It is unclear where some Asian states will lie on the spectrum between systematic authoritarianism and exploitation on the one hand and a deep regard for certain human rights under law on the other, once stability and a measure of prosperity are achieved. Alternative Asian perspectives may help intellectuals refine Western justifications for human rights; but some Asian nations seem to have farther to go in integrating human rights law into the elite consensus than South Korea.

Consider, for example, the overwhelming complexity of Indonesia next to the relative simplicity of Korea. The Constitution and the official Pancasila (Five Principles) of Indonesia legitimize human rights in providing the documentary basis for governing 180 million people on over 13,660 islands spread over 4,000 miles of ocean with hundreds of distinct ethno-linguistic groups and fewer than 1,000 lawyers. Indonesia, like India, Malaysia, Bangladesh, and Pakistan, must balance, and eventually integrate, human rights law with modern reformulations of Islamic politico-legal thought as Islam emerges again as a coherent world force in the twenty-first century, and as deep cleavages within the Muslim community continue.[26] Thailand may be taken to symbolize the difficulty in some Asian countries besides South Korea—for example, the Philippines, Indonesia, Burma, Pakistan, and China—of integrating the military into a constitutional system sensitive to human rights; but the cosmo-magic kingship system and Buddhism of Thai constitutionalism again make Thailand's problem more delicate than Korea's need to integrate unofficial Confucianism into a democratic state. The Philippines, mixing American and post-colonial legalisms with Catholicism in a sophisticated understanding of constitutional democracy and human rights, is plagued with fractious politics rooted in regional and long-standing socioeconomic divisions which make Korea's divisions in the south seem simple and historically shallow by comparison. But Korea shares with the Philippines and with many East Asian and Southeast Asian countries a version of patron-client, quasi-paternal-filial, and familistic social structure which frames power relations and affects human rights performance importantly, often negatively.[27] Concrete loyalties have more bite than human rights abstractions or laws in many situations.

The current age of constitutional fluidity may end within a few decades. It is not clear in 1990 where Korea will stand as the wheels of time turn, whether constitutional stability will be attained, and, if so, whether freedom, personal security, and socioeconomic justice will coexist with governmental firmness, whether Confucianism will yield to the democratic elements in modern tradition, whether the military will withdraw from government and politics, and whether familistic loyalties will accommodate to human rights law.

TRANSCULTURAL HUMAN RIGHTS THEORY

The constitutional documents of nations have never been so similar to each other as now, and international human rights instruments are gaining increasing acceptance as customary international law (if only because few dare repudiate such unexceptionable statements), but their philosophical, ideological, or religious leanings and historical experiences often differ radically in some respects.[28] Long-dominant Western formulations of rights are undergoing transformation as non-Western experience impinges on dialogue in the West. This will surely continue as non-Western formulations of human rights and legal thought grow in influence in the next century. A stronger sense of integration will likely come with the maturation of Islamic human rights theory, and a stronger sense of community will infuse democratic legalism generally with digestion of the encounter between the West and other directions. John Locke, John Stuart Mill, and American liberals of both conservative and progressive inclination seem destined to recede in importance, as have the excessively dated and parochial views of Karl Marx and his heirs. It will likely puzzle future American students of human rights law how legal positivism could have so long dominated legal education in disregard of any rational justification for human rights. Out of Asia and other regions may come the strongest insistence upon what may be the crucial alteration of theoretical understanding of individual human rights: the replacement of an individualist notion of human rights with what I call a "mutualist" conception in a "transcultural" theory.

By "transcultural" I mean applicable to, relevant in any cultural context, intersubjectively and cross-culturally persuasive. An American conception of individualism, for example, is not transculturally valid; nor is it philosophically convincing, because it tends to reduce the individual to "a naked chooser" without context or natural relatedness to others, and because its attendant conceptions of law and society are peculiar to one nation, or at most to some in some Western countries, and to few elsewhere. Human rights pertain to individuals as "persons-in-community," not as "individuals-in-nature."[29] The term *individualism* has been a major barrier to cross-cultural communication about human rights between Asia and the United States.[30] American individualism is a myth; like Koreans and other Asians, Americans are, in general, social conformists. Moreover, cooperation, compromise, a "team spirit," and Judeo-Christian respect for each person are as essential as competitive politics to the protection of human rights in the U.S. constitutional system. Inaccurately, American rhetoric often presents "individualism" as essential to the possession of individuality, individual dignity, and/or individual rights.

What is essential to any human rights theory is that it be compatible with philosophical attribution of great, intrinsic, and equal value and dignity to each person as a human without qualifications based on differences of religion, race, sex, wealth, caste, ethnic group, or any other basis for distinction. Philosophically rigorous relativism is incompatible with any persuasive human rights theory. The human rights ideal seems best expressed by "mutualism" and democratic constitutionalism. *Mutualism*, unlike words such as *individualism* and *collectivism*, is unencumbered by cultural chauvinism and complex historical argumentation; it implies government and rights based on mutual respect for equal individual dignity. The term well expresses the inherently interdependent and relational nature of individual freedoms, rights, and responsibilities among citizens and between citizens and government.[31]

Among the practical consequences of mutualist respect for each person is a democratically constitutionalist system which institutionalizes the following or analogous features:

1 Constitutional division of governmental power among two or more organs.
2 Regularized limits on the amount of governmental power possessed by anyone and on the length of time power is legitimately possessed. In large systems, elections and other legal procedures are used to bring peaceful, routine passage from one national leader or group of leaders to the next.
3 Sufficient governmental authority and means of coercion under law and constitution to maintain public peace and national security within parameters defined by human rights.
4 Governmental involvement in socioeconomic problem-solving to meet citizens' subsistence needs and a life compatible with human dignity when the private sector fails to provide this minimum.
5 Legally protected freedoms of peaceful expression and silence regarding personal and group belief and opinion.
6 Procedural rights in criminal and civil justice for each citizen equal to the rights of all others within the national community.
7 Acceptance of the constitution and human rights as the supreme law of the land, by the government and by the general public.

HUMAN RIGHTS IN SOUTH KOREA

The other contributors to this volume illuminate the sociohistorical context. They convey a dramatic sense of conflict between traditional Neo-Confucian thought and government and early modern efforts of intellectual politicians to revolutionize Korea toward modern statehood and protection of human rights under law. They also explain with empathy and dismay that this goal had not yet been achieved in the 1980s. How should we assess the Korean human rights situation from a comparative perspective?

South Korea seems to have remained a country under rule by military men or "military occupation" through most of its twentieth-century history. Today, the military leadership of the Republic of Korea continues to occupy a position of supra-constitutional power; in choosing its own candidates for national leadership it has shown recurrent disregard for the normal legal accoutrements of constitutional government. In Korea, the supremacy of the military, not the Constitution, has been the dominant pattern, at least since 1961. Yet the legitimacy of this supremacy is widely questioned. Like Park Chung Hee before him, President Chun Doo Hwan resigned from the military to assume the presidency as a civilian, in recognition of the inappropriateness of military rule in Korean constitutional understandings. Roh Tae Woo left the military in 1981, holding a variety of civilian posts in and out of the government before receiving his party's nomination and being elected to the presidency.

Basic living standards among the generality of Koreans have improved markedly in the past twenty years, but the rights of unions and workers have been circumscribed. Studies in this volume and elsewhere[32] indicate relatively strong public support for constitutional rights, and students and other dissenters have proved to be perennially irrepressible. In fact, the degree to which international human rights ideas have been indigenized in South Korean society, even without the aid of consistent official encouragement, may be unusual among non-Western countries. Contrary to the distinctively American fixation on absolutist wording (as in the First Amendment) as significant to legal protection of rights, defective performance is not traceable at all to constitutional phraseology allowing limitation of rights under law; that phraseology seems unimportant, viewed in comparative perspective. All democracies limit under law all but a few freedoms of the spirit in all traditions of legal draftsmanship.[33]

In Korea, the problem since liberation is that a way has not yet been found in Korean law and politics to divide and restrain governmental power sufficiently to guarantee individual rights. Law itself may not yet have the autonomy necessary for legal protection of rights. Perhaps the judiciary and the National Assembly are not yet institutionalized in relation to the presidency, and administrators and police are not yet democratically professionalized in such a way as to control under law violations of human rights.

But more than the above, the pivotal issue for human rights and for Korean constitutionalism in general may be the succession problem. Transitions are needed on three levels: (1) orderly passage under law and constitution from one president and leadership group to another; (2) peaceful transition from military supremacy to civilian sovereignty and the supremacy of the constitution; and (3) a generational change from current leaders who came to maturity in the 1940s and 1950s out of conditions of colonial oppression, war, indigenous authoritarianism (sometimes under civilians), and economic want, to the next generation of social and political leaders whose seminal experiences were in the 1960s and 1970s, and who would like liberty along with affluence, and somehow a less taut relationship with North Korea.

The issue of generational succession seems of vital concern throughout East Asia. Most dramatically, the People's Republic of China has been in transition since about 1975 from the era of Mao Zedong, Zhou Enlai, and others in a remarkable group of political leaders tracing their lineage back beyond the Long March of the mid-1930s. Twice purged before he assumed the mantle of leadership, Deng Xiaoping is of that earlier generation. His picked people now head the government (Li Peng) and the Chinese Communist party (Jiang Zemin).[34] Until Deng has passed and a new group of leaders has been confirmed in authority by a time of stability, China's succession process will not have ended. Almost concurrently with the generational succession, China is engaged in one of history's more comprehensive law-making efforts, both filling out the broad framework of a modern legal system and adding in the details with civil, criminal, commercial, and administrative laws and rules to replace the pattern of neglect and alegalism of the latter Mao years (1966–1976). How stable the leadership-succession system will prove to be under the living constitution combining the government Constitution of 1982 with party rules and practices remains to be seen. The Tiananmen Massacre of June 1989 only heightened uncertainty further.

On Taiwan, the generation of leaders who came with Chiang Kaishek from the mainland in the late 1940s is rapidly passing from the scene; the symbolic end of that regime was signaled when Chiang Ching-kuo, his son, passed away in 1988, and indigenous Taiwanese assumed greater authority in relation to mainlanders within the increasingly democratic political culture.

Whether durable North Korean leadership will pass simply from father to son, from Kim Il Sung to Kim Jong Il, is unclear, more so because there is no precedent since its founding in 1948 for leadership transition in the Democratic People's Republic of Korea, either individual or generational.

Since the end of the Pacific War forty years ago, once set on a new democratic course with Allied Occupation support, Japan has experienced at many junctures an independent and peaceful succession of leadership under law and constitution. The generational succession issue in Japan turns, in part, on the question of whether the emerging generation of political leaders will favor change like current "revisionists" who, in spite of overwhelming popular support for the Constitution, are uncomfortable with constitutional pacifism, democracy, and a powerless emperor; or will continue, with deep and quiet passion, adherence to the Constitution as the country's primary sacred writ, and with a revulsion to militarism and authoritarianism passed on to them by family and teachers who directly experienced the unprecedented horror, shameful aggression, and devastating defeat of World War II. As in South Korea, the form and content of constitutionalism in these other East Asian countries may continue as is or come into new or sharper focus by the turn of the century.

In the absence of a pattern over time of peaceful, predictable, rule-based transition from one national leader to the next, the human rights element in South Korea's constitutional order has tended to become lost in a recurrent military politics of force and alegal maneuver to secure the national leadership (as in 1961 and 1980), followed by aggressive manifestations of defensive anxiety about gaining full legitimacy and/or retaining presidential power, with the guidance of technocratic and military supporters. At times, there has been a jolting harshness about governmental violations of rights in Korea: dissenters have not just been arrested and detained, they have also at times been beaten and tortured; journalists and editors of newspapers and magazines have not simply been given coercive guidelines and advice on the political content of publications, they and/or their products have been banned if the level of their cooperation has been deemed inadequate; politicians perceived as possibly viable competitors in electoral politics, such as Kim Dae Jung and Kim Young Sam until 1987, have been subjected to a range of abusive measures to render them politically inoperative; hundreds have been banned from political life; unions have been severely restricted; procedural rights have been violated capriciously; and the freedom of peaceful assembly often denied. Granted that the modes of dissent have at times been quite provocative; political revenge, distaste for tolerance and compromise, and distrust of law as a basis for exercising governmental power may have been among the motivating forces. Authoritarian cowardice and cruelty have sometimes been matched by uncommon courage. But the tone of voice and political style of both government and opposition have often seemed marked more by stark confrontation over power than by practically oriented negotiations to achieve shared constitutional goals.[35]

Yet there have also been periods of political amnesty and relative freedom, as in the period following the assassination of Park Chung Hee in 1979 and 1980, and as in 1985 and 1987. More important perhaps than the strong electoral showing of the opposition in 1985 were the government tolerance of even harsh opposition criticisms of the regime, the absence of noteworthy violence in highly charged political campaigns, and the willingness of the government virtually to ignore widespread technical violations of the election-campaign law. The scale, persistence, and vehemence of the demonstrations and political rhetoric were seen as a sign that the expanded free speech of the February election period had broken a taboo and started the process of widespread popular expression of long-pent-up demands for democracy. Although the road from the 1985 elections to the autumn 1987 constitutional revision—returning to the direct popular election of the president in force in the 1960s—was by no means direct or predictable, the aura of freedom brightened with that campaign.

In comparative terms, it is unusual for a people to focus so explicitly and often on freedom and democracy themselves as the objects of practical concern in their major acts of political expression—most free speech in the world takes for granted the freedom itself and is for or against some type of concrete interest, such as better garbage collection, getting rid of the rascals in city hall, pollution control, or an end to nuclear weapons. Where freedom of expression is not protected under law, governments do not care to hear such demands to the degree found in South Korea, and so such speech is squelched with dispatch. Ambivalence is not a trait of the serious authoritarian. In Korea, the past pattern of inconsistency and unpredictability in government intent about human rights and democracy makes many wonder, with some doubts and suspicions but also with hope: Whither Korea now?

In the years ahead, should the government succeed in its gamble on restoring constitutional democracy and move towards elimination of torture (and ratify the 1984 U.N. convention against torture), political revenge, military dominance, and political intolerance, then the South Korean government might gain some of the human-rights legitimacy which eluded it as of the time President Chun Doo Hwan stepped down from office in 1988. But human rights seem likely to remain in a precarious position until the ruling group and the opposition leaders become accustomed to peaceful transfers of power under the supreme law of the land, until they leave behind harsh confrontation, and move on to mutualist democratic compromise on the road of constitutional politics.

NOTES

1 William Shaw, "Korea Before Rights" in this volume. For analogy in less-Confucian feudal Japan, see Lawrence W. Beer, *Freedom of Expression in Japan: A Study in Comparative Law, Politics and Society* (New York, Kodansha International/Harper & Row, 1985), Chapter 3; hereafter cited as *Freedom.*
2 On problems of liberty where well institutionalized, see Harry Street, *Freedom, the Individual and the Law*, 5th ed. (New York, Viking Penguin, 1982); Beer, *Freedom*; and William Spinrad, *Civil Liberties* (Chicago, Quadrangle Books, 1970).
3 David P. Forsythe, *Human Rights and World Politics* (Lincoln, University of Nebraska Press, 1981), pp. 1–21.
4 On the development of human rights in the West, see Richard P. Claude, ed., *Comparative Human Rights* (Baltimore, Johns Hopkins University Press, 1976), Chapter 1. On the Western need for revivification of its legal tradition by interaction with the non-West, see Harold Berman, *Law and Revolution* (Cambridge, Harvard University Press, 1984).
5 C. G. Weeramantry, *Equality and Freedom: Some Third World Perspectives* (Colombo, Hansa Publishers, 1976).
6 The founding by Richard Pierre Claude of *Universal Human Rights* (now *Human Rights Quarterly*) in 1979 may be taken to mark the growth of the interdisciplinary field of human-rights studies into healthy adolescence.
7 Forsythe, pp. 6–8.
8 Ibid., pp. 6–7; Hurst Hannum, ed., *Guide to International Human Rights Practice* (Philadelphia, University of Pennsylvania Press, 1984), pp. 4–6; generally, Paul Sighart, *The Lawful Rights of Mankind: An Introduction to the International Legal Code of Human Rights* (Oxford, Oxford University Press, 1985), and Albert P. Blaustein, ed., *Human Rights Source Book* (New York, Paragon, 1987).
9 Arnold Brackman, *The Other Nuremberg: The Untold Story of the Tokyo War Crimes Trials* (New York, William Morrow, 1987).
10 Forsythe, p. 8; United Nations, *United Nations Action in the Field of Human Rights* (New York, United Nations, 1980), pp. 5–6; hereafter cited as *UN.*
11 Resolution 217 A(III) of the General Assembly, 10 December 1948; UNIFO (ed.), *International Human Rights Instruments of the United Nations, 1948–1982* (Pleasantville, UNIFO Publishers, 1983), pp. 5–7, hereafter *UNIFO.*
12 Ibid., pp. 86–100; *UN*, pp. 12–14.
13 *UN*, pp. 8–10.
14 United Nations General Assembly Resolution 34/180, 18 December, 1979; entered into force on 3 September, 1981. *UNIFO*, pp. 150–154. This source also includes the record of each nation in ratifying the major human-rights instruments.
15 United Nations General Assembly Resolution 39/46 of 10 December, 1984; *Amnesty International Report 1985*, pp. 10–11, 353–357; Sieghart.
16 Forsythe, pp. 15–18; *UN*, pp. 8–22 especially.
17 For information on the Human Rights Committee, contact LAWASIA, 170 Phillip St., Sydney, NSW 2000, Australia.
18 *UNIFO*, p. 170; *Amnesty International Report 1985*, p. 11.
19 Ibid., pp. 163, 167.
20 J. S. Auerbach, *Unequal Justice: Lawyers and Social Change in Modern America* (New York, Oxford University Press, 1976).
21 Beer, *Freedom*, pp. 21–28.
22 Max Rheinstein, "Legal Systems: Comparative Law and Legal Systems," *International Encyclopedia of Social Sciences* (New York, Macmillan, 1968), IX, 208. He sees the tasks of law as social control,

conflict resolution, adaptation and social change, and norm enforcement. Though hope is essential for the human-rights revolution, whether there are grounds for optimism in a given case is an empirical question not to be facilely answered.

23 The ratification dates of constitutions were provided by Albert P. Blaustein, Rutgers University Law School, Camden, January 1990.

24 On Asian constitutions, see Lawrence W. Beer, *Constitutionalism in Asia: Asian Views of the American Influence* (Berkeley, University of California Press, 1979, and Baltimore, *OPRSCAS*, University of Maryland School of Law, 1989), especially pp. 4–8; hereafter *Constitutionalism*. See also, Lawrence W. Beer, ed., *Constitutional Systems in Late Twentieth-Century Asia*, forthcoming.

25 Lawrence W. Beer, "Freedom of Expression in Japan and Asia: Some Comparative Prespectives," in M. Shimizu, ed., *Nihonkoku Kempo no Riron* (Tokyo, Yuhikaku Publishing Co., 1985), p. 730; Harry M. Scoble & Laurie S. Wiseberg, eds., *Access to Justice: Human Rights Struggles in Southeast Asia* (London, Zed Books, 1985); B. Obinna Okere, "The Protection of Human Rights in Africa and the African Charter on Human and Peoples' Rights: A Comparative Analysis with the European and American Systems," *Human Rights Quarterly* 6.2:141 (May 1984); L. J. Macfarlane, *The Theory and Practice of Human Rights* (London, Maurice Temple Smith, 1985). Macfarlane's book is outstanding for clear conciseness and realistic balance.

26 Majid Khadduri, *The Islamic Conception of Justice* (Baltimore, Johns Hopkins University Press, 1984).

27 Lucian Pye, *Asian Power and Politics* (Cambridge, Harvard University Press, 1985).

28 Richard P. Claude, "The Case of Joelito Filartiga and the Clinic of Hope," *Human Rights Quarterly* 5.3:275 (August 1983).

29 Beer, *Freedom*, pp. 30–37; Macfarlane.

30 Robert Bellah et al., *Habits of the Heart* (Berkeley, University of California Press, 1985).

31 Beer, *Freedom*, pp. 28–37.

32 L. L. Wade, "South Korean Political Culture: An Interpretation of Survey Data," *Journal of Korean Studies* 2:1 (1980).

33 John Henry Merryman, *The Civil Law Tradition* (2nd ed. Stanford, Stanford University Press, 1985).

34 Zhao Ziyang, confirmed as General Secretary of the Chinese Communist Party at the 13th National Party Congress, 1 November 1987, has since been replaced by Jiang Zemin.

35 Among sources are the annual *Amnesty International Report*, U.S. Department of State's *Country Reports on Human Rights Practices*, Raymond Gastil's *Freedom in the World* (Freedom House), and publications of the Human Rights Committee of LAWASIA, and Asiawatch. See Asiawatch, *Human Rights in Korea* (New York, Asiawatch Committee, 1985).

■ First published in Eastern Asia, in A. Anghie & G. Sturgess (eds.), *Legal Visions of the 21st Century: Essays in Honour of Judge Christopher Weeramantry*, The Hague, Kluwer Law International, 1998, pp. 145–165.

5

Human Rights Theory and "Freedom Culture"

⌘

INTRODUCTION

In gazing across the ocean of the twenty-first century trying to discern the contours of freedom of expression around the world, one cannot know whether the iceberg whose tip one sees will melt away or grow to gigantic proportions in future decades. Is the present a golden age for free speech, fated to end in later militarist or technocratic authoritarianism on the Internet? Or is humankind at the threshold of ever-improving protection for each person's right to express peaceably ideas, feelings, beliefs and convictions with impunity in the public and private sectors? How is free speech likely to fare in Eastern Asia, that region of the non-West rising most rapidly towards equality of global influence with the West? "Eastern Asia" here refers to Japan, China, Taiwan, North and South Korea, and the ASEAN—Association for Southeast Asian Nations—countries, Brunei, Malaysia, Philippines, Thailand, Indonesia, Singapore, and Vietnam, with the eventual addition of Cambodia, Laos, and Burma (Myanmar).

One can extrapolate on the current sociolegal status of freedom to adduce possible future patterns of violation and protection of free speech in a nation. One can also try to formulate intersubjectively and transculturally persuasive theory regarding freedom of expression as a human right to guide normative judgments in concrete cases. General principles and cross-cultural perspectives can help one determine accurately and fairly in a world of thousands of diverse cultures whether a given restraint upon expression, in the public sector or in the private sector, is essentially compatible with human rights principles. This essay attempts such theory about human rights and free speech, bearing in mind the Eastern Asian context, and then focusing primarily on Japan to illustrate themes developed.

In Eastern Asia, one finds the cutting edge of many technologies and some of the world's oldest and greatest living civilizations. Dynamic democracies exist alongside communist and anticommunist authoritarian regimes. Democratic Japan, South Korea, Philippines, Taiwan and Thailand coexist with China, North Korea and

Vietnam as well as the somewhat repressive elected governments of Indonesia, Malaysia and Singapore. Well institutionalized freedom of expression and rigorous systematic repression both fit rather easily with the region's varied shades of capitalism and socioeconomic development.

The West's principal contributions to world dialog on constitutional free speech rights seem to have been made. With colonialism and imperialism but also with voluntary study of the law and political ideals of the West, vast numbers of non-Westerners have a reasonably solid grasp of relevant Western intellectual and institutional resources,[1] and Asian Studies in the West and East have made Eastern Asia more accessible in European languages. It is time to ponder how Eastern Asia might enrich the world's comprehension of freedom regarding expression.[2] However powerful and long-lasting in their appeal to some, the political liberalism and economic liberalism of the West, like Confucianism, communism, and cultural relativism, provide many insights but inadequate theoretical foundations for twenty-first century freedom of expression and other human rights. A reformulation melding the Eastern Asian emphasis on the home, family and quasi-familial relations with a transcultural and philosophical recognition of the transcendent inherent value of each person may provide a more solid undergirding for freedom and would accord with the thrust of international human rights law.

Educated elites in most countries know about and accept as relevant for public discourse the human rights specified in the United Nations Universal Declaration of Human Rights (UDHR, 1948), the International Covenant on Economic, Social and Cultural Rights (ICESCR, 1966), the International Covenant on Civil and Political Rights (ICCPR, 1966), and other refinements of human rights provisions addressing such specific problems as racial and gender discrimination, torture, treatment of refugees, and exploitation of children.[3] Different elements of the freedom of expression are set forth in Articles 18–20 of the UDHR and Articles 18–22 of the ICCPR. Article 19 in the former is basic.[4]

> Everyone has the right to freedom of opinion and expression; this right includes freedom to hold opinions without interference and to seek, receive and impart information and ideas through any media and regardless of frontiers.

Nevertheless, cross-cultural dialog on human rights is somewhat primitive, in that some governments champion only those human rights they effectively protect and promote internally, while denying to other rights importance or even the status of human rights, and attacking the policies of nations which emphasize other human rights under a different set of domestic priorities. This great divide in perception is reflected in the UN's need for two basic covenants rather than one, the ICESCR and the ICCPR. Human rights debate among some Asia Pacific countries and some Western nations has been an occasion for obfuscating rather than clarifying shared human values, diverse cultural preferences, and national legal resources. Competitive triumphalism rears its head and is prone to exaggeration, unfairness, and both cultural and official cover-up of serious violations of transcultural values and legal rights. At its worst, such triumphalism arrogates to one's own culture an exceptionally authentic humanity or denies the relevance of any general moral principles to the affairs of state and/or economy. For example, some East Asian officials and commentators (e.g. in Malaysia and Singapore) claim to attribute much more value to family and to survival rights to food, clothing and shelter than some nations in the West, while downplaying freedom of expression and criminal justice rights.

The United States, on the other hand, stresses expression rights while not ratifying as human rights the survival rights in the ICESCR. There is no right to cultural privacy, no legitimate national claim to immunity from scrutiny under international human rights law. However, myriad cultures are less often divided than united in according sacred status to "the family" and "a family spirit" with diverse but relatively few conflicting definitions of family structure and virtues. (Below I employ "home" and "family" as a culture-bridging metaphor for analyzing freedom and tolerance.) Any good government concerns itself with the physical well-being of its citizens, as a rigorous condition for being well thought of at home and abroad. Cultural triumphalism and political obscurantism are inevitable, but exaggerate the effects of diversity on human rights fundamentals.[5]

International covenants, NGOs (non-governmental organizations), national constitutions and laws and statements such as the Johannesburg Principles on National Security, Freedom of Expression, and Access to Information provide practical guidelines for many situations, but they need a foundation in transculturally relevant theories of human rights.[6]

PHILOSOPHICAL AND MOTIVATIONAL FOUNDATIONS OF HUMAN RIGHTS

Freedom of expression is a *human* right; so such freedom should be theoretically analyzed as an integral part of a comprehensive human rights theory, not only as a discrete area of positive constitutional law or sociopolitical theory. The transcendent and equal inherent value of each human is commonly posited as the adequate foundation value in human rights theory and in international human rights documents; the value of a human is much more often presupposed than demonstrated or accounted for. Responsiveness to this value requires that each person's freedom of expression be respected and tolerated.

The term "freedom of expression" is sometimes used narrowly to denote a protected right to express political ideas and opinions; but it is also used in many other contexts, such as: a general freedom of speech, freedom of the press, advertising and other mass media; free access to information; freedom to engage in election campaigning; freedoms of assembly and association; freedoms of religion and thought; freedom of artistic expression; academic freedom; and the freedom of employees to organize, bargain collectively and engage in strikes and other group activities. Myriad related legal, political and cultural issues arise, but at root freedom of expression means a *freedom of choice regarding expression.*

"Freedom regarding expression" seems a better term for human rights theory than freedom of expression, because the right to be silent rather than to express oneself is a major issue when a state or community compels a person to lie about his/her agreement with an orthodoxy or policy or leader. Private and informal regulation, suppression, and promotion of freedom are as important to freedom regarding expression as actions of government under formal law. Both government and community contribute to problems for freedom and to their solution. The state's duty to encourage expression of grievances and to systematically promote free speech in the public and private sectors is too rarely stressed. Revelation of leaders' criminal activity or gross inefficiencies and inequities at one's workplace more commonly leads to retaliation than to reward. This is sometimes the case where "whistleblowing" is nominally encouraged within the bowels of corporations and other institutions and where government protective mechanisms exist.[7]

To accommodate free choice regarding expression and silence, cultural variation, and public and private influences on expression and silence, an ecological, interdisciplinary approach to study is preferable to a focus on freedom in formal law and judicial decisions.[8] The object of study thus becomes a community's or a nation's "*freedom culture*," that is, the concrete status of freedom regarding expression in the ecological interplay of history, constitution, laws, public values, and government as well as social structures, processes and customs.

In human rights theory, gender, ethnicity, social role, race, age, wealth, health and other bases for distinguishing among humans have no effect whatever on a person's intrinsic dignity. However, if respect is not shown for each human as he/she lives within a concrete cultural and socioeconomic context, talk of human rights will seem to many in various cultural zones of the world to be vacuous, unintelligible, foreign, even repugnant and wrong. *Respect* is the empirical test: is the claim that a given behavior (expressive or silent) or normative judgment is respectful of, compatible with human rights principles intersubjectively persuasive to indigenous, authoritative human rights advocates? Culture is one factor defining the meaning of behavior. At the micro level, a slap on the back may be an expression of respectful friendliness or a deadly insult, depending on one's culture. Aggressive verbosity may be a condition for success in one culture and a sure road to failure in another. Such diversity in cultural symbolism does not argue for relativism, but for the crucial need to attend to specific cultural context when assessing freedom regarding expression.

Analogously, at the macro level, constitutional cultures seem to stress different values as primary while subscribing to the same or very similar basic principles. For example, Donald Kommers suggests that human dignity is primary in Germany, fraternity in Canada.[9] Liberty and "the sale" seem most sacred in the United States, consensus and socioeconomic equality in Japan, and in Australia perhaps the "fair go" (fairness to all affected). Under China's different principles of government, stability seems the crucial value; but China officially accepts the indivisibility of human rights.[10]

The ecology of free speech also varies with national legal traditions. The very meaning of "law" and "constitution" differs not only among the civil law tradition, the common law tradition, the Islamic law tradition, and the Confucian legal tradition, but also among countries within each tradition. Moreover, in Eastern Asia, these great legal traditions are mixed together. Japan, for example, is affected by all but Islamic law. Despite the above diversities, courts of one country can produce abstract phrases which are then usefully reworked in other judicial cultures; examples are the U.S. standards "clear and present danger" and "less restrictive alternative" commonly used in Japan's constitutional discourse.[11]

While allowing for great diversity among freedom cultures, a theory of freedom regarding expression needs to be grounded in a philosophical justification of the full range of political, economic and cultural human rights, a law and governance theory of "human rights constitutionalism".[12] As posited earlier, the adequate foundation for human rights law is attribution of transcendent public value to each person as a person, from womb to death.[13] Such an attribution is also necessary to *motivate* individuals, groups, communities and governments to honor freedom regarding expression. If one has no intersubjectivily persuasive reason for such an attribution, one has no basis for insisting human rights be respected, however emotively satisfying it may be for some to care about others of our species. The physical and social sciences and philosophy can clarify and refine questions, categories and data, but seem unable to gain wide acceptance for any analysis convincingly and/or inspiringly explaining *why* human rights should be honored.

Recognition of transcendent value in each human first renders reasonable the project of working persistently for enforcement of human rights law on a global basis. However, only a few universalist religions seem to provide coherent, principled explanations of that value and sources of motivation sufficiently powerful for the task. Throughout history and today, religion has been used both as the reason for impressively humane behavior and as an excuse for barbaric violations of human rights. Adherents of the same faith vary in the compatibility of their views with human rights;[14] but at the end of the twentieth century it is much more characteristic of the great religions to condemn and combat rather than to condone or to encourage inhumane behavior. A religion peculiar to one national culture may have within it imperatives which encourage respect and concern for humans as humans. However, much more than national religions (e.g. *Shinto* in Japan) or secular theories,[15] the few major universalist religions have the wherewithal to motivate adherents to honor human rights and rise above nationalist and ethnic limitations. Secular humanist and Marxist critiques of religion have pointed to historic weaknesses effectively, but too often they have been accompanied by *a priori* hostility and seriously inadequate knowledge of the objects of criticism; some such, perhaps most such, have failed to take sufficient note of the potential of religions for the cause of global human rights. In the next century, the academic secular bias against religion may well diminish, as the sobering inadequacy of modern intellectuality to convince or motivate for human rights stands out in ever sharper relief.

In particular, Christianity, Buddhism and Islam[16] may well provide increasingly in many countries the main rationale for unselfishly insisting on or passively assenting to public policy and law according greater respect for each human. Mutual understanding among the major world religions will continue as in recent decades to significantly improve. If these religions serve the cause of human rights and free speech, the continuing epidemics of barbaric ethnicism and torture will be less tolerated than now.[17]

This is not to suggest that unconscionable manipulation of religion in the cause of hatred will cease altogether. Rather, leaders of the great religions seem likely in the next century to integrate human rights more explicitly and more effectively into the core of moral demands made on their faithful than in the past, and this would further increase the importance of religious motivation in the advancement of the human rights movement.

Christianity is an example of a religion with the doctrinal resources to buttress secular systems of human rights protection. The logic is simple: It provides an unequivocal and uncompromising basis for honoring human rights. God is seen as *commanding* love of every individual without exception, and as radically intolerant towards a contrary or qualifying opinion. God, as accepted by most Christians, created and thus finds a value in each person which justifies Christian love, the corollaries of forgiveness and kindness, and, in general, the unselfish, ethically sensitive behavior required for protection of human rights. God is seen as "Father," the Spirit who created and maintains in being the universe with unfathomable power, absolute intelligence, and a mysteriously unlimited and gratuitous love for humans. Humans are even seen as "children of God" with heavy fraternal and filial duties to God and each other. In the view of many Christians, reason unaided by divine revelation provides no adequate reason to care much about human rights and surely no sufficient motivation to act on their behalf.

In fact, consistent individual effort on behalf of human rights is generally an unattractive, demanding life path and is often grounded in a religious faith (as in the Catholicism of Judge C.G. Weeramantry). On the other hand, putting aside philosophy and motivation for the moment, only secular institutions like the United Nations and national and international human rights law can supply the adequate *enforcement mechanisms* for freedom regarding expression. Belief in God in the Judeo-Christian-Islamic tradition and Buddhist and other religious humanisms influences billions worldwide; they may come to agree on many human rights issues, but achievement of consensus on one world religion is impossible for the species, so secular laws and institutions are needed to implement the human rights imperatives of the religions themselves, using transcultural and ecumenical formulations and methods. Human rights constitutionalism provides a kind of "secular religious" framework for human rights protection in the next century: it requires authoritative national and international agreement on credible institutions and justice processes and on tolerance, commonly motivated by religious conviction.

Freedom and Tolerance in Community

Freedom regarding expression assumes and depends on the existence of tolerance of diversity and dissent; tolerance rests in turn on recognition of the equal inherent value of each person; and that value justifies respect of all for all, and for the humane values of divergent communities. Tolerance is grounded in respect for the person as such, not in respect for the beauty or truth-value of the opinions, belief or convictions of other individuals or communities, which may have much or little transcultural, intersubjectively persuasive value. The distinction between respect for every person and respect for their views is crucial to justification of tolerance and to a reasonable middle ground between liberal relativism and objectivism.

Tolerance is most challenged in peacetime by open consideration of the foundation values of one's own community and of radically different cultures, their presuppositions. It seems harder than commonly assumed for communities and even for independent-minded intellectuals to look at, let alone tolerate or, better yet, *welcome* the peaceful presence of basic ideas thought to undermine the legitimacy to the *status quo* or to challenge a sociopolitically powerful consensus. Tolerance and freedom regarding expression as a human right invite diversity on profundities, not just policy differences. The custodians of democratic regimes find it difficult to ensure the openness they trumpet.

In the omnicultural twenty-first century a new framework for thinking about freedom and other human rights seems called for. One possibility is to speak less of the brittle difference between "individualism" and "collectivism" and more of "*mutualism*," a transculturally neutral term which expresses well the ideal of tolerance and freedom in a constitutional culture which honors human rights.[18] The rights of an individual exist only along with those of other individuals within concrete relationships, not in a detached monad. Participants in the relationship are in equal need of awareness of their own prerogatives and those of people affected by expression. Rights consciousness is thus balanced with awareness of a duty to reciprocate by honoring the other's rights. One's own expression and exercise of choice are humanized by the self-restraint needed to assure the other's equal enjoyment of rights. Respectful, responsive mutualism is at the core of a healthy community system of freedom regarding expression.

A FREE HOME FOR IDEAS, NOT A MARKETPLACE

Communications technology has dropped the universal relatedness of humans out of the sky of ideals onto the laptop computers on earth. The people to whose human rights one may feel obliged to treat responsively may live anywhere, not just in one's own town, city or nation. A mutualist understanding of freedom of expression and tolerance supports freedom more powerfully in this context than individualist notions in "a free marketplace of ideas," especially perhaps in Eastern Asia and the non-West generally.

The metaphor of "a free marketplace of ideas," so influential in the United States, poorly expresses the realities and ideals of freedom regarding expression. The existence of an idea in "a marketplace" is not a reason to tolerate it and is not an indicator of its value; that the idea is held by a human, who by virtue of being human deserves respect, is the basis for tolerance. The comprehensive analogy between non-material ideas and the goods and services found in a free market is colorful but inappropriate. Historically, "good sales" of an idea have often been a poor measure of its validity (e.g. hoop skirts, slavery, racism); "the sale," not truth or inherent value, is the ultimate goal of the marketplace.

The modern technology of selling has made the fate of an idea in the marketplace more dependent on engineering and money than on open debate. Edward Bernays, founder of Public Relations, saw advertising and democracy as the "engineering of consent," with marketing the sure road to good policy and leaders in a democracy. But substantive content matters. Although their repetitive presence and influence on minds are incomparably more pervasive, ads about a Coke or a cigarette are not as important as great music, profound insights, or public discourse on health care policy and foreign affairs.

The argument that the best solution to abuse of expression rights is "more expression" of more ideas makes expression the goal and sets aside issues of truth, competence, reason on behalf of fairness and balance, respect for those affected, and diversity of wealth and access to the social mind, as through the world's general mass media and scholarly and other intellectual publications. In domestic practice, "more expression" usually means not more ideas but repetitive expression to sell the same few ideas or products, with little or no attention to alternatives. Only a narrow spectrum of socioeconomic and political ideas is welcome in the U.S., for example, compared to Japan and other democracies.[19]

A better metaphor than "free marketplace" for freedom regarding expression in Eastern Asia and elsewhere in the twenty-first century is "home," "*a free home for ideas*," and more broadly, a free home for diversity in the humane contents and modalities of expression ("humane" by international human rights standards). For most, "home" makes family the prime analog for human relations and for community and home is where the ideals and intimate spirit of family are most fully challenged and realized and most comprehensively observable. It is remarkable how transculturally common is analogical reference to "family" as the explicit or implicit appropriate starting point for analyzing human relationships whether in the public sector or in the private sector. "We are family" is one of the many formulations used by non-familial groupings of many types: for example, nation states, local communities, companies, associations, unions, crews, military units, teams, ethnic groups, schools, and friends. Also at the core of human discourse are such related terms as "paternal," "maternal," and "fraternal" in non-family contexts.

The family-home has structure, differences of role, and authority, like a nation state. Confucianism, the Fourth Commandment ("Honor your father and mother"), and other family-oriented value systems of the world continue to define patterns of interpersonal expression within the family; but so should the heightened respect for the individual proposed for all cultures in the new synthesis represented by human rights principles for this and the next century. Thus, females are equal to males. Children are to be respected, heard, and protected. Essential are respect for parental authority, a sense of responsibility on the part of both children and parents, and strong bonds which ease the long process of individuating children into strong adults.

At home in the family is where it is most crucial to have a free home for ideas, freely but respectfully and responsibly expressed, in an ethos of mutual caring and acceptance, and with a great collective capacity for honesty, tolerance, shame, forgiveness, and reconciliation. If human rights ideas such as freedom regarding expression and tolerance are nurtured by spouses and parents in the nuclear family, in the multi-generational family, and in the local and national community as part of the assumed legacy of humankind, not as something foreign and culturally threatening, they will take hold and tenaciously last. A deep horror of intolerance, intergroup hatred, and their consequences must be instilled, sometimes paradoxically by adults warped toward intolerance by past experience; that is how a culture can improve its long-term compliance with human rights law. The key imperative is the conditioning of the young from a very early age to unequivocal condemnation of intolerant behavior based on clear familial, community and/or state commitment to powerfully motivating principles; for example, human rights constitutionalism fused with obedience to the Will of God. In a legal culture, the strength of a system of freedom of expression is proportionate to the unequivocally legitimate enforcement of tolerance among the young based on the dignity of each person. Of course, mutualist respect for the other implies interest in accurately understanding his expressed ideas, but not necessarily acceptance of the truth or other value in those ideas.

Families and communities have their own cultural values and customs to pass on to the young, but they should also teach the young to *welcome* the existence of myriad humane alternatives in the world and oppose any youthful tendencies toward spurious cultural nationalism. Just as a hospitable family welcomes a guest, and just as a good guest honors the host family's sensibilities regarding matters of importance to them, so should diverse ideas be welcomed courteously into the household and the community. Mutualist tolerance should govern. While taking pride in their own identities and heritages, families and nations should welcome the expression of new ideas and diverse cultures as they would welcome a visitor with hospitable treatment. Diversity should delight. The world is more than a marketplace; it should be a home for many "families of ideas," where respectful free expression is tolerated and nurtured by governments and more importantly by families.[20] Thus freedom could be newly appreciated under the great human traditions of courtesy and hospitality.

FREEDOM CULTURE IN EASTERN ASIA: THE CASE OF JAPAN

Study of the freedom cultures of Eastern Asia, with their family and quasifamilial values, social processes, law, problems and strengths with respect to freedom, provides a suggestive new family-centered paradigm for global understanding and support of freedom and tolerance. Perhaps in the twenty-first century mutualist personalism will spread along with a strengthened human rights law regime. Cynicism may be the easier attitude for many; but hope is more useful. As Gerard Manley Hopkins wrote: "And for all this, nature is never spent; There lives the dearest freshness deep down things."

Exaggeration of diversity seems the more common enemy of tolerance and free speech than cultural differences themselves; but seminal differences of perspective do exist. Around the world, but most noticeably in the United States perhaps, both political liberals and economic liberals seem to think only in terms of the individual, incapable of imagining any community unit as equally essential to analysis of individual freedom of expression.[21] On the other hand, some in Asia, Europe, Africa and Latin America find it immensely challenging to consider the individual as in some degree analytically separate from the family, other face-to-face communities, and familial patron-client relations.

Of Asia's countries Japan has the longest modern experience of freedom under law. Here I describe a few Japanese characteristics affecting the ecology of freedom there, its freedom culture, which are distinctive or which are suggestive of possible developments elsewhere in the next century. The most unique element in Japan's freedom culture is its quasi-pacifism under Article 9 of the Constitution of Japan:[22]

> Aspiring sincerely to an international peace based on justice and order, the Japanese people forever renounce war as a sovereign right of the nation and the threat or use of force as a means of settling international disputes.
>
> 2. In order to accomplish the aim of the preceding paragraph, land, sea and air forces as well as other war potential, will never be maintained. The right of belligerency of the state will not be recognized.

Before defeat in August 1945, Japan's political system was extremely nationalistic, aggressively militaristic, and thoroughly repressive.[23] With Japanese participation and the catalytic support of the United States, Japan began a constitutional revolution of freedom and peace during the Allied Occupation (September 1945–April 1952) which continues today.[24] Under the "Peace Constitution" Japan has not fought abroad since 1945, the military ("Self-Defense Forces") is geopolitically small and excluded from politics. Japan has shown even a great power can demilitarize. Japanese have not felt threatened, but support the Mutual Security Treaty with the U.S. Many take pride in Japan being "a conscientious objector nation" which leads the world in non-military aid and strongly supports the United Nations. They see freedom, not military strength, as promoting their "comprehensive national security".[25] Japan has no national security law system under which freedom of expression is subject to special restraints in time of crisis of war.[26] Civil servants are legally required to preserve secrets learned in the course of their duties. Any perception of the slightest political threat to free speech is met with vigorous and usually effective opposition, especially if a military factor is involved. Pacifism and freedom are linked in the public consensus.

Most generally, the self-realization of the individual Japanese is seen as achieved *within* rather than over, against or separate from the community, the family or the in-group. Individual obligations and rights are correlative, mutualist. The Constitution says: "All of the people shall be respected as individuals" but "to the extent that it does not interfere with the public welfare" (Article 13). Part of the public welfare is freedom of expression (Article 21):[27]

> Freedom of assembly and association as well as speech, press and all other forms of expression are guaranteed.
>
> 2. No censorship shall be maintained, nor shall the secrecy of any means of communication be violated.

For fifty years the independent judges of the Supreme Court and lower courts have been building a strong infrastructure of authoritative case law delineating the parameters of freedom.[28] In Japan's freedom culture, the status of freedom may be less dependent on government regulation or protection than on private-sector intra-group and inter-group relationships. In-groups encourage, regulate and restrain the freedom of expression of their members and effectively represent group interests in the public realm. The in-group is quasi-familial in nature; belonging, loyalty, and harmony with one's group is of fundamental importance. The nuclear family and one's primary in-group are Japan's central social structures. Typically, in-group membership (e.g. within a company, agency or organization) is long-term and loyal, and sharply divides one cluster of humans from other individuals and groups, giving rise to endemic factionalism and intergroup competition. Achievement of consensus on both trivial and important contentious questions is emphasized. Hierarchy and equality coexist. The group leader (*oyabun*, parental role figure) is not usually authoritarian but a builder of harmony, group cohesion and consensus. All members (*kobun*, filial role) are encouraged to participate in and take pride in group projects and decision-making processes. Once a decision has been made, the small minority who may still disagree are expected to selflessly and enthusiastically join in group actions to implement the decision. Open post-decision dissent or failure to cooperate with the group seems a key point in Japan's freedom culture. Freedom-friendly and community-friendly values require reconciliation in each case. Every individual contributes to group dialogue, whereas in some freedom cultures one or only a few may speak at a meeting, people join and leave groups casually, and special individual assertiveness is often needed to be heard at all. In the

U.S., for example, political power seems to come out of the mouth; listening is less crucial than in Japan.

A second characteristic which maximizes freedom of expression in Japan is the powerful sense of in-group rights. Factionalism is commonly called a curse of the system; but that seems rarely the case, only when one group's self assertions bring unwarranted harm to others, with what I call excessive "individualistic groupism". A recent regrettable example is *ijime*, group bullying of school mates.[29] The unfettered autonomy of multitudes of competing in-groups in a vast array of areas of human endeavor – party politics, company relationships, "schools" of various arts and crafts, universities, student organizations—gives creative and stable vigor to Japan's constitutional culture and tends to limit the power of all groups in government and society.

The fictive kinship of Japan's in-groups is predominantly occupational and contrasts with the more dominant roles of Confucian blood-related family relationships in such countries as China, Korea, Taiwan, Vietnam, and Singapore, and with other patron-client systems in the Philippines, Indonesia and Thailand.[30] Also noteworthy is the contrast between the stronger authority of leaders and fathers elsewhere in Eastern Asia and the deep egalitarian strain in Japan's groupist, consensual leadership. The leader who is thought to be authoritarian, too self-assertive, or unskilled in molding consensus and harmony loses much of his/her legitimacy. Japan's individualism is "soft;" her leaders are more impressive for group accomplishments than individual achievements. Anonymity is preferred in many contexts.[31]

Conciliation and publicity sponsored encouragement of freedom of expression also affect Japan's freedom culture.[32] Since at least the Tokugawa period (1600–1868), Japan has had formal procedures for settling disputes by conciliation. In earlier history, conciliation was compulsory; but under the present Conciliation Law (*Chōtei Hō*), conciliation procedures are voluntary and usually cheap and effective. In innumerable situations, Japanese prefer to settle disputes with the help of respected neutral third parties rather than by frontal confrontation in courts of law. Conciliation encourages fuller exercise of freedom of expression under light-handed guidance.

Finally, Japan has other institutions to encourage citizens to express grievances and concerns which enhance free speech and may be useful elsewhere in the next century.[33] Two such systems are the Human Rights Commissioners (*Jinken Yogo lin*, lit. Human Rights Protectors; more commonly but inaccurately "Civil Liberties Commissioners") and the Local Administrative Counselors (*Gyōsei Sōdan Iin*).

Over 13,000 unpaid laypeople, average age 64, throughout Japan serve for renewable three-year terms as Human Rights Commissioners.[34] These occupationally diverse men and women are meticulously and democratically selected for their human rights commitment and local credibility. The percentage of women Commissioners rose from 11% in 1967 to 23.2% in 1995. They are readily available. Each year they handle over 350,000 rights complaints at the town and neighborhood levels. They are low key problem solvers with no police powers; they rely on their skills in listening, conciliating and persuading. Rights violations are established in roughly 15,000 cases a year; for example, cruelty to the sick or elderly, community ostracism (*mura hachibu*), discrimination, environmental pollution, violation of freedom of expression. Commissioners refer problems beyond their competence to appropriate agencies.

With training and resources from the Human Rights Protection Bureau (*Jinken Yogokyoku*) of the Justice Ministry, Commissioners provide consultation services (e.g. at department stores) and educational programs during celebrations of Human Rights Day (December 10) and Constitution Day (May 3).

Local Administrative Counselors are respected local elders (average age over 60) who operate at the local offices of the Administrative Inspection Bureau of the Administrative Management Agency, the central organ monitoring the bureaucracy.[35] The Counselor system was established by statute in 1955 to improve public administration. However, their main task is to listen sympathetically to citizen complaints against civil servants and government services on a basis of confidentiality and impartiality. Problems are usually solved by explanation, discussion or conciliatory remedial action. About 5,000 Counselors deal with some 200,000 cases a year. Each October during "Administrative Counseling Week," Counselors and administrators offer programs explaining common problems and urging use of the system.

The Commissioners and Counselors have contributed to the change from the haughty authoritarianism ("*kanson minpi*", look up to officials and down on the people) of prewar bureaucrats to egalitarian democracy. In the 1980s and 1990s, private sector human rights efforts expanded, through the Human Rights Committee of the Japan Federation of Bar Associations, the Japan Civil Liberties Union (JCLU), Amnesty International, women's organizations, and specialized groups opposing pollution, military bases, value-added taxes and the death penalty. As a party to UN Covenants, Japan submits periodic reports to the UN Human Rights Committee, and these are vigorously supplemented by JCLU critiques. Since the later 1940s the bulk of constitutional law scholarship has focused on issues of rights and freedoms. Human rights legal research as a separate subfield has burgeoned in the 1990s with establishment of the International Human Rights Law Association (*Kokusai Jinkenho Gakkai*)[36] and the Kyoto Human Rights Research Institute (*Sekai Jinken Mondai Kenky Sentah*).[37]

In 1996, all of Japan's prefectures (*ken*) and some 230 cities have passed freedom of information and privacy ordinances; in 1998 the Diet is expected to pass a national Freedom of Information Law.[38] In government and law, Japan is one of the freest of nations.[39] The status of free expression depends primarily on its interplay with self-restraint in the community, as with the self-regulatory industry mechanisms of the mass media (e.g. the Motion Picture Ethics Commission (*Eirin*) and the Japan Newspaper Editors and Publishers Association (*Nihon Shimbun Kyōkai*) and distributor associations.[40]

CONCLUSION

In the twenty-first century, the interplay of legal culture and government described above will likely continue in Japan's freedom culture. Human rights constitutionalism seems to be the wave of the present and future in most parts of Eastern Asia, from Mongolia to Thailand. The obstacles to tolerant freedom in China, Indonesia, North Korea, Malaysia, and other nations are grounded less in culture than in leaders' unease about their power or public order, repressive policy, or resources insufficient to enforce a freedom regime. Their modern traditions include both authoritarianism and participatory democracy.

A modern legal system, trained law professionals, and independent courts are among the essentials for freedom regarding expression once a policy commitment has been made. Perhaps the recent legal developments in China and Vietnam augur well for freedom in this respect;[41] but they may, like Singapore, still opt for repression rather than free speech. However, the status of freedom of expression under law in Eastern Asia may more depend on the home, the development of free homes where parents nurture and defend freedom and tolerance, and on public and private institutions at the grass roots and sidewalk levels which encourage such families. The goal is a regime providing a free home for ideas and diversity, with strong families, strong individuals and strong community, and positive, sustained, multifaceted governmental nurturing of hospitality towards diverse ideas and peoples.

The success of this endeavor may rest ultimately on the sociopolitical power of a credible motivating principle; for example, recognition of a necessary linkage between tolerance and freedom regarding expression on the one hand and family nurturing and God's command to respect the dignity of all humans on the other. However sobering and burdensome this demand for respect may be, no obvious persuasive transcultural alternative presents itself on the twenty-first century horizon to justify tolerant freedom regarding expression.

NOTES

1 Illustrations are the Asian scholarship in L.W. Beer (ed.), *Constitutional Systems in Late 20th Century Asia* (1992) [hereinafter *Constitutional Systems*] and the publications of the Law Association for Asia and the Pacific (Lawasia).

2 Few law graduates of the West have been introduced to even one Asian legal system, even as diplomatic and commercial demand for expertise on Asian law burgeons.

3 Center for the Study of Human Rights, Columbia University, *Twenty-five Human Rights Documents* (1994). *See* Human Rights Watch/Asia, *Human Rights in the APEC Region:* 1994 (1994); L. Beer, Current Human Rights Issues in Asia, *Vital Speeches of the Day*, June 1, 1995, 506; E. Friedman (ed.), *The Politics of Democratization: Generalizing East Asian Experiences* (1994); Asian Human Rights Commission, *Eradication of Poverty as a Basic Human Rights Issue* (Colombo, Sri Lanka, Dec. 1995).

4 Article 18 of the UDHR provides for freedom of religious expression, and Article 20 for freedom of peaceful assembly and association. Articles 18–22 of the ICCPR are more detailed; for example:
"Article 19. Everyone shall have the right to hold opinions without interference.
2.Everyone shall have the right to freedom of expression; this right shall include freedom to seek, receive and impart information and ideas of all kinds, regardless of frontiers, either orally, in writing or in print, in the form of art, or through any other media of his choice.
3.The exercise of the rights provided for in paragraph 2 of this article carries with it special duties and responsibilities. It may therefore be subject to certain restrictions, but these shall only be such as are provided by law and are necessary:
a.For respect of the rights or reputations of others; . . .

5 A. Milner (ed.), *Perceiving "Human Rights,"* Australian-Asian Perceptions Project, Working Paper No. 2, University of New South Wales, December, 1993; A. Milner (ed.) *Australia in Asia: Comparing Cultures* (1996); 4 *Human Rights Dialogue*, Carnegie Council on Ethics and International Affairs, March, 1996.

6 The Johannesburg Principles (Dec., 1995), UN Doc. E/CN.4/1996/39 Annex. (For a copy, contact Malcolm Smart, *Article 19*, 1601 Connecticut Ave., NW, Washington, DC 20009, USA.) J. Fitzpatrick, *Human Rights in Crisis* (1994).

7 M.P. Glazer & P.M. Glazer, *The WHISTLEBLOWERS: Exposing Corruption in Government and Industry* (1989).

8 Excessive focus on judicial decisions can skew understanding of issues in one's own legal culture, but especially in others. *See* F. Brennan, The Bill of Rights and the Supreme court: A Foreigner's View, America, April 15, 1995, 1996.

9 Correspondence with Donald Kommers, 1995.

10 "Global Issues: Political and Economic Communities," *Draft Final Document*, Chapter 2, Tenth Conference of Heads of State of Governments of Non-Aligned Countries, Jakarta, September 1–6, 1992, NAC/Doc 1, September, 1992; Milner, *Perceiving "Human Rights"* 27.

11 Nobuyoshi Ashibe, Human Rights and Judicial Power, in Beer, *Constitutional Systems* 224. *See also* Bryant Garth, Transnational Research: Rethinking Scholarly Approaches, 7 *Research Law* No. 4, 1996, 2.

12 L. Beer, Introduction: Constitutionalism in Asia and the United States, in Beer, *Constitutional Systems*, 1. I distinguish human rights constitutionalism from other usages as follows:

"Constitutionalism" refers to systemic restraint on and division of government power under law on behalf of one or more fundamental national values.

"Documentary constitutionalism" means establishment of a single-document national constitution setting forth the principles, structures and processes of government. All but a very few nations have adopted such documents; over 130 of the current 181 constitutions have been ratified since 1970. A.P. Blaustein, *The Blaustein Register of Latest Constitutional Revisions*, Rutgers Univ. Law School, Camden, NJ (1994).

"Non-constitutionalism" points to a system which does not in fact limit government power, without reference to whether or not a written constitution has been ratified.

"Democracy" is government under the principle of popular sovereignty exercised in decision-making by a majority will, and without reference to the effect on human rights not directly related to discovery and implementation of the authentic majority position, such as voting and free speech rights.

"Judicialist constitutionalism" refers to systems profoundly, even primarily dependent on courts for the definition of basic principles and rights (e.g. the U.S. and Australia).

13 Medical research seems to undercut any persuasive fundamental distinction between the full humanity of a person in early pregnancy and after birth. The distinctly human and unique being simply continues to develop then in a more easily observable manner. On the conflicting philosophical presuppositions about personhood behind pro-life and pro-choice provisions, *see* F.J. Beckwith, Philosophical Commitments, Public Policy, and Family Law, 12 *Focus on Law Studies*, No. 1, Fall, 1996, 3. For comparative perspective, *see* Mary Ann Glendon, *Abortion and Divorce in Western Law* (1989).

14 Milner, *Perceiving "Human Rights"* 15–22.

15 On *Shinto*, *see* Beer, *Constitutional Systems*, 183–84; L. Beer & H. Itoh, *The Constitutional Case Law of Japan, 1970 Through 1990* (1996) 7, 48, 478, 492 [hereinafter *Case Law*]; J. Rawls, *A Theory of Justice* (1971); C. Bay, *The Structure of Freedom* (1968); R.E. Flathman, *The Practice of Rights* (1977); H. Shue, *Basic Rights* (1980); L.J. Macfarlane, *The Theory and Practice of Human Rights* (1985); and for transcultural views, *see* C.G. Weeramantry, *Equality and Freedom: Some Third World Perspectives* (1970) and R. Claude (ed.), *Comparative Human Rights* (1976).

16 A. Mayer, *Islam and Human Rights*, 2nd ed. (1995); D.E. Apter, *Rethinking Asian Development* (1987).

17 E. Peters, *Torture* (1985); R. Crelinsten & A. Schmid (eds.), *The Politics of Pain* (1993).

18 " 'Mutualism' integrates both the individual and the social sides of freedom and other rights more organically than either 'individualism' or 'groupism' ('collectivism'). 'Mutualism' points to the inherently reciprocal nature of individual rights, the mutual regard and respect they demand, and their existence within concrete interpersonal relationships of specific communities, not in individualist isolation, in an imaginary universalist world, or in groupist submersion."
L. W. Beer, Freedom of Expression: the Continuing Revolution, in P. Luney & K. Takahashi (eds.), *Japanese Constitutional Law* (1993) 247. *See also* Gabriel Marcel, *The Existential Background of Human Dignity* (1963) and *Being and Having* (1965); Martin Buber, *I and Thou* (R. G. Smith, trans.) (1958).

19 Mary Ann Glendon, *Rights Talk: The Impoverishment of Political Discourse* (1991) and *A Nation Under Lawyers* (1995).

20 Discussions with John Braithwaite, Australian National University, Canberra, July, 1996.

21 James Buchanan, at a symposium, "*Human Rights in Asia: the Current Debate*," Lehigh University, April 11, 1995; Brennan, *supra* no. 8 and Glendon, *supra* n.19.
22 *Case Law* 655.
23 H. Cook & T. Cook, *Japan at War: An Oral History* (1992); S. Harris, *Factories of Death: Japan's Secret Biological Warfare Projects in Manchuria and China*, 1932–1945 (1993); G. Hicks, *Comfort Women* (1995); R. Linner, *City of Silence: Listening to Hiroshima* (1995); and R.H. Mitchell, *Janus-faced Justice: Political Criminals in Imperial Japan* (1992).
24 L. Beer, Constitutionalism and Rights in Japan and Korea, in L. Henkin and A. Rosenthal (eds.), *Constitutionalism and Rights: The Influence of the United States Constitution Abroad* 225–43 (1990); L.W. Beer, *Freedom of Expression in Japan: A Study in Comparative Law, Politics and Society* chapter 2 (1984).
25 K. Chuma (ed.), *Kokusai Kyōroku to Kempō* (1995); K. Ogura, The Rupture between Japan and the United States: Exploring the Communication Gap between a Disoriented People and an Idealistic Empire, *Japan's Post Gulf War International Initiatives*, Ministry of Foreign Affairs, August, 1991, p. 47. On pacifism, *see* T. Fukase, *Sensō Hōki to Heiwateki Seizonken* (1987); N. Bamba & J. Howes (eds.), *Pacifism in the Japanese Christian and Socialist Tradition* (1976); T. Nardin, *The Ethics of War and Peace* (1996); and R. Musto, *The Catholic Peace Tradition* (1986).
26 J. Auer, Article Nine: Renunciation of War, in Luney and Takahashi, *supra* n. 18, 69.
27 The Constitution of Japan (*Nihonkoku Kempō*), 1947, in *Case Law* 656.
28 For judicial decisions in translation, *see* J. Maki, *Court and Constitution in Japan: Selected Supreme Court Decisions 1948–1960* (1964); H. Itoh and L. Beer, *The Constitutional Case Law of Japan: Selected Supreme Court Decisions 1961–1970* (1978); and L. Beer and H. Itoh, *The Constitutional Case Law of Japan, 1970 Through 1990* (1996).
29 On "individualist groupism" *see* Beer, *Freedom of Expression in Japan* 105–220. In the 1990s schoolyard bullying played a role in suicides.
30 L. Pye, *Asian Power and Politics: The Cultural Dimensions of Authority* (1985); Friedman, *supra* n.1; Apter, *supra* n. 16; J. Heuval & E. Dennis, *The Unfolding Lotus: East Asia's Changing Media* (1994).
31 M. Yamazaki, *Individualism and the Japanese: An Alternative approach to Cultural Comparison* (1994) (B. Sugihara, trans.); V.L. Hamilton & J. Sanders, *Everyday Justice: Responsibility and the Individual in Japan and the United States* (1992).
32 D.F. Henderson, *Conciliation and Japanese Law: Tokugawa and Modern* (1967).
33 L.W. Beer, *Human Rights Commissioners (Jinken Yogo Iin) and Lay Protection of Human Rights in Japan*, International Ombudsman Institute, Occasional Paper No. 31, Oct., 1985; K. Takamura, *Jinken chōsei senmon iin seido no dōnyū*, *Hōgaku Kyōshitsu* No. 193, Oct. 1996, 2; materials provided by the Human Rights Protection Bureau, 1970–1990; and Ian Neary, The Civil Liberties Commissioner System and the Protection of Human Rights in Japan, unpub. paper, June, 1996.
34 *Id.* This Commissioner system was established by Cabinet Order 168 in July 1948 to expand the very limited resources of the Human Rights Protection Bureau. A statute set the maximum number of Commissioners at 20,000; *Law* 139 of May 31, 1949, *Jinken Yogo Roppō* (1996).
35 Administrative Inspection Bureau, *Administrative Inspection and Administrative Counseling*, Administrative Management Agency, 1980–1995.
36 International Human Rights Law Association, *1990 Human Rights International* (in Japanese), No. 1, 1990.
37 Kyoto Human Rights Research Institute, *The Bulletin of Kyoto Human Rights Research Institute* (in Japanese), No. 1, March, 1996.
38 Hideo Shimizu, Tokyo; *see* his Masu Mejia No Jiyo to Sekinin (1993) and *Terebi To Kenryoku* (1995); and Y. Suzuki, Reformers Urge Sweeping Disclosure Law, *The Nikkei Weekly*, November 4, 1996, 4.
39 Beer, *Freedom of Expression and Freedom of Expression: the Continuing Revolution and Case Law*. Key issues in civil liberties law are the ban on vote canvassing, restriction of civil servant political activities to voting, and Education Ministry review of optional high school history texts.
40 On *Eirin*, *see* Beer, *Freedom of Expression* 340–45 and Hideo Shimizu, *a Brief Synopsis of Our Organization*, Eirin, Tokyo, 1995; Japan Newspaper Publishers and Editors Association, The Japanese Press (an annual); and J. Weinberg, Broadcasting and the Administrative Process in Japan and the United States, 39 *Buffalo L. Rev.* 3 (1991) 615.
41 For example, in 1995 Vietnam's National Assembly passed the country's first Civil Code;

B. Wormack, Vietnam in 1995: Successes in Peace, *36 Asian Survey*, Jan. 1996, 73. China's severe human rights problems are widely known. In 1996 China passed legislation establishing for the first time the principle of presumption of innocence in criminal law and limiting administrative detentions, commonly interminable in the past. H. Chiu, Institutionalizing a New Legal System in Den's China, *OP/RSCAS*, No. 3 (1994); *Lawasia Comp. Constitutional Law Newsletter*, No. 13, March, 1996, 2–6.

PART II

JAPAN

■ First published in *Asian Survey*, Berkeley, University of California Press, January, 1970, pp. 43-55.

6

Japan, 1969: "My Homeism" and Political Struggle

⌘

In the works and days of the world's third-ranking economic power during 1969, the university crisis and Okinawa reversion were central issues in domestic politics. Among the other preoccupations of Japan's leaders were demands for political party reform and Diet "normalization"; the year-end general elections; disputes concerning the courts; external pressures for complete import liberalization; rationalization of industry and agriculture to strengthen Japan's competitive position, at home and abroad; the labor shortage and rising prices; a rice surplus problem and city air pollution; fishery and territorial problems with Russia; far-reaching plans for tapping the resources of such areas as Siberia, Southeast Asia and Alaska; Japan's future role in Asia; and the Security Treaty with the United States, concerning which debate was expected to peak in 1970.

Most Japanese were well informed by the media of these events and issues, as well as of the Apollo moon-landings, the gradual expansion of the Tokyo-Osaka Hikari super express into a nationwide futuristic rail network, the ban on cyclamates, the near miss in Japan's attempt to orbit a satellite, and the discovery of Molotov cocktail production at the Institute of Space and Aeronautical Science.[1] Both the political apathy implied by "my homeism" and the radicalization of student politics were in part, products of the increasing prosperity, if not yet affluence, of Japanese society.

The main concerns of the man-on-the-street were likely to be better food and housing, pleasure excursions, perhaps a color TV purchase, and the local PTA. Virtually every family possessed a television, most had washing machines and refrigerators, around 65% owned their housing, 36% had private telephones, 24% stereo sets, and about 20% a family car.[2]

Often discussed was "my homeism": heightened emphasis on the privacy of nuclear family life; keener interest in the newest product and styles than in what others did in, for, or against society; a form of individualism which, while often criticized, persistently shook the intricately demanding structure of Japanese social mores. Standing over against the leadership and general populace, in their violence if not in some of their concerns, were faction-ridden student organizations.

THE UNIVERSITY PROBLEM

1968 and especially 1969 were traumatic years of unprecedented "struggle" for the world's second largest higher education system. Student demonstrations, common in Japan for decades, were not directed against the universities themselves until very recent years.

A few thousand students, collectively referred to as the "Anti-Yoyogi Groups" (i.e. opposed to the Japan Communist Party (JCP)-related *Minsei)*, were allowed to disrupt scores of universities throughout the nation.[3] By June, 1968, sixty colleges were under siege. At the dramatic and pivotal time of January 18–19, 1969, when the Yasuda Auditorium of prestigous Tokyo University was cleared of radical students, the number of disrupted schools was down to thirty-three; but the crisis then showed an upward curve.

The early 1969 entrance examinations were cancelled at some schools, and campus buildings across the country were occupied and barricaded for many months. Countless faculty meetings were held in search of policies which would accommodate some of the more broadly supported student demands, while protecting university autonomy, property, and educational processes from student radicalism and from undue police and political involvement. Many radicals were less interested in university reforms than in global attack on the political system, which was one reason long negotiations failed. Riot police were eventually called in, but buildings were at times reoccupied or resumed classes disrupted after the police left. College officials resigned; a few committed suicide. Temporary lockouts and gate checks were instituted.

The "struggles" continued through the summer. A controversial University Law was passed by the Diet on August 3, giving the Education Ministry temporary power to close or shut down schools which did not deal firmly with campus disorders. Since January, the number of currently disrupted colleges had steadily risen to 110, not counting a number of troubled high school campuses. By late November, through university and riot police efforts, the number had dropped dramatically and only five schools were still designated "seriously ill with dispute." In 1968, riot police were dispatched to campuses thirty-one times; in August, 1969, alone, thirty-six times, and the figure exceeded 300 at year's end, when most schools were functioning in relative quiet, at least for the time being.

Why, it may be asked, were prolonged campus disruptions, sometimes lasting over a year, allowed to continue? Only a few factors can here be tentatively suggested. For a long time, and for the most part, the Japanese government and people simply watched, urged university restoration of order, and waited. The academic community, including the mass of unorganized students, seemed afflicted with abulia and confusion for some time, though patience and other factors were in the mix. Professors and administrators had little or no analogous experience in terms of which to view the crisis. Many had been sympathetic toward anti-establishment student actions until they and their places of employment became objects of attack; and many found it hard even then to act decisively against a movement which was, at least in some ways, both politically "progressive" and on the side of needed university reforms. Numerous concerned but non-activist students shared this sentiment, and were as critical of the "my homeism" of "*non pori*" (politically apathetic) students as of the violent radicals. Finally, only the radicals were well-organized and armed.

Among the principal causes of the crisis adduced in opinion polls were the antiquated nature of the university system (19.9%; 28.6% of college students), followed in order by student disaffection with society, student political discontent, and *"masu puro"* (mass production) education. In another poll, 29% attributed the problem to a lack of student-professor communication, 20% to the radicals' desire for revolution, 15% to national neglect of educational problems, and 12% to inadequate school facilities.[4]

Of critical importance to most students was the "examination hell" and all it implied. A young man's success or failure in the excruciatingly difficult entrance examinations of the good universities (each school has its own exams) quite often determines his social and economic status for life. From early boyhood, disciplined, memory-oriented preparation for these tests has preoccupied the youth, his parents and schools. During his university years, a young man has enjoyed privileged status and considerable freedom (e.g. to demonstrate if he chooses), before settling down in the orderly adult world of Japan.

The university crisis hastened some reform proposals by the Education Ministry and leading universities, but the extent and effectiveness of change remain to be seen. Most universities are now firm, but moderate in dealing with disruptions. Somewhat paradoxically, the ultra-radical violence may have constricted the hitherto free atmosphere of Japanese student politics, while strengthening the hand of the radicals' enemies—the shrewdly moderate communist *Minsei* and the rightist elements. The time and property losses of some schools were rather substantial, as were the losses of hundreds of thousands of none-too-affluent students forced to mark time during the crisis. Use of the riot police was usually accepted as a regrettable necessity; but many academicians felt the new University Law showed a worrisome trend toward greater government involvement in university affairs.

In mid-September, 50% of a national sample either supported the University Law as is (8%), thought it unavoidable (21%), or favored sterner legislation (21%), while 40% answered "don't know" (hereafter, DK). Only 15% (25% in December, 1968) thought a solution could be negotiated; 12% wanted the solution to be left to the universities; while 57% considered government assistance necessary, and 31% DK.[5]

Almost no positive support seems to have existed in any age or occupational group for student violence, on or off campus (from .5% to 2%); but many sympathized with some of the radicals' positions on university problems, the University Law, Okinawa reversion, the Vietnam War, and/or the Security Treaty, all of which were stirred in with the students' various leftist ideologies. 70% of those in their 20s (slightly higher for older age groups) considered current police measures either too mild (33%) or appropriate (37%), while 17% (8%, of all age groups) thought the police too harsh.

DEMONSTRATIONS, PEACEFUL AND VIOLENT

Demonstrations make good newscopy, but some aspects of Japanese demonstration style that is important in assessing 1969 (and perhaps 1970) Japanese politics may not stand out clearly in press and TV reports reaching the United States. Demonstrations and group violence are two distinct issues in Japan. Not demonstrations, but the increase in student violence was a problem in 1969, and even the level of this violence could be easily exaggerated. Though the net political power of student activists has generally been negligible over the years, they have often dramatized domestic and foreign policy problems, and have only occasionally been a bit violent in the past. Demonstrations provide outlets for youthful idealism and/or exuberance in a socially, if not governmentally, restricted society. These roles should perhaps be taken more seriously than their announced goals, which are almost never achieved. During the university crisis, radicals constituted a very minute segment of a massive student population, and had little capacity to resist the police.

"Geba" (Gewalt) student violence contrasted sharply with the usually peaceful though much larger union demonstrations. A cause of wonderment for many Japanese may have been the radicals' failure to "play according to the rules." Demonstrations seem regulated less by law than by the unwritten but generally well understood rules of social propriety applied to that type of activity. For example, during brief slowdown strikes during 1969 opposing (with some success) the release of thousands of assistant engineers, railway union employees usually apologized repeatedly for the inconvenience caused (and were widely criticized if they did not apologize); this was expected of them, as was ample prior notice. In the largest union mobilization in Japan's history, some 1,240,000 employees participated in an almost uniformly peaceful and orderly national joint action (November 13) concerning Okinawa reversion and the Security Treaty.

On and off campus the radical students acted differently. When the university crisis developed, an early end to student violence was commonly expected, but was not forthcoming. On the night of November 16–17, over 1,700 (the largest arrest in postwar history) radicals were taken into custody for violence attendant to Prime Minister Sato's departure for Washington. Typically, though some eighty persons were injured (in descending order: bystanders—some from the neighborhood "Self-Defense Group"—police, students), damage to property was not widespread, and shortly train schedules were back on punctual schedule.

Regarding the style of 1969 student radicalism, though emotions ran quite high at times, serious injury was not common and deaths, as over the years, exceedingly rare and almost always accidental. Neither students nor police employed knives or guns. The Anti-Yoyogi factions were often as intent on fighting each other or the ideologically benighted *Minsei* (the JCP youth mass organization, currently strongest) as on confronting the establishment. Factions could be identified by varicolored helmets and banners held high; they were equipped with towel masks, whistles and/or bullhorns, long 2/2 sticks, rocks, shields, home-made Molotov cocktails, and, on rare occasions, acid. Faction leadership tended to be single-minded and self-righteous; but followers often moved rather casually from faction to faction or in and out of the movement.

The elements of meticulously organized pageantry, festival *(matsuri)* street dance, and flambuoyant melodrama were often dominant, rather than a "guerrilla warfare" atmosphere; and Japan's cartoonists made good humor of students' loose use of revolutionary garb and slogans.

Battle preparations by both sides were well publicized. The well-armored riot police, symbol of the hated establishment, overwhelmed their adversaries by sheer numbers, after responding with tear gas to a hail of rocks and Molotov cocktails. Clashes usually occurred on campus or around train stations, though, as on "Okinawa

Day" (April 28), students were chased at times through busy city streets. The scenario was acted out again and again, while a somewhat annoyed society continued about its business.

PARTY POLITICS AND THE DIET

The most dramatic legislative struggle of 1969 concerned the University Law. On May 24, the Cabinet presented a bill on the university problem to the Diet. Demonstrations against the bill were frequent. A joint statement was issued July 12 by public and private university presidents opposing passage. With virulent opposition protest at each stage, the ruling Liberal-Democratic Party (LDP) brought the matter to an affirmative vote in the Education Committee of the House of Representatives (July 24), the full House (July 29), the House of Councilors Education Committee (August 2), and the House of Councilors (August 3). The University Management Emergency Measures Law went into effect on August 17.

A common pattern of Diet controversy was followed: rather prolonged debate on a government-sponsored bill, in committee and/or on the floor, resolving into a form of opposition filibuster, which terminates with the LDP "ramming through" the legislation with party-line voting amidst protests and at times scuffles; and subsequent calls for "self-examination" and "normalization" from the press and the political parties, which become in time less urgent under the pressure of other political business.

The electorate continued to be generally uninterested in party membership, but a fall 1969 poll indicated current party preferences: LDP, 33.5%; Japan Socialist Party (JSP), 14.3%; Democratic Socialist Party (DSP), 3.1%; Komeito, 3.2%; JCP, .9%. Another 7.4% preferred a conservative party over a reform party, given that additional choice; and 6.9% preferred a reform party; while 30.9% gave DK or no preference as answers. The slight majority who supported a particular party most often gave as their principal reason opposition to some other party, or "I just do; no very clear reason."[6] Local popularity, personal connections, campaign funds, and other factors remained more crucial to election than party affiliation.

Prime Minister Sato returned from the U.S. in late November with an Okinawa reversion agreement; the House of Representatives was dissolved in early December, and a general election called for later in the month. With the 1969 revision of the Public Offices Election Law, which formerly prohibited TV campaign speeches, each candidate was allowed two radio broadcasts and four telecasts. The government claimed that its financial sponsorship of such a system was a world first, and anticipated a rise in voter interest and participation in elections. Over 900 local constituency candidates for the House made 4½ minute TV appearances paid for by the government and the TV companies, after being advised and lectured on the art of TV speech delivery by television personalities.

The LDP gained an impressive victory in the December elections, winning an absolute majority (288 seats plus another 12 pro-LDP independents), but only about 48% of the popular vote. With the exception of Yoshida Shigeru (over six years, from October 1948), Sato Eisaku had held the Premier's position for a longer continuous period than any man in prewar or postwar Japanese history (over five years). Throughout 1969, about 40% of those polled supported the Sato government, while an almost equal number did not; a not unusual phenomenon.[7] Sato hardly enjoyed immense popularity, but, as often in modern Japan, major national political figures who did were exceedingly rare.

The JSP, under Eda Saburo and Narita Tomomi, had lost ground in the 1967 general election, the 1968 upper house election and the July 1969 Tokyo Assembly election. The December general election was a near disaster, with the party losing more than 50 seats in the Diet. Their platform called for unarmed neutrality and policies serving the common man's needs, rather than business interests. There was increasing discussion of "multipartyism" possibly maturing in the 1970s, giving Komeito and the DSP a more pivotal position. Some Japanese analysts viewed the LDP and the JSP as the "old establishment" parties, incapable of dispelling the "black mist" from party politics. Perhaps a new party is in the offing.

THE JUDICIAL YEAR

Here we can recount only a few of the many controversial decisions and incidents which made 1969 perhaps the most eventful year in Japanese judicial history. On September 27, a Tokyo District Court quashed a 1967 suit against the Prime Minister for his unprecedented overriding of a court injunction permitting a demonstration in the Diet environs. The court held that the law legitimizing Sato's act was a political matter determined by the Diet.

Also in September, twenty-nine defendants in a 17-year-old case involving violent demonstration were acquitted by a Nagoya District Court on the unprecedented grounds of unconstitutional denial of a speedy trial (Takada case). But on November 11, another Nagoya court convicted over 100 men of committing a "crime of riot" in 1952 on a finding of "joint intention" to resort to violence (Osu case).

Perhaps the most bizarre matter before the Japanese courts in 1969 was the Tokyo University case *(Tōdai jiken)*, arising from the January campus violence. Counsel for about 500 defendants demanded they all be tried in one group (allegedly to make the courtroom a political forum), rather than in small groups as determined by the Tokyo District Court. Loud sympathy demonstrations occurred within the courtroom; both students and their lawyers refused to come to the courtroom. Some students chained themselves to their cells or disrobed to dissuade court officers from bringing them in. Appeals from the bar association and judges were to no avail. The trials finally went on in the absence of the defendants and defense counsel, who maintained their absence voided any judicial decisions. Like the universities, the court was notably reticent about decisive action against the students; but the first five convictions, handed down on November 28, were not attended by the usual lenient sentences.

The news media, who provided comprehensive coverage of all demonstrations and related court actions, themselves became involved in a number of disputes with the courts. Most notably, the Fukuoka District Court ordered (August 28) four TV companies to present film gathered during a 1968 student-police confrontation for use as evidence in a student suit against the police. This court order elicited nationwide cries of protest from the news media. "Escalation" was charged when a prosecutor's office monitored TV news broadcasts of Kyoto University clashes (October 20–21), and presented the videotape to the courts for use in the case against student radicals.

The media maintained their constitutional right to determine when freedom of reporting will permit use of film and still photos as court evidence; they feared loss of neutrality and interference with their freedom to gather news, due to possible loss of "the people's trust" (especially perhaps, students during public disturbances), and an attendant infringement on the people's "right to information."

On November 27, the fifteen Judges of the Supreme Court unanimously quashed their appeal, maintaining the great importance of freedom of reporting as a part of freedom of expression, and setting forth conditions under which film evidence may be used. But it also held that the fear of future limitation in gathering news is outweighed in the case at hand by the constitutional right to a fair trial, for which the film in question is necessary in the absence of other sufficient third-party evidence (Hakata Station film case).

Such cases, arising within Japan's unified court system, reflected and were an important part of the political environment of 1969. The courts and prosecutors were also busy devising methods for processing rapidly vast numbers of demonstrators, anticipating large-scale "struggles" in 1970. As from other mass arrest cases. they gained experience from those taken during the October 21 "Anti-War Day" (about 1,000 suspects) and the mid-November Kamata Station (about 1,700) disturbances.

Finally, in another unprecedented controversy, the Supreme Court (September 20) disciplined Chief Judge Hiraga Kenta of the Sapporo District Court for sending a letter of advice to a Judge Fukushima concerning disposition of the pending Naganuma Nike Missile Site suit. This suit against the government involved the highly political questions of land acquisition and use for defense purposes. Both the independence of the judiciary from the executive branch and the independence of an individual judge in decision-making were at issue. An article supporting Hiraga by Chief Judge Iimori of Kyushu, which subsequently appeared in an LDP-related organ, also brought public outcry and punitive action.[8]

OKINAWA REVERSION, THE SECURITY TREATY, AND DEFENSE

Armin Henry Meyer, a career diplomat new to Asian affairs, was appointed U.S. Ambassador to Japan in the spring. United States-Japan relations continued in 1969 to be a more crucial aspect of domestic politics in Japan than in America. The American people, if not their government, may only be beginning to take amicable relations with Japan less for granted. While government and business in both nations were alert to trade opportunities and problems, Okinawa reversion and Security Treaty extension were more central to Japanese political debate.

Since Japanese independence in 1952, America has recognized Japan's "residual sovereignty" over the Ryukyu Islands, and has returned to Japan the smaller territories of the Amami Islands and the Bonin Islands. Although perhaps ambivalently worded on some points, the Nixon-Sato communique (November 21) indicated that Okinawa will be returned to Japanese administrative control in 1972, that nuclear weapons will be removed from Okinawa, that U.S. bases on Okinawa will be subject to the same conditions as bases on the main islands of Japan, and that Japan considers Taiwan and South Korea important to her own security. According to Sato's understanding, Japan's three "non-nuclear principles" (no manufacture, possession or entry of nuclear weapons) were reconfirmed, and nuclear weapons would, once removed, never be allowed back into Okinawa, even under the "prior consulation" clause. Agreements to effectuate the transfer of power were to be worked out as soon as possible.

The JSP, Komeito, DSP and JCP attacked the communique as ambiguous regarding, among other things, possible reentry of nuclear weapons under the "prior consultation" clause of existing agreements. Many in the opposition had called for immediate, complete, and unconditional reversion. This implied immediate cessation of Okinawa's use in connection with the Vietnam War, early departure from Okinawa of American military men and material, and immediate removal of all nuclear weapons with no possibility of their return with "prior consultation" or in case of aggression in the area.

The Ryukyu Islands and their nearly one million people may prove to be more an economic and social liability than a valuable acquisition, at least initially. The islands are even less well-endowed with natural resources than Japan proper, and Okinawans are concerned lest (as before) mainland Japanese treat them as less than equal. The issue of reversion arose from natural feelings of political nationalism, and in part as a symbol of more complete Japanese independence *vis-à-vis* the United States. Full Diet representation and economic aid are planned for the Ryukyu Islands.

1969 was the year of final preparations for 1970's anticipated "Anti-Security Treaty struggles," which may or may not prove to be a serious problem, depending on the astuteness of Japanese and American politicians, the international climate next spring, and the amount of energy left in the student movements. As of June 23, the ten-year Japan-United States Treaty of Mutual Cooperation and Security, so dramatically debated in 1960, becomes open to automatic extension (the government position, formally approved by the LDP on October 14), revision, or notice by either party of termination after one year (favored by the JSP and other opposition groups).

Okinawa reversion, the Security Treaty, the changing situation in Vietnam and America's attendant policy modifications, the cutback of American bases in Japan (generally welcome, though difficult for released base employees), trade relations, and Asian developments were interrelated in the accelerating redefinition of U.S.-Japan relations. While substantially increasing trade and aid relations with Southeast Asia and easing loan and tariff terms, Japan's government and people seemed wary of suggestions that Japan play a politico-military role in Asia, beyond providing gradual conventional force increments for the defense of Japan itself.

American restraint in speaking about Japan's defense responsibilities might prove useful for minimizing future U.S.-Japan and U.S.-Asian and Japan-Asian tensions and for maximizing the chances of a long-term Japanese-American competitive friendship, whether or not Japan decides to become a major military power. For twenty-four years, Japan has been happily free from military threats and expenses, and largely free from international responsibilities and conflicts that tangibly affected the daily lives of the Japanese people. Domestic political debates, except within the factional context of the ruling party, have often been meaningful primarily in terms of internal political configurations; but then Japan may not have felt pressed to answer questions which her power may pose only in the 1970s.

If at times politically manipulable, Japan's largely non-philosophical popular pacifism, rooted in defeat and the atom bomb, has been unique in the world, and more perhaps than a curious "nuclear allergy." This pacifism is institutionalized in Article 9 of the Constitution, in literature and cinema, and in political discourse.

Whether, to what degree, and how it may affect Japan's domestic and international politics in the future seem rather moot questions, in the absence of genuinely analogous precedents. Pacifism is often linked with the desire for a neutralist foreign policy, and is one factor contributing to the framework of public opinion on certain foreign policy issues.[9]

In a September poll, 37% felt the Security Treaty benefitted Japan, while 34% felt it did not; 31% (42% in December 1968) favored phased abolition of the treaty after 1970, while 24% (15%, December 1968) favored automatic extension, and 14% opted for early abrogation. Asked in a June poll whether Japan should give the U.S. notice of termination in 1970, 24.1% said "yes," 31.7% "no," 44.2% DK.

When those favoring abrogation were asked how Japan's security should be assured, the following views were expressed, representative of more widely supported government opposition views: by means of a clear statement of Japan's neutrality and by her Self-Defense Forces (34.5%); by gaining assurances of non-aggression from Russia, the People's Republic of China, and the U.S. (21.4%); by a statement of neutrality combined with reliance upon the United Nations (26.6%); by building a new security system with a nation other than the U.S., such as Communist China or Russia (5.4%); DK (12.2%).

In mid-September, 46.1% favored Japan's continued identification with the "free world," while .8% preferred the "communist camp," 29.3% opted for neutrality, and 23.8% DK. Without exaggerating the importance of such popularity polls, or other polls, and allowing for the 40% without clear positions, when asked to name up to three of the nations they liked best, 34.9% mentioned the U.S. and 34.1% Switzerland, with the rest of the world far behind. Easily the three "most disliked" countries were Japan's neighbors, Russia (40.9%), mainland China (34%), and Korea (22.8%).

Only Russia (20.4%) and mainland China (15.6%) were mentioned as potential threats by a notable proportion in another poll, but the Japanese do not feel particularly threatened as of now. Moderate concern about Japan's defense problems was expressed by 63%; 63.8% supported the maintenance of the Self-Defense Forces at at least their present levels, while only 2.5% thought they should be abolished (usually because considered contrary to the Article 9 "no war" clause). On the other hand, the draft Defense Agency White Paper (September) drew fire from the opposition for stressing Japan's need to contribute more to her own defense.

When queried about their willingness to defend Japan in case of direct armed attack, 85.5% answered affirmatively, but only 20.2% would do so at cost of life (a much larger number would lend moral or economic support); a little less than half thought the Japanese people capable of uniting for the nation's defense in case of military aggression.[10]

JAPAN AND THE WORLD

Preparations for the "Expo '70" World Exposition neared completion in Osaka. Foreign Minister Aichi's UN speech in the fall hinted at Japan's desire for permanent membership on the UN Security Council. Japan raised its International Monetary Fund (IMF) contribution, and looked forward to inclusion in the IMF "Big Five." The ship-building industry continued to set the pace, producing around half of the world's tonnage. On October 30, the government approved the merger of

Yawata and Fuji into the "New Japan Steel Corporation," which is expected to be the world's largest steel concern within a year or so.

Persistent calls came from the OECD and the U.S. for very early liberalization of food, auto, capital and other imports into Japan, in light of Japan's rapid GNP growth, shift from debtor to creditor nation status, and generally favorable international financial situation. Though Japan has benefitted greatly from technology imports over the years, it should also be noted that only in very recent years have Japanese exports to the U.S. pulled even with U.S. exports to Japan.[11] American demands for restraint on textile exports were a sore point in negotiations; but more symbolic of the massive, mutually profitable, and generally amicable economic relations of Japan and the U.S. were the Mitsubishi-Chrysler Corporation joint venture agreement, and the arrival in November of the first of many shipments of LNG (liquified natural gas) under a long-term agreement with Alaskan interests.

After a twenty-day delay, Russia reported an August 9 patrol boat collision with a Japanese fishing boat in which eleven of the twelve aboard were killed. (Since 1946, Russia has captured 1302 boats and 10,987 Japanese crewmen.) All media and political parties in Japan attacked the "murderous" action. A movement, centered in Hokkaido, demanding the return of the Russian-held Northern islands, was slowly gathering broad sympathy; but attempts at negotiating the issue again met with a wintery Russian response. On the other hand, as a partial answer to Japan's great energy needs, plans looking toward Russian-Japanese construction of a 900-mile gas pipe-line from Sakhalin to Hokkaido industrial centers went ahead, as did negotiations for an annual import of six million kilowatts of electricity in exchange for Japanese construction of a large thermal power plant in Siberia.

The Sino-Soviet border conflicts caused generally quiet consternation. The unofficial "Memorandum Trade" agreement with Communist China ran out at year's end, and renewal negotiations had not yet begun; but "friendly firm" trade showed some increase.[12] Particularly interesting, perhaps, among innumerable 1969 agreements for Japanese factory construction, resource exploitation, trade, and technical assistance to Asian, African and other nations, was the unexpected Tanzanian request that Japan cooperate in the overall industrial and agricultural development of the Kilimanjaro area. This was seen as an opportunity to create a showcase for Japanese technology in Africa.

CONCLUSION

Japan in 1969 was girding for the socio-economic impact of full liberalization. Though wages and GNP rose faster than prices in general, rising prices were an issue of importance, and the older employed were feeling the stresses at times of Japan's economic restructuring process. On the other hand, the labor shortage in some sectors was such that six jobs awaited each high school graduate, and restraints on pre-graduation "recruiting" were thought necessary. Ending a four-year suspension of regular meeting, the government-sponsored Consultation Council, expanded to include not only union representatives but also "learned men" and employers, prepared to grapple with the labor and labor-management problems of the 1970s.

The expansion of industry into less prosperous rural areas continued. In response to the rice surplus and increasing competition from food imports, the Japan

Economic Council bared imaginative proposals for "mechanization and systematization" of agriculture, which may lead to the most far-reaching changes since the Occupation land reform.

As a world maritime nation, Japan continued to trade with any nation that could and would trade, regardless of political system. This separation of politics and economics also operated, in a way, within Japan during 1969. Student violence erupted and enormous union demonstrations occurred, and Diet debate was at times heated. But the economy of Japan was never importantly affected, not because the Japanese is an "economic animal" (as other Asians sometimes suggest), but because as a rule he is not only energetic, but also practical and orderly. With these qualities, Japan may prove to be as alert and nimble as a Tokyo pedestrain in making her way through the 1970s.

SELECTED READING

James Dator, *Soka Gakkai, Builders of the Third Civilization: American and Japanese Members* (Seattle: University of Washington Press, 1969).

Donald Hellmann, *Japanese Domestic Politics and Foreign Policy: The Soviet Peace Agreement of 1956* (Berkeley: University of California Press, 1969).

Dan Fenno Henderson (ed.), *The Constitution of Japan: Its First Twenty Years, 1947–1967* (Seattle: University of Washington Press, 1969).

"University and Society," *Journal of Social and Political Ideas in Japan* (Tokyo: Center for Japanese Social and Political Studies, 1969; dated Dec. 1967, Vol. V., Nos. 2–3).

Nathaniel Thayer, *How the Conservatives Rule Japan* (Princeton: Princeton University Press, 1969).

J. A. A. Stockwin, *The Japanese Socialist Party and Neutralism* (Melbourne: Melbourne University Press, and N.Y., Cambridge University Press, 1968) (available in US in 1969).

Gekkan Seron Chōsa (The Japan Opinion Research Monthly), available through Seifu Kankobutsu Sabisu Sentah, Tokyo; began publication in 1969; a monthly compilation of poll data gathered by Japan's various public & private opinion research agencies.

NOTES

* The author is indebted to Japanese and western colleagues in Japan for the benefit of their perspectives.

1 *Asahi Shimbun*, November 8 & 14, 1969. Throughout this article, references are made to specific dates. Full accounts of the matters discussed will be found in the *Asahi Shimbun, Mainichi Shimbun*, and *Yomiuri Shimbun* issues of those dates.

2 "Kokumin Seikatsu," *Gekkan Seron Chosa* (The Japan Opinion Research Monthly) (Tokyo, Okurasho Insatsu Kyoku), June, 1969, pp. 68–73; October, 1969, pp. 2–21. Also, Ministry of Health and Welfare, *White Paper*, October 31, 1969; *Asahi Shimbun*, evening ed., October, 31.

3 Ichiro Sunada, "The Thought and Behavior of Zengakuren: Trends in the Japanese Student Movement," *Asian Survey*, June, 1969; *Journal of Social and Political Ideas in Japan*, "University and Society," double issue, (Vol. V., Nos. 2–3), March, 1969. For a chronology of the crisis, see *Asahi Shimbun*, October 18, 1969; and for the genealogy and present status of student factions, see *Asahi Shimbun*, October 9, 1969.

4 "Daigaku Mondai," *Gekkan Seron Chosa*, op. cit., July, 1969, pp. 56–59, and November, 1969, pp. 75–78; "Gakusei Undo," *Gekkan Seron Chosa*, June, 1969, pp. 20–47.

5 "Daigaku Mondai," *Gekkan Seron Chosa*, November 1969, pp. 75–77.

6 "Jiji Seron," *Gekkan Seron Chosa*, November 1969, pp. 78–80.

7 *Asahi Shimbun*, November 8, 1969.

8 Sato Isao, "The Hiraga Letter Question and the Independence of Judges," *Hogaku Seminah* (Tokyo), November, 1969, No. 164, pp. 2–9. Concerning Hakata Station film case, see "Criminal Justice and the Freedom of Information," (a special issue) *Jurisuto* (Tokyo), December 1, 1969.

9 Kendell Whitney, "Pacifism and Japanese Politics," (unpublished thesis), University of Colorado, 1969.

10 *Asahi Shimbun*, October 1, 1969; "Kokumin no kuni ni taisuru ishiki," *Gekkan Seron Chosa*, July, 1969, pp. 12–14; "Nichibei Anpo—Kokumin no ishiki," *Gekkan Seron Chosa*, October, 1969, pp. 81–90. The monthly Jiji Press poll on current problems, as well as party and nation preferences, appears in *Gekkan Seron Chosa*.

11 "Japan," OECD Economic Surveys, (Paris), August, 1969; *Bank of Tokyo Weekly Review*, November 4, 1969: "White Paper," Ministry of International Trade and Industry, November 21, 1969, summarized in *Asahi Shimbun*, November 21.

12 Lawrence W. Beer, "Some Dimensions of Japan's Present and Potential Relations with Communist China," *Asian Survey*, March, 1969.

■ First published in Lawrence Ward Beer, *Freedom of Expression in Japan: A Study in Comparative Law, Politics, and Society*, New York & Tokyo, Kodansha International, 1984, pp. 100-128.

7

Social Patterns and Freedom of Expression

⌘

During Japan's current constitutional revolution of freedom, aspects of social structure and social value affect and are affected by the legally protected right to expression. Social rules condition the unofficial and official status of freedom of expression and the ways in which individual expression is encouraged and discouraged. These patterns, like the modern history of liberty, define in important part present strengths and weaknesses of free speech. They also mold the mind-set of decision-makers in public and private life responsible for issues of freedom.

I. ASSUMPTIONS AND CAVEATS

Some clarifications seem in order at the outset. First, the aim of this chapter is not a comprehensive discussion of Japanese character or even of patterns that affect human rights. Rather, the purpose is to provide a suggestive analysis of some social tendencies that seem particularly relevant to an understanding of freedom of expression in Japan. Although later sections present a somewhat distinctive slant on freedom and expression in Japan, most of what is said herein will be familiar to most Japanologists (though to few others), and they may wish to skip on to Chapter 4.

Second, the Japanese are in some ways pluralistic, with much variety in their political viewpoints, interests, living environments, and beliefs; but compared to most other large nations, they are quite homogeneous. This may make the effort to delineate social foundations less temerarious than it would be in the case of more heterogeneous countries like India, Indonesia, or the United States. These tendencies and others can legitimately be called Japan's "national character," but with no implication of uniformity or lack of exceptions. My main concern here is not epistemological precision but cross-cultural statement intelligible or at least empathetically useful to those who are not Japan specialists.

Third, many Japanese and some other observers have claimed that Japanese society is "unique" and peculiarly difficult for foreigners to understand. Such contentions are not persuasive. All nations and many subnational groupings are distinctive, even unique in some respects; and many nations, such as the United States, seem far more opaque than Japan.

Fourth, the intent is neither to condemn nor to praise Japanese patterns. Depending on which aspect of the nation's culture or legal doctrine one stresses, one may see Japan as somewhat oppressive or supportive of freedom. The same is found by sociolegal analysis of any democracy. All cultures are defective in upholding the right to expression.

The fifth caveat is that (as explained in Chapter 1) free speech is not presumed to be the highest priority in the ecology of all cases in which it is an issue. In some cases, only analysis of the intended and unintended social or economic effects of free speech and its denial may yield a persuasive assessment. Other substantive reason, rather than advocacy of a protected right to expression, is usually behind the exercise of a felt-right to expression.[1] But even where power-holders or ideologies do not value a functional equivalent of a legal right to expression, peoples have recognized the rightness of dissent from injustice and expressive promotion of justice. Severely repressive governments and societies are commonly out of tune with the ideals of their own cultures. Japanese have publicly expressed themselves, on occasion as individuals but usually in organized groups,[2] or through newspapers and other communication systems as the media have emerged in the history of technology.[3] Yet it is also true that Japanese have seemed to many to be docile, submissive, and quiet before authority.

II. SOCIAL STRUCTURE, VALUES, AND FREEDOM, PAST AND PRESENT

Present cultural patterns bear traces of the historical past. Perennial tendencies found in the Tokugawa era (ca. 1600–1868) still affect the Japanese understanding of freedom rights, though less than the dynamic modern mixture of indigenous and foreign legal, political, and intellectual forces. Radical social, constitutional, and economic adjustments have not eliminated the perennial importance of sociality and group-orientation as opposed to autonomy and individualism, a stress on duty and loyalty rather than on rights and a right to change, a preference for consensual rather than majoritarian decision-making, and respect for hierarchy, seniority, and family. Stirred in with these patterns has been a sensitivity to those lower on the social scale in the common pursuit of group harmony.

The pervasive imperative in Tokugawa Japan was to fulfill one's duties according to one's place in a feudal hierarchy with an elaborate differentiation of hereditary status. At the top of the social ladder were the nobles and samurai; then, in order, came farmers, craftsmen, merchants, and those in outcaste trades. Law, justice, authority, administration, and custom were tightly interwoven rather than clearly differentiated and separated. There was no imperative to recognize the rights of the individual. Indeed, as explained later, no word for "a right" existed in the Japanese language until the nineteenth century.

> The standards of correct conduct were elaborately implemented by a complex of practical rules, centering around the five Confucian relationships, which were quite suited to implement the controls of the Shogunate. These relation-

> ships—lord-man, father-son, husband-wife, older-younger brother, friend-friend—provided a fabric of detailed and fixed rules to handle most situations of daily life in such a way as to reduce volition, self-assertion, and choice—hence personal responsibility—to a minimum. As taught in the village and family circles, they engendered conformity and submissiveness at such a tender age that these characteristics became the outstanding features of the personality. They tended to negate individuality; even the superior was not an individual, but the most important part of the group. Yet the superiors could be held strictly accountable to the Shogunate for the conduct of their groups which was convenient for authoritarian control.[4]

Relations between lords and followers involved reciprocal obligations. In many villages local customary law probably admitted little gap between the equivalents of perceived and protected rights. However, the traditional view of the functional group from very early times was that since all, regardless of status, were in the same boat, everybody enjoyed communal rights. As Nakane Chie observes of the traditional peasant outlook: "There is strong opposition to the formation of status groups within a single community, although the order of higher and lower in relationships between individuals is readily accepted."[5]

Every Japanese had some recognized duties under *dōri* (natural justice, reason),[6] and Confucian duties were understood to be in some degree reciprocal. Duties differed with one's status, but persons in a higher status had duties to peers and to those above and below them. Though rights of individual commoners were generally not enforceable through the functional equivalent of suits against authorities in a higher status, irresponsibility on the part of superiors was not accepted in Tokugawa law and government.[7]

The mutual loyalty so essential to the operation of the social system, then as now, was to be given by inferiors in return for adequately benevolent treatment from above. Within limits, those below had an expectation of, a sense of entitlement to, paternal concern by superiors in return for loyalty and service. Thus, a real right-consciousness existed, however much rights and duties were skewed in favor of higher status. To some extent, these traditional perceptions, which can be termed "reciprocal duty consciousness," condition present perceptions and practices. In such a context, self-realization is achieved by freely fulfilling duties to other persons with a correlative expectation that others will fulfill their duties to oneself.

The *desideratum* for the Japanese was and commonly is not the right to a high degree of autonomy but the right to belong to a world of loyalties and duties which, while demanding much at times, surrounds, stimulates, provides for, and protects the individual person. There have been various types of duty and obligation (e.g. *giri, on*) in Japanese culture and language. The mutual awareness of duty is often of diffuse, interpersonal responsibilities, rather than of clearly and narrowly defined duties to be carried out within a specific time frame (as in a U.S. contract, for example). The manner of repaying debts of either limited scope or unlimited nature (*on*, as to parents) is generally flexible in content, depending on concrete context and the wishes and resources of those involved in the relationship.

For centuries a major theme of Japanese literature has been the dilemmas created by conflicting duties of an individual to different people, and by the sometimes incompatible demands of duty (*giri*), to family for instance, and of "human inclination" or "feeling" (*ninjō*).[8] "*Ninjō*" allows for the expression of spontaneous individual emotion and sympathy, but not with any attendant legal or moral "right" to do so; it concerns private personal relations, not public matters; it serves as "an escape valve in a regimented society."[9]

Officials considered adherence by all to *giri* obligations essential to maintenance of the *status quo*, social peace, and public order. Personal wishes or feelings are clearly subordinate and are to be repressed, if that is demanded by *giri* obligations. Feelings are there, but *giri* must be honored. The person enduring frustration, suffering, or love due to *giri* conformity had best not show his feelings, but the observer may note the existence of the situation and sympathize. Thus, the social system sharply distinguishes between expression where *giri* is involved and expression related to *ninjō*. It distinguishes between the public and private arenas of life, as between duty and personal emotion.

Another essential element in the context of expression rights is the relationship between the duty—feeling factor and common understandings of government. In the past there was no clear differentiation between the public and the religious spheres, except that Buddhism taught early rulers that government should not intrude into matters of conscience. Victor Koschmann notes the linkage from early times to the present between the group, the sacred, and leadership, understanding of which seems to be critical to perspective on the Japanese "groupism" analyzed later:

> The function of the sacred here is not to judge, deny or negate the world, but to renew its productive energy through affirmative, communal participation. In addition, the sacred—in the sense of communion with the divine—is a group, rather than individual, enterprise: "The gods appear in the course of communal worship." Sacred and profane are both immanent in group life. . . . Rather than encouraging negation and transcendence of the temporal world, loyalty to the sacred reinforces an affirmative view of society. Indeed, separation from the community through ostracism can be a fate worse than death. . . . A pattern of political authority based on the sacred quality of group life, and the special position of the group leader as link with the divine, remains influential to the present day. . . ."[10]

The development in Japan of a central government over time, whether in very early or more recent historical eras, did not involve the replacement of local kinship group authority by some different or abstract notion of government, but rather an extension of the notion of the sacred group as coincident with *ōyake* (the public sector) to the entire nation with the emperor serving as the formal "link with the divine."[11] This understanding continued even after the imperial institution lost its actual governmental power. Harootunian explains:

> *Ōyake* was always associated with high-sounding purpose: public tranquility and order, fairness, and the "consultation of public opinion" (*kōgi*); *watakushi* [I, private] was identified with irregular dealings, bad faith, selfishness, personal feelings, and private desires. . . . [Yet,] it is essential to emphasize that *watakushi* was a necessary adjunct of *ōyake*. No conflict was intended. But in the inevitable encounter between the realms, individuals were admonished, as a kind of moral imperative, "to dissolve the personal and honor the public (*messhi hōkō*)."[12]

Similarly, in Japan today official power clothes itself in the mantle of the Constitution and law as righteousness, and pursues the collective good as seen by leaders, while sometimes downplaying the duties of leaders to citizens and "selfish" individual wishes and rights.[13] The common people have not successfully revolted against an incumbent regime. They were conditioned at least till recent times to view what is "public" (*ōyake*) as naturally authoritative, even sacred, and morally superior to what is "private" (*shi, watakushi*). In turn, what affects the group as a whole was held much more important than the interests of an individual member.

The "public" today includes leaders and officials of national and local government, but not politicians in general. Politicians other than the representative of one's own constituency tend to be seen as venal and self-serving, while one's favorite elected politician tends to be viewed as the natural "public" leader.[14] Government is seen as something "given" by nature, and as basically good and necessary, not as something separate from, over against, and possibly inimical to the interests of the people; selfish politicians and special interests are the problem, not the bureaucracy.

Officialdom has generally inspired respect, even some awe among ordinary citizens, and this was sanctioned by prewar regimes in such dicta as *kanson minpi*, "look-up-to-officials-and-down-on-the-people." In part by reason of this mental context, careers in government generally carry great prestige, and élitist collectivism there may weaken both the protection and the exercise of freedom of expression. On the other hand, the constitutional revolution since 1945 has given sovereignty to the people and has identified the dignity and rights of the individual as such with the sacred public sector. This identification of the individual as the sacred public value has legitimized freedom and called for unprecedented government attention to the individual's concerns. Thus, in government-citizen relations, though not necessarily in society, service of the "private" (individual) has become the sacred imperative of the "public" (government).

A further value pattern that influences the free speech of individuals and groups is respect for "*makoto*," single-minded sincerity and correspondence between exterior and interior. As Joseph Roggendorf observes:

> "Truth" signifies, in ordinary parlance, not much more than a vague personal opinion which should, of course, be respected, but does not denote the idea of a demonstrable reality or of a valid assertion about the nature of things. . . . The place of "truth" is taken by "sincerity," for which there are several neologisms (*shini, seii*) but also an old classical word, *makoto*.
>
> You are sincere if you outwardly express what you subjectively think. . . . How is one to determine it? The Japanese accentuate the appearance. They insist on "sincerity" as evidenced through one's contrite look, lowly posture and modest language. That has something humanly attractive about it. But how is one to be sure that sincerity is what it seems, and not mere play-acting? A student caught in the wrong may be forgiven provided he shows "the color of reflection" (*hansei no iro*). That . . . will then show. . . . by the deep bow, the sharp intake of breath, and the rattling off of a few polite phrases.
>
> Excessive stress on sincerity easily leads to theatricals, hence to hypocrisy. We have all seen on television (in Japan) a politician, a trade union leader, or a business tycoon, caught in the act of wrongdoing, kowtow abjectly and apologize. The Japanese tell many a funny story about abuses of publicly displayed "sincerity."[15]

It is the degree of stress on a type of appearance that seems distinctive, not the emphasis or occasional hypocrisy. The seriousness of "sincerity" is evident in public life from the fact that a cabinet minister may feel it necessary to resign with abject apologies to the public to atone for a natural disaster over which he has had no control.[16]

Subjective dedication to a cause expressed in direct action is much admired, whether or not the cause is thought rational or for the common good, and whether or not the goals pursued are accomplished. The young military officers on trial for assassinating prominent leaders in the 1930s were admired by many for the "sincerity" (*makoto*) of their pronouncements in court on ultranationalist loyalty to the emperor. Other things being equal, justice, in both political and nonpolitical cases, can be less harsh for defendants who have acted "sincerely," even where others have been victimized, as during the 1968–70 university crisis. Heroic sincerity may be viewed with admiration, even popular awe, but that does not imply that either government or citizens think such "heroism" should generally be condoned or succeed. In fact, in a tradition explicated by Ivan Morris, failure itself carries its own nobility when attended by sincerity:

> [This] represents the very antithesis of an ethos of accomplishment. He is the man whose single-minded sincerity will not allow him to make the manoeuvers and compromises that are so often needed for mundane success. . . . Flinging himself after his painful destiny, he defies the dictates of convention and common sense, until eventually he is worsted by his enemy, the "successful survivor," who by his ruthlessly realistic politics (or, empirically, for other reasons) manages to impose a new, more stable order on the world. Faced with defeat, the hero will typically take his own life in order to avoid the indignity of capture, vindicate his honour, and make a final assertion of his sincerity. His death is no temporary setback which will be redeemed by his followers, but represents an irrevocable collapse of the cause he has championed: in practical terms the struggle has been useless and, in many instances, counterproductive. . . . In a predominantly conformist society, whose members are overawed by authority and precedent, rash, defiant emotionally honest men . . . have a particular appeal. . . . [T]he fact that all their efforts are crowned with failure lends a pathos which characterizes the general vanity of human endeavor and makes them the most loved and evocative of heroes.[17]

Such an ideal offers an antidote to any conformist, success-worshipping culture, or one that unrealistically assumes that justice will out in the end. This Japanese tradition of respect for sincerity and noble failure has remained vigorous; many public political acts of individuals and groups—whether Saigō Takamori's abortive samurai rebellion in 1877 or thousands of student demonstrations since the 1950s—have been predestined to failure. Opposition political parties since 1948 seem to have systematically avoided taking control of the government by refusal to compromise "sincerity" and coalesce with similar-minded groups to achieve broader electoral appeal. So in many cases an imperative for self-expression in Japan, whether by a group or by an individual, is not closely linked with an expectation of success or "results."

Japan's social structure and values have undergone fundamental alteration since the Tokugawa period.[18] There are no longer authoritarian government or clearly discernible and sanctioned classes to which one belongs by heredity. However, a meticulously and minutely differentiated hierarchy continues to exist, based on position, education, occupation, age, genealogy (occasionally), and quasi-parent–child (*oyabun–kobun*) relationships, a type of patron–client relationship. An individual's web of relationships may be endlessly complicated, and who one knows now modifies the impact on one's status of the usual determinants. In male society, one's hierarchical position in relation to another, if unknown at time of first meeting, is quickly discovered and fixed with the exchange of *meishi* (name cards which indicate both occupation and affiliation) and with bows of greeting which signal mutual recognition of relative social standing. Among the qualifications necessary, one's perceptions of another's status may change as one learns more of his web of human relationships. For example, the relative prestige of one's university, where relevant, may raise or lower one's status in another's view. Those in high position are commonly reluctant to rush into an exchange of *meishi*, because it may entail future impositions. In any case, one's hierarchical position *vis-à-vis* another, and the existence or absence of prior obligations (*giri*) or an *oyabun–kobun* relationship, importantly affect the relative freedom of each party in a relationship to speak, as well as the legitimate content of that expression.

In an *oyabun–kobun* relationship, "[T]he *kobun* receives benefits or help from his *oyabun*, such as assistance in securing employment or promotion, and advice on the occasion of important decision-making. The *kobun*, in turn, is ready to offer his services whenever the *oyabun* requires them."[19] The quasi-familial nature of the in-group system derives from the quasi-parental–filial quality of the modal superior-inferior relationship. Today, very cohesive groups are usually formed by the multiplication of vertical relations between two individuals, according to the structure in Figure 7.1.[20]

In-group ties tend to become close, through the common bond with the leader, but also through relations of varying intensity among subgroup leaders and among other group members. This creates an interlocking network centered on the leader, as represented in Figure 7.2. A subgroup leader mediates between subgroup members and the group leader. In general, one's hierarchical place in the group is fixed or deeply affected by time of entry. In a sense, then, the building block of society is not the family or the individual, but the small group of people bound together by feelings of quasi-familial loyalty and obligation to each other and fealty to a common leader.

Loyalty is another principal ingredient in Japan's social cement, and in this emphasis we find one of the most striking contrasts between Japanese and U.S. values. The social system of the United States, for a number of reasons, seems to put

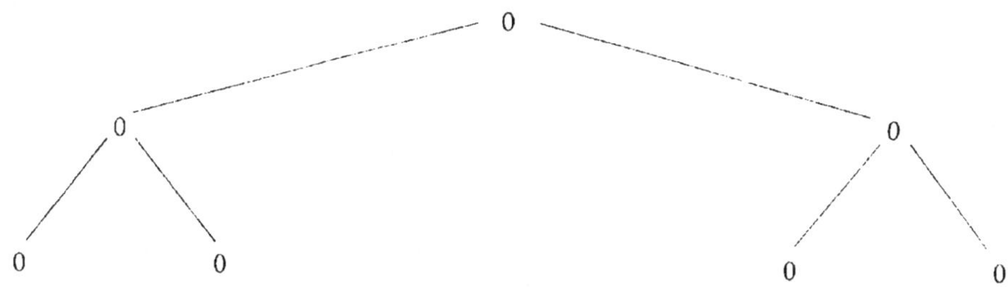

Figure 7.1 Japan's Vertical Social Structure

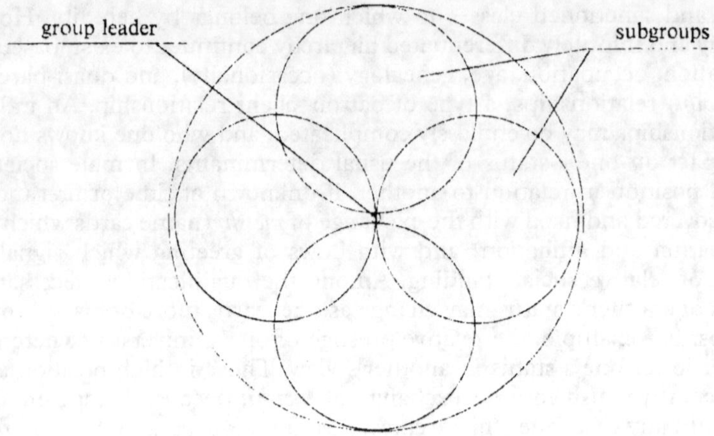

Figure 7.2 Subgroup Linkages within the Group

comparatively little store on deep and persistent loyalty, whether in the family, the political world, or the economic arena. Nagao Ryūichi suggests that a better understanding of the enigmatic urge to absolute loyalty—not simply to loyalty—may be a key to understanding the history of Japan's sociopolitical ideas.[21] History, literature, and present sociopolitical life abound with tales of loyalty and betrayal in high and low places. The frequency of betrayal as a theme in literature and as a problem in group life, and the seriousness with which it is taken, should be understood not to imply that loyalty is not really an intensely operative social value, but that disloyalty and betrayal are among the ugliest names of evil in a persuasive universalist ethic, as understood by the Japanese. Preoccupation with betrayal indicates deep appreciation of its opposite, loyalty, as essential to personal integrity and to harmonious group life.

The pull of nuclear family loyalties today is quite strong, and increasingly so, but it can be overpowered in some cases by the tug of the occupational group, especially among white-collar workers.[22] Even where family concerns are in fact primary to the individual, he will normally honor in practice the quasi-feudal social structure and mores for career reasons.

The present styles of loyalty often seem to continue in analogous form patterns of feudal times, when duty to feudal lord or village could come before duty to family and feudal lords formed and broke alliances, as well as patterns of earlier times when the group and its leader partook of a sacred public nature.[23] In fact, Japan might be called a "feudal democracy." The term "feudal" here is meant not in an ideological or pejorative sense, as often in Japanese usage, nor in a European sense, but as descriptive of the historically accumulated and intersecting aspects of Japan's present organizational ethos, groupism, feudalism, and constitutional democracy.[24] What "democracy" and "freedom" mean in this context differs significantly from what they mean in the freedom culture of the United States.

According to Doi Takeo, the comparative psychiatrist, a major motive force that permeates this group-oriented and "vertical society" (*tate shakai*) is *amae* (dependency; verb form, *amaeru*), a powerful drive for dependency.[25] *Amae* has been described as an individual's need and desire, conscious or unconscious, to be passively loved, to be sheltered, cared for, and indulged, to be able "to depend and presume on another's love," "to remain warmly wrapped in" an optimistically conceived environment. Or, as George De Vos says, it is "a passive induction of nurturance towards one's self from others" which "cannot be expressed in an active intransitive verb in Western languages. . . . To *amaeru* is to produce passively the state of being loved and indulged or appreciated by another, a form of emotional *judo*."[26] To some extent, this type of orientation, so characteristic of mother–child relationships from early infancy in most cultures, is often in Japan "prolonged into and diffused throughout adult life," shaping perspectives on adult relationships much more than in the West.[27] Maturity does not imply personal independence in Japan, but appropriate patterns of reciprocal dependence. Robert Ozaki captures the contrast rather well:

> The voice of Western Culture would then suggest: "Be independent. Be an adult. Do your own thing and go your own way." Japanese culture says it differently: "Search for the ideal. The ideal may be rare, but the rare is not impossible. Find your group and belong to it. You and the group will rise or sink together. Without belonging, you will be lost in the wilderness. Apart from dependence there is no human happiness. Contentment through independence is a delusion." . . . As a Japanese looks around, he realizes that he has no other alternative.[28]

The traditional understanding of "freedom" (*jiyū*) can best be seen in the context of reciprocal duties, loyalty, and *amae*. "Freedom" meant the freedom to *amaeru*, "to behave as one pleases, without considering others."[29] A duty consciousness is not intrinsic to the *amae* mentality but can derive from a benevolent sense of duty to indulge the *amae* of others. It generates the feelings that a person must fulfill duties to others in one's circle, if he is to be indulged by them, and that cold formalism is generally more appropriate with strangers (*tanin*).[30]

The individual does not transcend the group; rather, group life powerfully raises the self from a sense of relative emptiness to greater felt significance. This sense may be strongest when the individual is swept up in collective actions, most visibly in political demonstrations.[31] The force of general philosophical or religious principle is less obvious. The individual prefers a context enabling uninhibited presumption on others but is disciplined in carrying out duties to the in-group and the family. Both are often referred to by the term "*uchi*" ("my home," "our house," but derivatively "my company," "my group," "my organization," or simply "we"). In this social context, the insider often opts for individual anonymity and may show sensitive shyness when dealing with strangers or "outsiders" (*autosaidah*). Thus, there exists a patterned stress on self-restraint, ritual politeness, and rigorous propriety in expressing oneself as an individual before outsiders, particularly about matters of in-group life.

The status of freedom of expression in Japan depends primarily on relationships of the individual with his/her in-group and with the key quasi-parental (*oyabun*) and parental figures in his/her life, not on relations with government, the law, or the community at large, and on the relationships of the in-group with the community, not with government or the law. The individual is oriented more towards expressing himself *in* and *with* the group as an individual in the larger community. The individual's right to free expression may face its most pervasive restraints in pressures to conform with the group which amount to psychological coercion. Such sociopsychological force is legitimized by unwritten rules supporting *amae*, loyalty, and reciprocal duty consciousness, and opposing the "egotism" of excessive self-assertion. Still, such force is rarely attended by governmental, legal, or theoretical sanctions, or by physical coercion.

A few contrasts with right consciousness in the United States, which is also an influence on present-day Japan, will further clarify Japanese emphases. Americans, and some other peoples, stress the autonomy of the individual and the propriety or legitimacy of maximum self-assertion consonant with law and the autonomy of others.[32] The stress is upon individual rights, the imperative "to stand up for one's rights," the right casually to join or to leave an association or even a job, the right not to belong or conform. Freedom from the encroachments of other persons or government is considered essential for self-realization.

The notion of duty is often seen in a somewhat negative way in the United States. To do something because it is a duty may be thought to imply that the action is not done freely, but because one "has to." To act with questionable freedom is in many minds to act with less authenticity as a person. Freedom and spontaneity, not just in expression under law, but in general, have been raised to a remarkably high level as U.S. ideals, rightly or wrongly. Spontaneous expression is often confused with freedom as a value. Duties are carefully curtailed and defined lest they interfere with the right to fulfillment through individual freedom and independence. Among other values less honored in the United States than in Japan are long-term and deep loyalty and persistence, anonymity, harmony and interdependence within the group, self-discipline, silence, nonverbal or roundabout expression, intuitive communication, decision by consensus rather than by majority will,[33] and settlement of disputes by conciliation and unobtrusive mutual compromise. De-emphasis on human interdependence by excessive individualism has been as detrimental to freedom and reasonable order in communities as extreme self-restraint, conformism, or group dependency.

In contrast with the United States is the major role of conciliation. Amicable settlement of disputes is of course a central imperative of most societies, and particularly of religions in the United States,[34] but the interplay of modern forms of individualism with the formal U.S. legal system has encouraged frontal conflict in social life and litigation in court more often than a drive for harmony through mediated compromise. As Marc Galanter notes, the forms of conflict and its settlement that are sanctioned by a polity's legal system tend to become reflected over time in the ways people think about, act out, and settle disputes in that society.[35] Law and legal procedures affect social practice; not just the reverse is true. Disputes in Japan from the Tokugawa period to the present have been settled by voluntary or compulsory conciliation (mediation) more commonly than by arbitration or adjudication.[36]

The aim of the conciliator, traditionally a local community status-bearer, has been to involve disputants in a quasi-group relationship of harmony, as a means of restoring at least external, and ideally emotive, interpersonal harmony between the parties. Both sides are expected, *a priori*, to be willing to compromise. Most Japanese still seem to prefer conciliation or informal adjustment to litigation or arbitration, even when the court system becomes involved.[37] It may be that black-and-white court judgments—ending confrontations and backed by official force—carry less moral authority than the results of informal discussions and leave a more bitter aftertaste. This preference for what might be termed "conciliable rights" (i.e. rights effectively safeguarded in disputes by means of a conciliation process) very often meshes with a modern legal consciousness; parties in civil cases generally expect that official mediation will result in a solution conforming with objective facts and reflecting their legal rights.[38] Though traditionally common, compulsory conciliation is no longer legal; but social pressures encourage compliance with mediated dispute solutions.

III. Some Tensions Among Values Affecting Freedom of Expression

Western ideas of freedom have not quickly and easily joined with Japanese notions of duty, *amae*, and freedom.[39] The elements of duty and right, freedom and restraint, independence and *amae*, conciliation and litigation, the individual and the group, and group welfare and the public welfare all collide with each other in daily life. As noted above, "freedom" (*jiyū*) traditionally carried a pejorative implication of selfish willfulness, because it meant the freedom to *amaeru*; it did not mean freedom from *amae*. So "freedom" carried critical overtones, unlike the notion of freedom in the West; but it was not simply the equivalent of "license." Today, the word *jiyū* ambiguously partakes of both its positive Western sense and its negative traditional Japanese meaning. Doi Takeo contends:

> In the West . . . people have always looked down on the type of emotional dependency that corresponds to *amae*. . . . [T]he spirit of *amae* and freedom of the individual would seem to be contradictory with each other. If this is true, then contact with Western-style freedom must have been a considerable shock for the Japanese following the Meiji Restoration . . . [and] since Meiji times the Japanese have been obsessed by a conflict concerning freedom clearly illustrated in modern Japanese literature.[40]

The word "right" (*kenri*) equally carries cross-currents of meaning. The term *kenri* was created and first employed in Japanese constitutional and legal thought in the mid-nineteenth century to express legal concepts brought in from Dutch, French, and other Western law.[41] Previous uses of *ken* (the first ideograph in the compound *kenri*) implied might or power without a connotation of moral or legal claim. Although *ken* is now also commonly employed in such terms as *jinken* (human rights) and *jiyūken* (civil liberties), the term *kenri*, used to mean a right in constitutional law, took on full strength only in recent decades, and is unrelated to the traditional usage of *jiyū*.

A. Consensus, authority, and free speech

An individual rights consciousness is vigorously operative in Japanese democracy, especially in the sense of a reciprocal duty consciousness and an awareness of the right to expect something from superiors and peers—for example, the right to speak. An awareness of individual legal rights under the Constitution seems to be growing stronger. Nevertheless, very often the group's sense of its rights *vis-à-vis* the individual and society are incomparably stronger. As Nakane Chie explains, the group expects its sense of social hierarchy to be honored:

> At any meeting or gathering ... [t]he frequency with which a man offers an opinion, together with the order in which those present speak at the beginning of the meeting, are ... indications of rank. A man who sits near the entrance may speak scarcely at all throughout the meeting. In a very delicate situation those of an inferior status would not dare to laugh earlier or louder than their superiors, and most certainly would never offer opinions contradictory to those of their superiors. To this extent, ranking order not only regulates social behavior but also curbs the open expression of thought. . . .[42]

In a less general context, Nakane opines:

> Japanese scholars . . . never escape from the consciousness of the distinction between *sempai* and *kōhai* (i.e. based on who graduated first from university). It is very difficult for a Japanese scholar to disagree openly with a statement of his *sempai*. Even a trifling opposition to or disagreement with the *sempai*'s views involves an elaborate and roundabout drill. First, the objector should introduce a long appraisal of . . . the *sempai*'s work in question, using extremely honorific terms, and then gradually present his own opinion or opposition in a style which will give the impression that his opposition is insignificant, being afraid to hurt his *sempai*'s feelings. The ranking of *sempai* and *kōhai* thus stifles the free expression of individual thought. . . .
>
> Even if there are others who share a negative opinion, it is unlikely that they will join together and openly express it, for the fear that this might jeopardize their position as desirable group members. Indeed, it often happens that, once a man has been labelled as one whose opinions run contrary to those of the group, he will find himself opposed on any issue and ruled out by majority opinion. . . .[43]

Although deference is commonly paid to the group leader's opinions and feelings in decision-making (for example, in companies, unions, university departments, and ministries), the "good leader" is not arrogantly "one-sided," authoritarian, or even obviously strong by comparative standards. Rather, his/her very authority may rest more on capacities to listen, encourage consensus and harmony, mediate disputes, put a final stamp of authoritative approval on the group's felt-needs for action, and otherwise satisfy the psychic and material needs of members.

Less store is placed on public proclamation than on privately transmitted messages. The prime minister, for example, is not one of the world's strong and eloquent executives, and requires much support from his own group and other faction leaders within the ruling Liberal Democratic Party to maintain his position. (Arguably, Prime Minister Kishi was driven from office by his own party in 1960 for unpopular arrogance during the public debates on the U.S.–Japan Security Treaty; while Prime Minister Suzuki Zenkō retained an unusually high level of popularity in 1981 because of his notably quiet, conciliatory style of leadership.) This restraint on executive power by the group seems part of the unwritten constitution and operates in the private sector as well.

The leader's influence is essential to group cohesion, but he is not equally important in determining the views of the group.[44] Commonly, the leader is obliged to consult the views and sentiments of other group members, those both high and low on the hierarchical ladder. Democratic freedom of speech is "the freedom of the lower or the underprivileged to speak out. . . ."[45] Nakane Chie explains:

> What the Japanese mean by "democracy" is a system that should take the side of, or give consideration to, the weaker or lower; in practice, any decision should be made on the basis of a consensus which includes those located lower in the hierarchy. Such a consensus—reached by what might be termed maximum consultation—might seem a by-product of the post-war "democratic" age; yet it is not at all new to the Japanese, representing as it does, a very basic style of the traditional group operation. The exercise of power or unilateral decision-making on the part of the top sector of a group co-existed with unanimous decision-making on the basis of maximum consultation. . . .[46]

The group as such has much more authority than its leader in many circumstances. On the other hand, the style and views of an effective leader can notably affect the mood, viewpoints, and actions of the group as a whole. In large groups, the leadership often has limited time for consultation and for reasons of efficiency falls back on its authority and on the use of the "undemocratic" principle of majority vote; whatever his motivation, the skilled leader evidences a preference for a more "democratic" approach. In some public and private contexts, there is much rather formal speech-making, with little comment or discursive consultation in decision formation. Although quite influential in familial decision-making, women are generally excluded from significant roles in the decision-making of élite in-groups in such sectors as government, higher education, and business. But "democracy" in decision-making processes means active, multilateral consultation within the group, at whatever level of society, in an atmosphere in which deference does not substantively interfere with reasonable openness, and where each member feels he is taken seriously by the leader and the group.

The qualities deemed desirable in a leader do not appear to have changed significantly in recent decades. Every five years since 1953, the Institute of Statistical Mathematics in Tokyo has conducted survey studies of Japanese national character; the results of these and other studies suggest a continuing preference for traditional values, albeit with modifications.[47] The results of a 1978 study of the attitudes of 1,500 Tokyo voters also illustrate this point that the qualities deemed desirable in a leader do not appear to have changed much.[48] The single most important determinant of political choice (the key factor to 29 percent of voters, and a major factor to 53 percent) was the image of the candidate as expressing and supporting traditional values and what might be termed "the good Japanese way" of doing things.

However, a striking contrast to this preference for traditionalism in the personal style of candidates is found in the analysis of the positive elements in voter images of liberalism, capitalism, socialism, and communism: the most likely to succeed were candidates, ideologies, and parties presenting an image of flexibility, modernity, conservatism, and economic egalitarianism somehow combined. Ideology and party preference by themselves were relatively unimportant. Forty-two percent of the voters studied considered themselves entirely unaffected by political ideologies such as the four above; only 1 percent considered the pairing of socialism-communism preferable in general to liberalism-capitalism, but only 10 percent rate the latter pairing preferable to the former. For maximum legitimacy, a leader must combine great respect for traditional values and modes of human interaction with concern for constitutional freedoms and economic equality.

In public life, subservience, passivity, or "internalized dissidence" seems more common than open, penetrating criticism of leaders or persistent pursuit of policy change. "Expressive protest," whether by peaceful demonstration, by riot, by press campaign, or by assassination or suicide, may depend less on a lively sense of natural or legal right than on *amae* assumptions or a hope to shame superiors into the desired action.[49] As Koschmann says:

> Rebellion breeds isolation from the social and political hierarchy, which remains the primary source of wisdom and paternal care. Therefore, inherent in the system are the preservation of harmony through repression of conflict and the failure of a universal concept of individual rights to fully replace power as the central principle of hierarchical relationships.[50]

To dissent on grounds of honest disagreement from a group consensus once reached—a consensus of, say, 70 percent—is to fail to understand the higher moral values of group harmony and loyalty. One may of course retain his private views (though the traditional ideal was to conform not only with law but with intent and thought), but they must not interfere with group action and should not be overemphasized. A longing to be a nonconformist or independent, an *ippiki ōkami* (lone wolf), is common, but the fear of offending the group is much stronger. A Japanese saying has it that "the nail which sticks out is hit." Nakane writes: "An individual, however able, however strong his personality and high his status, has to compromise with his group's decision, which then develops a life of its own."[51] In practice, majoritarian Americans also like a consensus or a cooperative minority when a task is to be done but stress more the right to maintain one's opinion, at least in principle.

The consequences of serious deviation from loyalty to consensus, by word or action, can be painful ostracism. Being cut off from the group in a society where *amae* and belonging are so central can be both shameful and frightening. The painful shock of ostracism can be better understood by noting how carefully "lonely" (*sabishii*) states of separation from the group are avoided, at times with a sense of near metaphysical dread. Loneliness is seen as evil, yet as the condition of humans as part of nature. This attitude is shown when a beautiful moon or a flight of geese going South is referred to as "*sabishii*" and when a great deal is made of departures. There is strong peripheral awareness that the present is both precious and poignantly fleeting, in human relations as in nature. The pain of ostracism and loneliness in Japan may be less intense in the United States, where group relationships are less dense and where most humans see themselves as somehow separate from nature, but with a benevolent personal God behind nature. In Japan, the group may serve as the principal object of "religious devotion" in a Western sense.

Be that as it may, the forms and contexts of ostracism in Japan are many.[52] The phenomenon cuts across ideological, generational, occupational, and urban-rural lines. In the newspaper industry, a newsman may have to be transferred to a new assignment if his reporting offends the consensus of his peers on the same beat from ostensibly competing newspapers. In schools, a student group may beat and ostracize a member who violates consensus on a minor matter. In the countryside, a village may harass an entire family, if a disloyal member cooperates with authorities in criminal investigation of one of its own, or otherwise offends community sensibilities (*mura hachibu*).[53]

Pathological examples are useful to bring out tendencies in sharp relief, as some incidents occurring in the 1970s illustrate: in a number of cases, students in school athletic clubs (there are no "teams") quite severely beat, and hospitalized or killed, a member who wished to leave the club or to quit before the end of a practice; the extremist Rengō Sekigun (United Red Army) killed a number of its own members for slight alleged deviations in loyalty or ideology. In Japan, one does not casually join or leave a group, or deviate from its position; this colors one's perception and exercise of the freedoms of association and assembly, as well as other aspects of free speech.

B. "Individualistic groupism" and individual expression

The stress on conformity encourages the individual to identify his sense of personal rights with the rights of his group. As Western ideas of individualism and litigiousness have become influential in Japan, they may have combined with the tendency to identify deeply with the group so as to encourage an exaggerated sense of group rights. Emphasis after 1945 on the individual and on his/her rights seems to have heightened a sense of the "group's rights" as much as consciousness of individual rights, though the group as such enjoys no technical legal right.

The group as a whole tends to be acutely conscious and assertive of its rights as a collectivity in dealing with "outsiders" (*autosaidah*), that is, with all individuals, groups, and agencies that are outside the in-group. "Outsiders" are normally to be met with indifference or, especially if they are in the same occupation or sphere of activity, with intense competition.[54] The "soft" approach of in-group life gives way to "hard" and rigid posture towards other groups.[55] A sense of radical separateness from outsiders and secrecy about the quasi-familial private life of the in-group are also common; candor and easy give-and-take with nonmembers do not often come naturally, but formal propriety is generally respected.

This collective mind-set can be called "individualistic groupism," an analogy with a myopic sort of individualistic right-consciousness found more often in some other countries, such as France, India, and the United States, than in Japan. The group unit tends to be less aware of legitimate restraints on its rights based on outsiders' rights. There is much less conciliation, harmony, conformity, and duty consciousness between groups than within groups. Important exceptions exist insofar as leaders of a cluster of groups are occasionally able to constitute a secondary group themselves (e.g. faction leaders of political parties, unions, industries, or student groups).[56] The group tends to be cliquish, exclusive, and closed rather than open, emphasizing internal cohesion and collective maintenance of the honor, rights, and interests of the group. The group's sense of its rights tends to be limited only by its power, untempered by the strong social awareness displayed within groups and in the politeness of individual relations. "Whereas intragroup conflict is dealt with emotionally, as a threat to familistic unity, intergroup conflict goes unregulated due to the general lack of emotional bonds between groups."[57] This individualistic element in group rights consciousness may in some cases add virulent intensity to intergroup conflict and ideological oppositions in labor, education, business, government, and politics.

One dramatic example of individualistic groupism in the decade following World War II was *seisan kanri* (production control), illegal worker seizure and operation of a place of business, and ejection of management and owners.[58] More generally, a former director of the Civil Liberties Bureau once noted:

> [A]mong the intelligentsia and the classes which provide leaders there is a tendency for violation of human rights . . . to be used as a stick with which to beat one's adversary or the organization to which he belongs. One example of this is, as everyone knows, where in labor disputes, etc., one union fights another . . . whereas one's adversary's violations of human rights are listed with neurotic precision, one is almost indifferent to the violation of human rights by one's own union. . . . We have a mixture of undue sensitivity to human rights on the one hand and complete indifference on the other.[59]

This indifference, or even hostility, to the rights of others may have softened somewhat over the postwar decades, with prosperity and the impact of the constitutional revolution; but harsh confrontations continue to recur. Such patterns have been most striking since the late 1960s in "gang warfare" conflicts between radical student factions such as the Kakumaruha (Revolutionary Marxist Faction) and the Chūkakuha (Core Faction), with a cycle of group killings and reprisals.[60] In another arena, during the 1970s tense opposition between schools of thought in psychology burst out in violence in a few cases (e.g. fist fights at an academic conference and seizure by force and prolonged occupation of facilities at Tokyo University).

In many contexts, the individual may be transformed from reticence or silence to exuberant or vehement expression by involvement in a group, as in the laughing and jostling of carrying a portable shrine (*omikoshi*) during a Shintö festival or in the rhythmic chants of students on a political snake dance through Tokyo streets. The individual taken alone does not often tend to assert publicly his/her rights, views, feelings, complaints, petitions, or protest but instead tends to be rather passive and long-suffering, especially *vis-à-vis* social authorities.

Silence, listening, indirection, and understatement are valued in themselves much more than in many Western and non-Western countries; eloquence, directness, and individual assertiveness may be greeted with suspicion, even disdain.[61] What is important is getting along with others and avoiding conflict. Individual powers of verbal communication, particularly oral expression, are not fostered and are not often an index to a person's accomplishment and power.

A few examples will illustrate how parsimonious expression or secrecy are sometimes required of individuals and groups, particularly when dealing with outsiders. At regular meetings of a group of leading world bankers in the 1970s, the Japanese representative—a person fluent in English, the language used by all present—was typically the only completely silent partner to substantive discussions. Analogously, at a binational academic seminar on problems in U.S.–Japan relations, after various possible positions on a particular problem were elaborated by the other side, the Japanese group sat silent for minutes. Finally, one stood up, tersely indicated one alternative, and said "*That* is the correct position." He then sat down and no further Japanese comment was forthcoming. Another type of incident shows the sensitivity that may be required of a group member in dealing with outsiders: A company employee was severely reprimanded by colleagues and superiors because, during telephone pleasantries with an acquaintance in another company, he recounted a public fact of international business, the telling of which could have no negative effect on his company's interests. Free-wheeling and open exchanges involving one or more outsiders do occur, but rarely.

Another dimension of the universe of expression is the relationship between the surface meaning and the substantive meaning of expression, between the wrappings and the content. Japan may be termed a "wrappings culture," in which packaging and politenesses are highly refined arts but where the contents are often ambiguous. Perhaps no other people places more emphasis in everyday life on beauty in "wrappings," for products both simple and elegant. As with the polite gradations and overtones of Japanese language and bowing, there is intrinsic charm and meaning to exquisite wrappings and other artistic externals, not mere frivolous formality or shallow aestheticism. Unwrapping the intent of expression can be a delicate or difficult task, since elliptic and intuitive communication and pleasant ambiguity have their merits and uses, and are valued.

Chalmers Johnson, in analyzing the distinction between "*omote*" (explicit, surface, or what is publicly manifest) and "*ura*" (implicit meaning or what is behind what is said), writes of political speech at Diet hearings:

> All cabinet members and officials have *sōtei mondōshū* (hypothetical question-and-answer booklets) in front of them, prepared by the ministries, and except for an occasional *bakudan shitsumon* (bomb question), everything is prearranged. Bureaucrats refer to Diet members as *sensei* [teacher].
>
> Masters of the political *omote* world can speak at these hearings politely and at length without saying anything of substance. Shiina Etsusaburō . . . was such a master. . . . [W]hen he was MITI minister he filled Diet records with his correct but only rarely substantive remarks. . . . As a young section chief . . . Shiina had to *hankō* (stamp a seal) daily on numerous documents that flowed across his desk . . . he did the job "looking at knotholes in the ceiling, using as little physical strength and intelligence as possible. . . ." [T]he language of bureaucratic *omote*, even of *menjū-fukuhai* (follow orders to a superior's face, reverse them in the belly), is among the hardest political Japanese to read—or to translate.[62]

The beautiful wrappings are essential to the legitimacy of the contents, but the statements leading to élite decisions are commonly made elsewhere in small group contexts.

Outside of government, the ordinarily quiet individual often becomes aggressively assertive and vocal, or "individualistic," as a member of an activist group, with an organized support group (as in court cases) or when the interests of his group seem threatened or otherwise at stake. Thus, the term "individualistic groupism" can be applied both to the group as a whole and to the individual as a member of the group. Without this very strong group sense of a right to express grievances, views, and interests, Japan's system of freedom of expression might well be but weakly supported by deeply imprinted patterns of social value and organization. In any case, the entire context of public and private infringement and protection of human rights would be quite different. As Thomas Blakemore observed in 1946: "A more fundamental and difficult problem than that of legislative reform is the creation of groups militantly anxious to maintain liberties not merely for themselves but for the public in general."[63]

Among the manifestations of individualistic groupism most visible to the world have been the thousands of demonstrations, enormous to small in size, by workers and students since the 1950s[64] and the numerous demonstrations by effective anti-pollution groups in various parts of Japan, especially since 1970.[65] Full of color and emotion, they have generally been quite well organized and nonviolent by comparative standards. The mass media have played a support role in many cases by quickly disseminating awareness of group actions, concerns, and opinions around the nation, and thus advancing debates towards consensus. Assertive groupism, as later chapters indicate, appears in many other contexts of daily life as well. Unions, women's groups, student groups, offices within ministries and businesses, villages, political groups, artists, educational and medical groups, and other types of face-to-face groups manifest with some consistency variations of the above patterns in their intragroup and intergroup behavior.

C *"Inclusionary groupism"*

A final feature of groupism to be discussed, which also affects freedom of expression, is the capacity of normally conflicting in-groups in a given sector of activity to combine with each other in an expanded group framework for limited goals and for a limited time. Such combinations occur under circumstances of perceived common external threat to or special common benefit with the larger grouping. In this process, the in-group's boundaries expand outward for a time, then contract inward. Factions within a political party or union and subdivisions within a business firm, a ministry, a university, or a mass media company compete among themselves with considerable intensity under ordinary circumstances; but unanimous loyal support of the larger unit is normally expected in dealings with "outsiders," that is, those external to the temporary larger cluster of groups. The shifting demarcation of group parameters, "outward" to include all the units within a single industry, for example, and "back inward" to the small face-to-face group of company workers, depends on concrete circumstances and temporary alliance between the quasi-feudal leaders of different groups. When an overarching consensus emerges that a cluster of groups should cooperate on an issue or project, cohesive and effective action soon follows. The process of group coalescence and later dissolution into constituent groups sometimes appears to take place with remarkable suddenness, but a complex web of personal, mass media, and organizational linkages among élites in Tokyo and other key urban areas is always in place for activation as need arises. This system of overlapping relationship facilitates communication among relevant leaders when necessary for cooperation in a given sector, so that relevant groups can sometimes be brought quickly to the "critical mass" of consensual action.

The national mass media system—newspapers, TV, radio, and magazines—has unsurpassed resources and density of coverage. It also regularly presents to the public, in print and on the air, the guidance of élite views on national issues in *zadankai* (roundtable discussions). Most important in the present context is that the life of the more inclusive in-group, however short its existence may be in a given case, takes on much of the intensity and cohesion of a small in-group, and feelings of mutual indifference or even stark competition give way to effective cooperation and stress on consensus. One example occurred in 1969 when a court ordered some television stations to present previously broadcast TV film for use as evidence in a case alleging abuse of police authority during a student demonstration.[66] No "newsman's privilege" issue was involved, but the order triggered instant media unanimity in opposition. Fair debate of the problem in the media was very rare till well after Supreme Court resolution of the issue months later. The face-to-face in-group serves as the model in the dynamics of this inclusionary groupism, which counterbalances individualistic groupism in special circumstances of challenge.[67] On the other hand, members of a trade union or other group may at times be too loyal to their own company to join forces with other unions even on issues of common worker interest.[68]

The capacity to transcend the in-group for the benefit of the "larger we" and to transfer the intense and dutiful life of the in-group to the quality of participation in the larger group is not limited to special interest sectors. The process of combining into ever-larger pyramids can extend all the way upward and outward until the primary tight-knit in-group is the Japanese people as a whole, as a national, quasi-familial group facing the world of "outsiders." Put otherwise, all the face-to-face groups at the base of the social pyramid give firm foundation for impressive collective strength and cohesion all the way to the top of the national pyramid. However, this can happen only when élites see it as necessary in order to deal with international relations or severe internal problems. More often than not, the nation coalesces in this manner after drawn-out, multilateral consultations; it does not result from sudden and authoritarian government action.

These abilities to identify individual with group interests and group interests with national interest, and to act as a unified state (*kokka*, literally "national family"), have been demonstrated often in modern Japanese history. A colorful custom of daily life may symbolize this familial togetherness. Every weekday afternoon, music is played on the radio and over loudspeakers at many points around the country at the same time. In thousands of offices work is stopped and virtually everyone joins unself-consciously in doing calesthenics to the music. It is a marvel to behold from across the street thousands of employees in hundreds of offices through the glass windows of a many-storied ministry building, all bending and swinging in time. A few other examples[69] are: the dynamic preparation processes for Japan's Summer (1964) and Winter (1972) Olympics and for "Expo '70," the Osaka World Exposition; the striking progress made in combating air and water pollution once consensus was reached in 1970 on the serious need for action;[70] and Japan's effective adjustment when the 1973 Organization of Petroleum Exporting Countries (OPEC) "oil shock" threatened energy supplies. This "national groupism" seems to give special intensity to Japan's nationalism. At the same time, it may encourage the exaggerated sense of separateness from, and disinterest in communicating with, the "outsiders" of foreign countries.[71]

On analogy with the Tokugawa feudal system, with much multilateral consultation, the leaders of major and minor "feudal domains" today have the ability, through hierarchical networks of *oyabun–kobun* relationships among themselves and their followers, to form useful temporary alliances on behalf of clusters of in-groups or even the nation. Thus, massive attention to intragroup and intergroup consultation can build temporary cooperation in the larger community, but the normal pattern is intense loyalty to the leader and small in-group, and communication blockage with outsiders.[72]

IV. A SCALE OF RETICENCE AND FREEDOM

Japanese attitudes and problems concerning expression itself and free speech rights can be summarized in terms of the different degrees of reticence (*enryo*) they tend to feel in different types of context about expressing themselves in a manner at variance with the views or feelings of the target of expression. The nature of the variance may be expression of a new or different idea, or opposition, dissent, or protest against an idea, decision, situation, or action. On a rough scale of reticence and freedom, one can chart at least seven levels:

1 Inhibition is greatest about oral expression of opposition or dissent as an individual to an authoritative superior. The superior may be in a public or private position, and in a one-to-one or in-group circumstance. Most inhibited seems expression of opposition to the leader of one's group in a group meeting after the group has achieved a consensus on an issue.
2 Difficult, but a little less so, seems written dissent or protest as an individual in circumstances akin to those mentioned above. (In some contexts, Japanese tend to be more easily communicative when writing than when speaking, witness biographical and epistolary style; but in decision-making, oral consultations seem preferred.)
3 Less inhibited is a group's oral dissent or protest against its own leader.
4 Still less reticent is the expression, oral or written, of a group as such when pursuing its interests and communicating its views to "outsider" authorities or agencies viewed as groups.
5 Next down the scale of reticence is expression directed at an individual outsider who is socially higher than the group, but not in a position of operative authority over the group.
6 Less inhibited yet is group expression *vis-à-vis* a group, or an individual as a member of a group, which is on the same level as, or on a lower level of the social hierarchy than the in-group. In such contexts, *oyabun–kobun* and *amae* relationships, as well as other social restraints, tend to be weakly operative.
7 Least reticent is in-group expression directed at an individual member of the group who does not occupy a position of social authority in the group.

In light of the patterns of social value, structure, and process discussed in this chapter, the following are among the aspects and contexts of freedom of expression in Japan which seem to deserve emphasis:

1 The freedom of the individual to dissent during the consensus-building process within his/her group.
2 The freedom of the individual (often with group support) and of the group as such to protest against perceived injustice and to petition private or public authorities for benevolent, paternal response to collective concerns.

3 The freedom of both primary groups and more inclusive clusters of groups—in both the public and private sectors—to compete in public for general public support on issues affecting the larger local or national community.
4 The freedom of stable association.
5 The freedom to assemble and demonstrate peaceably but exuberantly, even vociferously.
6 The freedom to publish, to broadcast, to exhibit film and pictures, and to entertain, based on the rights to know, enjoy, and communicate.
7 The freedom of religious, academic, and political in-groups to maintain and express their beliefs, convictions, and ideas with impunity and without discrimination.
8 The freedom to bring individual rights problems to such publicly sponsored agents as Civil Liberties Commissioners, Local Administrative Counselors, and the courts.[73]

V. THE EXPANSION OF THE DUTY OF TOLERANCE

The Japanese structural system tends to protect the freedom of expression of groups better than that of individuals. The problem for individual freedom presented by the group is different in degrees, not in kind, from that in the United States. The problem is balancing the rights of individuals or, as in Japan, harmonizing the rights of all involved in a group situation. In the United States, a greater emphasis on the social context of freedom is as much needed as stress on individuality in Japan.

Analytically, in addition to general impunity for peaceful expression and the more specific sociolegal issues referred to in later chapters, two questions surround individual freedom of expression in Japan. The first is whether the individual's right to self-determination in preconsensus discussion is honored and whether diversity is tolerated in the content of the discussion. Allowances should be made for the fact that in many instances the verbal expression of opinion may seem less crucial to meaningful participation for the Japanese than for the American. Moreover, within the group, an idea for policy or action, to have full legitimacy, must not be overtly recognized in most cases as arising from a single individual's mind; it must rather be seen as emerging into effective existence from the dynamic interplay of communications among group members about the topic. The second problem is whether variance from the group's will, such as postconsensus dissent, is punished without persuasive reason. For example, a person might be temporarily or permanently ostracized not because his dissent from the group has had any negative effect on the group, but simply for the act of dissent itself. This confers upon the act of the group an unreasonable degree of intrinsic sacredness.

A call for more individualism of a Western or other sort does not seem helpful and could be ecologically destructive of social characteristics healthily supporting constitutional democracy and national identity. Rather, in a dialog situation, sensitivity to the requirements of respectful treatment of the individual within the group framework of reciprocal duties seems an appropriate emphasis. Deepened responsiveness to the value of the person as such does not imply abrogation of stable interdependence in a social world characterized by groupism. It does imply some expansion of duty consciousness beyond the particularistic confines of any group context to encompass some awareness of duty to Everyman.

Such expanded consciousness implies recognition of a duty to be tolerant of the right of an individual or of another group to its self-determination regarding expression, and it may imply a system of diffuse, reciprocal duties that is less demanding. Responsiveness to substantial demands on time, energy, and resources is expected by the Japanese, in what they term their "wet" (close and emotional) human relations. These contrast sharply, in the Japanese perception, with the "dry" (casual and less emotional and binding) relations of people in the United States.

In many cases, the demands upon the individual implied by the Japanese model of responsive relationships are so great that they can be engaged in with only a very limited number of people, lest the burdens on total resources become impractical and intolerable. The right of the moral person to refuse to respond to the desires and needs of people in one's circle seems much more limited in Japan than in the United States. Paradoxically, the higher one's location in the feudal pyramid and the greater one's social influence and resources, the more one may be constrained by peers and supplicants seeking filial or other obligational access to paternal favor. These complex burdens of duty often act as healthy and effective restraints on power under the unwritten constitution.

Expansion of duty consciousness may strain binding loyalties or diminish demands in a model relationship, which, in turn, may loosen particularistic group bonds. The loosening of such bonds might facilitate more widely diffused trust, conciliation, and tolerance in interpersonal and intergroup relations. However, this would be so only if such a nexus were seen as natural within the ever-changing system. The rights of others in the community might come into peripheral vision more easily, if the individual person, as such, were not conceived of as a basically incomplete entity, a submerged part of a group or an outsider, but as an end in himself/herself, a social whole and as such the ultimate reference point in public life.

The closed nature of groups sometimes militates against their recognizing and accepting, not only the rights of individual "outsiders," but also the legitimacy of laws and community standards, unless they sense their own participation in consensus-building through representative consultations within the most inclusive group, Japan. Demonstrations and many other modes of group activity outside of election times provide that essential sense of free participation for many in present-day Japan.

Whatever the forms of future rights consciousness and social organization, it is likely that freedom of expression in Japan will be maintained and frequently exercised. Free expression has the support of pluralized group interests and it is reinforced by a powerful mass media system which relishes its freedom. Moreover, it is supported by highly professional police, prosecutorial, and judicial systems; by respected intellectual élites who rationalize freedom in the Japanese milieu through the education system and the mass media; and by leaders and citizens who, at least, vaguely support legally protected freedom and, at most, consider it essential for Japan. The general law of freedom and its official support systems are considered next.

NOTES

1 See Chapter 1, *supra*; and William Spinrad, *Civil Liberties* (Chicago: Quadrangle Books, 1970), pp. 5–26, 292–306.

2 Hugh Borton, "Peasant Uprisings in the Tokugawa Period," in *Imperial Japan, 1800–1945*, ed. John Livingston et al. (New York: Random House, 1973), pp. 49–55.

3 See, for example, J. V. Koschmann, ed., *Authority and the Individual in Japan* (Tokyo University Press, 1978); Wagatsuma Sakae et al., *Nihon seiji saiban shiroku*, 5 vols. (Daiichi Hōki, 1970); Tanaka Jirō et al., eds., *Sengo seiji saiban shiroku*, 5 vols. (Daiichi Hōki, 1980); Irokawa Daikichi, *Meiji no bunka* (Iwanami Shoten, 1970); Roger W. Bowen, *Rebellion and Democracy in Meiji Japan* (Berkely: University of California Press, 1980); Nobutaka Ike, *The Beginnings of Political Democracy in Japan*, (Baltimore: Johns Hopkins University Press, 1950); Shioda Shōbei et al., eds., *Nihon shakai undō jinmei jiten* (Aoki Shoten, 1979); and Irwin Scheiner, *Christian Converts and Social Protest in Meiji Japan* (Berkeley: University of California Press, 1970).

4 Dan F. Henderson, *Conciliation and Japanese Law: Tokugawa and Modern*, Vol. 1 (Seattle: University of Washington Press, 1967), p. 41. Henderson's work is the most important basis for comments on the Tokugawa period. Elsewhere, Henderson touches on Tokugawa rights consciousness:

> Since individual rights have been accorded a new degree of justiciability under the Japanese Constitution (1947), I see Japanese attitudes toward law vastly changed, and changing daily before our very eyes. Indeed, even in Tokugawa village transactions which I have studied, I find the logical and rational qualities of the Japanese nowhere near so underdeveloped as they may appear from general works which illuminate "Japan" relying on poetry, painting, court diaries, and the like. Then as now, the common folk knew their due (right) and how to get it in a logical, rational way, though, of course, at that time there was rare resort to "court."

Review of Y. Noda, *Introduction to Japanese Law (1976)*, in *Monumenta Nipponica*, Vol. 32, No. 4, Winter, 1977, p. 537. See also John H. Wigmore, *Law and Justice in Tokugawa Japan*, 10 vols. (University of Tokyo Press, 1969–80); Dan F. Henderson, *Village "Contracts" in Tokugawa Japan* (Seattle: University of Washington Press, 1975); and Hajime Nakamura, "Basic Features of the Legal, Political, and Economic Thought of Japan," in *The Japanese Mind*, ed. C. A. Moore (Honolulu: East–West Center Press/University of Hawaii Press, 1967), pp. 143–62.

5 Chie Nakane, *Japanese Society* (Berkeley: University of California Press, 1970), p. 147.

6 Henderson, *Conciliation and Japanese Law*, p. 58. The modern term for "reason" (*jōri*) corresponds to *dōri*; ibid., p. 210.

7 Concerning court jurisdiction and the status hierarchy in Tokugawa Japan, see ibid., pp. 63–97.

8 Masataka Sugi, "The Concept of *Ninjō*," in J. Bennett and I. Ishino, *Paternalism in the Japanese Economy* (Minneapolis: University of Minnesota Press, 1963), pp. 267–72.

9 Ibid., p. 269.

10 Koschmann, ed., *Authority and the Individual*, p. 9. The sacred public group in Japan has an analogy with the notion of worship as a public work (*liturgos*, or liturgy) of "the people of God" in Judaeo-Christian tradition, though the modern secular nation-state is at odds with this sensibility in the West.

11 Ibid., p. 10.

12 H. D. Harootunian, "Between Politics and Culture: Authority and the Ambiguities of Intellectual Choice in Imperial Japan," in *Japan in Crisis: Essays on Taisho Democracy*, ed. H. D. Harootunian and Bernard S. Silberman (Princeton: Princeton University Press, 1974).

13 Kamishima Jirō, *Jōmin no seijigaku* (Dentō to Gendaisha, 1972).

14 Hayashi Chikio, "Seiji ishiki no seitai," *Asahi Shinbun*, December 16, 1978, p. 4. Only a small percentage (ca. 20 percent) of Japanese are reported as expressing much trust in politicians compared to tax officials (45 percent), judges, teachers, police, doctors, newspapers, and weather forecasters, among whom the last in the ascending order are the most trusted. *Asahi Shinbun*, October 22, 1978 and January 1, 1979.

15 Joseph Roggendorf, "The Group-Key to the Japanese Mentality," *Japan Times Weekly*, January 3, 1981, p. 3.

16 Concerning the institution of public apology as a remedy in defamation cases, see Chapter 9.

17 Ivan Morris, *The Nobility of Failure* (New York: The New American Library, 1975), pp. xiii–xiv. Morris states:

> In Japan the weaker side acquiesces in those instances, set by group structure, in which negotiation is considered wrong. But even where it is considered correct, the notion of *compromise* will be avoided, because it connotes a surrender of principle . . . compromise . . . is indeed possible but must be interpreted as forced by an impersonal, uncontrollable situation.

Steven A. Hoffmann, "Faction Behavior and Cultural Codes: India and Japan," *Journal of Asian Studies*, February, 1981, p. 247. On the distaste for compromise in labor-management relations, see Chapter 6, below.

18 Nakane says:

> The change from "feudalism" to "democracy" is not structural or organizational; it is rather a change in the direction of the motion of energy within the pipeline [from downward to upward], this energy exerted by the same kinds of people.

Nakane, *Japanese Society*, p. 144. The point is well stated, but understates the modifications of structure and value that have taken place. See also Tadashi Fukutake, *The Japanese Social Structure*, trans. Ronald P. Dore (Tokyo University Press, 1982).

19 Ibid., pp. 42–43. On patron–client relationships elsewhere, see Clark D. Neher, *Politics in Southeast Asia* (Cambridge, Mass: Schenkman Publishing Co., 1979), pp. 89–142; E. Gellner and J. Waterbury, eds., *Patrons and Clients* (New York: Duckworth, 1977); J. Woo and L. Wade, "A Study on Current Korean Political Culture," *Journal of East Asian Affairs*, Vol. 1, No. 1, 1981, p. 118.

20 Nakane, *Japanese Society*, pp. 40–62. Figure 1, above, is an adaptation of Nakane's figure 2, at p. 42. Steven Hoffmann, in contrasting Indian and Japanese factional structures, de-emphasizes the subgroup relations in Japan, as represented in the figures below:

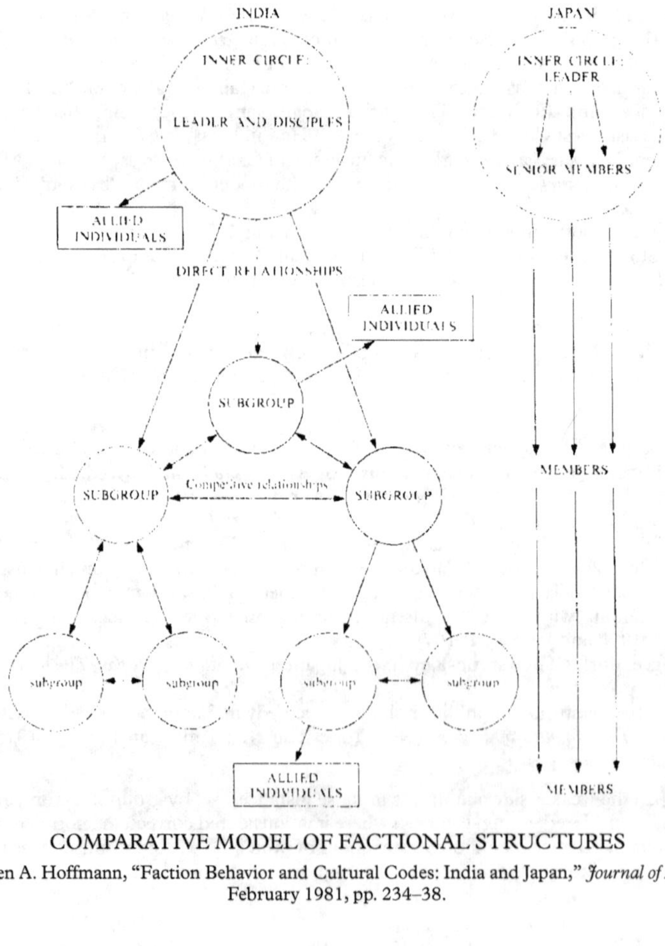

COMPARATIVE MODEL OF FACTIONAL STRUCTURES

Source: Steven A. Hoffmann, "Faction Behavior and Cultural Codes: India and Japan," *Journal of Asian Studies*, February 1981, pp. 234–38.

21 Ryūichi Nagao, in a review of R. Minear, *Japanese Tradition and Western Law* (Cambridge, Mass.: Harvard University Press, 1970) in 5 *Law in Japan* 225 (1972). Comparative study of the meanings and objects of loyalty would help clarify the bases of intercultural disagreements. See also Gino K. Piovesana, *Recent Japanese Philosophical Thought, 1862–1962* (Tokyo: Enderle Bookstore, 1962), for modern philosophical reflections on loyalty and other basic values.

22 Thomas Rohlen, *For Harmony and Strength, Japanese White-Collar Organization in Anthropological Perspective* (Berkeley: University of California Press, 1974).

23 Henderson, *Conciliation and Japanese Law.*

24 The term "feudalism" in Western law

> included a contractual element, the personal homage of a man to his lord, symbolized by the oath of fealty and the reciprocal property right in an enfeoffment of land or other property. The term is often used, especially in Japanese writings, to refer pejoratively to the "old regime."

Dan F. Henderson and James L. Anderson, "Japanese Law: A Profile," in *An Introduction to Japanese Civilization*, ed. A. E. Tiedemann (New York: Columbia University Press, 1974), p. 570. The term "feudal" now applies not so much to the law of Japan's feudal period as to the family and group systems which predated feudalism by centuries and which made Japanese feudalism different from Western feudalism; it can also be used to stress relations among present "feudal domains" of modern society. See Peter Duus, *Feudalism in Japan* (New York: Alfred A. Knopf, 1969). Japanese-style "feudalism," as it functions today, is not necessarily a detriment to freedom.

25 Takeo Doi, *The Anatomy of Dependence*, trans. John Bester (Tokyo: Kodansha International, 1973), his "*Giri-Ninjo*: An Interpretation," in *Aspects of Social Change in Modern Japan*, ed. R. P. Dore (Princeton: Princeton University Press, 1967), p. 327, and his "*Amae*: A Key Concept for Understanding Japanese Personality Structure," in *Japanese Culture*, ed. R. J. Smith and R. K. Beardsley (Chicago: Aldine Publishing Co., 1962), p. 132.

See also R. P. Dore, *City Life in Japan* (Berkeley: University of California Press, 1958); Douglas D. Mitchell, *Amaeru: The Expression of Reciprocal Dependency Needs in Japanese Politics and Law* (Boulder, Colo.: Westview Press, 1976); Y. Scott Matsumoto, *Contemporary Japan: The Individual and the Group, Transactions of the American Philosophical Society*, vol. 50 (Philadelphia, 1960); Nobutaka Ike, *A Theory of Japanese Democracy* (Boulder, Colo.: Westview Press, 1978), pp. 21–24; Robert J. Ozaki, *The Japanese: a Cultural Portrait* (Rutland, Vt.: Charles E. Tuttle Co., 1978), part II, especially, pp. 181–201; David K. Reynolds, *The Quiet Therapies* (Honolulu: University Press of Hawaii, 1980); Kazuko Tsurumi, *Social Change and the Individual: Japan before and after Defeat in World War II* (Princeton: Princeton University Press, 1970); and Ken'ichi Tominaga, "An Empirical View of Social Stratification," *Japan Interpreter*, Vol. 12, No. 1, Winter, 1978, pp. 9–12. Tominaga found "Status inconsistency resulting from democratization of a distribution criteria [sic] for social resources and rewards" (p. 10). That is, high prestige does not imply economic rewards, and vice-versa.

In Japanese see Miyagi Otoya, *Ningensei no shinrigaku* (Iwanami Shoten, 1968), and his *Nihonjin no seikaku* (Asahi Shinbunsha, 1969); Nihon Chiiki Kaihatsu Sentah, ed., *Nihonjin no kachikan* (Shiseidō, 1970); Nihon Bunka Kaigi, ed., *Nihonjin no hōishiki* (Shiseidō, 1973); and Kobayashi Naoki, *Nihonjin no kenpō ishiki* (Daigaku Shuppankai, 1968), especially pp. 15–20.

26 George A. De Vos, *Socialization for Achievement* (Berkeley: University of California Press, 1973), p. 49.

27 Doi, *Anatomy of Dependence*, pp. 8–9.

28 Ozaki, *The Japanese*, p. 183. A somewhat harsh view of this is taken by Yoshiyuki Noda:

> Ben-Dasan, the author of *The Japanese and the Jews*, points out more than once that from the Jewish point of view, no other people are more coddled than the Japanese. I, too, believe that the Japanese as a people have been coddled and take others' good will or good faith too much for granted. This is not without reason. The Japanese are like a group of overprotected kids who have been brought up under greenhouse conditions; though they are highly good-natured, they have not been exposed to the rigors of the real world outside the confines of their island country. They expect to be treated leniently by everybody else, and expect to be so treated by the law as well . . .

In H. Tanaka and M. D. H. Smith, eds., *The Japanese Legal System* (Tokyo University Press, 1976), p. 304.

29 Doi, *Anatomy of Dependence*, pp. 84–87.
30 Ozaki, *The Japanese*, pp. 186–87.
31 Edwin O. Reischauer, *The Japanese* (Rutland, Vt: Charles E. Tuttle Co., 1977), pp. 135–65. On demonstrations, see Chapter 5, below.
32 This emphasis in the United States is sometimes read into Japanese ideals, as when an author judges Japan should develop "the aggressive individualism required for effective citizenship in a democracy." H. Quigley and J. Turner, *The New Japan* (Minneapolis: University of Minnesota Press, 1956), p. 175. See also T. Kawashima and R. Wargo, "Symposium on Law and Morality: East and West," *Philosophy East and West*, October, 1971, pp. 493–511. Although less blatantly than the quotation above, much Japanese and U.S. legal and political writing on Japan continues to mirror individualist premises. For good analyses of related values in nearby Korea, see Vincent Brandt, "Sociocultural Aspects of Political Participation in Rural Korea," *Journal of Korean Studies*, Vol. 1, 1979, p. 205; and Woo and Wade, "A Study."
33 This is not to say that the building of consensus is not a universal sociopolitical problem. For a welcome, though harsh, *caveat* against inadvertent suggestion that consensus-building is peculiarly Japanese, see Robert E. Cole's review of E. F. Vogel, ed., *Modern Japanese Organization and Decision-Making* (Berkeley: University of California Press, 1975), in *Journal of Asian Studies*, May, 1976, pp. 504–6. Vogel notes:

> What democracy and individualism mean to the Mamachi resident is that subordinates now have the right to expect something from their superiors . . . [But] it is still considered crude and selfish for a person to stand up for his rights. Few people in Mamachi consider it a higher morality to be concerned more with one's own benefit than with the welfare of one's group.
>
> One of the characteristics of loyalty as a basic value is that no principle is more important than regard for the other members of one's own intimate group. Hence, there is no fully legitimate basis for standing against the group. Once group consensus is reached, one should abide by the decisions.

Ezra F. Vogel, *Japan's New Middle Class* (Berkeley: University of California Press, 1971), pp. 147–48. Concerning decision-making styles in the Diet, see Hans Baerwald, *Japan's Parliament* (New York: Cambridge University Press, 1974), pp. 106–20, which illustrates the limits of compromise when "sincerity" is at issue.
34 John Owen Haley, "The Myth of the Reluctant Litigant," *Journal of Japanese Studies*, Summer, 1978, pp. 359–90.
35 Marc Galanter, "Justice in Many Rooms: Courts, Private Ordering, and Indigenous Law," *Journal of Legal Pluralism*, No. 19, 1981, p. 1. See also Stuart S. Nagel, ed., "Law and Social Change," *American Behavioral Scientist*, Vol. 13, No. 4, March/April, 1970.
36 Henderson, *Conciliation and Japanese Law*; Takeyoshi Kawashima, "Dispute Resolution in Japan," in *Law in Japan*, ed. A. T. Von Mehren (Cambridge, Mass.: Harvard University Press, 1963), pp. 41–72; and Kawashima T., *Nihonjin no hōishiki* (Iwanami Shoten, 1967).
37 On *wakai* (compromise) and the courts, see Chapter 4.
38 Kahei Rokumoto, "Problems and Methodology of Study of Civil Disputes," trans. Toru Mori, part 1, 5 *Law in Japan* 109 (1972), and part 2, 6 *Law in Japan* 111 (1973).
39 See Toyomasa Fuse, *Modernization and Stress in Japan* (Leiden: Brill, 1975); and Hadley Cantril, *The Pattern of Human Concerns* (New Brunswick, N.J.: Rutgers University Press, 1965).
40 Doi, *Anatomy of Dependence*, pp. 84–87.
41 See sources in Chapter 2, note 1, *supra*; Carmen Blacker, *The Japanese Enlightenment: A Study of the Writings of Fukuzawa Yukichi* (New York: Cambridge University Press, 1964), p. 105; Y. Noda, "Nihonjin no seikaku to sono hō-kannen (The character of the Japanese people and the conception of law)," in Tanaka and Smith, *Japanese Legal System*, pp. 304–6; Takeshi Ishida, "Fundamental Human Rights and the Development of Legal Thought in Japan," p. 39; and Yoshiyuki Noda, "Comparative Jurisprudence: Its Past and Present," 8 *Law in Japan* 5 (1975), p. 10. The earliest written use of "*kenri*" may be by Tsuda Mamichi in 1866; ibid.
42 Nakane, *Japanese Society*, pp. 33–35.
43 Ibid.
44 The late Prime Minister Ōhira Masayoshi spoke of the leader's role as like that of an orchestra leader. An example of the limited influence of authorities and the power of those in subordinate positions is the *ringisei* system, whereby lower functionaries in government and business "pile up" seals of their approval before a person in highest authority has an opportunity to judge a proposal.

See Tsuji Kiyoaki, *Nihon kanryōsei no kenkyū* (Tokyo University Press, 1969), and his "Decision-Making in the Japanese Government," in Ward, *Political Development*, pp. 457–76; and Nakane, *Japanese Society*, p. 65.

45 Nakane, *Japanese Society*, p. 147. Freedom to speak out in a group is affected by one's status in the group's organization.

46 Ibid., p. 144.

47 Hayashi Chikio et al., *Nipponjin no kokuminsei* (Shiseidō, 1970, 1975, and 1980), concerning which see *Asahi Shinbun*, July 18, 1979, and *Japan Times*, July 18 and 27, 1979, and January 20, 1980; Lewis Austin, *Saints and Samurai* (New Haven: Yale University Press, 1975); Kamishima, *Jōmin no seijigaku*; Bradley M. Richardson, *The Political Culture of Japan* (Berkeley: University of California Press, 1974); and William K. Cummings, *Education and Equality in Japan* (Princeton: Princeton University Press, 1980). On the felt-need for, but resistance to a sense of community in the United States, see Ralph Keyes, *We, the Lonely People* (New York: Harper & Row, 1973).

48 Hayashi, "Seiji ishiki no seitai."

49 Koschmann, ed., *Authority and the Individual*, especially "Introduction"; Kamishima, *Jōmin no seijigaku*. A Japanese film *Nihon no ansatsu hiroku* (1969) traced the modern Japanese history of political assassinations, contending that all such killings have been the result of group conspiracy, rather than the efforts of isolated individuals, in apparent contrast to the American style of assassination. Similarly, the political suicide of novelist Mishima Yukio in 1970 was a carefully planned group operation. Stuart D. B. Picken, *Nihon no jisatsu*, trans. Hori Taoko (Simul Press, 1979), provides a welcome comparative perspective on the context and ordinary frequency of suicide in Japan; see also, *Japan Times*, December 3, 1978.

50 Koschmann, ed., *Authority and the Individual*, p. 14.

51 Nakane, *Japanese Society*, p. 150.

52 See, for example, Chapter 9, concerning rights of the person.

53 For example, a Takushoku University student was killed by fellow *karate* club members in June, 1970. On these and other cases, see *Asahi Shinbun*, March 25 and 26, June 15 to October 15, 1970. Concerning a child gang beating of a young paralytic, see "*Koe*" section, *Asahi Shinbun*, October 31, 1978. On convictions for the United Red Army killings, see *Asahi Shinbun*, March 30, 1979; *Japan Times*, March 30, 1979; and *Japan Times Weekly*, November 15, 1980. On *mura hachibu*, see Chapter 9 see also Chapter 5, notes 94 and 121.

54 The medical profession illustrates the intensity and style of competition one sometimes finds. For a hospital administrator, a central problem is the harmonization or pacification of factions of medical personnel which identify with different medical schools, such as those of Tokyo University and Keiō University. On conflict between schools of traditional dancing, see *Japan Times Weekly*, March 8 and April 28, 1980. On other East Asian systems and conflict, see Alan Liu, *Political Culture and Group Conflict in Communist China* (Santa Barbara: Clio Books, 1976); Martin K. Whyte, *Small Groups and Political Rituals in China* (Berkeley: University of California Press, 1974); Brandt, "Sociocultural Aspects"; Woo and Wade, "A Study"; and Paul Crane, *Korean Patterns* (Seattle: University of Washington Press, 1967).

55 Kamishima, *Jōmin no seijigaku*; and Koschmann, ed., *Authority and the Individual*.

56 H. Fukui, *Party in Power: The Japanese Liberal Democrats* (Berkeley: University of California Press, 1970); R. Scalapino and J. Masumi, *Parties and Politics in Contemporary Japan* (Berkeley: University of California Press, 1962); Nakane, *Japanese Society*, *passim*; and Ike, *A Theory*, pp. 50–63.

57 Koschmann, ed., *Authority and the Individual*, p. 15.

58 K. Ishikawa, "The Regulation of the Employee–Employer Relationship," in *Law in Japan*, ed. Von Mehren, pp. 439–79; Tadashi Hanami, *Labor Relations in Japan Today* (Tokyo: Kodansha International, 1979), pp. 171–74; for other examples, see Chapter 6.

59 As translated by David C. S. Sissons in "Human Rights under the Japanese Constitution," *Papers on Modern Japan* (Canberra: Australian National University, 1965), pp. 68–69.

60 See, for example, *Asahi Shinbun*, March 5 (evening ed.) and April 12, 1979.

61 See Masao Miyoshi, *Accomplices of Silence* (Berkeley: University of California Press, 1977); and Nobuko Mizutani, "Communicating in Japanese: Rules for Expressing Oneself," *Center News* (Tokyo: Japan Foundation), Vol. 4, No. 2, June, 1979, pp. 2–4. Yukio Matsuyama put it with humor:

> While I lived in New York and Washington, I got the impression that Japan could be compared to a hare. A hare has long ears, symbolizing his avid curiosity to catch information quickly, while he cannot express himself with his very small mouth. His behavior is far from being

> majestic. He moves and jumps so unsystematically that no one can tell where he heads for. And mild and gentle as he may look, he is often disliked by others because of sneaking into another's field to eat carrots.

In an address, "An Advice to Americans," U.S.–Japan Business Forum, San Francisco, October 6, 1980, p. 5.

62 Chalmers Johnson, "*Omote* (Explicit) and *Ura* (Implicit): Translating Japanese Political Terms," *Journal of Japanese Studies*, Vol. 6, No. 1, Winter, 1980, pp. 110–11; see also Baerwald, *Japan's Parliament.*

63 Thomas Blakemore in *Nippon Times*, July 23, 1946.

64 Concerning demonstrations, see Chapter 5.

65 Robert L. Seymour, "Japan's Environment: The Legal Response to Pollution," *Selected Papers in Asian Studies*, Vol. 1 (Western Conference of the Association for Asian Studies, 1976), p. 207; J. Gresser et al., *Environmental Law in Japan* (Cambridge, Mass.: MIT Press, 1980); Lawrence W. Beer and C. G. Weeramantry, "Human Rights in Japan: Some Protections and Problems," *Universal Human Rights*, No. 3, July–September, 1979, pp. 30–31; *Asahi Shinbun*, July 28, 1979; the journal *Kōgai Kenkyū*; and Margaret McKean, *Environmental Protest and Citizen Politics in Japan* (Berkeley: University of California Press, 1981).

66 For a full discussion of the *Hakata Station Film* case, see Chapter 8, below.

67 Hoffmann alludes to the flexibility in what I have called "inclusionary groupism" in his reference to "permeable group boundaries" and other aspects of factional structure, while comparing Japan and India:

> *Japanese factional structure* is characterized by: (1) a less clear distinction between inner and outer circles, made so by promotion of individuals within a faction through seniority, competence, or other considerations and by maintenance of an unbroken descending chain of relations primarily between individuals rather than between subgroups; (2) more permeable group boundaries, in that identification can be shifted from an inner or outer circle to the whole faction, and even beyond the faction, according to situational considerations; (3) a more stable hierarchical ordering and often a higher degree of bureaucratization than in India; (4) roles and relationships patterned on several indigenous cultural models, namely, the *ie* (traditional extended family, a household), the village, the *gekokujō* ("control of the superior by the inferior") decisional method, and Japanese values concerning personal obligations and ties.

Hoffmann, *Faction Behavior*, p. 233.

68 Nakane, *Japanese Society*, p. 149.

69 *Tokyo Weekender*, August 10, 1979.

70 Lawrence W. Beer, "Japan Turning the Corner," *Asian Survey*, January, 1971; and Seymour, "Legal Response."

71 Beer and Weeramantry, "Human Rights," pp. 31–33; Reischauer, *The Japanese*, pp. 369–426; and Takao Suzuki, *Japanese and the Japanese*, trans. A. Miura (Tokyo: Kodansha International, 1978), pp. 140–47.

72 See note 24, *supra*, and accompanying text.

73. These agencies are described in Chapter 4.

■ First published in *Occasional Paper No. 31*, International Ombudsman Institute, Canada, October, 1985, 21 pp.

8

Human Rights Commissioners (*Jinken Yogo Iin*) and Lay Protection of Human Rights in Japan

⌘

INTRODUCTION

How best protect the rights of citizen's on a day-to-day basis? What is necessary for rights protection, in terms of resources and human skills and institutions? Wherever in the world one may live, whatever the nature of a given socioeconomic system, political culture, or legal tradition, such questions reflect serious practical concerns. The public and private origins of a rights problem are various but the goal of rights protection systems is low cost, efficient, just, and timely solutions in accordance with law and community standards.

Formal legal mechanisms and procedures, presided over by law-trained professionals, are of course necessary at the State level; but, I would suggest, in terms of the proportion of rights cases handled and in terms of determining the status of individual rights within a national legal system, less formal modalities for solution, in which professionals utilize clear but simple procedures in a manner responsive to local circumstances and culture can be and should be more important than law enforcement agencies, lawyers and the courts. Of course reasonably effective operation of the latter is an essential part of the backdrop.[1] In offering this broad hypothesis, I must add the important caveat that less formal systems are valuable in the cause of individual rights protection only insofar as related lay people and officials are deeply committed to rights protection and not in fact part of the problem of rights violation. For example, the local leader and the face-to-face community may in their autonomy and grass-roots identification with individual rights problems be a major force for or against human rights; only empirical research can tell us which in a given instance.

In this paper I will describe some roles of lay people in the protection and promotion of human rights in Japan, with particular empasis on the Civil Liberties Commissioner system. The Japanese term for these volunteers is "*Jinken Yogo Iin*," which can be literally translated as "Human Rights Protectors"; but, for historical reasons, they are usually referred to, in Japan and elsewhere, as "Civil Liberties

Commissioners,"[2] and the related government agency is referred to as the "Civil Liberties Bureau" (*Jinken Yogo Kyoku*). "Human Rights Commissioners" is linguistically and functionally more accurate; I will hereafter refer to them generally as "Commissioners." There are today about 11,500 men and women serving as Commissioners in virtually every town and city in Japan. Before saying more about the Commissioner system and how it has worked. I will briefly explain its origins, its social setting, and its legal and constitutional context.

CONSTITUTIONAL RIGHTS IN JAPAN

The human rights of Japanese citizens received unprecedented legitimation and protection as constitutional and legal rights when the present Constitution of Japan (*Nihonkoku Kempo*) came into effect in the spring of 1947.[3] Japan had entered into creative dialogue with the West on new ideas of law and politics such as human rights (*jinken*) in the 1850s, and lived under a monarchical, parliamentary constitutional system from around 1890 through the disastrous years of World War II.[4] Unlike most non-Western peoples, the Japanese have had an independent, indigenous national legal system since they ended almost 50 years of colonialist encroachments on their legal sovereignty at the turn of the century.

Modern law heavily derived from Western Europe took hold and gave currency to an untraditional emphasis on equal rights under the law (except for women and a very small aristocracy) and credence among a sizeable minority to democratic understandings of individual rights.[5] The early modern revision of the imperial tradition bestowed uncharacteristic constitutional centrality on the Emperor and, in practice, increasingly repressive power on functionaries who restricted rights in the name of the Emperor's modern law.[6] The present Constitution is technically an amendment, but actually a replacement of the Meiji Constitution, the 1889 Constitution of the Empire or Japan.[7]

The 1947 Constitution was clearly influenced by strong democratic and American "New Deal" forces within the apparatus of the Occupation of Japan (1945–1952); but the human rights revolution wrought during that period was and still is strongly supported by the overwhelming majority of Japanese.[8] The origins of a system of constitutionally protected rights are much less important than the question of whether the government and the overwhelming majority of the citizenry are united behind and contented with those democratic rights. In Japan, perhaps no other locus of sociopolitical theory or document carries such great popular legitimacy as the Constitution of Japan.

The conception of "eternal and inviolate" human rights (Articles 11 and 97) embodied in the constitution is comprehensive and is rooted in the transcendent intrinsic value of each person: "All of the people shall be respected as individuals"[9] (Article 13). The Emperor is now powerless; the people have sovereignity. The general and specific rights provisions of Chapter 3 (Articles 10 to 40) are not simply rhetorical or didactic pronouncements; they mandate national policies and laws and are enforceable in the courts.[10] Most rights contained in the 1948 Universal Declaration of Human Rights were guaranteed to Japanese a year earlier. Among their constitutional rights are freedoms of expression, conscience, and religion, freedoms of mobility and occupation, equality under the law, socioeconomic rights, educational rights, worker rights, property rights, and rights to equal procedural safeguards in crimminal justice. Such rights are to be "the supreme consideration in legislation and in other governmental affairs" unless they interfere with the "public welfare" (Articles 12 and 13); but the Supreme Court has defined the public welfare as "the maintenance of order and respect for the fundamental human rights of the individual."[11]

On balance, Japan's human rights record is very good; most rights problems arise from customary biases and the darker side of social culture (e.g. in-group violation of member rights) rather than from government policy or law.[12] The breadth and depth of support for human rights in Japan are due to many factors: to memories of prewar repression and the horrors attending defeat in 1945, to the earlier acceptance of human rights ideas by many influentials, to decades of internal peace, to an unusual ethnic homogenity along with vigorous intellectual heterogeneity, to the absence of deep political divisions grounded in competing religious or ideological legitimacies, to an era of exceptional economic prosperity, and to the simple fact that humans enjoy being treated with seriousness and respect more than having their dignity ignored and their rights violated. Unanswerable questions, as for any democracy, are whether economic disaster might lead to an overthrow of the human rights protection system, and whether the young (in Japan, the postwar generations) will be wary enough of aspects of the social and political culture inimical to democratic constitutionalism to avoid drift towards a mood of tolerance and/or passivity in the face of human rights violations. A large majority has little or no memory and often slight knowledge of the militarist and ultranationalist infringements on rights, in and by Japan, before her surrender of August 14, 1945.

On the other hand, the legitimizing organs of a constitutional culture, such as the education system, the family, the mass media, opinion elites, the bureaucracy, and most political parties stand clearly behind comprehensive protection of human rights in most respects. In addition, the Constitution of Japan (Article 12) *requires* that human rights "shall be maintained by the constant endeavor of the people, who shall . . . be responsible for utilizing them for the public welfare";[13] hence, the establishment of the Human Rights Commissioner system, by which laypeople join directly in human rights protection, promotion, and education, is firmly grounded in the basic law.

THE BEGINNINGS AND DEVELOPMENT OF THE COMMISSIONER SYSTEM

During the massive administrative reorganization of Japan's government under the 1947 Constitution of Japan, a "Civil Liberties Bureau"; *Jinken Yogo Kyoku*; lit., "Human Rights Protection Bureau" (hereafter referred to as the Bureau) began functioning within the Justice Ministry (*Homusho*) on February 15, 1948.[14] The idea for the Bureau derived from the nascent Civil Rights Section, Criminal Division, United States Department of Justice, which grew over the decades into the important Civil Rights Division; however, the Bureau's powers differ. Neither the Bureau nor the Commissioners who work under its aegis have police powers or authority to prosecute; but the scope of the human rights cases they handle is much wider than that of the American counterpart.[15]

The Bureau has never been a large government agency; in 1984, only 220 professionals staffed its national (15) and local (205) offices. The Commissioner system was established by a 1948 Cabinet Order[16] as a way to expand the Bureau's rights protection capacities by involving qualified lay volunteers. It should be noted in passing that the Commissioners system is only the most important of a number of officially sanctioned modes of lay involvement in problem solving and service.[17] Under this Cabinet Order the number of Commissioners nationally never exceeded 150; but the Civil Liberties Commissioner Law (hereafter, the Commissioner Law)[18] which went into effect on June 1, 1949, raised the authorized number to the present level of about 20,000 (19,915 in 1984).[19]

Although Japan's Commissioner system is in some ways unique, in the broader history of the international movement for human rights protection, the Commissioner Law represents an important positive instance of creative national legislation institutionalizing a system which, in at least some of its features, may well have relevance to other countries. The Law's purposes are "to ensure the full protection of human rights by the appointment of Human Rights Commissioners throughout the country . . . and to promote and make widely known the ideal of human rights in order to protect the fundamental rights guaranteed to the people" under the Constitution.[20]

Commissioners are appointed for each town, village and city but a Commissioner may also operate beyond his/her assigned boundaries if need arise. They serve for renewable three-year terms without pay. Towns have at least three Commissioners; cities up to 100; Tokyo 360. The duties of the Bureau and Commissioners include:[21] 1) to make human rights ideals better known and appreciated by the public through public information and education activities; 2) to foster the active involvement of others in community human rights activities; 3) to investigate and collect information regarding human rights violations such as giving advice or warning, to report such to the Bureau, and to recommend action by other agencies, if needed and appropriate; 4) to promote human rights efforts among the poor, such as legal aid.

To summarize, the Commissioners are to popularize human rights thought, to educate, and to involve themselves in the conciliatory settlement of disputes arising close to home. Although they can be quite effectively conscious of their rights when acting in groups, and although high valuation of harmony has not implied a weak rights consciousness, Japanese have tended to be reluctant to "selfishly" assert their rights as *individuals* in a way that could bother others or challenge the authority of those with social or governmental power.[22] The Commissioner system has significantly eased for the ordinary citizen the expression of grievances and the assertion of individual rights without resort to courts or other distasteful forms of prolonged, costly and/or public confrontation.

The number of Commissioners has only gradually increased over the years; in 1984, for a population of approximately 120 million there were 11,421 (1,546 women; 13.5%), while on January 1,1978 they totalled 10,626 (1,215 women; 11.4%).[23] As Table 8.1 indicates, Commissioners are ordinary people from a broad range of working and living environments.

Table 8.1 Occupations of Human Rights Commissioners as of January 1, 1983.

		percent 1/1/83	*percent 1/1/78*
agriculture, forestry, fisheries	3,171	27.7%	29.9%
no full-time occupation (e.g. housewives, retired people)	2,794	24.4%	19.3%
religious leaders	1,059	9.3%	10.3%
shopkeepers	764	6.7%	7.4%
company executives	792	6.9%	6.7%
officers of organizations	456	4.0%	3.8%
practicing attorneys	360	3.1%	3.4%
company white collar employees	287	2.5%	3.0%
public employees	225	2.0%	2.6%
manufacturing and processing workers	218	1.9%	2.2%
professors and school teachers	253	2.2%	2.3%
doctors and medical personnel	178	1.6%	1.8%
judicial scriveners, tax accounts, etc.	235	2.1%	1.9%
various kinds of government commissioners	195	1.7%	1.6%
legislators	120	1.0%	1.0%
press and television employees	27	0.2%	0.3%
others	300	2.7%	2.5%

HUMAN RIGHTS COMMISSIONERS: THEIR SELECTION AND ORGANIZATION

Organization

A brief look at the organization context within which the Commissioners work and the procedures by which they are chosen will set the stage for a description of some of their activities.

1. Organizational structure

The Civil Liberties Bureau of the Justice Ministry is headed by a Director-General and is divided into three parts:[24] the General Affairs Division, which promotes nongovernmental human rights activities and handles the Commissioner system; the Investigation Division, which looks into alleged rights violations and gathers information on such cases; and the office of the Human Rights Administrator, which promotes public information and education activities and coordinates legal aid for the financially disadvantaged.[25]

Helping the national Civil Liberties Bureau supervise the Commissioner system and the other human rights activities are the local Civil Liberties Departments within Legal Affairs Bureaus located in the eight major regional cities of Tokyo, Osaka, Fukuoka, Nagoya, Hiroshima, Takamatsu, Sendai, Sapporo, and Civil Liberties Divisions within 42 District Legal Affairs Bureaus. Although law and constitution provide for a significant degree of local autonomy in some matters,[26] Japan has a unitary, not a federal system of government. District courts (*chihosaibansho*) are the courts of original jurisdiction in most noteworthy human rights cases, and high courts (*koto saibansho*), the principal appellate level under the Supreme Court. The accompanying map shows the cities where one finds high courts and district

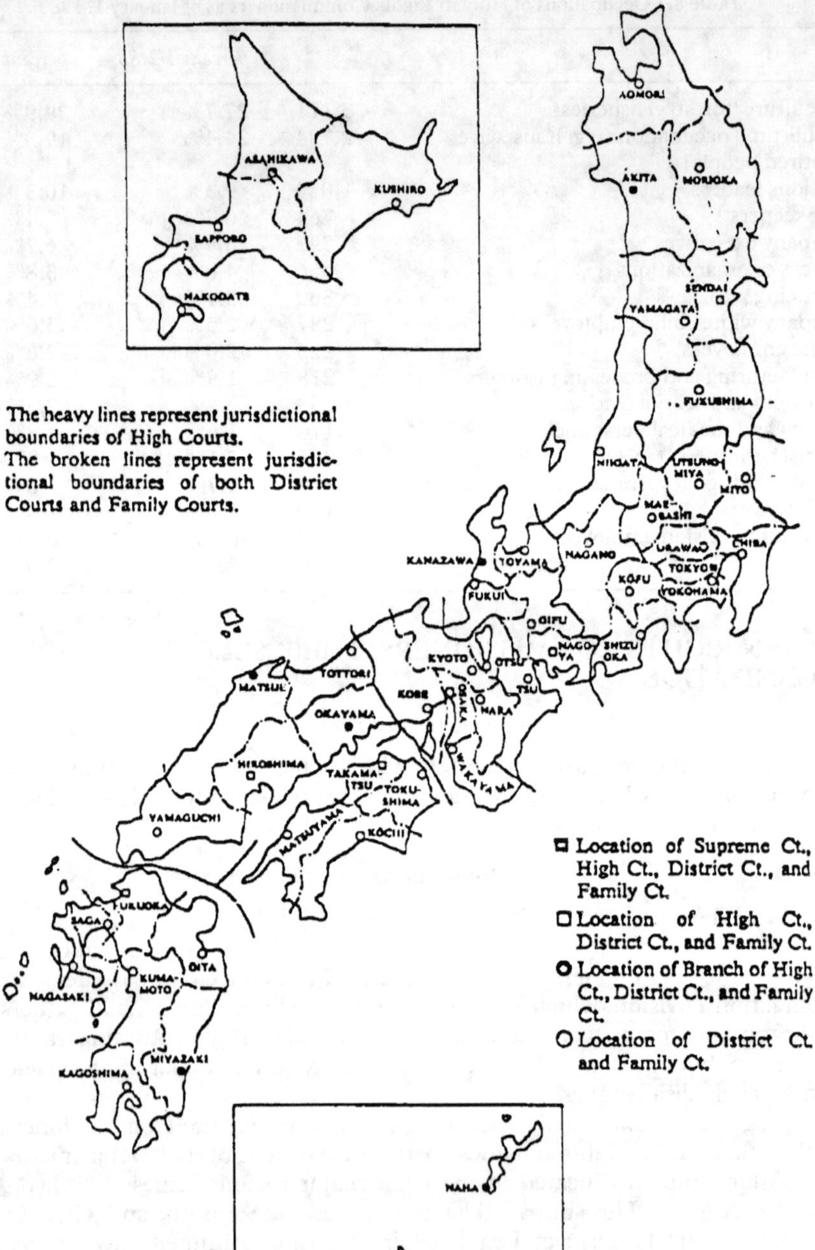

Map of Court Jurisdictions in Japan

Source: Supreme Court of Japan, *Justice in Japan, 1978*, Tokyo, 1978, p. 46.

courts and where regional Bureaus and the lower tier of forty-five Civil Liberties Divisions within District Legal Affairs Bureaus are located.[27] With the exception of the large northern island of Hokkaido, which has three districts, the sites of these district offices are also the seats of prefectural government. There are 260 additional "Branch Bureaus" connected to the regional and district legal affairs bureaus, and it is in relation to these offices that the Commissioners are organized into 319 Consultative Assemblies of Human Rights Commissioners (*Jinken Yogo Iin Kyogikai*).[28]

These local assemblies have in turn formed fifty Federations at the prefectual level. Capping the organizational hierarchy since 1953 has been the National Federation of Human Rights Commissioners (*Zenkoku Jinken Yogo Iin Rengokai*). Each Commissioner must belong to a local assembly, and must attend meetings and training sessions. The lay Commissioner carries out official duties on a part-time basis, but receives no recompense.[29] However, out-of-pocket expenses incurred in the line of duty (e.g. the costs of telephone, travel, and attendance at training sessions) are paid by the government. The functions of the consultative assemblies and their federations are mutual liaison and coordination of work among Commissioners, collection and exchange of information, research and publication on their work, and preparation of advisory opinions for interested agencies. Since they provide valued social services, the activities of local Commissioner organizations have been subsidized by related cities, towns and villages. National honors have been accorded outstanding Human Rights Commissioners.[30]

2. *The commissioner selection process*

We have seen their occupational backgrounds and organizational framework; we now turn to what is most crucial to this system of lay volunteers, the way they are chosen and the work that they do in every man's neighborhood or village.[31] A position as Human Rights Commissioner is prestigious, but not elitist. To preserve the prestige of the office and to enable the commissioner to function with a broad base of public support, great pains are taken in the selection procedures to pick outstanding individuals. What is sought is not one filled with self-importance or one who can sway an audience with eloquence, but one who has proven by word and action in his/her community an understanding of and commitment to human rights. Under Article 6, paragraph 6 of the Commissioner Law, discrimination in the selection of candidates on the basis of race, beliefs, sex, social position, or political view or affiliation is forbidden. Excluded from eligibility for commissioner status (Article 7) are those known for attitudes and conduct contrary to human rights principles (e.g. a person favoring discrimmination), anarchists, the legally incompetent, those convicted of crime meriting incarceration until such time as the term has passed,[32] those who form or belong to political organizations which advocate the violent overthrow of the constitutional system. The basic positive requirements for candidacy are substantial residence and qualified voter status in the area to be served, broad knowledge of local conditions, high moral character, the respect of the local community, and reasonable knowledge of and demonstrated support for human rights protection and promotion.

When a vacancy occurs, the Director-General of the Civil Liberties Bureau, on behalf of the Justice Minister, calls for a recommendation from the mayor of the affected city, town, village, or ward (as in the case of Tokyo). The mayor invites nominations, one each from a sometimes wide range of community organizations and agencies, such as the education committee, labor unions, the bar association, the mass media organization, and the political parties.[33] The mayor sorts out the nominees and brings a nomination to the elected local assembly of the city, ward, town, or village. With the advice and consent of the assembly, the mayor then submits a name to the Justice Minister for consideration. The Director-General must then solicit opinion on the candidate from the Justice Minister, the bar association, and the Federation of Consultative Assemblies of Human Rights Commissioners of the prefecture affected. The process is completed when the Justice Minister makes the appointment and informs the mayor and the individual. If a person recommended is deemed unsuitable by the Ministry, a call is made for submission of another recommendation within a given time period, using the original list of nominees; should this not issue in a satisfactory candidate, the Director-General may directly seek the advice of the prefectural bar and Federation on other persons nominated at the first stage of the process.[34]

THE WORKS AND DAYS OF HUMAN RIGHTS COMMISSIONERS

A. Dealing with violations of human rights

The Commissioner is someone nearby, who can be identified by a smart lapel badge and a plaque posted in a conspicuous place outside his/her home. Most Japanese live in cities; in cities most houses are close together, and most streets are narrow. It is easy to notice the location of the local commissioner walking to and from shopping, school and work, and posters giving the name, address and phone number of the commissioner are put up in neighborhood post offices, local government offices, meeting halls, and other well-frequented places.

The Commissioner is not a distant or threatening authority figure, but one who understands well the local scene and works easily with agencies and ordinary people to solve concrete problems in a quiet, flexible way on a day-to-day basis. Although Commissioners are commonly very generous in making themselves available to talk with people about their human rights problems, the actual hours they work under their "part-time" appointment varies from week to week and month to month, depending on the nature and number of cases that arise and the sorts of human rights educational activities on schedule.

The cases handled are divided generally into alleged rights violations by public officials and rights infringements by private individuals or organizations. Some examples of official infringements of rights are unlawful physical constraint, search, seizure, coerced confession, or assault by law enforcement agencies, improper treatment of inmates by prison officials, and corporal punishment by teachers. The number of such allegations coming to the attention of Commissioners is small and declining; for example, there were 345 such cases in 1976, 242 in 1982, and 243 in 1983.[35] Upon investigation, infringements were established in 167 of these cases in 1982 and in 165 cases in 1983.

It should be noted that law enforcement and administrative agencies have their own internal inspection systems, and a separate system of lay commissioners, the Local Administrative Counselors (*Gyosei Sodan Iin*) monitors official performance in light of human rights standards and receives citizen complaints.[36] The traditional elitism and bureaucratic disrespect for citizens found among earlier modern civil servants in Japan have markedly diminished under the current constitutional regime; but internal checks still must form an important part of the rights protection apparatus. The Administrative Inspection Bureau (Administrative Management Agency) and its local offices oversee the activities of the Counselors. The Counselor system was established in 1961; by 1965 they numbered 3,605 and handled 55,547 cases. In 1975, about 4,500 Counselors, average age 61, dealt with some 100,000 complaints, while in 1979 about 4,600 were consulted in over 120,000 cases; in 1982, 4,789 Counselors handled almost 200,000 cases.[37]

Local Administrative Counselors are respected local citizens who provide confidential and impartial service. Apparently, most problems are settled to the citizen's satisfaction by explanation, discussion, or conciliatory remedial action in cooperation with appropriate officials. The Counselor system has proven its value, but is not as widely known or used as the Commissioner system. There is naturally some overlap in the types of cases faced by Counselors and Commissioners, as with the work of local police in the neighborhood, social welfare offices, and the family courts (which involve both lay people and judges in the settlement to domestic conflicts and juvenile problems);[38] but the Human Rights Commissioners are the most active in noncoercive solution of rights issues problems for private parties.

Their legal context is somewhat delicate: the Commissioners and Bureau are limited by the principle that, as administrative entities, they should not intervene in private, civil matters. The primary intent of the Constitution is to guarantee citizen rights *vis-à-vis* the State, not in private dispute situations. However, the Supreme Court has held that the State has a legitimate interest in cases where private actions issue in infringement of freedom and equality rights that "go beyond the limits permissible in society."[39] For example, when the socially or economically influential infringe upon the rights of a socially disadvantaged individual, the Constitution and the Commissioners may come into play,[40] but the means used to resolve problems are meant to avoid compulsory intervention or any appearance of such.

A Commissioner takes up a case on the basis of a complaint or information provided by a victim or someone else, or when a newspaper, television or other report brings to light evidence of an apparent rights violation in his/her area. The main categories of private cases established by the Bureau are: cruelty to the sick or aged; restraint on physical freedom; community ostracism (*mura hachibu*); discrimination; violation of trust, good name or privacy; infringement of the freedom of speech, religion, association or assembly; violation of worker rights; denial of the right to security in ones's home; and environmental pollution and public hazards.[41] In most recent years, the number of cases of alleged (and, in parenthesis, established) rights violation has shown a gradual increase: in 1979, 16,385 cases (15,877 confirmed); 1980, 16,306 (16,140); 1981, 16,632 (16,479); 1982, 15,539 (15,329); and 1983, 13,923 (13,742).

The Commissioner reports each case to the local Bureau office and tries to help the victim and others involved solve the problem on a voluntary basis. The Commissioner investigates on his own without asking help of agencies with compulsory investigative powers, and then discusses the case thoroughly with the principals involved or affected. The aim is to defuse what is often a quite emotional local situation involving family or neighbors or co-workers. Where a culprit emerges, the Commissioner endeavors to help the person by quiet persuasion to cooperate, to realize that such rights violations are not acceptable, and to agree not to repeat the offense. Restoration of social harmony, insofar as humanly possible, is the deal. In the great majority of cases the Commissioner succeeds, with others lending moral support, in inducing the offender to desist and to express regret, repentence and/or apology. In more serious cases which elude solution, the Commissioner or the Bureau may issue a written "warning" to the rights violator. Although such warnings have only the force of informal advice, they are socially powerful in many of Japan's tight-knit communities, where a reputation for being inhuman and selfish can be socially devastating.[42] It should be noted that while Commissioners are required to refer offenses under Crimminal Code to the appropriate law enforcement agency, no such cases have arisen in recent years.

In addition to availing themselves of this avenue for relief from more serious problems of rights infringement, an increasing number of citizens have been making use of the *human rights consultative services* of the Commissioners and Bureau in the past decade. To illustrate, in 1976, 290,000 made such use of the human rights agencies, in 1977, the figure was 307,073; more recently, 358,737 consultations occurred in 1981, 368,802 in 1982, and 356,320 in 1983.[43]

A few salient characteristics of the Commissioner system of human rights problem solving merit emphasis. The Commissioner is not an official backed up by the coercive resources of the State, but a layperson trying to help his/her neighbors and fellow local citizens find a conciliatory way out of deeply troubling conflicts. In technical law, the conflict may or may not entail a violation of constitutional right. The Commissioner listens and empathizes a great deal, and tries to assist the parties to a less conflictual and more intersubjective and softened perception of the situation, but in light of the human rights standards involved. He/she is neither an arbitrator nor a judge, but a conciliator in a group context within a culture which recognizes the fitness of group problem-solution and the propriety of calling upon a prestigious third party to serve as a sympathetic presence facilitating dispute resolution with a minimum loss of face on the part of all concerned. "Black and white justice" is not descriptive of what is sought or what happens; "an intersubjectively persuasive and acceptable local resolution of conflict with substantive attention to human rights standards" seems better. In sum, the Commissioner system is low cost and high yield in all respects, and it re-enforces the legitimacy of both human rights and the constitutional regime by linking national law with the ordinary citizen's daily environment in a salutary manner.

B. Human rights education and promotion

Perhaps in few places are the ideals of human rights as unabashedly advertised and as systematically promoted as in Japan. A wide range of Commissioner and Bureau educational programs facilitates student and adult awareness of the importance of human rights. The Commissioners, as human rights elite of laypeople, buttress government, scholarly, and mass media support for human rights in ever more deeply institutionalizing Japan's human rights revolution, which began in 1945. Here I would only set forth a few of the many and sometimes colorful means used to diffuse human rights awareness throughout society. It is easier to bring one's problems to a Commissioner if one already knows of his/her readiness to help through effective educational propaganda.

Among the tools are special human rights consultation desks at department stores and other well-traversed locations, radio and television programs, local lecture and discussion meetings with Commissioners, publications, posters, bumper stickers, and so on.[44] National human rights essay contests are sponsored in the schools, with the Commissioners honoring local winners and the Bureau publishing an annual collection of the nationally best essays on human rights.

In a high-technology world small and inexpensive physical objects can be meaningful purveyors of human rights wisdom. In August, 1984 for example, I received from the headquarters of the Bureau a number of objects carrying human rights slogans:[45] colored marking pens, a mechanical pencil, calling cards and book marks with different human rights admonitions, calendar cards of various design, note pads, a triangle ruler in an attractive pack, leaflet handouts explaining the Commissioner system and the Bureau's mission, announcements of national poster contests on human rights, matchbooks.

There are also sincere, slick, and persuasive posters: with babies decrying discrimination (with clear identification of the problem: discrimination against the 1.5 to 2.5 million *burakumin*[46] descendants of traditionally outcaste occupational groups who now enjoy legally, though not always socially, enforceable rights); with celebrations of the 35th anniversary of the United Nations Universal Declaration of Human Rights in December, 1983; with calls couched in traditional art forms for observance of "Human Rights Day" on December 10; with internationalist pictures which link human rights with happiness and the Human Rights Commissioners; with a child's art and words asking all to think of the other person and the "mutual existence of human rights"; with an actress asking, "Aren't you forgetting what's most important?" in Human Rights Week theme.

During Human Rights Week, the Bureau organizes celebrations and school assemblies, festooned human rights sound trucks pass along the streets, public meetings and national poster contests are held, banners are strung across avenues, and panel discussions and public debates encouraged. Commemorative human rights stamps have been issued on occasion by the Postal Ministry. In a society permeated with modern advertising, all the above is not gimmickry but common sense.

All local and national government bodies are alerted to the importance of human rights during the December week and also with Constitution Day observances on May 3, when leading constitutional lawyers give solemn honor to constitutional rights at large and well-publicized public gatherings. It seems fitting to close by mentioning the impressive local and national observances in December, 1983, of the 35th anniversary of the Universal Declaration of Human Rights, when the Prime Minister's Office, the Justice Ministry, the Foreign Ministry, other public and private agencies, and every local government unit joined in grand public ceremonies to honor human rights. In short, human rights have entered sufficiently into the fabric of Japanese civilization to be an ordinary object of public education and annual national celebration.

CONCLUSION

Here it has been my intent not to analyze a number of Japan's specific rights problems, nor to underplay or exaggerate human rights violations,[47] but to focus attention on a low cost and relatively effective national system for protecting and promoting human rights which centers on the official utilization of locally respected, unpaid laypeople. Conciliatory, noncoercive, persuasive solution of rights problems and resolution of serious, private interpersonal disputes without excessive reliance on the courts, compulsion, or officialdom are needed in both industralized countries and in predominantly rural societies. Country studies, as of Japan's Human Rights Commissioners, and comparative studies of analogous systems[48] may well provide scholarly knowledge and insight useful to the general cause of individual human rights in many countries with a variety of types of regime and socioeconomic system. More generally, accurate and sensitive cross-cultural communication on various distinctive modes of rights protection and dispute resolution by laypeople at the level of the face-to face community may powerfully foster mutual understanding and intercultural respect.

Chart 1: Persons Doing Legal Work in Japan (1982)

Judges	2,700
Public Procurators	1,173
Practising Attorneys	12,233
Company Employees Doing Legal Work	1,320
Judicial Scriveners (*Shiho-Shoshi*)	14,572
Administrative Scriveners (*Gyosei-Shoshi*)	30,121
Patent Attorneys (*Benrishi*)	2,600
Tax Attorneys (*Zeirishi*)	40,860
Total Persons Doing Legal Work	105,579
Population of Japan (December 1981)	118,107,000
Population Per Person Doing Legal Work	1,119

Chart 2: Comparison of Population Per Person

Doing Legal Work in Several Countries	
France (1965)	4,026
West Germany (1971)	1,561
Japan (1982)	1,119
United Kingdom (1971)	1,023
United States (1978)	505

NOTES

1 See C.L. Pe and A.F. Tadiar, *International Survey of Conciliation Systems* (Manila: UST Press, 1982); Lawrence W. Beer, *Freedom of Expression in Japan* (Tokyo and New York: Kodansha International, 1984 (hereafter cited as *Freedom*; and Marc Galanter, "Justice in Many Rooms: Courts, Private Ordering, and Indigenous Law," *Journal of Legal Pluralism*, No. 19, 1981, p.1.

2 "Civil Liberties Commissioners" is the term used in English language publications of the Bureau, based on the creation of the term during the predominantly American Occupation (1945–1952).

However, the human rights guaranteed by the Constitution encompass much more than civil liberties. See, for example, Civil Liberities Bureau, "The Organization and Functions of the Organs for the Protection of Human Rights and the Legal Aid System in Japan, "Ministry of Justice, Japan, January, 1983 (hereafter referred to as "Organization and Functions").

3 The text of the Constitution of Japan can be found in Hiroshi Itoh and Lawerence W. Beer, *The Constitutional Case Law of Japan* (Seattle: University of Washington Press, 1978), p.256.

4 *Freedom*, chapter 2.

5 Lawrence W. Beer, "Constitutional Revolution in Japanese Law, Society, and Politics," *Modern Asian Studies*, Vol. 16, No. 1, 1982, p.33; Dan Fenno Henderson, "Law and Political Modernization in Japan," in Robert E. Ward (ed.), *Political Development in Modern Japan* (Princeton: Princeton University Press, 1968).

6 David A. Titus, *Palace and Politics in Prewar Japan* (New York: Columbia University Press, 1974).

7 Itoh and Beer, op. cit., p.3.

8 Beer, "Constitutional Revolution"; Prime Minister's Office, "Jinken Yogo," *Gekkan Yoron Chosa* January, 1984, p.33.

9 Itoh and Beer; p.258.

10 For many examples, see *Freedom*; Itoh and Beer; and Dan Fenno Henderson (ed.), *The Constitution of Japan: Its First Twenty Years, 1947–67* (Seattle: University of Washington Press, 1968).

11 *Japan* v. *Sugino*, 4 *Keishu* 2012, 2014 (Sup. Ct., Grand Bench, 1950).

12 Lawerence W. Beer, "Group Rights and Individual Rights in Japan," *Asian Survey*, April, 1981, p.437.

13 Itoh and Beer, p.258 The full text is: "Article 12. The freedoms and rights guaranteed to the people by this Constitution shall be maintained by the constant endeavor of the people, who shall refrain from any abuse of these freedoms and rights and shall always be responsible for utilizing them for the public welfare."

14 "Organizations and Functions," p.3.

15 Ibid., p.2.

16 Cabinet Order No. 168 of July, 1948.

17 See *Freedom*, chapter 4.

18 Law No. 139 of May 31,1949. See *59 nen Jinken Yogo Roppo* (*The 1984 Compendium of Human Rights Protection Laws*, hereafter, *1984 Compendium*) (Tokoyo: Nihon Kajoshuppan, 1984), p.31.

19 *Hoso Jiho*, Vol. 36, No.4, 1984, p.137; and materials kindly provided to the author by the Civil Liberties Bureau, Tokyo, August, 1984.

20 *1984 Compendium*, pp.31–34; "Organization and Functions," pp.2–5.

21 Article 11, Ministry of Justice Establishment Law, Law No. 193 of December 17, 1947; *1984 Compendium*, p.91.

22 *Freedom*, chapters 3 and 9.

23 L.W. Beer and C.G. Weeramantry, "Human Rights in Japan: Some Protections and Problems," *Universal Human Rights* (now *Human Rights Quarterly*), Vol. 1, No. 3,1979, p.7; "Organization and Functions," pp.3–4. The context of Japan's law personnel within which Commissioners fit is presented below. The source for the charts is Michael K. Young in "The Role of Law and Lawyers in Japan and the United States," *Occasional Paper No. 16*, East Asia Program, The Wilson Centre, Washington, D.C., 1983, p.10.

24 "Organization and Functions," p.2.

25 Ibid., pp.2, 11–20. This legal aid system is geared to help the poor in civil cases; in criminal cases, the court assigns defense councel for the poor upon application after indictment.

26 Articles 92–95, Constitution of Japan, Itoh and Beer, pp.267–268.

27 "Organization and Functions," pp.2–6.

28 Ibid., p.5.

29 Article 8, Commissioner Law, *1985 Compendium*, p. 32.

30 "Organization and Functions," p.5.

31 Ibid., and materials provided the author by the Bureau, 1984; discussions with Commissioner, 1979, Beer and Weeramantry, pp.9–10.

32 Only a few percent of those convicted of crime actually go to prison; much more common are fines and suspension of the execution of sentence (*shikko yuyo*). The person's attitude towards the crime and the probabilities with respect to recurrence of criminal behavior are primary determinants of penological decisions in Japan. See Government of Japan, *Summary of the White Paper on Crime, 1979* Research and Training Institute, Ministry of Justice, 1980, pp.23–28.

33 The major political parties are the perennially ruling Liberal Democratic Party, the relatively weak perennial second Japan Socialist Party, Komeito (Clean Government Party), the Democratic Socialist Party, and the peaceable Japan Communist Party.

34 Article 6, paragraphs 4 and 5, Commissioner Law, *1984 Compendium*, p.31.

35 Beer and Weeramantry, p.13; *Hoso Jiho*, op.cit., p. 144; and "Organization and Functions," p.7.

36 *Freedom*, p.143.

37 Ibid.; Beer and Weeramantry, pp.14–16; Kiyoaki Tsuji, *Public Administration in Japan* (Tokyo: Tokyo University Press, 1983), pp. 229–235.

38 *Freedom*, chapter 4; Supreme Court of Japan, *Justice in Japan 1978*, Tokyo, p.14.

39 *Mitsubishi Resin* v. *Takano*, 27 *Minshu* 1536 (Sup. Ct., Grand Bench, December 12, 1973; see translation Series of Prominent Judgments No. 15, General Secretariat, Supreme Court of Japan, "Judgment upon Case of Seeking Affirmation of the Existence of a Contractual Labor Relationship," Tokyo, 1980.

40 Ibid; "Organization and Functions," p.7.

41 Ibid; *Hoso Jiho*, op.cit. p. 146.

42 *"Organization and Function,"* pp. 8–9.

43 *Hoso Jiho*, op.cit. p. 159.

44 "Organization and Functions," p. 9; Beer and Weeramantry, pp. 10–12.

45 I am grateful to Hiroshi Suzuki and the leadership staff of the Civil Liberties Bureau, Justice Ministry of Japan for sharing generously with me written materials, sample promotional materials, and helpful perspectives concerning the Commissioner system, Tokyo, August, 1984.

46 Beer and Weeramantry, pp.16–19; Frank K. Upham, "Ten Years of Affirmative Action for Japanese Burakumin: A Preliminary Report on the Law on Special Measures for Dowa Projects," *Law in Japan*, Vol. 13, 1980, p.39.

47 Although Japan's homogeneity reduces the society-wide importance of interethnic conflict, problems of discrimination against Koreans (c. 670,000), Chinese (c. 50,000), *burakumin*, and women remain.

48 See sources *supra*, note 1.

■ First published in *Modern Asian Studies*, New York, Cambridge University Press, Vol. 16, No. 1, 1982, pp. 33-57.

9

Constitutional Revolution in Japanese Law, Society and Politics

⌘

Modern Japan has experienced two constitutional revolutions, one from the latter half of the nineteenth century until 1945, and the other since 1945. By "constitutional revolution" is meant a long process in which a fundamental shift takes place in constitutional values diffused throughout society by means of law, administrative actions, judicial decisions, and education, both formal and informal.

Previous to these modern constitutional revolutions, neo-Confucianism, already well known and understood in 1600, was adapted to produce what might be called the Tokugawa constitutional revolution.[1] In contrast to this, the two modern constitutional revolutions were not precipitated by the maturing of internal forces over a long period. They were assimilative reactions to Western legal traditions. As a result, contemporary Japanese law blends traditional elements with European (especially German) civil law and legal theory, and Anglo-American common law traditions.

In this article I offer some data and reflections on (1) prewar and present Japanese constitutionalism and the revision debate; (2) legal culture, embracing the legal system and values, as related to such issues as freedom of expression; and (3) some pending problems in Japanese constitutional law.

THE TWO MODERN CONSTITUTIONAL REVOLUTIONS

Pre-1945 concepts of constitutionalism and law affect legal interpretation and debate today. Many leading judges, prosecutors, legal scholars and lawyers have had to straddle mentally two constitutional eras, and received much of their formative training and experience under the pre-1945 legal system. The Meiji constitutional revolution (1868–1945)[2] institutionalized the system against which much of the post-1945 constitutional system has been a reaction, but also laid the foundation for aspects of the post-1945 revolution.

Study of the law, administrative practice and police developments affecting freedom of expression between 1868 and 1945 suggests that most parts of a thorough system for restraining free speech had fallen into place by 1913 after piecemeal development, and that enforcement of the Peace Preservation Law of 1925 and subsequent related law brought a final touch of unusual sophistication to the pre-1945 system of control, for which the military were not as responsible as sometimes assumed.[3] Neither the legal system nor traditional culture seems to have honored individual rights, as rights came to be understood in Japanese law under Western influence.

Rights and freedoms were quite new concepts in Meiji Japan. However, the absence in Japan of a long and coherent tradition of liberalism does not imply that the Meiji constitutional revolution did not vastly expand pre-existing group tendencies to assertion for and against policies in accord with their sense of justice and self-interest.[4] In general, the maintenance of civil liberties in a country does not depend on explicit emphasis in law or society upon rights and freedoms, as understood in the law and intellectual traditions of the West, but on: (1) a mixture of institutionalized values which taken together favor liberty; (2) the existence of competitive, as opposed to authoritarian, politics; (3) actual expression of agreement or dissent on substantive issues along with the possibility of dissent with impunity; (4) such a balance of social and political forces that those favoring rights outweigh those opposed.[5] The sociological interplay of such factors in Japan from the 1860s through the 1930s resulted in a growing awareness of individual legal rights, as understood today in Japanese and Western law, among many scholars, officials and other citizens at the same time that a modern system of political repression was being refined and increasingly enforced in service to the Emperor.

The constitutional system of Japan today, reflecting a quite different interplay of factors, stresses enforcement of individual rights. The present widespread acceptance of the constitution in Japan rests in part on a continuing reaction against a prewar system that failed in the mind-numbing defeat of World War II. It does not seem probable that Japan would soon have become a constitutional democracy without the shock of losing the Pacific War and without massive Occupation support for Japan's liberal forces.[6] Modern political systems which are systematically authoritarian, whether left or right in orientation and however inefficient in light of abstract goals, appear much simpler to maintain as regimes than constitutional democracies. Japan's authoritarian apparatus, by comparative standards, was efficient in its methods of political control during the militarist period, and not likely to evolve along more liberal lines.

The widespread, deep, and genuine loyalty to the emperor-nation of that earlier era is not much discussed in public today, and is perhaps remembered more often with embarrassment than with pride. The rejection now of significant military power under the pacifist provisions of Article 9[7] and the denial of power to the Emperor under Chapter I[8] of the constitution seem intimately linked in the Japanese mind to the utter national failure resulting from total and militant loyalty to the Emperor. Just as prewar children were programmatically indoctrinated in *kokutai* ideology, so postwar children have been conditioned systematically to believe in freedom ever since the first student was required to memorize the new constitution during the Occupation (1945–52).[9] The shock of those who had believed unquestioningly in the invincibility of the nation under the Emperor, although profound, is as difficult to convey to today's youth as it is to make real to America's affluent youth the depression years.

Closely associated in the collective memory of the "militarist period" is the severe, even irrational, limitation of the freedom of thought, the freedom of expression, and other individual rights. The radical postwar rejection by the overwhelming majority of the prewar military-bureaucratic system, which is seen as having misused the imperial institution for its own ends, explains in part why efforts to alter notably the status of Japan's Self-Defense Forces, *or* the Emperor, *or* individual rights are perceived by many liberal and leftist Japanese as an attempt to rip apart the entire fair fabric of the 1947 constitution, and not simply as an attempt to modify one of its elements. Whether or not this perception represents a persuasive assessment of relationships, the three parts are commonly seen as crucial and inseparable; no other components of the new constitutional structure arouse such noteworthy emotion. More power to the Emperor would mean, it is thought, more power to the military which would mean expanded police powers and less democratic freedom; and conversely, strict limitation of imperial and military functions in government is necessary to assure the maintenance and development of constitutional rights. In sum, the term "Peace Constitution" is used in Japan as a reference to the antimilitarist provisions of the constitution, its guarantee of individual rights, and imperial powerlessness.

THE REVISION CONTROVERSY

The Constitution of Japan has not been amended even once, as the constitutional revolution of postwar Japan has continued to take root. As it has been applied, it seems sufficiently flexible to remove any pressing need for amendment. The Meiji Constitution was never amended, unless the establishment of the present constitution is viewed technically as a constitutional amendment.[10] The aspects of perception described above seem a critical factor underlying the seriousness of academic, legal and political debate on questions of constitutional interpretation and revision over the past thirty years. A litmus test applied to scholars and politicians, as well as to laws and judicial decisions on many issues is how they relate to the tripartite revision issue. So thoroughly integrated into political and legal rhetoric is this constitutional sensitivity that court cases concerning a wide range of subjects—for example, history textbook certification, academic freedom, demonstrations, the rating of teachers, and the Japan–United States Security Treaty—have evoked references to all aspects of the tripartite image of Emperor, military, and individual rights.

Once the Allied Occupation ended in 1952, the revision controversy gathered momentum and reached a peak during the mid- and late-1950s following the formation of the Liberal-Democratic Party (LDP) and the Japan Socialist Party (JSP) by coalitions of smaller parties. Some powerful LDP leaders wanted revision precisely to strengthen the positions of the Emperor and the military and to limit individual rights; but this does not mean a widespread desire existed in the LDP for a return to the political system of the wartime period from the Manchurian Incident (1931) till late 1945, during which period bureaucrats and militarists decisively replaced elected party politicians as top leaders of the government.[11]

At least six factors seem to have virtually eliminated the probability of wholesale constitutional revision in Japan's near future, assuming no severe economic upheaval:

1 The Security Treaty Crisis of 1960 seems to have been more of a community rite affirming consensual democracy than an anti-treaty or revolutionary struggle.[12] It was the largest mass movement in Japanese history,[13] and it may well have suggested to LDP leaders such as Prime Minister Ikeda Hayato that an effort at major constitutional change, whether needed or not, would awaken organized opposition on a much grander scale than that of 1960.

2 The Sunagawa Decision of the Supreme Court[14] spoke of Japan's natural right of self-defense and held Japan's cooperation and security treaty with the United States to be constitutional under Article 9. This decision may have reduced the revisionists' sense of urgency about revision for the sake of Japan's military security. The present Security Treaty of 1960 was similarly upheld by the Supreme Court on April 2, 1969.[15] Two other aspects of Japan's politics tend to support Article 9's anti-militarism and Article 66-2, a constitutional requirement that "the Prime Minister and other Ministers of State must be civilians." First, over 80 percent of the Japanese people support Article 9 and the Security Treaty; 57 percent favor maintaining the Self-Defense Forces at present levels, while only 19 percent support an increase in military strength; and very few Japanese exhibit a sense of external military threat.[16] Most feel there are greater internal than external threats to the system, and even internal threats are minimal. Second, Article 9 has operated in such a way that the military has been removed from the political drama, and, barring an unforeseeable crisis, this has negated the possibility of a military *coup d'état* in Japan. If Japan had a conventional constitution, without Article 9, a strong military, whatever its political alignments, would have at its disposal the instruments of coercion which, Japanese history suggests, it would not be reticent to use politically.

3 The issuance in 1964, under the leadership of Professor Takayanagi Kenzō, of a non-committal final report by the Commission on the Constitution (1957–64; *Kenpō Chōsakai*) also discouraged further revision efforts, at least for some time. No recommendations for amendment were made after six years of hearings, study, and debate.[17] From its inception, many critics viewed the Commission as a revisionist tool; if such was the original intent of the LDP, it was frustrated. Many scholars and politicians refused to participate in or support the Commission's activities. Whether their participation would have added even greater force to the Commission's final refusal to recommend changes is a moot point. In any case, many opponents of the Commission were actively involved in parallel study groups, which included Commission members, during the long debate over every important and technical provision of the Constitution of Japan. In its function, this debate may be viewed as a Japanese-style *constitutional convention*, with long consultations at home and abroad, and widespread debates in pursuit of national consensus. Japan had had no opportunity for such a "convention" under the Occupation.

4 In the late 1940s and early 1950s, food, clothing, and other basic needs were the preoccupations of most, leaving a small minority to debate ideologies and constitutional ideas. The postwar revolution of thought had a slow start. By far the most frequently cited reason in 1979 for Japan's peace since World War II was "the personally experienced misery of war,"[18] and popular support for the "peace constitution" is perhaps equally attributable to that experience, at least

initially. The fact is that popular assimilation and support for the constitution has grown, and militates strongly against revision. This has been primarily the result of education, accumulating experience of the operation of the constitution, prosperity, the absence of any appealing alternative, the work of the Commission on the Constitution, and the long-term absence of a perceived external military threat.

5 The LDP lost in the late 1960s and 1970s the overwhelming parliamentary power necessary to revise the constitution. This, and factional differences within the LDP render revision very unlikely. Inside and outside the political parties, Japan has many power centers, groups organized along relatively non-authoritarian, quasi-familial lines. A few such centers seem dominant—such as the ruling political party, the Ministries (especially the Finance Ministry), the judiciary, mass media combines, and industry federations—with lesser interest groups or domains filling out the system. In general, loyalty to the small face-to-face group is primary,[19] and it is quite common for such groups or factions to be in competition with, or at best indifferent to, the others. But they can also freely enter into alliances of mutual benefit, usually for limited periods and for particular purposes. This often happens, for example, among factions of the LDP, and this capacity for making and breaking alliances makes the system dynamic and highly organized. But a consensus within the LDP to revise the constitution is certainly not readily foreseeable, and cooperation with other political parties is much more unlikely. The distribution of seats in the Diet remains fairly stable, the LDP's capacity to retain control of the Diet being primarily due to the absence of an alternative appealing to the voters. In July 1980, even after an atypical LDP landslide victory, the LDP's 286 seats out of 511 in the lower house and 135 of 252 in the upper house[20] are far short of the two-thirds majority required to amend the constitution.[21]

6 Also militating against constitutional revision is the institutionalization of the Constitution of Japan through law and judicial decisions. The district, high and Supreme Courts of Japan have been much too diverse in their ideological leanings and interpretive methods to allow blanket characterizations of judicial performance since 1947 with respect to constitutional law. But the net cumulative effect of their work in millions of cases, civil, criminal and administrative, has significantly strengthened the roots of rule of law democracy in Japanese soil.[22] In addition, family courts, Civil Liberties Commissioners, and Local Administrative Counselors have also brought the law of the constitution to bear in resolving millions of disputes in a quiet atmosphere.[23] District courts more often than appellate courts[24] have stressed civil liberties in their findings; but even the now conservative Supreme Court has notably nurtured procedural rights of the accused[25] while allowing creeping restraints on the rights of public employees, on and off the job.[26] (Other examples are discussed later.) The courts are restrained by an insufficiency of judges, dilatory trial proceedings, jurisprudence that is sometimes restrictive, and other factors touched on later. In general, the courts have guarded jealously their tradition since the Meiji period[27] of judicial independence in deciding individual cases; they have also upheld their institutional prerogatives in dealing with the Diet and administrators.

Legal professionals as well as politicians, ranging from rightists to moderate liberals to democratic socialists to those who view Marxists as rank conservatives, seem cautious about the intentions of their political foes on the revision issue. It is more a debate among elites who would speak on behalf of the citizenry than an issue like economics or education preoccupying the public in general. Many Japanese of otherwise differing views would like the revision controversy to cool down sufficiently to allow a complete rewriting of the Constitution of Japan into appropriate Japanese language without changing the intent of any important provision. That may of course be an impossible dream; but the present translation into Japanese of some parts originally in English is not adequate, and may be an unnecessary reminder of the document's Occupation-period origins.[28]

Some anti-revisionists maintain the LDP policies and the decisions of conservative courts have already revised the constitution in fact, if not formally, in pursuit of a "reverse course" preference for the prewar order.[29] Surely, in Japan as in past and present democratic law and politics the world over, one can find much evidence of an abiding preference for anti-democratic policies and judicial decisions at both the official and private levels of society; but the contention that substantive constitutional revision has occurred seems a doubtful political judgment and an oversimplification of the tasks of courts in Japan, unless by "revision" one really means "interpretation" which one finds needlessly restrictive. Moreover, the problems in interpreting the Article 9 "no war clause" are unprecedented in world judicial history; they cannot be solved or whisked away by too facile a use of "political question" doctrine, the view in law that courts have no right to decide certain politically sensitive issues such as those affecting national security.[30]

Japan's power centers criticize each other for wrong-headedness regarding the constitution, and in doing so they manifest the competitive politics essential to the maintenance of liberties. Anti-revisionists retain sensitivity to the repressive past and show awareness that democracy is a vulnerable system of law and government always in some respects in tension with its professed ideals.

JAPAN'S CONSTITUTIONAL THEORY

The Constitution of Japan is now the most authoritative reference point for public values in Japan and is, as Edward Seidensticker has noted, "among the Sacred Books of the East."[31] The constitution's theoretical thrust is based on natural law suppositions and on the attribution of intrinsic value to the individual person. So many formal philosophies and ideologies co-exist in Japan's political and intellectual worlds that it is hard to discern any agreed-upon general theory underpinning Japanese constitutional democracy. Among the pillars and struts of Japanese thought are traditional ideas drawn from Buddhism, Confucianism and Shinto, as well as theories related to Christianity and Marxism; but how they relate to each other, if at all, is elusive.[32] But it is clear that customary law has had a powerful influence. Though generally unwritten, these rules are partially expressed in such documents as company rules.[33] A sophisticated system of rules with effective sanctions governs *oyabun-kobun* (quasi-parental-filial) group structures[34] and gives specificity to such motive forces as *amae* (reciprocal dependency)[35] and loyalty. Nagao Ryūichi suggests that a better understanding of the enigmatic urge to absolute loyalty—not simply to loyalty—may be a key to understanding the history of Japanese social and political ideas.[36]

Every five years the Institute of Statistical Mathematics in Tokyo conducts comprehensive surveys of Japanese national character. The results indicate that there has been no appreciable modification of a clear Japanese preference for traditional values since 1953. Among the possible approaches to clarifying the principles underpinning or at variance with the constitution is analysis of the reasons given by voters for their voting preferences. An attitude study of 1,500 Tokyo voters was made in 1978 by a team of Japanese scholars.[37] Analysis indicated that ideology and party preference were relatively unimportant. The single most important determinant of political choice (the key factor to 29 percent of voters, and a major factor to 53 percent)[38] was the image of the candidate as expressing and supporting traditional values and what might be termed "the good Japanese way" of doing things. But a most striking contrast to this preference for traditionalism in the personal style of candidates is found in the analysis of the positive elements in the images which voters entertained of liberalism, capitalism, socialism, and communism: the most likely to succeed were candidates, ideologies, and parties presenting an image of flexibility, modernity, conservatism, and economic egalitarianism somehow combined. For maximum legitimacy, a leader was seen as combining great respect for traditional values and modes of human interaction with concern for constitutional freedoms and economic policies promoting equality. Forty-two percent of the voters studied considered themselves entirely unaffected by political ideologies such as the four above; only 1 percent consider socialism-communism preferable in general to liberalism-capitalism, but only 10 percent rate the latter pairing preferable to the former.

Along with the strong support for Article 9 pacifism (*not* a general philosophy of pacifism) referred to earlier, values such as hierarchy, equality, groupism, freedom and loyalty form at least part of the structure of operative constitutional theory in Japan. Replacing in some measure and without much emotion their earlier loyalty to the Emperor, perhaps the generality of Japanese now share a loyalty to the constitution, not as a formal document, but as a summation of preferred values and guidelines for public action. What the constitution rejects seems as important as the rights it guarantees, but the whole structure rests on a recognition of the equal dignity of each individual. As the late constitutional lawyer Miyazawa Toshiyoshi once expressed it, while contrasting prewar and postwar Japan, "Every day I enjoy breathing freedom again."

CONSTITUTIONAL CULTURE AND LAW

The core new element in post-1945 Japanese constitutionalism is legally protected freedom and individual rights, based primarily on the Preamble and Chapter III (Articles 10 to 40) of the constitution.[39] Japan would very likely be a well-organized (some might say, over-organized) nation under almost any imaginable governmental system; but much was added to order by the present constitutional revolution. The Preamble proclaims that "sovereign power resides with the people," and Article 13 that "all of the people shall be respected as individuals." This abstract latter provision has been invoked by the courts as the textual basis for both establishing and limiting certain constitutional rights. The individual person has replaced the

Emperor as the highest public value. The Emperor is a "symbol of the State and of the unity of the people" (Article 1); and "he shall not have powers related to government" (Article 4). This is the first time the powers of the Emperor have ever been legally limited, although historically he seldom, and, since 1868, almost never, actually exercised any political powers. Although continuities do exist which link present and prewar institutions, significant changes have been made in their organization and function.[40] The Cabinet has no military membership and is collectively responsible to the Diet (Article 66). Constitutional rights, although in fact sometimes subordinate to informal in-group pressures and bureaucratic presumptions, are more freely exercised than in prewar Japan, vastly expanded in scope, usually honored by the police, and justiciable or conciliable in public tribunals.[41] The mass media serve more adequately than before as a quasi-constitutional Fourth Estate, a power center relatively independent of any political party or Ministry, without which Japanese democracy might crumble.[42] The Diet is the "highest organ of State power" (Article 41) except for the ruling political party, yet subject to judicial review (Article 81) of the constitutionality of its official acts.[43] The court system, supervised by the Supreme Court, is judicially and administratively independent. Finally, the status of women has improved markedly, in both fact and law.[44]

The Supreme Court and lower courts have the "power to determine the constitutionality of any law, order, regulation or official act";[45] but like most court systems, they exercise this power against other branches of government only rarely. They are further restrained by predominantly civil law perceptions of the judicial role in government, a role of democratic deference to the elected parliament.[46] The technical effect on future law of a judgment of unconstitutionality is still debated, but a "conclusion in a decision of a superior court shall bind courts below in respect of the case concerned," and not in general.[47] For example, if a legal provision is held unconstitutional by the Supreme Court, it is nevertheless possible that the same or other courts may rule differently in other cases on the same issue, and it is possible that the Diet will not pass remedial legislation to remove the offending provision. A judgment of unconstitutionality does not necessarily trigger among lawyers, legal scholars, mass media leaders or politicians the requisite sustained pressure on the Diet to take legislative action to support such a judgment.[48] If the judicial decision is that an official action is invalid, no court doctrine has resolved the scholarly debate on whether some legal provision enables a court to order an administrative agency to take remedial action.[49] Article 37 of the constitution guarantees the accused in a criminal case "the right to a speedy and public trial"; but some controversial cases have languished in the courts for a decade or even two (e.g. the 1952 May Day Incident decisions of the 1970s), and years of delay are commonplace. Widely spaced trial sessions characterize Japan's civil law system, courts have been used at times as political forums, causing additional delays, and judges are generally meticulous in moving slowly towards a decision. These factors may constitute a systematic obstacle to quick justice.

The conviction rate in Japan is extremely high, approaching 99 percent. But in recent years criminological reasons, rather than insufficient evidence have led prosecutors not to prosecute around 40 percent of serious violations of the Criminal Code. A lay Inquest of Prosecution regularly reviews a prosecutor's determinations on whether or not to file charges; these organs recommend a change or indictment or a reinvestigation of the case about 10 percent of the time, and such recommendations are accepted by the Chief of the District Public Prosecutor's Office in 30 percent of the cases.[50] "In Japan in 1971 less than 4 percent of persons convicted were given a jail sentence and almost two-thirds of those were suspended. Over 96 percent of persons convicted of a crime were punished only with a fine," usually a small fine. Forty-four and seven-tenths percent of the convicted went to prison in the United States that year, and for much longer periods than the Japanese sentenced. Criminal justice in Japan is generally not severe.

Freedom of expression is a *sine qua non* of any constitutional democracy. A review of the status of freedom of expression will thus be a particularly useful way of conveying reasonably reliable perspectives on the state of Japan's democratic law. Issues to be touched on include the freedom to demonstrate, mass media freedom, privacy, obscenity, and textbook certification.

THE LAW OF DEMONSTRATIONS

In any assessment of the strength of freedom, we need to study judicial decisions, which are the backbone of the law on liberty, but especially where values differ from Western ones, we need to understand the society in order to comprehend how law is perceived and how it functions. For example, the Japanese commitment to groupism instead of to individualism has not, and does not, prevent people from resorting to the law to protect their rights and interests.[51] Nor has it been an obstacle to the people's support for the freedom of expression.[52] But it has affected the forms that these take.

There is a strong sense of *group* right rather than individual right in public contexts, analogous to an individualist sense of right in the West. Largely due to this, privately and freely organized demonstrations have been very frequent in postwar Japan. Freedom of association and freedom of assembly have been central aspects of freedom of expression in Japan, and contrast sharply to the prewar suppression of these freedoms. Highly vocal but nonviolent group dissent or advocacy by groups seems more fully accepted public behavior in Japan than in the United States.[53] Even peaceful marches sometimes arouse considerable public ire in the United States, as they did during the civil rights and anti-war movements of the 1960s and 1970s.[54]

A number of agencies and laws regulate demonstrations in Japan,[55] but the most important are the local "public safety ordinances" (*kōan jōrei*) and "public safety commissions" (*kōan iinkai*) of prefectures or cities.[56] The key constitutional provision on freedom of expression is Article 21:

> Freedom of assembly and association as well as speech, press, and all other forms of expression are guaranteed.
>
> 2. No censorship shall be maintained, nor shall the secrecy of any means of communication be violated.

Basic Supreme Court doctrine on demonstrations and other "collective activities" was laid down in the landmark Tokyo Ordinance Decision in 1960,[57] which held that local authorities are obliged under public safety ordinances to grant permits with "maximum respect for freedom of expression." Denial of a permit is legitimate only when a collective activity "will directly endanger the maintenance of the public peace" and thus contravene "the public welfare" (*kōkyō no fukushi*).

Later judicial decisions have followed and refined *Tokyo* doctrine.[58] Although the "public welfare" was defined early (1950) by the Supreme Court as "the maintenance of order and respect for the fundamental human rights of the individual,"[59] for many years the judicial use of the term has evoked unease and protest from many constitutional lawyers and opposition politicians. "Public welfare" has reminded them of terms used during the ultra-nationalist period to urge all to forget their own interests and revere the Emperor.[60]

One of the most significant developments in constitutional law since 1947 may be the decreased use, especially in the lower courts, of abstract formulations of public welfare doctrine, and increased specificity since 1965.[61] The courts have honed more concrete criteria for determining what the public welfare is in each class of cases. These technical developments are in some cases due more to changes in judicial education, the influence of legal scholars, and accumulated judicial experience under the 1947 constitution than to liberalism. For example, *Tokyo* doctrine, which was handed down in the aftermath of the 1960 Security Treaty Crisis, deemphasized the place where demonstrations are held. In fact, *Tokyo* upholds the right of authorities to regulate mass demonstrations "in any place whatsoever," contending that debate on such matters as place is "completely profitless." But a 1970 Supreme Court decision hinged upon the meaning of "public place" (*kōkyō no basho*) in the Hiroshima prefectural ordinance. It was defined by the judges as "a place which in reality is generally open and can be used and entered freely by unspecified persons."[62] The ordinance requires a permit only for a demonstration which is to take place in a public place. The accused were public employees who staged a demonstration outside the prefectural capitol building without obtaining a permit. They contended the ordinance did not apply, since the location of the demonstration was not a public place; the judges disagreed, and they lost their case.

Vigorous exercise of the freedom to demonstrate by groups representing local and national interests will likely continue little affected by adverse court decisions. Most public group actions in Japan are orderly and peaceful, and are often attended with colorful pageantry and a festival spirit, a healthy blend of seriousness and play. Convictions for illegal collective activities are usually for physical obstruction or violence which would be held illegal in most or all of the world's other democratic courts; and as noted earlier, Japan's courts are quite lenient in sentencing. On the other hand, the Supreme Court has been criticized when it has overturned acquittals handed down by both a trial court and an appellate court; this it did about twenty times between 1974 and 1979 in civil liberties cases. The ever-clearer restriction in the political activities of public employees to voting alone deserves special mention. In the late 1960s, the Supreme Court recognized that different degrees of restraint are appropriate to a management-level official in a Ministry and a janitor in the public monopoly tobacco corporation.[63] But between 1973 and 1978, decisions of the Supreme Court affected adversely the political freedom of public employees.

In the famous *Sarufutsu* Case,[64] for example, a postal employee was convicted for putting up six political posters on a public bulletin board during his leisure hours. The issues still debated include the proper delineation of limits on the rights of teachers, postal workers, telecommunications workers, and transportation workers to strike or to engage in political activities, and whether administrative discipline (most common), criminal penalties or no punishment should be applied for related violations of the laws governing public employees.

Some Aspects of Freedom for the Mass Media

Along with group activism, freedom of the press is particularly close to the core of Japanese democracy, because the mass media may represent the only power centers that are effectively organized, separate from the government, linked with important people and groups, especially in Tokyo and Osaka, and whose influences spread throughout the nation.

Japan's print and broadcast media are mammoth in scale, technologically impressive, and socially pervasive.[65] Daily newspapers with nationwide circulation like the *Asahi Shinbun, Mainichi Shinbun, Yomiuri Shinbun*, and *Nihon Keizai Shinbun* print over fifty million copies each day, about twenty percent of which are distributed in Tokyo. The newspapers' political roles are complex, although the major papers do not endorse political candidates. For example, the press helped to sustain the crisis atmosphere for a time during the 1960 Security Treaty Crisis, they moderated the tension in most cases during the nationwide University Crisis of 1968–69, they massively publicized the Lockheed scandals and trials during the 1970s after disclosures were made in the United States, and they have played a major role in activating, publicizing and supporting the consensus against pollution since 1970. The principal organization for newspapers, television and radio is the *Nihon Shinbun Kyōkai* (Japan Newspaper Editors and Publishers Association), which at times when a need is felt can form a cohesive power center by alliance among its leaders in the face of external threat. For example, during the Hakata Station Film Controversy of 1969, the media united to oppose a court order for evidence to be presented (TV film of a student–police confrontation) in the alleged absence of other or better evidence. The Supreme Court upheld the courts' prerogatives after months of well-organized media reistance.

The University of Missouri world survey of press freedom rates Japan highly, but has noted industry centralization and self-regulation as problems. On the latter score, the "*kisha kurabu*" (press clubs) attached to politicians or agencies may be mentioned. Reporters from competing papers do not so much compete for news, as they form a coherent group which may determine when what news is suitable for release to their respective papers. Stable ties can develop between a "reliable source" and a press club; the wishes of both the club and the source may heavily influence what a reporter decides to convey to the public. (Foreign correspondents are not welcome.) There is some merit in the system, because secrecy-loving officials would probably obstruct access to information more substantially, if the cordial relations of mutual trust with the press did not exist. On the other hand, this system of agency–media and reporter–reporter relations too effectively limits the freedom of information, and is one reason why news of such affairs as the Lockheed scandals derived first from foreign sources rather than from Japanese investigative journalism. The right of access to information (*akusesuken*) and the individual's right to know have been major themes studied by specialists such as Itō Masami, Shimizu Hideo, Okudaira Yasuhiro, and Horibe Masao.

In the *Nishiyama* Decision of 1978,[66] the Supreme Court made its first ruling on the relationships between state secrets and newsgathering. While attached to the

Foreign Ministry, Nishiyama Takichi, a reporter for the *Mainichi Shinbun*, gained access to secret cables on the negotiation of terms for the reversion of Okinawa to Japan. Nishiyama had received this information from Hasumi Kikuko, a girl friend working in the Ministry. At a Diet committee meeting on March 27, 1972, a Socialist (JSP) member made the contents of the cables, received somehow from Nishiyama, a part of his attack on government policies. The documents contradicted the government's earlier assurances that no secret agreements had been made with the U.S. The Supreme Court held: (1) that the courts have the authority to determine what constitutes a state secret under the National Public Employees Law (and what, for example, is merely a political secret); (2) that the government's secrecy regarding international negotiations in this case was appropriate; (3) that the government's failure to bring the full facts before the Diet did not conflict with the constitutional order or constitute illegal secrecy; and (4) that although free news-gathering and reporting are of special importance to the people's democratic right to know and freedom of expression generally, Nishiyama violated the legal prohibition against inducing divulgence of official secrets by a public employee in his ethically questionable relationship with Hasumi, a married woman.

The right of privacy has been another noteworthy issue in recent law. Expanded press freedom since 1945 has occasioned an increase in journalistic excursions into the private lives of political leaders, other public figures, and ordinary citizens (unknown but for a cruel *exposé*).[67] The former have served the people's right to know about and criticize the famous and the powerful. According to a survey, both well-known and unknown victims of defamation and violation of privacy more often suffer in silence and "go to bed weeping" (*nakineiri suru*) than assert their legal rights as individuals. The consensus among scholars seems to be that there have been too few legal charges lodged by victims. Where any redress has been sought, the more common solution has been a conciliatory out-of-court settlement with public and private apologies and monetary compensation by publishers.

Courts and scholars alike have strongly supported the rights to privacy (*puraibashiï*) and good name, but there seems to have been a low demand for the legal protection of these rights at least until the 1970s. In sharp contrast to official secrecy, the right of privacy seems to have been less honored in group-oriented Japan than the right of families, occupational groups or other groups or communities to know about the affairs of their members, and to impose sanctions for deviance. For example, the institution of ostracism from the community (*mura hachibu*) for non-conformity is a persistent problem, according to Japan's Civil Liberties Bureau.[68] On the other hand, if one values the positive aspects of the strong Japanese sense of community, one must hope that a stress on privacy rights will not unduly disturb it.

The constitutional right of privacy was first established in Japan not by a law, but by a 1964 Tokyo district court decision against Mishima Yukio in a case involving his novel *Utage no Ato (After the Banquet)*.[69] The novel, serialized in *Chūō Kōron* in 1961, dealt in thinly veiled fashion with marital affairs of Arita Hachirō, a Socialist (JSP) politician and unsuccessful gubernatorial candidate in the 1960 Tokyo elections. Arita sued Mishima, who was ordered to pay a substantial amount in damages. The emergence of the right of privacy is an example of the considerable influence of Japanese legal scholars on some areas of the law, the fruitful interaction of campus and court, and the importation of a legal concept from American law into Japanese legal discourse.

The constitutional basis for the privacy right is found in the sentence, "All of the people shall be respected as individuals" in Article 13, while code law provision is detected in Articles 709 and 710 of the Civil Code, under which a person is bound to make compensation for intentional or negligent violation of the right of another, whether "injury was to the person, liberty, or reputation of another or to his property rights." Among other noteworthy privacy cases are the following:

1 A 1969 Supreme Court decision held that, as an aspect of the right of privacy, one has the right not to be photographed against one's will during an illegal demonstration unless the photography was necessary to a criminal investigation.[70]
2 A 1969 Tokyo high court decision in the Kato Case required a weekly magazine to pay remuneration and to apologize publicly in a national newspaper, on grounds of damage to good name and privacy rights.[71] The magazine at issue claimed that two famous TV and film personalities cohabited before marriage, which was denied.
3 In 1970, an injunction to ban the showing of an art film on the grounds of privacy violation was denied.[72] The film dealt with the early amorous and political affairs of an elderly feminist politician, Kamichika Ichiko; but she herself had publicized her private life on a number of prior occasions, thus negating in the court's view the confidentiality factor necessary for a valid claim of privacy violation.
4 The 1977 *Kawabata* Case was settled out of court with public apologies for lack of circumspection. The bereaved family of the late Nobel Prize-winning novelist, Kawabata Yasunari, sued the publisher and author of a novel which suggested that Kawabata's 1972 suicide was linked to indiscreet relations with the family maid, apparently an outcast *burakumin*.[73]

Incidentally, the increase in civil defamation suits in the early 1970s exemplifies the utility of analyzing the side effects of specific legal changes.[74] An important but unintended and unforeseen byproduct of legal change in one issue area affected the effects and applications of law in another. Prior to 1970, very few civil defamation suits had been brought to court compared, for example, to German and French experience under similar defamation laws.[75] In the early 1970s, the success of groups and individuals bringing civil suits against companies for injury or illness caused by pollution was thoroughly publicized. As a result, popular awareness of the possibility of effective court action against newspapers and other media enterprises for civil defamation rose dramatically, and so did the number of successful suits.[76]

The obscenity question is another media-related issue affected by the second modern constitutional revolution. Under Article 175 of the Criminal Code, various laws regulating the media, the police laws, obsçenity regulation, public security maintenance and thought control were sometimes linked in the Japanese official mind before 1945.[77] Today, such connections are seen by few officials and citizens. Since the Occupation period, Japan has been again rather tolerant, producing large numbers of erotic books, pictures, magazines, comic books, advertisements, TV broadcasts, motion pictures and tape recordings.[78]

There have been two major Supreme Court decisions on obscenity, both concerning translations of foreign works: the 1957 *Lady Chatterley's Lover* Case[79] and the 1969 *de Sade* Case.[80] Article 175 provides penalties for "a person who distributes or sells an obscene writing, picture or other object or who publicly displays the same . . .".[81] In *Chatterley* the Supreme Court held that twelve obscene passages at issue infected D.H. Lawrence's entire work with obscenity, and defined obscenity as follows:[82] "In order for a writing to be obscene, it is required that it wantonly arouse and stimulate sexual desire, offend the normal sense of shame, and run counter to proper concepts of sexual morality."

The *Chatterley* decision has continued to draw criticism from liberal scholars for arrogating to the courts "a clinical role" in the event society's moral views become lax. In *de Sade*, the court generally followed *Chatterley* doctrine, but seemed to some analysts to stress artistry and intellectual values more than *Chatterley* in the following passage:[83]

> There may be cases where the artistry and intellectual content of a work may diminish and moderate the sexual stimulus caused by its portrayal of sex to a degree less than that which is the object of punishment in the Criminal Code, so as to negate obscenity. . . .

Dissenting opinions denied the obscenity of the partial translation of de Sade's *In Praise of Vice* either because of its artistic and intellectual content, or because its sadistic repulsiveness reduced its erotic appeal to insignificance. Majority doctrine is regarded by commentators as somewhat restrictive.[84]

While providing binding guidelines for official Japan, judicial decisions do not give much hint of the systems for purveying and regulating obscenity in Japan. Critical to freedom of erotica are public agencies and private regulatory agencies connected with different industries. For example, the major motion picture producer-distributors abide by decisions of their own Motion Picture Ethics Committee (*Eiga Rinrikitei Kanri Iinkai*, or *Eirin*) in applying the industry's code of ethics and their understanding of what is legally permissible.[85] The film *Kuroi Yuki (Black Snow)* was shown with the approval of *Eirin*, but was held obscene by the Tokyo high court in 1969.[86] For some years after that, the courts did not accept *Eirin*'s view as a basis for immunity from prosecution. *Black Snow* depicted the life of prostitutes in the environs of an American base. The accused were acquitted on grounds that until this judicial decision, they could assume reasonably that if *Eirin* approved of a work, it was indeed legal. On the other hand, the Tokyo district court held in the 1978 Nikkatsu Romantic Sex Film Case[87] that *Eirin* was an instrument for determining what is in accord with prevailing community standards, and acquitted the Nikkatsu company of obscenity charges based on *Eirin* approval of its films. However, scores of "eroductions" appear annually, unregulated by *Eirin* and rarely restricted by officials.

The Customs Bureau censors imported films and pictures,[88] particularly those brought in for commercial purposes, with the assistance of a committee of citizens of "learning and experience."[89] The constitutionality of this system is questioned by scholars, and some judges. In the first test case reaching the appellate level—one involving a challenge to a denial of permission to import nude picture books—the Supreme Court in 1979 ordered a retrial favoring the challenge, but did not clearly present its own doctrine.[90]

Frank and undisguised pornographic writings with the traditional designation of *shunpon* (literally, springtime books), can be found in specialized shops and do not often generate widespread concern. Weekly pulp magazines, poster advertisements, pornography vending machines, and lewd comic books for children present the most noteworthy problems today. Their content is often strongly erotic and presents a degraded image of humanity, especially women.

About sixty percent of Japan's popular magazine sales take place in newsstands in railway stations, where concession privileges are controlled by the private Railroad Benefit Association (*Tetsudō Kōsaikai*).[91] The RBA can forbid the sale of a magazine or a particular issue of a magazine which its officials feel might be obscene. Among other sanctions, should police seize a magazine under obscenity law, the RBA may ban the next three issues from all its newsstands.

Local systems for regulating reading material outside train stations vary. For example, the private but powerful Tokyo Newspaper Sellers Commission (*Tokyoto Shinbun Sokubai Iinkai*)[92] determines the permissibility of distributing certain magazines to member newsstands and bookstores, and makes periodic spot checks to assure compliance with its policies. If objectionable material is found, a review committee considers the case and may issue a warning. Three warnings in a single year or one police seizure of a magazine may bring suspension of the seller's franchise. In addition, the Publications Ethics Council (*Shuppan Rinri Kyōgikai*) has been the publishing industry's main self-regulatory agency since 1963; but it does not appear very vigorous and it is helpless *vis-à-vis* "outsiders", who do not belong to the Magazine Publishers Association (*Zasshi Kyōkai*) or other industry organizations.[93]

The above and other private-sector systems of restraint combine in a complex web; they are supplemented by 39 local youth protection ordinances.[94] Ordinances such as Tokyo's encourage primary reliance upon self-regulatory systems. The Tokyo Governor may give warnings which, if not heeded, are followed by an order to stamp "unfit for youth" on the cover of offending publications. In some cases, a dozen or more official cautions or warnings have been given before any other enforcement action was taken against pornography affecting children.[95] In 1979, parental and official concern focused on pornography vending machines within easy access of young children, and on objectionable TV advertisements and films shown during children's usual viewing hours.[96] Efforts to solve the latter problem have been led by local TV branches of the Federation of Commercial Broadcasting Labor Unions (*Minpō Rōren*).[97]

As in other areas of regulation, so in restraining obscenity, particularly on behalf of children, Japanese regulatory authority is spread around among many public and private agencies, while the courts and interested scholars debate rather abstract definitions. The picture that emerges is not one of clear or simple leniency or restrictiveness, but relations between law and society resembling in complexity a *kanji* ideograph of 25 strokes. As William Spinrad notes in his sociology of civil liberties, formalized and just legal structures are essential to freedom, but are "never a carbon-copy reflection of the libertarian or anti-libertarian attitudes of politicians or any general public consensus."[98] This applies to Japan.[99]

Government certification of pre-collegiate textbooks has been another object of controversy for many years, in part in reaction to the very stringent controls of prewar days. In the complicated processes of writing, publishing, local selection, and marketing of such textbooks may be found unintended restrictions on freedom which may be more important than censorship,[100] and these problems are further complicated by the polarization of debate on some educational issues along rigid political lines. The textbook certification process takes place within the Ministry of Education. The *Ienaga Textbook Review* Cases significantly challenged administrative review criteria and processes with respect to textbooks, but also dramatized the continuing sensitivity of many Japanese to anything even faintly reminiscent of the thought control exercised by the prewar government. Professor Ienaga Saburo brought two suits, in 1965 and in 1967, against the Ministry of Education for requiring him to make changes in the manuscript of his revised high school history text under the Ministry's textbook certification system. Both cases[101] were on appeal in 1980, one to the Supreme Court against a 1975 high court ruling[102] that the Ministry had failed to adhere to its own criteria in assessing Ienaga's book.

Among the issues raised by the Ienaga cases are freedom of expression, academic freedom, the educational rights of parents, children and the state, and the question of whether the controversies themselves are among the great constitutional cases of modern Japan (a view this writer shares) or exclusively matters of administrative and civil law. A key point of contention was whether Ienaga's book was unfairly critical of the imperial family in discussing the mythological and historical origins of the Emperor system, so as to imply, to some, authoritarian unconcern for the people. The relevant passages are of less interest to Japanese school children than tonight's TV programs; but the length of the Ienaga controversy and the intensity of feeling supporting Ienaga well illustrate the concern of Japanese intellectual élites, if not necessarily the generality of citizens, about possible reversion to reverence for the Emperor and an overturning of the postwar constitutional revolution. The treatment accorded pre-1945 history, domestic and international, in many school textbooks does gloss over a great many unpleasant facts, and Ienaga is not alone in complaining about this tendency.[103] Ienaga's special concern is understandable, as he was a principal co-author of the first official history text for the compulsory grades in postwar Japan.[104] Moreover, official systems for restricting freedom of thought and expression in prewar Japan were realistically seen as coercive measures secondary to and supplementary to the desired natural effects of a modern public education system permeated with the imperial orthodoxy over a period of decades.

CONCLUSION: SOME PROBLEMS AND PROSPECTS

Japan is now in a constitutional era when concern about reversion to the prewar system may recede into the background for the salaried man and his family.[105] Among noteworthy constitutional issues now pending are: the constitutionality of the Self-Defense Forces; limits on the freedom of expression of public employees; delayed justice in the courts; unreviewed internal rules and processes of regulatory agencies which affect individual rights; the extent of expanding environmental rights; discrimination against *burakumin* (traditional outcasts), women, Okinawans, and resident aliens; and serious malapportionment of seats in the Diet.

In substance, the Supreme Court will most likely concur with the Sapporo high court in upholding the constitutionality of the Self-Defense Forces in the *Naganuma* Case.[106] The debate on this case in the past decade has helped to refine and clarify positions on this unique issue. Article 9's pacifist provisions may well continue to be meaningful in law and politics as a unique symbol of self-restraint on military power and the constitutional order under the "Peace Constitution," and needs to be understood by Japan's allies. Whether a similar confluence of history, internal law and politics, and geopolitics will enable pacifism to occur in another nation-state remains to be seen.

Discrimination is a significant constitutional and human problem in Japan, although it does not receive much attention from scholars and is of interest to relatively few lawyers, politicians and citizens as yet. The Civil Liberties Bureau works imaginatively to combat discrimination through educational means and the Civil Liberties Commissioner system.[107] Social discrimination against the million Okinawans is likely to continue. The *burakumin*, numbering something over 1.5 million by government estimates and 3 million according to the Burakumin Liberation Movement, have been helped, as Japanese citizens, by remedial discrimination in the 1970s which has provided them with educational and other aid.[108] However, resident aliens, legal and illegal, have little recourse under Japanese law, and are not eligible for aid from the Civil Liberties Commissioners.[109] Most notable are roughly 650,000 Koreans, 50,000 Chinese, and the 2,500 unwelcome refugees from Indochina in and out of Japan since mid-1975.[110] For the above and for women, employment discrimination is the most discussed problem. Many *burakumin* and aliens also suffer private restraints on their choice of a marriage partner.[111]

Revised rules of the LDP for the selection of the party president (and, as a consequence, the Prime Minister) which were used for the first time in late 1978 have established something comparable to a primary election system, though not preliminary, as in the United States, to a popular election for public office, but to a run-off election for party leadership. This may be viewed as a quasi-constitutional innovation, as previously the electors were limited to the parliamentary party, plus prefectural party leaders. Votes were cast by registered LDP members throughout the country in November, 1978, and Ōhira Masayoshi received perhaps the highest total (more than 550,000 votes) ever received in an election by a single aspirant to the premiership.[112] Ōhira became party president, when the second-ranking vote-getter (of four candidates), Fukuda Takeo, declined to participate in a run-off election. The new system encourages broader popular participation in LDP politics.

However, the malapportionment of seats in the House of Representatives and the less-powerful House of Councilors under the Public Office Election Law is an unresolved constitutional problem the political parties have chosen not to solve by legislative action. In 1976, the Supreme Court held unconstitutional the distribution of lower house seats in 1972.[113] The *degree* of malapportionment was against requirements for equality under the law and universal adult suffrage, and against the prohibition on discrimination against any particular candidates for public office.[114] (Candidates, for example, who must get twice as many votes as candidates in another district in order to be elected are suffering a form of discrimination.) But the court invalidated neither the election nor the subsequent actions of the malapportioned Diet, as requested by the plaintiffs. In 1975 the Diet added twenty seats, bringing the total to 511;[115] but the apportionment as of the December 1976 general elections were also challenged, in two cases decided in 1978. The first decision, handed down by the Tokyo high court,[116] upheld the constitutionality of the apportionment; while the second, much more widely supported,[117] struck it down as a violation of the Article 14 requirement of equality under the law. Both holdings were on appeal to the Supreme Court before October, 1979, when the next lower house election was held.[118] The apportionment as of the 1979 elections was challenged, and the apportionment as of the subsequent June 22, 1980, elections is also expected to be challenged. Some LDP leaders have expressed their disagreement with the "one man—one vote" thinking behind the 1976 and 1978 judgments of unconstitutionality and the repeated challenges; but opposition politicians also see a threat to their political positions in change.[119] In September 1978, the apportionment caused discrepancies in the effective weight of a vote, depending on election district, ranging up to 3.74 to 1 in the lower house and 5.31 to 1 in the upper house, with 1 representing the minimum weight.[120] The interplay of the Supreme Court and the Diet on the malapportionment issue will merit close attention in the 1980s.

In addition, a November 1979 district court decision raised the spectre of Japan's imperial past in sentencing two radicals to death for killing eight and injuring close to 200 people in a series of bombings between 1972 and 1975, and for plotting the assassination of the Emperor. Although neither law nor constitution recognizes any difference between attempted murder of the Emperor and of an ordinary citizen, the presiding judge raised political hackles by suggesting, to many, a basic difference in holding the conspirators "had a firm intent to assassinate the Emperor, the symbol of the unity of the people of Japan, with bombs."[121]

On balance, however, despite political and judicial problems, the second modern constitutional revolution of Japan is likely to be guarded with vigilance by substantial forces in the public and private sectors. In Bonn, Matsuyama Yukio, international journalist with the *Asahi Shinbun*, put well the hopes of many Japanese:[122]

> We want to be peaceful, and we want to remind you that Japan is next to none in her love of freedom, after having enjoyed its sweetness in these recent years. And we will not have it taken away by any government of any form. I still remember being deeply impressed with President Kennedy's remarks on his visit to the Berlin Wall, when he said, "*Ich bin ein Berliner.*" He meant, of course, that he was a free man, dedicated to liberty. And I still remember being deeply impressed by Martin Luther King, when he raised a vision for all mankind and said, "I have a dream." For man to be free and at peace with his neighbors. *I* have a dream that the day will come when I shall be able to say to the world at large, "*Ich bin ein Japaner.*" And the world will know that such is a man who tries to keep his liberty through peaceful means.

I share those hopes for Japan, and believe that constitutional democracy will probably continue without further constitutional revolution, barring a severe economic dislocation, the resurgence of extreme nationalism, or a holocaust. The reasons for optimism in 1980 are that competing constitutional structures and some values of Japanese law and society give substance to such hopes, and that the balance of political forces for and against stable Japanese-style democracy seems more likely to weigh increasingly on the side of responsible freedom.

NOTES

1 David M. Earl, *Emperor and Nation in Japan* (Seattle: University of Washington Press, 1964); John Fairbank et al., A History of East Asian Civilization—East Asia: The Great Tradition (Boston: Houghton-Mifflin, 1960); and Dan Fenno Henderson, *Conciliation and Japanese Law: Tokugawa and Modern*, 2 vols (Seattle: University of Washington Press, 1968), vol. I.

2 Dan Fenno Henderson, "Law and Political Modernization in Japan," in Robert E. Ward (ed.), *Political Development in Modern Japan* (Princeton: University Press, 1968); and Hideo Tanaka (ed.), assisted by Malcolm D. H. Smith, *The Japanese Legal System* (Toyko: University of Tokyo Press, 1976), pp. 194–253. For a concise historical analysis of rights in the West, see Richard P. Claude, "The Classical Model of Human Rights Development," in Richard P. Claude (ed.), *Comparative Human Rights* (Baltimore: Johns Hopkins University Press, 1976), pp. 6–50.

3 Yasuhiro Okudaira, *Political Censorship in Japan, 1931–1945* (Philadelphia: University of Pennsylvania Law School Library, 1962), esp. pp. 1–50.

4 Probably the most valuable compilation of detailed studies and official trial records of group political actions in Japan from the 1860s till the Pacific War is *Seiji saiban shiroku*, 5 vols (Daiichi Hōki, 1969–70), edited by Daiichi Hōki publishing co. An additional five volumes on recent decades were published in 1980. These studies amply illustrate preferences for group, as opposed to individual, assertiveness, and for other traditional values (referred to later in this paper) which antedated but are not integrated with Western legal ideas of justice.

5 William Spinard, *Civil Liberties* (Chicago: Quadrangle Books, 1970), pp. 5–26, 292–306. See Okudaira, *Political Censorship in Japan*; Richard Mitchell, *Thought Control in Prewar Japan* (Ithaca: Cornell University Press, 1976); and Patricia Steinhoff, "Legal Control of Ideology in Prewar Japan," unpublished paper, International Congress of Orientalists, Canberra, Australia, 1970.

6 See *Legal Reforms in Japan during the Allied Occupation*, special reprint volume, *Washington Law Review*, 1977.

7 "Article 9. Aspiring sincerely to an international peace based on justice and order, the Japanese people forever renounce war as a sovereign right of the nation and the threat or use of force as a means of settling international disputes.

"2. In order to accomplish the aim of the preceding paragraph, land, sea, and air forces, as well as other war potential, will never be maintained. The right of belligerency of the state will not be recognized." *The Constitution of Japan*, in Itoh and Beer, *The Constitutional Case Law of Japan* (Seattle: University of Washington Press, 1978), p. 258. According to Chalmers Johnson, the Japanese *senryoku*, the usual Japanese translation of war potential in paragraph 2 of Article 9, is a mistranslation, as *senryoku* means fighting power or strength, something more limited than war potential. The constitution does not, therefore, limit *senbi* or *gunbi* which have the wider meaning implied in war potential, and which, owing to Japan's industrial potential, is considerable. C. Johnson, "*Omote* (Explicit) and *Ura* (Implicit): Translating Japanese Political Terms," *Journal of Japanese Studies*, Vol. 6, No. 1 (Winter 1980), p. 114.

8 "Article 4. The Emperor shall perform only such acts in matters of state as are provided for in this Constitution and he shall not have powers related to government." Ibid., p. 257.

9 Lawrence W. Beer, "Education, Politics and Freedom of Expression in Japan: the Ienaga Textbook Review Cases," *Law in Japan: An Annual*, Vol. 8 (1975), 67–90; Ronald Suleski, "A New Generation of Japanese Intellectuals," *Japan Foundation Newsletter*, 6, No. 4 (October–November, 1978), pp. 10–12.

10 The Constitution of Japan was promulgated on November 3, 1946, and went into effect on May 3, 1947. The amendment provision in The Constitution of the Empire of Japan was as follows: "Article 73. When it has become necessary in future to amend the provisions of the present Constitution, a project to the effect shall be submitted to the Imperial Diet by Imperial Order.

"2. In the above case, neither House can open the debate, unless not less than two-thirds of the whole number of Members are present, and no amendment can be passed, unless a majority of not less than two-thirds of the Members present is obtained." Tanaka, *Japanese Legal System*, p. 23.

11 On the history of the revision controversy, see Haruhiro Fukui, "The Liberal Democratic Party and Constitutional Revision," in David Sissons (ed.), *Papers on Modern Japan* (Canberra: Australian University Press, 1968), and "Twenty Years of Revisionism," in Dan Fenno Henderson (ed.), *The Constitution of Japan: Its First Twenty Years* (Seattle: University of Washington Press, 1969), pp. 41–70; and Reinhard Neumann, "The Inaba Affair, Constitution Day and Constitutional Revision," *Law in Japan: An Annual*, Vol. 9 (1976), pp. 129–43.

12 Max Gluckman's distinction between "rituals of rebellion" and "revolution" may apply to the 1960 Security Treaty Crisis and to some aspects of the University Crisis of 1969. Revolution seeks to overthrow the whole existing order, while ritual rebellion, which may be a luxury limited to societies like Japan with a stable established order, reaffirm the system in venting tensions between leaders and led and between viewpoints. In this connection, see Max Gluckman, *Custom and Conflict in*

Africa and *Politics, Law, and Ritual in Tribal Society*; and Takeo Doi (John Bester, trans.), *Anatomy of Dependence* (Tokyo: Kodansha International, 1973).

13 On the Security Treaty Crisis, see George R. Packard III, *Protest in Tokyo: The Security Treaty Crisis of 1960* (Princeton: Princeton University Press, 1966); Richard Rabinowitz, "Law and the Social Process in Japan," *The Transactions of the Asiatic Society of Japan*, Third Series, Vol. 10 (1968): 54–71; John M. Maki, *Government and Politics in Japan* (New York: Praeger Publishers, 1962); Robert Scalapino and Junnosuke Masumi, *Parties and Politics in Contemporary Japan* (Berkeley and Los Angeles: University of California Press, 1962).

14 *Japan v. Sakata*, 23 *Keishū* 3225 (Sup. Ct., Grand Bench, December 16, 1959). For a translation, see John M. Maki (ed.), *Court and Constitution in Japan* (Seattle: University of Washington Press, 1964), pp. 298–361.

15 *Japan v. Sakane et al.*, 13 *Keishū* (No. 5) 685 (Sup. Ct., Grand Bench, April 2, 1969). A translation appears in Itoh and Beer, *Constitutional Case Law of Japan*, pp. 103–30.

16 See the opinion poll survey reports in *Asahi Shinbun*, November 1, 1978, and January 1, 1979.

17 Kenzō Takayanagi (John Maki, trans.), "The Conceptual Background of the Constitutional Revision Debate in the Constitution Investigation Commission," *Law in Japan: An Annual*, Vol. 1 (1967): 1–24; Robert E. Ward, "The Commission on the Constitution in the Prospects of Constitutional Change in Japan," *Journal of Asian Studies*, Vol. 24 (1965): 401–30; John M. Maki, "The Documents of Japan's Commission on the Constitution," *Journal of Asian Studies*, Vol. 24 (1965): 475–89; and the final report of the Commission on the Constitution, *Kenpō Chōsakai Hōkokusho (Ōkurashō Insatsukyoku*, 1964). For commentaries, see *Hōritsu Fihō* 419 (August, 1964): 363–74, and *Furisuto* 303 (August, 1964): 10–26. A study group, *Kenpō Mondai Kenkyūkai*, opposing the Commission on the Constitution, *Kenpō Chōsakai Hōkokusho (Ōkurashō Insatsukyoku*, 1964). Iwanami Shoten, 1964).

18 *Asahi Shinbun*, November 1, 1978, and January 1, 1979.

19 Such loyalty is especially emphasized among white collar workers. See Sepp Linhart, *Arbeit, Freizeit und Familie in Japan*, with a summary in English (Weisbaden: Otto Harrassowitz, 1976), and Thomas Rohlen, *For Harmony and Strength, Japanese White-Collar Organization in Anthropological Perspective* (Berkeley: University of California Press, 1974).

20 The distribution of seats in both Houses of the Diet in July 1980 was as below. For perspective, statistics after the prior two lower house elections and the last upper house election are included. The sudden jump in LDP strength in 1980 was attendant to the unexpected death of Prime Minister Ōhira Masayoshi on June 12 during the election campaign. Voter turnout on June 22 was the highest since 1960, 74.57%, as citizens rallied around the strongest party and, perhaps, honored the deceased by supporting his party, especially candidates of factions allied with Ōhira. See *Asahi Shinbun*, June 23–26, 1980.

	House of Representatives			*House of Councilors*	
Party	*1980*	*1979*	*1976*	*1980*	*1977*
LDP	286	253	254	135	125
JSP	107	107	118	47	53
Kōmeitō	34	58	56	27	28
Democratic Socialist Party	33	36	28	12	11
Japan Communist Party	29	41	19	12	16
New Liberal Club	12	4	17	2	5
Shaminren	3	2	3	2	3
Independents	7	10	6	14	4
Vacancies			10	1	2
	511	511	511	252	247

In the 1970s, independents usually joined with the LDP, thus assuring it a parliamentary majority. The New Liberal Club is a moderate conservative group which split off from the LDP in the mid-1970s, but often votes with it.

21 *The Constitution of Japan*, Article 96:
"Amendments to this Constitution shall be initiated by the Diet, through a concurring vote of two-thirds or more of all the members of each House and shall thereupon be submitted to the people for ratification, which shall require the affirmative vote of a majority of all votes cast thereon, at a special referendum or at such election as the Diet shall specify.
"2. Amendments when so ratified shall immediately be promulgated by the Emperor in the name of the people, as an integral part of this Constitution." Itoh and Beer, *Constitutional Case Law of Japan*, p. 268.

22 Lawrence W. Beer, "Nihon no saibankan," *Jurisuto*, no. 700, September 15, 1979. Annually, *Hōsō Jihō* (Hōsōkai) publishes authoritative statistical reports on cases dealt with by the courts, and *Hōritsu Jihō* (Nihon Hyōronsha) carries reviews of both constitutional case law and constitutional studies (*kenpōgaku*). Although the Supreme Court's share in the judicial caseload is only a small fraction of the whole, by the end of 1977, it had "taken cognizance of 183,496 cases, out of which 1,045 cases were referred to the Grand Bench [by petty benches], and in 263 cases the Court declared a law, order, regulation or official act unconstitutional." *Justice in Japan* (Tokyo: Supreme Court of Japan, 1978), p. 19.

23 Family courts, summary courts, and various modes of lay participation in dispute resolution are briefly described in *Justice in Japan*. pp. 14–17, 23–6. Concerning the Civil Liberties Bureau and Commissioners, see Lawrence W. Beer and C. G. Weeramantry, "Human Rights in Japan: Some Protections and Problems," *Universal Human Rights*, No. 3, 1979, pp. 1–33.

24 Concerning Japan's court system and judges, see Itoh and Beer, *Constitutional Case Law of Japan*, pp. 7–21, 250–5; and, on barriers to civil litigation, John Owen Haley, "The Myth of the Reluctant Litigant," *Journal of Japanese Studies*, (summer, 1978): 359–90. In Japanese, Wada Hideo, *Saikō saibansho ron* (Nihon Hyōronsha, 1970), and *Saikō saibansho* (Hōgaku seminah-Nihon Hyōronsha, 1977).

25 For example, *Abe v. Japan*, 20 *Keishū* (No. 6) 537 (Sup. Ct., Second Petty Bench, July 1, 1966), translated in Itoh and Beer, *Constitutional Case Law of Japan*, pp. 167–8.

26 See, for example, *Japan* v. *Ozawa*, 28 *Keishū* (No. 9) 393 (Supreme Court, Grand Bench, November 6, 1974); for comments, see Lawrence W. Beer, "Recent Developments—Constitutional Law," *Law in Japan: An Annual*, Vol. 8 (1975): 205–8, and Nobushige Ukai, "The Significance of the Reception of American Constitutional Institutions and Ideas in Japan," in L. W. Beer (ed.), *Constitutionalism in Asia* (Berkeley and Los Angeles: University of California Press, 1979), pp. 123–6. See generally "Kenpō no sōten," *Jurisuto zōkan* (May, 1978); "Nihonkoku kenpō," *Jurisuto rinji zōkan*, 638 (May, 1977); "Kenpō 30nen no riron to tenbō," *Hōritsu Jihō rinji zōkan* (May 1977); Kobayashi Naoki, *Kenpō handan no genri*, 2 vols (Nihon Hyōronsha, 1978); and Ashibe Nobuyoshi (ed.), *Kenpō* (Yūhikaku, 1978), Vol. 2.

27 The Ōtsu Case (1891) and the Meiji Constitution established judicial independence for the first time in Japan. As Kenzō Takayanagi notes: "In a sense, the Ōtsu Incident and its legacy contradict the basic thesis advanced by the Western scholars interviewed by Kaneko: the inclusion in the Constitution of an institution quite foreign to the Japanese scene provided the foundation on which a tradition of judicial independence very quickly emerged." Takayanagi, *supra* n. 17. See also Marc Galanter, "The Displacement of Traditional Law in Modern India," *Journal of Social Issues* 24 (1968): 65–91.

28 See Tanaka (ed.), *Japanese Legal System*, pp. 642–85 and works cited therein.

29 A good presentation of these views is Reinhard Neumann, "The Inaba Affair, Constitution Day and Constitutional Revision," *supra*, n. 11.

30 Hiroshi Itoh, "Judicial Decision-making in the Japanese Supreme Court," *Law in Japan: An Annual*, vol. 3 (1969): 128–61; Kisaburo Yokota, "Political Questions and Judicial Review," Henderson (ed.), *Constitution of Japan*, pp. 141–66; Hideo Wada, "Decisions under Article 9 of the Constitution: The *Sunakawa*, *Eniwa*, *Naganuma* Decisions," *Law in Japan: An Annual* 9 (1976): 117–28; "Recent Developments," ibid.: 153; Robert L. Seymour, "Japan's Self-Defense: The Naganuma Case and Its Implications," *Pacific Affairs*, Vol. 47 (1974–75): 421; and Kenneth M. Tagawa, *Justiciability and Judicial Power in Japan*, unpublished Ph.D. dissertation, University of Colorado, 1979.

31 Edward Seidensticker, "Japan After Vietnam," *Commentary* (September, 1976): 56.

32 Gino Piovesana, *Recent Japanese Philosophical Thought* (Tokyo: Enderle Bookstore, 1961); Charles A. Moore (ed.), *The Japanese Mind* (Honolulu: East-West Center Press, 1968); Miyazawa Toshiyoshi, *Kenpō* (Yūhikaku, 1962).

33 Carl Steenstrup, "The Company Code," *Asian Law Forum*, Vol. 1 (1976): 21–5.

34 Chie Nakane, *Japanese Society* (Berkeley and Los Angeles: University of California Press, 1970).

35 The term "reciprocal dependency" is taken from Douglas D. Mitchell, *Amae: The Expression of Reciprocal Dependency Needs in Japanese Politics and Law* (Boulder, Colorado: Westview Press, 1976). Mitchell seems to this writer to present Takeo Doi's important views on dependency more systematically and more clearly than Doi himself. See also Takeo Doi, *Anatomy of Dependence*.

36 Ryūichi Nagao, in a review of R. Minear, *Japanese Tradition and Western Law* (Cambridge, Mass.: Harvard University Press, 1970), in *Law in Japan: An Annual* 5 (1972): 224. A comparative study of the meanings and objects of loyalty would be very helpful as a step toward clarifying the bases of intercultural disagreements.

37 Hayashi Chikio et al., *Nipponjin no kokuminsei* (Shiseido, 1970); and Hayashi Chikio, "Seiji ishiki no seitai," *Asahi Shinbun*, December 16, 1978, p. 4. See also the comprehensive survey report in *Asahi Shinbun*, January 1, 1979, pp. 1, 10–13.

The term "feudal," often used pejoratively to criticize traditional aspects of modern Japan, is usually applied to factors such as the family system which predated feudalism by centuries and which made Japanese feudalism different from other feudalisms such as those of Western Europe. See F. Joüon des Longrais, *L'est et l'ouest, institutions du Japon et de l'occident comparées* (Paris and Tokyo, 1958). This writer does not share a uniformly negative view of Japanese-style "feudalism" as it functions today.

38 Hayashi, "Seiji ishiki no seitai." Only a small percentage (*c.* 20%) of Japanese expressed much trust in politicians in late 1978 compared, for example, to tax officials (*c.* 45%), judges, teachers, police, doctors, newspapers, and weather forecasters, among whom the last in the ascending order were the most trusted. *Asahi Shinbun*, October 22, 1978, and January 1, 1979. My only explanation for the extraordinary trust of forecasters is good-humored Japanese stress on distrust of other categories. Newspapers are trusted institutions, but the results may have been skewed to their advantage by the fact that the newspapers did the polling.

39 *The Constitution of Japan*, Article 97 in the "Supreme Law" chapter of the constitution reads: "The fundamental human rights by this Constitution guaranteed to the people of Japan are fruits of the age-old struggle of man to be free; they have survived the many exacting tests for durability and are conferred upon this and future generations in trust, to be held for all time inviolate."

40 On the severe limitations on the emperor's political role as an individual in the Tokugawa period (1600–1868), see Herschel Webb, *The Japanese Imperial Institution in the Tokugawa Period* (New York: Columbia University Press, 1968), and for the period 1868–1946, see David A. Titus, *Palace and Politics in Prewar Japan* (New York: Columbia University Press, 1974), and *Modern Asian Studies*, 14, 4 (1980), p. 529.

41 Regarding the police, who enjoy considerable public respect and trust in Japan, see David H. Bayley, *Forces of Order: Police Behavior in Japan and the United States* (Berkeley: University of California Press, 1976).

Takayanagi Kenzō noted that prewar debates on constitutionality involved political rhetoric, but rarely justiciable rights; *supra*, n. 32. "Conciliable rights" is meant to express the prevalent style of dispute resolution, involving a third-party status bearer (informal or official) pursuing compromise and formal harmony. On Japanese right consciousness, see Lawrence W. Beer, "Freedom of Expression in Japan with Comparative Reference to the United States," in Claude (ed.), *Comparative Human Rights*, pp. 101–9; Henderson, *Conciliation and Japanese Law*.

42 Discussions in 1978 and 1979 with Itō Masami and Shimizu Hideo. They consider press freedom more critical to democracy in Japan than in most countries.

43 *The Constitution of Japan*, "Article 81. The Supreme Court is the court of last resort with power to determine the constitutionality of any law, order, regulation or official act." Itoh and Beer, *Constitutional Case Law of Japan*, p. 266. Lower courts, by judicial decision and Article 76, also have the power of judicial review.

44 Beer and Weeramantry, "Human Rights in Japan."

45 Article 81 of the *Constitution of Japan*. Article 76 is also critical: "The whole judicial power is vested in a Supreme Court and in such inferior courts as are established by law.

"2. No extraordinary tribunal shall be established, nor shall any organ or agency of the Executive be given final judicial power.

"All judges shall be independent in the exercise of their conscience and shall be bound only by this Constitution and the laws." Itoh and Beer, *Constitutional Case Law of Japan*, p. 265.

For a study of the prewar administrative court system, to which paragraph 2 of Article 76 is in part a reaction, see Hideo Wada, "The Administrative Court under the Meiji Constitution," *Law in Japan: An Annual* 10 (1977): 1–64.

46 For comparative perspectives, see Beer (ed.), *Constitutionalism in Asia*; Ivo Duchacek, "Constitutions: Adapting to Change," *Power Maps: Comparative Politics of Constitutions* (Santa Barbara: ABC Clio Press, 1973), pp. 210–32; Claude, *Comparative Human Rights*; David H. Bayley, *Public Liberties in the New States* (Chicago: Rand McNally & Co., 1964). On judicial roles in civil law systems, see John Henry Merryman, *The Civil Law Tradition* (Stanford: Stanford University Press, 1969); Rudolf B. Schlesinger, "Common Law and Civil Law: A Historical Comparison," *Comparative Law*, 2nd edition (Brooklyn: Foundation Press, 1959), pp. 179–98.

47 Article 4, Court Organization Law, Law No. 59 of April 16, 1947. See Itoh and Beer, *Constitutional Case Law of Japan*, pp. 7–11, 251–5; Haley, "Myth of the Reluctant Litigant," pp. 381–9; and on the effect of an unconstitutional judgment, Ukai in Beer, *Constitutionalism in Asia*.

48 Discussions with judges, Tokyo, 1978–1979.

49 Haley, "Myth of the Reluctant Litigant," pp. 387–90.

50 Conversation with Matsuo Kōya, specialist in criminal procedure law, 1979. Bayley, *Forces of Order*, pp. 141–4. Civil liberties lawyer Ōno Masao says police brutality is very rarely a problem; ibid., pp. 165–6.

51 Haley, "Myth of the Reluctant Litigant"; Kahei Rokumoto, "Problems and Methodology of Study of Civil Disputes," pt 1, *Law in Japan: An Annual* 5 (1972): 97–114, and pt 2, 6 (1973): 111–27.

52 Beer in Claude (ed.), *Comparative Human Rights*, pp. 101–9.

53 On the other hand, *individual* dissent and post-consensus dissent from the views of one's in-group seem notably limited in Japan. However, pre-consensus debate within one's group is relatively uninhibited (except by the seniority order of presentation), as is expression of group disagreement with government policies or the opinions of "outsiders" of whatever kind. See Beer in ibid.

54 See Bayley, *Forces of Order*, pp. 172–83.

55 Freedom of assembly can be regulated under Article 7 of *Dōrō Kōtsūhō* (Law 105 of 1960), Article 19 of *Densenbyō yobōhō* (Law 36 of 1897), Articles 5 and 7, *Hakai katsudō bōshihō* (Law 240 of 1952), Articles 106 and 107, *Keihō*, and Article 4 of Ministry of Welfare Order No. 19 of 1949 (*Official Gazette*, No. 938); and by public safety ordinances.

56 On public safety ordinances and their use, see Beer in Claude (ed.), *Comparative Human Rights*.

57 *Japan* v. *Itō*, 14 *Keishū* 1243 (Sup. Ct., Grand Bench, July 20, 1960). For a translation and the ordinance in question, see Maki (ed.), *Court and Constitution in Japan*, pp. 84–116. For an analysis, see Beer in Claude, *Comparative Human Rights*, pp. 115–18.

58 The Supreme Court can and does on occasion reverse its own precedent. For examples, see Cases 7 and 24 in Itoh and Beer, *Constitutional Case Law of Japan*.

59 *Japan* v. *Sugino*, 4 *Keishū* 2012, 1014 (Sup. Ct., Grand Bench, 1950).

60 See Miyazawa Toshiyoshi, *Nihonkoku kenpō* (Nihon Hyōronsha, 1963), p. 205; and Yamamoto Keiichi, "Kōkyō no fukushi," in Tanaka Jirō (ed.), *Nihonkoku kenpō taikei*, Vol. 8 (Yūhikaku, 1961), p. 16. On legal theories in Japan on the public welfare, see Satō Isao, *Kenpō Kenkū Nyūmon*, 3 vols (Nihon Hyōronsha, 1966) 2: 25–117.

61 Ashibe Nobuyoshi et al., "Kenpō hanrei no 30nen," *Jurisuto*, special issue (May 3, 1977): 452, 453, and in the same issue commemorating the thirtieth anniversary of Japan's constitution, see Itō Masami, "Kenpō kaishaku to rieki kōryōron," p. 200, on the increased judicial use of an interests-balancing approach. See in general this issue of *Jurisuto* and *Kenpō sanjūnen no riron to tenbō, Hōritsu Jihō, rinji zōkan* (May, 1977), on Japan's constitutionalism.

62 See *Asahi Shinbun*, July 17, 1970 (Sup. Ct., Petty Bench, July 16, 1970); conversations with Justice Irie Toshio, January, 1971.

63 See, for example, *Japan* v. *Sakane et al., supra* n. 15, and *Toyama et al.* v. *Japan*, 20 Keishū (No. 8) 901 (Sup. Ct., Grand Bench, October 26, 1966), in Itoh and Beer, *Constitutional Case Law of Japan*, pp. 85–130. See also *Rōdō to jinken* (Hōgaku seminah-Nihon Hyōronsha, 1978).

64 *Japan* v. *Ozawa*, 28 *Keishū* (No. 9) 393 (Sup. Ct., Grand Bench, November 6, 1974). For comment, see Ukai in Beer (ed.), *Constitutionalism in Asia*, pp. 122–5; and "Recent Developments—Constitutional Law," *Law in Japan: An Annual* 8 (1975): 205–8.

65 On the courts and media, see Lawrence W. Beer, "Freedom of Information and the Evidentiary Use of Film in Japan. . . .," *The American Political Science Review* 65 (1971): 1119–34; *Genron to masu komi* (Hōgaku seminah-Nihon Hyōronsha, 1978); *Gendai no masu komi, Jurisuto, sōgōtokushū* No. 5 (October 1976); Masami Ito et al., *Broadcasting in Japan* (London: Routledge and Kegan Paul, 1978); Horibe Masao, *Akusesuken towa nanika* (Iwanami Shinsho, 1978).

66 *Nishiyama* v. *Japan, Hanrei Jihō* 887 (July 11, 1978): 14–41 (Sup. Ct., First Petty Bench, May 31, 1978); Ronald G. Brown, "Government Secrecy and the 'People's Right to Know' in Japan: Implications of the *Nishiyama* Case," *Law in Japan: An Annual* 10 (1977); 112–39. See also the final report of the Secrecy and Disclosure Subcommittee, Senate Select Committee on Intelligence, October, 1978, U.S. Senate.

67 Lawrence W. Beer, "Defamation, Privacy and Freedom of Expression in Japan," *Law in Japan: An Annual* 5 (1972): 192–208; Itō Masami, *Puraibashii no kenri* (Iwanami Shoten, 1963); Shimizu Hideo, *Hō to masu komyūnikēshon* (Shakai Shisōsha, 1970); and *Meiyo-puraibashii no shintenkai, Jurisuto* 653 (December 1, 1977). On rights of the person in the United States, see Don R. Pember, *Privacy and the Press* (Seattle: University of Washington Press, 1972); and Arthur R. Miller, *The Assault on Privacy* (Ann Arbor: University of Michigan Press, 1971).

68 Conversation with Onizuka Kentarō, Head, Civil Liberties Bureau, Justice Ministry, October, 1978. See Beer and Weeramantry, "Human Rights in Japan," p. 13. *Mura hachibu*, ostracism from the village, was the prototype of this powerful sanction, but for the Tokugawa period, *machi hachibu* (ostracism from commercial districts of towns and cities) was also common. See *Nihon Keizai Jiten* (Nihon hyoronsha, 1943), p. 1844. Today *mura hachibu* is the official catch-all term for illegal ostracism. In the cities, *mura hachibu* may even include ostracism of a housewife in a modern apartment complex by other women living there.

69 *Arita* v. *Mishima*, 15 *Kakyū Minshū* (No. 9) 2317 (Tokyo district court, September 28, 1964). For Donald Keen's translation of the novel at issue, see Yukio Mishima, *After the Banquet* (New York: Alfred A. Knopf, 1963). On private enforcement of rights, see Hideo Tanaka and Akio Takeuchi, "The Role of Private Persons in the Enforcement of Law: A Comparative Study of Japanese and American Law," *Law in Japan: An Annual* 7 (1974): 34–50. The Civil Code provisions are:

"Article 709. A person who violates intentionally or negligently the right of another is bound to make compensation for damage arising therefrom.

"Article 710. A person who is liable in compensation for damages in accordance with the provisions of the preceding Article shall make compensation therefore even in respect of a nonpecuniary damage, irrespective of whether such injury was to the person, liberty or reputation of another or to his property rights."

A theory which would directly apply such constitutional guarantees as good name and privacy without reference to code provisions seems to have little support. See Ukai in Beer, *Constitutionalism in Asia*, p. 122; and Ashibe, *Kenpō*, pp. 39–97.

70 *Hasegawa* v. *Japan*, 23 *Keishū* 1625 (Sup. Ct., Grand Bench, December 24, 1969). For a translation, see Itoh and Beer, *Constitutional Case Law of Japan*, pp. 178–82. Similar specification of the public welfare as what is necessary for criminal justice is used by the same court in *Kaneko* v. *Japan*, 23 *Keishū* 1490 (Sup. Ct., Grand Bench, November 26, 1969), translated in ibid., pp. 246–50.

71 *Katō* v. *Shūkan Jitsuwa, Hanrei Jihō* 537 (1968) 28 (Tokyo district court, November 25, 1968), and *Shūkan Jitsuwa* v. *Katō, Jurisuto* 449 (1970): 128 (Tokyo high court, December 25, 1969).

72 "*Eros + Gyakusatsu*" Case, *Kamichika* v. *Art Theatre Guild, Jurisuto* 449 (1970): 21 (Tokyo district court, March 14, 1970), and 23 *Kōminshū* (No. 2) 172 (Tokyo high court, April 13, 1970). See also, *Asahi Shinbun*, April 13 and 14 (morning and evening edns).

73 *Kawabata* v. *Chikuma Shobo et al.*, Tokyo district court, 1977. See *Japan Times Weekly Edition*, August 27, 1977. *Burakumin* are still discriminated against socially, despite laws to the contrary, as noted in the concluding section of this paper.

74 See the statistics for both civil and criminal defamation in annual reports in *Hōsō Jihō (Hōsōkai)*.

75 For example, at least until the 1970s, on a *per capita* basis France and Germany had roughly 200 times as many defamation suits and ten times more convictions than Japan. See K. Igarashi and H. Tamiya, *Meiyo to puraibashii* (1968), pp. 74–78; *Jurisuto* 332 (1965): 60; and *Jurisuto* 653 (1970).

76 Conversations with Judge Mutō Shunkō, Legal Training and Research Institute, in July, 1973 and December, 1978. The sharp rise in civil defamation suits peaked in 1973 and thereafter leveled off.

77 The term "*waisetsu*" (obscenity) and punishment of its "public display or sale" first appeared in Article 259 of the Criminal Code of 1880. Article 175 of the 1907 revised Criminal Code remains today the primary legal provision for restraint of obscenity, amended only in 1947 by the addition of imprisonment of fines as possible penalties. See Shimizu, *Hō to masu komyūnikēshon*, and Okudaira Yasuhiro, *Hyōgen no jiyū towa nanika* (Chūōkōronsha, 1970).

78 Shimizu, *Hō to masu komyūnikēshon*, pp. 170–89, presents historical perspective on Japan's obscenity law.
79 *Itō et al.* v. *Japan*, 11 *Keishū* (No. 3) 997 (Sup. Ct., Grand Bench, March 13, 1957); a translation is in Maki, *Court and Constitution in Japan*, pp. 3–37.
80 *Ishii et al.* v. *Japan*, 23 *Keishū* (No. 10) 1239 (Sup. Ct., Grand Bench, October 15, 1969); all opinions are translated in Itoh and Beer, *Constitutional Case Law of Japan*, pp. 183–217.
81 Ministry of Justice, Japan, *Criminal Statutes* (n.d.), Vol. 1, p. 39.
82 See Maki, *Court and Constitution in Japan*, p. 7.
83 Itoh and Beer, *Constitutional Case Law of Japan*, p. 184. See also Chin Kim, "Constitution and Obscenity: Japan and the U.S.A.," *American Journal of Comparative Law* 23 (1975): 255.
84 Itō Masami and Shimizu Hideo (eds), *Masu komi hōrei yōran* (Gendai Jānarizumu Shuppankai, 1966); Shimizu, *Hō to masu komyūnikēshon*; Okudaira, *Hyōgen no jiyū towa nanika*.
85 Discussions with Itō Masami, a member of *Eirin*, August, 1979. Concerning *Eirin*, see Masu Komi Rinri Kondankai (ed.), *Masu komi no shakai sekinin* (Nihon Shinbun Kyōkai, 1966), hereafter cited as *Sekinin*. On Japan's film industry see also J. I. Anderson and D. Richie, *The Japanese Film: Art and Industry* (New York: Grove Press, 1960).
86 *Japan* v. *Murakami et al., Hanrei Jihō* 571 (November 11, 1969): 19 (Tokyo high court, September 17, 1969).
87 *Japan* v. *Nikkatsu Co., Hanrei Jihō* 897 (October 11, 1978): 39–53 (Tokyo district court, June 23, 1978); *Asahi Shinbun*, June 23 (evening edn), 24, 1978. "Black Snow" was also a Nikkatsu film. In the 1970s Nikkatsu turned out a series of sexually explicit films allegedly to help clear up debts due to legal fees in an earlier case, and due to the depression of Japan's film industry. *Japan Times*, November 4, 1977; *Asahi Shinbun*, January 28 (evening edn), (evening edn), February 11, May 25, and June 21, 1972; and Fujiki Hideo, "Eirin jiken o meguru hōritsu mondai," *Jurisuto* 504 (May 1, 1972): 56. For "Poruno sangyō toshite no Nihon eiga," see *Asahi Jānaru* (April 28, 1972): 38; also *Jurisuto*, special issue (December 10, 1970).
88 This was done under the Customs Standards Law (*Kanzei teiritsu hō*), Law 54 of April 11, 1911, Article 11, which is in Itō and Shimizu, *Masu komi hōrei yōran*, p. 75.
89 For examples of seizures at airports, see *Asahi Shinbun*, January 17, 1979.
90 *Hanrei Jihō* 707 (1973): 16 (Tokyo high court, April 26, 1973).
91 *Sekinin*, pp. 51–75. (This book, available only at the offices of the Nihon Shinbun Kyōkai, remains a principal source of information on private regulatory systems.) In addition to the criminal and customs law provisions already mentioned, obscenity is also regulated under *Kōgyō hō* (Law 137 of July 10, 1948), *Fuzoku eigyō torishimari hō, Kankyō eisei hō, Denpa hō, Hōsō hō*, and local youth protection ordinances.
92 *Sekinin*, pp. 273, 64.
93 *Asahi Shinbun*, January 22, 1979, an interview with Nunokawa Kakuzaemon, President, Publication Ethics Council, and member, Tokyo Youth Protection Council.
94 *Sekinin*, p. 208; and *Nihon Keizai Shinbun*, July 12, 1978.
95 *Nihon Keizai Shinbun*, July 12, 1978. For example, amidst widespread parental and public concern, pornography vending machines in Saitama Prefecture increased from 887 in August, 1977 to 2,116 on July 31, 1978. After a great many warnings, police seized two machines in October, 1978. *Asahi Shinbun*, October 10, 1978.
96 For example, occasionally imported Western films restricted to adult-oriented theatres in the United States are shown on commercial television in Japan. See also *Asahi Shinbun*, September 22, 23, and December 12 (evening edn), 1978.
97 Ibid.
98 Spinrad, *Civil Liberties*, pp. 5–26, 292–306. On the law and experience of the United States, see *The Report of the Commission on Obscenity and Pornography* (New York: Bantam Books, 1970), especially pp. 346–442.
99 For related opinion poll data, see *Asahi Shinburn*, January 3, 1979, p. 7.
100 See Lawrence W. Beer, "Education, Politics and Freedom of Expression in Japan: The Ienaga Textbook Review Cases," *Law in Japan: An Annual* 8 (1975): 67–90.
101 *Ienaga* v. *Ministry of Education, Hanrei Jihō* 604 (1970): 35 (Tokyo district court, July 17, 1970); and *Ienaga* v. *Ministry of Education, Hanrei Jihō*, special issue (October 15, 1974) and *Jurisuto* 569 (1974): 14 (Tokyo district court, July 16, 1974).
102 *Ministry of Education* v. *Ienaga, Hanrei Jihō* 800 (1976): 19 (Tokyo high court, December 20, 1975).
103 Private discussions with Japanese textbook authors at various times during the 1970s.

104 Ministry of Education (ed.), *Kuni no ayumi* (October, 1946). For a recent expression of Ienaga's views, see *Rekishi no naka no kenpō* (Tokyo Daigaku Shuppankai, 1977), 2 vols. Ienaga sees the issues in broad constitutional and political terms, as part of efforts on behalf of Article 9 and against constitutional revision. Correspondence with the author, December 10, 1978.

105 See *Asahi Shinbun*, January 1, 1979, pp. 1, 9–13. Survey results therein indicate middle-class pre-occupation, not with large political questions, especially those of the past, but with work, inflation, children's education, and other immediate problems.

106 See sources cited *supra*, n. 30.

107 Beer and Weeramantry, 'Human Rights in Japan'.

108 *Tōkei Nenkan* (Ōkurashō Insatsukyoku, 1977), p. 26.

109 Discussions with Onizuka Kentarō (Head, Civil Liberties Bureau), Nakadaira Kenkichi (attorney), Sasahara Keisuke (attorney), and Andō Isamu (Head, Asian Relations Center, Sophia University, Tokyo), in 1978 and 1979.

110 Japan came under some international pressure in 1978 and 1979 to allow some refugees to reside in Japan. However, as of July 1979, only 12 Southeast Asian refugees had been given visas for a year or so of residence. Of wider interest in Japan with respect to rights of foreigners in Japan was the McLean Case, *McLean* v. *Japan, Hanrei Jihō* 903 (December 1, 1978): 3–20 (Sup. Ct., Grand Bench, October 4, 1978). The Supreme Court denied McLean, a teacher active in peaceful and legal activities opposing the American involvement in Vietnam in 1969–1970, the renewal of his visa, saying that while foreign residents in Japan have the same freedom of expression under the Constitution as Japanese citizens, the Justice Ministry has discretionary authority to take into account whatever factors it thinks appropriate, including legal political activities, when determining whether or not to renew a visa. See Katsuhiko Okazaki, "Foreign Nationals in Japan and the Human Rights Question," *The Japan Times*, December 17, 1978; *Kokusaikajidai no hōritsu mondai, Jurisuto* 681 (January 1, 1979), especially pp. 13–26, 66–70.

111 Sources cited *supra*, n. 109; *Asahi Shinbun*, January 21, 1979; Joyce C. Lebra *et al.* (eds), *Women in Changing Japan* (Boulder: Westview Press, 1976); see n. 114, *infra*.

112 The LDP rules provide that one electoral point is assigned to a prefectural party chapter for every 1,000 party members. The two national party candidates with the most votes in each prefecture divide the points in proportion to the number of votes each receives in the "primary." No other candidates are allotted electoral points. The voting for the four candidates in the 1978 primary election was as follows: Ōhira Masayoshi 550,891 (748 points); Fukuda Takeo, 472,503 (638); Nakasone Yasuhiro, 197,957 (93); Komoto Toshio, 88,917 (46). *Asahi Shinbun*, morning and evening edns, November 27, 28, and December 8, 1978. After the first round in a primary with more than two candidates in which no one has received a majority of the points, the top two vote-getters compete in a run-off election. In 1978, Fukuda withdrew his candidacy before the run-off. See also Minoru Shimizu, "LDP Reform Movement Retrogresses," *The Japan Times*, May 24, 1979.

113 *Kuroka* v. *Chiba Prefecture Election Commission*, 30 *Minshū* 223 (Sup. Ct., Grand Bench, April 14, 1976). See "Recent Developments," *Law in Japan: An Annual* 9 (1976): 151–2.

114 *Constitution of Japan:*

"Article 14. All of the people are equal under the law and there shall be no discrimination in political, economic or social relations because of race, creed, sex, social status or family origin. . . ."

"Article 15. The people have the inalienable right to choose their public officials and to dismiss them.

"2. All public officials are servants of the whole community and not of any group thereof.

"3. Universal adult suffrage is guaranteed with regard to the election of public officials.

"4. In all elections, secrecy of the ballot shall not be violated. A voter shall not be answerable, publicly or privately for the choice he has made."

"Article 44. The qualifications of members of both Houses and their electors shall be fixed by law. However, there shall be no discrimination because of race, creed, sex, social status, family origin, education, property or income." Itoh and Beer, *Constitutional Case Law of Japan*, pp. 258–9, 261.

115 Law 63 of 1975 added twenty seats to the House of Representatives, and created new election districts in Tokyo, Chiba, Saitama, and Kanagawa, areas severely afflicted with malapportionment.

116 *Hanrei Jihō* 902 (November 21, 1978): 24–34 (Tokyo high court, September 11, 1978).

117 *Koshiyama* v. *Election Commission, Hanrei Jihō* 902 (November 21, 1978): 34–51 (Tokyo high court, September 13, 1978).

118 *Asahi Shinbun*, September 7, 12, 13, 14, 17, and October 30, 1978.
119 *Asahi Shinbun*, September 27, 1978.
120 Sources cited *supra*, n. 118.
121 Tokyo district court, November 13, 1979; *Asahi Shinbun*, November 13 (evening edn) and 14, 1979; *The Japan Times*, November 16, 1979. On the face of it, the judge was merely stating a fact and quoting the constitution, but the fact that it was made into an incident is another example of the supersensitivity, among many opposition politicians and opinion purveyors, of the issue of the Emperor.
122 Yukio Matsuyama, "What Has Been Changing in Japanese Politics and What Not?," unpublished speech, Trilateral Commission, Bonn, West Germany, October 23, 1977, pp. 9–10.

■ First published in P. Luney & K. Takahashi (eds.), *Japanese Constitutional Law*, Tokyo, Tokyo University Press, 1993, 221–254.

10

Freedom of Expression: the Continuing Revolution

⌘

In August 1989, at his first press conference, Emperor Akihito defended the democratic right of individuals to comment on and criticize the imperial institution or a particular emperor, even his father, Hirohito. In so doing, the Emperor reaffirmed the constitutional revolution on behalf of freedom of expression and other human rights that began in the autumn of 1945, and encouraged uninhibited public discourse on politically sensitive subjects. By soft-spoken implication, he attacked the rightists making death threats against Mayor Motoshima Hitoshi of Nagasaki, a critic of Emperor Hirohito's role in World War II.[1] One might look in vain through the sixty-two years of the Shōwa period for a similar instance of unequivocal imperial advocacy of free speech and an open society.[2] Rather, without reference to the personal views of Emperor Hirohito, conservative revisionists and extreme rightists may have depended on the expressive silence of the imperial household as implicit approval of their efforts since the 1950s to restore the Emperor to greater constitutional prominence and to discourage open discourse on the imperial institution and in general. Both silence and expression reveal the status of freedom of expression in a country, and that freedom is a critical test of constitutional democracy. The other side of an orthodoxy is its attendant taboos—topics on which silence is enforced or powerfully encouraged—such as the emperor system in Japan and socialism in the United States.

For over four decades, the prewar orthodoxy of emperor-centered, repressive nationalism seems to have contended among political elites with the orthodoxy of the 1947 Constitution, which is characterized by popular sovereignty, quasi-pacifist internationalism, freedom of expression, and other human rights. Much of Japan's Liberal Democratic Party leadership during this period seems to have found it hard to reconcile the earlier nationalistic orthodoxy in which they were educated with the revolutionary orthodoxy of freedom, which insists on tolerating diverse, even contradictory, views on basic public values and other issues.

The passing of Emperor Hirohito on January 7, 1989, seems part of a major transition from the postwar generation of leaders to a new generation educated in the past half century. This generational succession is part of a broad pattern of leadership changes in Asia during the 1980s. The emerging leaders of Japan are more apt to be matter-of-fact than passionate about the Emperor and Shinto, more comfortable than some of their predecessors with the 1947 Constitution, and increasingly confident about Japan's prominence among nations, if not about its precise implications. At this juncture of generational leadership succession, the revolution of freedom may be as firmly institutionalized in Japan as in virtually any other constitutional democracy.

Why freedom of expression is relatively strong in Japan or any country cannot be ascertained simply by looking at laws, constitutional provisions, and judicial decisions. The reasons and reality are most effectively unearthed by empirically well-founded, *ecological* analysis of factors such as social culture, institutions of government and law, economic conditions, political value commitments, and historical serendipity. Free speech is nowhere permanently established and uniformly or fully enjoyed. Opinion research suggests that while a majority in the United States, for example, supports freedom of expression in the abstract, a majority also opposes much free speech for those espousing views quite different from their own.[3] Other survey research indicates that in Japan college-educated adults now express more confidence in the 1947 Constitution than in any other national institution.[4] Freedom of expression on a particular topic at a given time exists in a constitutional culture in part because of widespread trust in the system and a national consensus that the inherent equal dignity of each person requires protection of each individual's freedom in law and politics. Freedom of expression also exists because the balance of competitive sociopolitical forces favors expression rather than repressed silence on the subject, at least for the moment. The test of freedom is whether, in general, citizens actually have the option of expressing themselves peacefully or remaining silent about a subject without negative social, legal, or economic consequences. These perspectives are useful for examining Japan's record. After setting forth relevant constitutional provisions and touching lightly on the institutional and social context of freedom of expression in Japan, this essay surveys judicial holdings on freedom of assembly and association, the expression rights of workers, and the freedom of the mass media.

CONSTITUTIONAL PROVISIONS ON FREEDOM

Social culture affects law, and widely accepted legal norms and institutions affect the status of freedom of expression in society. The 1947 Constitution sets forth the broad array of rights guaranteed to Japanese citizens.[5] In general terms, Article 11 guarantees "the fundamental human rights" as "eternal and inviolable rights," while Article 97 refers to these rights as "conferred upon this and future generations in trust, to be held for all time inviolate."

Article 21 is the primary provision affecting freedom of expression: "Freedom of assembly and association as well as speech, press and all other forms of expression are guaranteed. No censorship shall be maintained, nor shall the secrecy of any means of communication be violated."

Article 15 establishes the people's "inalienable right to choose their public officials and to dismiss them," implying rights of election campaigning. Article 16 guarantees the right of peaceful petition and forbids discrimination against a petitioner for opposing or advocating a particular official action. The 1947 Petition Law[6] implementing this provision has seldom been invoked in a free speech case, but organized citizen demands on government are commonplace. Freedom of religious expression and the right not to "be compelled to take part in any religious act, celebration, rite or practice" are established in Article 20.[7] With Article 23, Japan's Constitution was the first to guarantee academic freedom. Workers have the right "to organize and to bargain and act collectively" under Article 28. Under Article 51, Diet members cannot be held liable outside parliament "for speeches, debates or votes cast inside." Significantly, Article 82 requires that "trials of political offenses . . . involving the press or cases wherein the rights of people guaranteed in Chapter 3 . . . are in question shall always be conducted publicly."[8]

Counterbalancing individual rights in the Constitution is "the public welfare" (*kōkyō no fukushi*), a phrase found in Articles 12 and 13:

> Article 12. The freedoms and rights guaranteed to the people by this Constitution shall be maintained by the constant endeavor of the people, who shall refrain from any abuse of these freedoms and rights and shall always be responsible for utilizing them for the public welfare.
>
> Article 13. All of the people shall be respected as individuals. Their rights to life, liberty, and the pursuit of happiness shall, to the extent that it does not interfere with the public welfare, be the supreme consideration in legislation and in other governmental affairs.

Officials and constitutional lawyers have long debated how, if at all, courts and other government agencies should use the public welfare clause in decisions affecting freedom of expression and other individual rights. Definitions of the phrase have ranged from abstract references to public order, the collective good, or state policy, to specific criteria related to one category of court cases. For example, provisions for parade regulation are designed to serve the public interest of smooth traffic flow. In general terms, a 1950 Supreme Court statement reflects the spirit of self-disciplined liberty in the Constitution: "[T]he maintenance of order and respect for the fundamental human rights—it is precisely these things which constitute the content of the public welfare."[9] The courts use the clause as a positive law standard, not merely as a hortatory statement of an ideal.

Society, Government, and Freedom

In Japan, judges and prosecutors play roles of great importance to the ecology of free speech. Leaders in other establishment systems serve important functions as well. For decades, educators from primary school through the university have effectively indoctrinated students into believing democratic principles are part of the Japanese way. The overwhelming majority of constitutional lawyers and other legal professionals continually reaffirm the legitimacy of freedom of expression. Artists of many categories and the mass media confidently assume their expression rights, as do private associations of all sizes throughout the country. And in their competitive political discourse and internal rules, most of Japan's diverse political parties take for granted and generally confirm by practice the right to freedom of expression.

But does the ordinary citizen enjoy the right to freedom of expression in everyday life? The answer to this question often depends more on society than on government and law. Social values and behavior patterns specific to each culture affect both the degree and the characteristics of free expression in a country's sociopolitical life.[10] In Japan, for example, homogeneity, group orientation, social hierarchy, quasi-parental-filial relationships (*oyabun-kobun*), reciprocal dependency patterns (*amae*), and ethnic separatism join the civil law, common law, and conciliation traditions to affect freedom and restraint of expression.

Japan is a nonindividualist, group-centered society in which vigorous expression of diverse views emanates from very cohesive groups rather than from isolated individuals. The individual's self-realization is assumed to occur within rather than apart from his or her primary group. Powerless individuals anywhere are less effective defenders than are well-organized groups of both free speech in general and specific interests. Thus, "groupism" may be more supportive of democratic freedom under law than is individualism. Two test points for the individual's freedom of expression in Japan's group-structured society, where the ideal of consensus rather than majority rule governs, are: (1) whether an individual in-group member is allowed free expression of views at the preconsensus stage of group decision-making or consensus formation on an issue, and is not sanctioned after consensus is reached for having earlier advocated a contrary position, and (2) whether a competitive-minded group excessively presses its own interests in complete disregard of the rights of other groups, individuals, or the public—an "individualistic groupism" that is analogous to the extreme individualism shown by one who is blind to others' rights in an individual-oriented society such as the United States.

Japanese culture values individual reticence and, in many contexts, views aggressive assertion of personal opinion as reprehensible; therefore, Japan's system of freedom of expression requires modalities of dispute resolution and politics that encourage citizens to assert their rights under law freely. Conciliation by a third party is often preferred to adjudication in a court of law.[11] Officially sanctioned mediation of disputes, both public and private, is well established. Welfare Commissioners (Min'ei Iin), neighborhood police, family courts, and other agencies assist parties in reconciling differences without resort to complex, expensive, and time-consuming legal processes, and without loss in the quality of justice.

As elsewhere, individuals, more than groups, need free speech law that encourages, not merely allows, the expression of concerns. In the ecology of freedom in Japan, two distinctive examples of systems that encourage the assertion of citizen rights are the Jinken Yōgo Iin and the Local Administrative Counselors (Gyōsei Sōdan Iin).[12] Probably for historical reasons,[13] the government has translated Jinken Yōgo Iin as "Civil Liberties Commissioner"; however, that term is inaccurate and misleading. Jinken Yōgo Iin literally means "Human Rights Protector"; and "human rights" encompass far more under Japanese law than "civil liberties."[14] Perhaps Jinken Yōgo Iin may be best rendered as "Human Rights Commissioner." These local commissioners, meticulously selected for their human rights credentials, serve for renewable three-year terms. Their duties include consultation by individuals regarding human rights problems, human rights education, conciliatory settlement of neighborhood disputes, and referral of serious rights violations to the appropriate authorities. They are typically very approachable, non-elitist, respected men and women.

Local Administrative Counselors, like the Human Rights Commissioners, are unpaid volunteers. They average sixty years of age and work for renewable two-year terms under the Bureau of Administrative Inspection of the Administrative Management Agency (AMA). The AMA began entertaining thousands of citizen complaints a year against government offices around 1955, more as a means of improving the quality of administration than as a technique of human rights enforcement. Amendments to the 1948 AMA law in 1960 and 1961 first empowered the AMA to use Local Administrative Counselors to resolve complaints against government agencies. In the 1980s, about 5,000 of these respected counselors were dealing on an impartial and confidential basis with roughly 200,000 complaints each year against public officials.

The Human Rights Commissioners and Local Administrative Counselors play a small but significant part in a complex sociolegal system generally favoring freedom of expression. They are useful, well institutionalized, and worthy of emulation; their task would be even more impressive if the Human Rights Bureau received more adequate funding. They serve as examples of well-focused, officially supported, and socially supported volunteerism that transcends narrow interests and government bureaucratism, costs little, and brings relief to millions of citizens suffering from ostracism, discrimination, official arrogance, environmental disruption, cruel treatment due to age or illness, and other afflictions to which the flesh is heir.

SOME JUDICIAL DECISIONS ON FREEDOM OF ASSEMBLY AND ASSOCIATION

The competitiveness and nonindividualism of Japan's sociopolitics seem to make the freedoms of assembly and association particularly critical to the infrastructure of the nation's constitutional democracy. Both freedoms were effectively suppressed, especially during the wartime period of 1930 to 1945. Now, demonstrations and campaigns of protest regarding tax and trade issues, environmental pollution, airport expansion, working conditions, and other problems enliven national discourse, irrepressibly reaffirm freedom to act, and only rarely degenerate into violence.[15]

Since 1948, the content or application of public safety ordinances (*kōan jōrei*) has been at issue in much of the litigation involving freedom of assembly. Sixty such city and prefectural ordinances establish local public safety commissions (*kōan iinkai*) composed of three to five locally respected citizens; fifty-three ordinances require a permit, and the remaining ordinances require prior notification. Denial of a permit almost never occurs, but conditions have often been attached regarding the time, place, and manner of a public gathering, parade, or demonstration under both permit and notification systems. The reasonableness of restraints attendant to such conditions or the prima facie constitutionality of ordinance provisions has been disputed in a series of court cases. In addition, article 77 of the Road Traffic Law (Dōro Kōtsu Hō) authorizes local public safety commissions to require a police permit for parades and demonstrations in the interest of orderly traffic flow (as around construction sites), and the Criminal Code covers various types of group violence, such as riots, insurrections, and obstruction of the performance of police duties.[16]

Perhaps the most important judicial decision on freedom of assembly is the 1960 Grand Bench judgment of the Supreme Court in the Tokyo Ordinance case.[17]

Under the ordinance, group representatives apply to the police for a permit. If the police deny permission or attach conditions (for example, changing the route or time of a demonstration), they must justify their decision to the Tokyo Public Safety Commission for final disposition. However, many groups have held demonstrations without applying for a permit, particularly during the late 1940s and the 1950s.

The particular historical backdrop to the Tokyo Ordinance case is as follows. In 1959 and 1960, Japan's "consensual democracy" was powerfully confirmed during the Security Treaty crisis by the largest mass movement in the nation's history. Millions were involved for months in passionate but usually nonviolent political demonstrations in Tokyo and other cities; only one life was lost, and that by accident. Whether or not Japan should cast its lot indefinitely with the United States was much debated; but more central to the maelstrom may have been the allegedly undemocratic arrogance of Prime Minister Kishi Nobusuke and the ruling Liberal Democratic Party (LDP), who were "ramming through" the revised U.S.–Japan Treaty of Mutual Cooperation and Security[18] with their parliamentary majority. Apparently, premature reliance on the majority vote without giving adequate hearing to all views, and thus possibly achieving a partial consensus, deprived the decision of unquestioned legitimacy.

In related 1959 cases, Tokyo district courts refused to allow police to detain students demonstrating without a permit, but the government won a reversal in mid-1960 on direct appeal to the Supreme Court. In an extended opinion affecting subsequent judicial reasoning, the Court held that a freedom such as freedom of assembly "is the most important feature that distinguishes democracy from totalitarianism," and that the courts are required under law "to draw a proper boundary between freedom and the public welfare."[19] The potential for violence in collective activities such as demonstrations justifies public safety ordinances to establish "the minimum measures necessary to maintain law and order."[20] The Tokyo Ordinance is constitutional because it requires the Public Safety Commission to issue a permit unless a proposed demonstration would "directly endanger the maintenance of the public peace."[21] It is "profitless," the Court said, to debate whether the ordinance's regulation of gatherings "in any place whatsoever" is unconstitutionally broad.[22] Nor does the ordinance create "a general prohibition" on demonstrations by not allowing them when officials fail to act on an application by the scheduled time of the event.[23]

The Tokyo Ordinance decision continues to be a powerful precedent, but subsequent lower and appellate court holdings have refined procedural standards and made more concrete the guidelines for applying the ordinance to the place and circumstance of a collective activity. Since the mid-1960s, many lower court judges have taken a more relaxed view of the dangers posed by crowds. In the 1975 Tokushima Ordinance case,[24] the Supreme Court seemed more positive in its assessment of political demonstrations. In that case, Teramae Manabu, a union official and antiwar activist, was convicted under the Road Traffic Law and the Tokushima Public Safety Ordinance for a 1964 demonstration against visiting U.S. nuclear submarines, for leading a snake dance down city streets in a 1968 protest against the presence of B-52 bombers in Japan, and for attendant violence. The district court held article 3 of the ordinance unconstitutionally vague in requiring demonstration leaders to "maintain orderly traffic." The majority in the highest tribunal reversed on the grounds that "a person of ordinary common sense" would be able to apply article 3 to "a concrete case," but some justices acknowledged a deficiency in the article's wording.

A 1977 decision of Judge Terao Shōji of the Tokyo High Court,[25] confirmed by the Supreme Court in 1979, was less ambiguous in its appreciation of demonstrations and labor union campaigns than the Tokyo Ordinance case, the Tokushima Ordinance case, and many other appellate holdings. In a decision handed down sixteen years after the demonstrations and eleven years after trial, Judge Terao upheld convictions for illegal demonstrations, but reduced the sentences from imprisonment to mild fines. He wondered in his reasoning about the constitutionality of prior restraint under the Tokyo Ordinance, and pointedly criticized those who exaggerate the dangers inherent in democratic collective activities.

The Narita Airport case,[26] decided in 1986, involved a rare instance of substantial violence and provides further illustration of a pattern of delayed justice in politically sensitive cases. Tortuously long trials are the exception in Japan's criminal justice system. In the occasional political case, delays sometimes occur. A protracted trial may be intended by defense attorneys using the court as a forum, or it may be a natural, unintended effect of civil law judicial process in which a trial takes place in a number of court sessions strung out over a considerable period of time. The prospect of an interminable trial may dampen enthusiasm for collective activities more than some other legal and administrative restraints. In a 1971 clash, some 260 mobile police (*kidōtai*) confronted 700 opponents of government land acquisition for the Narita International Airport near Tokyo. Three police officers were killed, and many on both sides were injured. (Typically, the effective mobile police outnumber protesters, and injuries are few.) Not until October 1986 did the Chiba District Court issue its decision, giving fifty-two protestors suspended sentences (ten months to three years in duration) and acquitting three, in part because their confessions were inadmissible as evidence. The prosecution did not appeal, for lack of further evidence.

Freedom of association is routinely enjoyed in Japan. Alexis de Tocqueville's point about America 150 years ago might be made of Japan today (admittedly, without adequate comparative data in either case): "In no country in the world has the principle of association been more successfully used or applied to a greater multitude of objects."[27] Among the laws enabling and regulating associations, certain provisions of the Subversive Activities Control Law (Hakai Katsudō Bōshi Hō) of 1952 have been challenged.[28] The law has not often been invoked in constitutional litigation because terrorist acts are quite rare in Japan and because the constitutionality of the law is questioned by lawyers. Mindful of the prewar thought-control system, legislators who supported the law were opposed to controlling ideas, but thought it necessary to regulate the terrorist actions of antidemocratic organizations. Early in the Occupation (1945–52), extreme rightist groups were the primary concern; with the advent of the Cold War and instances of communist violence between 1947 and 1952, leftist organizations were targeted for restraint, as in prewar Japan. At present, terrorist acts by extremists are of minor concern.

Prior restraints on collective activities, violent group actions, and too harsh or excessively lenient sentences for related crimes do not negatively affect the enjoyment of freedom in Japan. Rather, over-reliance on confessions at the preindictment stage, excessive detention without bail or adequate legal representation, and needlessly long trials in political cases affect the quality of the system regulating the freedoms of assembly and association. These restraints have not inhibited the strong drive to group self-expression through demonstrations, factional in-fighting, intergroup intolerance, and a multitude of autonomous associations. Groupism seems to reinforce rather than weaken the individual's rights to associate with like-minded people in minicommunities and to participate in the vigorous expression of collective views.

EXPRESSION RIGHTS OF EMPLOYEES

Union workers in Japan enjoy constitutional rights "to organize and to bargain and act collectively," in addition to the freedoms of collective activity they enjoy as citizens.[29] Some of these protections do not extend to many public employees (*kōmuin*). Under article 7 of the Labor Relations Adjustment Law,[30] private sector unions may engage in "dispute activities" (*sōgi kōi*) such as "strikes, slowdowns, lock-outs, and other acts and counteractions carried out by parties in labor relations to achieve their objectives, which obstruct the normal conduct of business." "Other acts" are union actions interfering with business operations in order to activate the law's dispute settlement procedures.[31] Acts are "proper" and immune from legal sanctions if they are nonviolent and are undertaken for economic rather than political gains. The Supreme Court has tended "to regard only the collective refusal to work as a proper act of dispute."[32] However, the Labor Union Law, which covers over 70 percent of union members, clearly recognizes the propriety of "other acts" in articles 1, 7, and 8, and unions make use of a colorful array of obstructive activities during labor disputes.

For decades, the denial to civil servants of both freedom of political expression, except through the ballot box, and worker rights to engage in collective bargaining or dispute activities has engendered bitter controversy.[33] In general, and especially since 1973, Supreme Court decisions have upheld the constitutionality of restrictive laws such as the National Public Employees Law (NPEL), the Public Enterprise Labor Relations Law (PELRL), and the Rules (*kisoku*) of the National Personnel Authority (NPA) (*Jinjiin*). Typically, the justices have comprehensively denied expression rights to public workers by relying on constitutional provisions with respect to the public welfare, the concept of "the collective benefit of all the people," and the need for political neutrality lest citizen trust be lost. During the latter half of the 1960s, however, the Supreme Court stressed worker rights in its statutory interpretation and, where alternative sanctions were available, imposed a lenient administrative reprimand rather than, for example, a harsh one-year suspension from employment.[34]

In its 1966 Tokyo Central Post Office decision,[35] the Supreme Court required the high court to reconsider whether postal union leaders' incitement of workers to leave work and hold a rally during the 1958 "spring labor offensive" was "justifiable." The Court upheld the constitutionality of article 17 of the PELRL, which forbids such incitement, but gave the court below interpretive guidelines, for instance: "[T]he fundamental rights of workers engaging in public services or in public enterprises involve restrictions different from that of private enterprise only according to the nature of their duties."[36] The majority maintained that distinctions should be made between types of work, between legitimate labor dispute acts and political activities, between degrees of illegality and public inconvenience caused, and between mild sanctions and criminal penalties that would be disproportionate for failure to perform a contractual obligation.

With the 1973 All-Japan Agriculture and Forestry Workers Union (Zennōrin) case,[37] the Supreme Court shifted decisively to a more restrictive policy based on literal interpretation of the statutes, acceptance of the authority of NPA Rules, and rejection of all distinctions among public employees on the nature of their work. In 1958, Zennōrin, other unions, and opposition political parties successfully opposed a revision of the Police Duties Law, which they feared might lead to repression of the labor movement, as in prewar Japan. A union leader issued a call for some 3,000 members to hold a two-hour political rally during work hours, and other political activities were organized. The union leaders were convicted for "political strike" activities, illegal for both public and private workers. Like all litigants in subsequent cases, the union leaders unsuccessfully challenged the NPEL and other laws as violating constitutional provisions governing workers' right, expression rights, and/or procedural rights.

In the famous 1974 *Sarufutsu* case,[38] the Supreme Court reversed an acquittal and convicted a postal worker for putting up six political posters on a public bulletin board during leisure hours. The majority reasoned, first, that public officials must be politically neutral in order to retain public trust in their impartiality. Second, although the law does not intend restraints on expression of opinion, that may be an inevitable side effect. Third, the Court rejected the view of lower court decisions that administrative sanctions should be seen as "less restrictive means" or preferable to criminal penalties. Four dissenting justices argued that criminal penalties, as contrasted with administrative punishment, are constitutional only when the political acts of public employees cause grave and direct harm, or the danger of such harm, to the state or to social interests. Neither threat was present in this case. This view has been supported by many constitutional lawyers. Unfortunately, the controlling judicial doctrine has been that public workers may be criminally liable even if their acts do not impair performance of duty and are performed away from official premises, by off-duty, nonmanagerial employees, in a peaceful manner.[39]

For many years, the National Personnel Authority (NPA) has punished thousands of public employee union members for illegal dispute activities or political acts. Most NPA disciplinary actions have consisted of a reprimand, but many have also included a pay cut or temporary "suspension from duty." A few have resulted in firings. Other government bodies also mete out penalties short of criminal prosecution to activist employees.

Occasionally, members of public employee unions mount a successful challenge in court. For example, on December 18, 1986, the Supreme Court upheld a lower court order quashing a reprimand issued by the Hokkaido Education Commission against five high school teachers.[40] These union members had used half of an annual school holiday in 1965 to participate in a rally with colleagues from other schools. The gathering was part of labor's annual springtime "joint struggle." When the teachers notified the principal of their intention three days beforehand, he and the education commission forbade their attendance as a dispute activity violating the Local Public Employees Law.[41] The Supreme Court denied that such use of a holiday amounted to a strike, since it did not interfere with classes and other schools had allowed the activity. The officials' felt need to litigate to reassert control over innocent activities is more noteworthy and typical than the Supreme Court's vindication of the teachers.

In 1989, a historic unification of most public and private sector unions under one umbrella organization took place. The Japanese Private Trade Union Confederation (Rengō) established local chapters in forty-seven prefectures in March. In November it joined with the General Council of Trade Unions (Sōhyō) to form the ten-million-member Japanese Trade Union Confederation (Shin Rengō). In 1993, it was not yet clear how this consolidation of labor forces would affect long-term patterns of worker political power, worker rights assertion, and worker rights regulation.

MASS MEDIA RIGHTS AND RESPONSIBILITIES

Due in part to the vigor, freedom, and power of the mass media, a wide range of issues affecting their rights and responsibilities has been raised in public debate and in the courts. Freedom lives and is moderated in the interplay of formal law, politics, and social culture in daily life. After a few comments on obscenity, a more detailed sketch is presented of rights regarding freedom of information, secrecy, media privileges, and textbook publishing problems.

Japanese society is rather tolerant of erotica in print, in pictures, and in other media. Regulatory authority is spread among many public and private agencies. Since 1907, article 175 of the Criminal Code has punished lightly the distribution and sale of obscene matter.[42] Since 1910, under article 21 of the Customs Standards Law, the Customs Bureau has censored imported "written material and pictures harmful to public order and public morals,"[43] a system of disputed constitutionality. The Supreme Court has held that obscene passages in a book infect the whole and that a judgment on obscenity should be made with respect for the public welfare according to "prevailing social ideas" or "the common sense of society," without too much attention to a work's artistic or social values.[44] In a mid-1980s poll, 80 percent of Japanese adults (up 19 percent since 1980) said they felt that mass-media portrayals of sex—particularly in weekly magazines, television, and films—were excessively explicit. Of these 80 percent, 73.3 percent preferred that minors under eighteen not be exposed to these portrayals. Close to 90 percent of all respondents complained about the public sale of pornography in vending machines.[45] To this writer, permitting private adult access to virtually any media material seems the best general guideline; nonetheless, in order to protect minors' development rights (however "minor" is defined chronologically in a given culture), moderate restraint on obscene, excessively violent, or otherwise degrading material seems reasonable.

Defamation, privacy, and press freedom

The rights to reputation and privacy have been balanced against press freedom under articles 709 and 710 of the Civil Code, which require compensation for intentional or negligent violation of another's right.[46] No distinction is made between libel and slander; defamation (*meiyō kison*) is prohibited under both article 723 of the Civil Code and articles 230 and 230–2 of the Criminal Code. Damage awards and fines have been moderate or small. A published apology is also required in some cases.[47] Supreme Court interpretations in the late 1960s moved away from punishing the simple public allegation of facts (whether true or false) as defamation. This interpretation had resulted from a literal reading of the codes. The Supreme Court has moved to a doctrine in both criminal and civil cases under which one escapes liability for an otherwise defamatory comment when the allegations, even if factually mistaken, concern a matter of public interest, were made for public benefit, and were published in a belief that they were true, based on what the Court considers sufficiently objective evidence.[48] Two cases decided in the 1980s illustrate debated issues.

In 1976, the monthly magazine *Gekkan Pen* published articles critical of Soka Gakkai, the lay Buddhist organization, and its leader, the well-known public figure Ikeda Daisaku. In 1981, the Supreme Court[49] overturned the lower court's finding of defamation. The Court held that Ikeda's affairs were not private, but rather matters of public interest calling into play article 230–2. The highest tribunal noted the public importance of Soka Gakkai and the social influence of Ikeda as a public figure, and directed the lower courts to reexamine the facts objectively. The Tokyo courts then convicted the accused on a finding that the truth of the magazine's allegations was not proved, and that the accused lacked sufficient grounds for believing them true.[50]

The rather intricate *Hoppō Jānaru* (The Northern Journal) case involved a provisional injunction against publishing an issue of a magazine without giving its representatives a hearing. The April 1979 issue was to carry an article harshly critical of Igarashi Kōzō, a well-known Socialist member of parliament and former mayor of Asahikawa City who was about to run for Governor of Hokkaido, Japan's large northern island. The Supreme Court[51] approved this use of an injunction to prevent defamation against the claim of Ona Takao of the journal that it was illegal prior restraint and censorship, violating Article 21 of the Constitution. The Court argued that, in general, a hearing was procedurally required and that prior restraint was improper, but that in this instance the article, "A Power Seeker's Temptations," was so extreme in its insults, vulgarity, and personal attack as obviously to lack credibility on a first reading. The injunction did not constitute censorship in the meaning of Article 21 because it was a judicial act, not the result of an administrative process. As a rare exception, the Court held that a provisional injunction was appropriate because the article's contents were untrue, the article was not written solely for public benefit, and Igarashi's reputation would have suffered severe and probably irreparable damage if it had been published. The article was a lively blend of political and strictly personal comment on Igarashi. To the Court, character assassination trumped the public-interest value of comment on a candidate for public office. Would its publication have affected the election's outcome? If it was so extreme, would not quick rebuttal have been relatively easy? To anyone familiar with the effect of the Willie Horton advertisement of U.S. television during the 1988 presidential campaign and the powerful effectiveness of negative campaigning, the answers are not obvious or simple.

The right of privacy (*puraibashii no kenri*) was first recognized in Japanese law in a 1964 Tokyo District Court decision involving Mishima Yukio's *After the Banquet* (*Utage no ato*), a "model novel" mixing fact and fiction in its depiction of the marital affairs of Arita Hachirō, a noted Tokyo politician. Mishima had received Mrs. Arita's consent, but not Mr. Arita's, before serializing the story in a major magazine (*Chuō Kōron*). The names of the principals were disguised by pseudonyms, but upon reading the novel, both Aritas were outraged, and Mishima was successfully sued for what became the largest damage award until then (approximately $2,220 in U.S. currency).

The court defined the right of privacy as "the legal right and assurance that one's private life will not be wantonly opened to the public," applying it to both individual and family life and basing it on the Constitution's Article 13 requirement that "[a]ll of the people shall be respected as individuals."[52] A privacy right is violated when: (1) fear exists that a work may be taken as factual or close to the facts of one's personal life; (2) the average person would not want the matters publicized; and (3) the work presents material that is generally unknown. Four considerations, on balance, may negate illegality: (1) artistry; (2) freedom of expression; (3) the public position of the aggrieved party; and (4) the prior consent of the party. Mishima lost, but the court denied the Aritas' request that a published apology be required on grounds that in a privacy case, in contrast to an instance of defamation, restoration of the *status quo ante* is impossible.

A right to one's own image (*shōzōken*) has been discussed in and out of court as a type of privacy right.[53] The inventively snoopy photo magazines have continued to enrage or humiliate entertainers and other public figures over the decades; but the will to regulate seems weak, and the felt right to know is strong in this area.

Mass media freedoms and information rights

The mass media industry in Japan is free, organizationally strong, self-regulating, technically sophisticated, and diverse. It is about as informative, entertaining, and educational as any nation's system. The national newspapers and television news programs enjoy much more public trust—particularly among the college-educated—than any sector of government except the Supreme Court.[54] Sustained investigative newspaper, magazine, and television reporting on sensitive matters has been infrequent, as in other democracies. On the other hand, the national newspapers, such as the *Asahi Shimbun*, *Yomiuri Shimbun*, *Mainichi Shimbun*, and *Nihon Keizai Shimbun*, have been major actors in political and policy debates at a few critical junctures, for example, during the Security Treaty crisis in 1960, the diffusion of the antipollution consensus in 1970, and the exposure of the Recruit Cosmos stock scandal in 1988 and 1989.[55]

SECRECY AND PRESS FREEDOM

Some parameters of press freedom have been clarified by appellate court decisions in the Hakata Station Film case in 1969,[56] the Nishiyama State Secrets case in 1978[57] and the Hokkaido Newsman's Privilege case in 1980.[58] In *Hakata*, four television stations in southwest Japan refused to comply with a court order to present (*teishutsu meirei*) for use as criminal evidence film they had taken in 1968 during a train station clash between students and police. The students were on their way home from demonstrations in southern Japan protesting a visit of the aircraft carrier U.S.S. *Enterprise*. The television companies, backed by the Japan Newspaper Editors and Publishers Association (Nihon Shimbun Kyōkai), and virtually the entire mass media industry, argued that "the use of this film as court evidence might render free and impartial newsgathering and reporting impossible." The Grand

Bench unanimously disagreed, but confirmed that Article 21 of the Constitution guarantees the freedom to gather news and to report facts and ideas in service of the public's right to know, and that freedom of information is at the foundation of democracy. Since the film in question had already been used in news broadcasts, the Court said, its purpose was achieved; so the court order did not directly affect newsgathering freedom. The Court reasoned that although the use of the film for another purpose might lead someone not to cooperate with reporters sometime in the future, hypothetical harm must be balanced against the need for evidence to assure a fair trial. Other sources of evidence had proved inadequate, the justices continued, and the film was virtually indispensable to a determination of guilt or innocence.

The television stations subsequently refused to obey the Supreme Court. In the absence of other alternative, a seizure order was issued by the district court and the film was used as evidence. In 1970, the district court upheld the students' contention that police had abused their authority, but dismissed their case on grounds that, even with the videotapes, the identities of the individual police officers involved were not clear. In this struggle between the courts, the media, and the police, the responsible police officials did not cooperate with the courts and were not disciplined by higher authority for keeping secret the names of the guilty police officers.

Japan has no freedom of information statute, but in the 1980s a national movement for greater openness in the bureaucratized government has resulted in approximately 140 local ordinances on information control. Conversely, no law forbids spying or otherwise adequately protects state secrets. The state secrets bills proposed repeatedly by the ruling LDP party in the mid-1980s met strong and successful opposition, in part perhaps because they manifested little sensitivity to citizen rights such as freedom of information. Some law is necessary to deal with security problems attendant to the worldwide transfer of commercial technology, whether the technology be military or civilian in nature. This was illustrated in recent years by the Soviet Union's purchase of state-of-the-art milling machines for submarine propellers from a Norwegian company and a division of Japan's Toshiba. The citizen's right to know is more essential to democracy than international commercial freedom and should be given more serious consideration in debates on what legal limits on freedom are the minimum necessary. But how to balance freedom of information with legitimate national security concerns and how to distinguish in law the narrowly political secret from a state secret are difficult questions.

The Supreme Court first ruled on state secrets and a reporter's newsgathering rights in the 1978 *Nishiyama* case. Nishiyama Takichi, a *Mainichi* political reporter, violated a solemn promise to his source, Hasumi Kikuko, a Foreign Ministry employee, in leaking sensitive information she had provided to an opposition member of the Diet. In 1971, Nishiyama induced Hasumi, his lover, to give him the contents of secret cables sent during the U.S.–Japan negotiations for the 1972 reversion of Okinawa to Japanese sovereignty. Shortly after the exchange of ratification documents but before reversion, the parliamentarian revealed that, contrary to government assurances that no secret agreements had been made, Japan had secretly agreed to pay $5 million to Okinawans in land-damage claims. Prime Minister Satō Eisaku took "deep responsibility" for the incident but did not admit any improper suppression of information. Nishiyama and Hasumi (both married) were soon exposed, arrested, and convicted of violating the National Public Employees Law.

Article 100(1) prohibits revealing secrets learned while carrying out official duties. Nishiyama was charged with inducing a civil servant to commit a crime. The maximum sentence for secrecy violations—hypothetically including those seriously harmful to Japan and/or other nations—is only one year in prison and a small fine.

Nishiyama appealed on grounds of press freedom. The Supreme Court, in rejecting his appeal, held that: (1) the courts have the authority to determine what is a state secret under the NPEL and what is a legally unprotected political secret; (2) the government's secrecy during the negotiations on Okinawa was appropriate; (3) the government's failure to bring the facts before the Diet did not violate the constitutional order or constitute illegal secrecy; and (4) while free newsgathering and reporting are critical to the people's right to know and to freedom of expression, Nishiyama's ethically questionable relations with Hasumi involved illegal inducement. The Supreme Court's questionable legitimation of unnecessary and patently political secrecy and official lying to the parliament and public was matched by Nishiyama's violation of both family ethics and the professional ethics of a journalist. Though adultery was not the issue in the case, the Court seemed to take more note of Nishiyama's violation of family ethics than of professional ethics. "Overlooked in the later uproar about the relationship between Nishiyama and Hasumi was that Nishiyama's employer, the *Mainichi Shimbun*, chose to remain silent about a controversial issue of public importance despite its own brave words about a 'people's right to know.' "[59]

What if Hasumi had brought forth the story of government deception on her own, as a conscientious whistleblower? In the *Hakata* case, suppose an informed police officer had exposed his guilty colleagues. Or imagine the early intervention of a responsible public or private employee to reveal the Recruit Cosmos scandal. It is not clear that such whistleblowing would result in reward or neutral acceptance rather than punishment. In addition to ordinary mechanisms to assure accountability (for example, the Administrative Management Agency), encouragement in law for concerned but vulnerable employees is needed. Public disclosure of executive wrongdoing will be rare indeed in a system relying on the heroism of subordinates. In Japan, as elsewhere, a formidable future challenge to the freedoms of expression and information is the development of effective legal protections for employees in both the public and private sectors who are willing to expose illegal activities at their places of work. One possible support for such responsible citizenship may be legal recognition of a "newsman's privilege" not to divulge confidential sources.

A newsman's privilege (*shōgen kyozetsuken*—literally, the right to refuse to testify) was first recognized in a 1979 civil case by the Sapporo District Court, but the issue has been debated for decades. In 1949, Ishii Kiyoshi of the *Asahi* newspaper published an article about the impending arrest of a local tax official before the police had made it public. At the official's trial, Ishii, with the strong support of his employer and the Publishers Association, refused to be sworn to testify regarding the name of his source. In 1952, the Supreme Court[60] denied his claim that a reporter's communications with a confidential source are "privileged," as are certain other professional confidences under article 105 of the Code of Criminal Procedure.[61] Withholding this prerogative does not violate free press guarantees under Article 21. Rather, the Court said, such a newsman's privilege could obstruct criminal justice and lead to improper favoritism in the treatment of reporters and other writers.

On the other hand, the Sapporo District Court, sustained by the appellate courts,[62] held that article 281 of the Code of Civil Procedure[63] protects a newsman's privilege as a witness to refuse to divulge information on a source as "an occupational secret" (*shokugyō no himitsu*) unless it blocks access to evidence necessary for a fair trial. In an article for the *Hokkaidō Shimbun* in June 1977, Shimada Hideshige alleged that parents were complaining about child abuse in Sasaki Masako's nursery. Sasaki sued Shimada and his newspaper for erroneous and defamatory reporting, and asked for payment of damages and publication of an apology. Under questioning, Shimada declined to identify his sources. The courts upheld his privilege on grounds that, when a fair trial is not at issue, revealing confidential sources would improperly impair a reporter's pursuit of his profession.

Courtroom note-taking and reporters' clubs

In 1989, the Supreme Court[64] again granted a special prerogative to the news media by holding that the equality requirements of Article 14 of the Constitution are not violated when judges allow only news reporters to take notes in court during a trial. The judicial policy was not persuasively grounded in Article 21 or in Article 82's provision for public trials. Since the 1960s, however, Japan's courts had generally denied permission to take notes in the courtroom to all but members of the "reporters' club" (*kisha kurabu*—commonly, but inaccurately translated as "press club") attached to the courts. Judges have "courtroom police powers" (*hōtei keisatsuken*) under article 71 of the Court Organization Law, but no strong contempt or subpoena powers (as illustrated by the *Hakata* case).[65] The restrictive policy on note-taking may have arisen in reaction to courtroom disruptions during politically charged trials in earlier postwar decades.[66]

The courts' policy was challenged in 1985 by an American lawyer, Lawrence Repeta, who began attending trial sessions in Tokyo District Court in October 1982 as part of a research project. Like other judges in Japan, the presiding judge prohibited note-taking in court as a general policy. Before each session, Repeta asked the judge's permission to take notes and was denied. However, the judge did allow note-taking by reporters belonging to the local judicial press club.

Repeta sued the government, claiming that the judge's denial of permission violated a trial spectator's right to know under Articles 14, 21, and 82. He also cited article 19 on freedom of expression in both the United Nations Universal Declaration of Human Rights and the International Covenant on Civil and Political Rights.[67] Repeta argued that a citizen's right to information about government is fundamental to democracy and that a right to take notes in court or in any public place (in abbreviated form, *memoken*, a "memo right") is implied by the right of anyone to attend a trial under Article 82. Moreover, the gathering and communication of information are essential to the enjoyment of freedom of expression and the right to know. "In reality," he maintained, "if people do not take notes, they cannot fully understand trials nor transmit knowledge concerning trials." One might substitute the word "lectures" for Repeta's "trials" and draw a parallel with a college student's need for lecture notes to pass a course.

The Tokyo District Court and High Court disagreed with Repeta's position, emphasizing the authority of a judge to decide whether a particular activity in a courtroom would in some way interfere with an orderly and fair trial. Although trials are generally open to the public, the individual does not have a right to attend a particular public trial. On March 8, 1989, the Grand Bench, in a complex opinion, unanimously upheld judicial prerogatives and refused to recognize a new constitutionally protected right to observe a particular trial or to take notes in court. The Court did not formally hold illegal the district judge's refusal to allow Repeta to take research notes—because the judge was merely following the general practice in Japan at the time. However, the justices did shift policy decisively toward greater respect for freedom of note-taking in court. They characterized the judge's denial of permission to Repeta as "an exercise of the courtroom police power poorly grounded in reason," which did not show proper appreciation of the importance of taking notes in Court. While the Court denied that a legal right to take notes arises from Article 82's open-trial provision, it did recognize that a freedom of courtroom note-taking should be respected in light of Article 21 freedom of expression. The Court's language was reminiscent of the affirmation of newsgathering freedom (*shuzai no jiyū*) in the *Hakata* decision.

Until this decision, according to a survey of major democracies taken by the Japan Federation of Bar Associations, Japan and South Korea were alone in virtually banning note-taking in court. The other democracies have long taken for granted a freedom to take notes in court. Although the Court's wording gave preferential position to the public importance of news reporters, its recognition that all, citizens and foreigners alike,[68] have a virtual right to take notes opens the courtroom to scholars, freelance and magazine writers, novelists, and others hitherto denied the right because they did not belong to reporters' clubs. The Repeta case and the reporters clubs illustrate the pattern of tension in Japan between democratic openness and self-protective groupism.

It is a paradox that, due to the organized restraints on freedom attendant to the reporters' clubs, a free press with such impressive resources should be a symbol of a closed society in an age of burgeoning internationalism. The system deserves to be more widely known. Hundreds of reporters' clubs provide the main source of news for Japan's mass media.[69] First organized by reporters in the 1920s to ease liaison with news sources in government and politics, the clubs became government tools for controlling the news during the authoritarian militarist period, from about 1930 until September 1945. With the postwar revolution, the media and their reporters' clubs became free and have operated independently under the self-regulatory guidelines of the Publishers Association. Now, each of the major newspapers, news agencies, and radio-television networks assigns one or more reporters to each major reporters' club. Reporters' clubs, by custom, have their own offices at government ministries, the Diet, political party headquarters, the police department, economic organizations, the courts, the Prime Minister's Office in Tokyo, and at other strategic locations throughout the country.

Reporters' clubs meet with representatives of such agencies at least once daily; they also call press conferences. Typically, reporters go from home to the reporters clubs', not to their employers' offices. They file their stories by messenger or electronic means. Over time, many reporters develop close ties with their sources and with their colleagues from competing media companies. Four problems for press freedom in this otherwise excellent and efficient news-producing system may be:

1 In the newsgathering relationships between reporters—who cover one "beat" for only two or three years—and agencies, the reporters may not be a match for the well-briefed government or business "spin artists" who slant the news.
2 Reporters from different media companies do not compete for news, but may rather form a consensus on what should and should not be reported by the club, and may ostracize a reporter who deviates from the shared view (occasioning perhaps a transfer of the reporter rather than vigorous support from his editor's office).
3 Nonmembers, domestic and foreign, are excluded from the main national newsgathering process.
4 The group-dependent context of newsgathering may discourage independent investigative journalism.

Foreign correspondents, even if competent in Japanese and Japan's affairs, have not been admitted to reporters' clubs. Nor have they been welcome at reporters clubs' press conferences as nonmembers, with few exceptions. For example, foreign correspondents have been welcome at the Prime Minister's Official Residence Reporters' Club since 1965. To ameliorate this restrictive situation, the Publishers Association issued new guidelines in 1985, urging that "[t]he press clubs extend cooperation, where possible, for foreign correspondents stationed here with certain accreditation, and give assistance to them, such as allowing them to attend the official press conferences sponsored by the clubs."[70] A Tokyo English-language paper editorialized:

> Now it is one small step to admit them to press conferences, another to allow them to ask questions there. However, we all know that the most significant news does not come out of these meetings but instead at nonattributable briefings, and for the present at least there is absolutely no thought of ever admitting foreigners to these.[71]

For reasons both good and bad, democratic governments are generally more at ease about leaking political secrets to domestic newsmen than to foreigners. The organizational system of the reporters' clubs, however, makes newsgathering in Japan more than ordinarily difficult for "outsiders." The assertive groupism and competitive factionalism of the social culture, which encourages free and diverse discourse in many other settings, and which characterizes the competition among newspapers for subscribers, does not often extend into news-reporting processes.

History Textbooks and Nationalism

The final media-related controversy touched on, the Ienaga textbook review cases,[72] illustrates the impact that nationalism and bureaucratism can have on freedom of expression, in particular on the freedom to write and publish history textbooks for precollege students. Japan's education establishment seems to lack a consensus on how to treat history and "State Shinto"[73] in the schools and in political discourse. Students learn little about Japan's World War II history at school, in part because university entrance exam questions focus on earlier history. For about twenty-five years, Ienaga Saburō, a distinguished historian, has struggled in court with the Education Ministry over its tampering with the content of different editions of his high school history text, which takes a critical view of the country's history. As the representative of the democratic state, the Ministry emphasizes its own authority and duty to assure accuracy, quality, and balance in precollege texts, as opposed to any rights of parents and educators. Ienaga, like some others, has long worried about a reversion to prewar aggressive nationalism and statist government rooted in Shinto. It may well be that the complicated processes of writing, editing, certifying, publishing, locally selecting, and marketing history textbooks contain unintended restraints on freedom more important than intentional bureaucratic censorship by the Education Ministry. In any case, ideological polarization accentuates the disagreements.[74] Since school textbooks may convey to young people the most authoritative version of the nation's history they encounter, the issues are worthy of great constitutional controversy.

In court, Professor Ienaga challenged the Ministry's textbook-review criteria and procedures as unconstitutional interference with his freedoms of thought and expression and his academic freedom, as well as with a child's right to education.[75] He also challenged recommended or required changes of content. Under the certification system, a textbook author must submit a manuscript for review by the Ministry's examiners. A certain point total is necessary for approval, and points are taken off for factual errors, lack of balance, and other deficiencies. Even when a manuscript is approved, examiners commonly suggest or require changes in many places. Regarding content, three of the points on which the Ministry and Ienaga sharply disagreed were his text's references to: (1) all of Japan's earliest mythological Shinto writings as simply a means of legitimizing control of the government by the Emperor; (2) workers and farmers as the more important makers of history rather than some better-known historical figures; and (3) the Russo-Japanese Neutrality Pact of the early 1940s as a means used to strengthen Japan's position for a strategy of advancing into southern Asia. The Ministry deleted picture captions referring to ordinary people as "the mainstay of history" and insisted that the reference to the neutrality agreement with the Soviet Union include the phrase "after an overture from the Soviet Union."

The complex judicial decision-making since 1970 has resulted in victories and defeats for both sides. The courts have affirmed the author's freedom and the need for great Ministry caution lest examiners tamper improperly with content, while also recognizing the duty and prerogatives of the state as representative of the sovereign people in precollege textbook certification. In some instances, as in the 1982 Supreme Court Ienaga decision, judges have avoided most of the great issues by reliance on legal technicalities.

On October 3, 1989, the Tokyo District Court[76] ruled on Ienaga's 1984 suit against government tampering with his coverage of modern history in the 1980 edition of his text. While awarding compensation for an abuse of authority on one point, the court upheld the Ministry's position on seven other disputed passages, deleting, for example, discussion of wartime experiments on thousands of Chinese by "731 Unit" in Manchuria. In out-of-court negotiations, Ienaga seemed more successful. The Ministry yielded on two key points: "Japan's invasion" of China was called an invasion, not an "advance," and the Nanjing Massacre (1937) of "many Chinese civilians and soldiers" was attributed to "the Imperial Japanese Army," not "chaos."

Over the years, politicians and officials on the right have sought change in the content of history textbooks in order to further cloud the mythological, ahistorical nature of very early writings on Japan's origins and the imperial institution, and to gloss over Japan's colonialism in Korea (1905–45) and wartime aggression against China and Southeast Asian nations. For example, in the 1980s, revised Education Ministry guidelines for history textbook writers drew not only domestic criticism but also expressions of outrage from Asian neighbors at Japan's dishonesty and insensitivity. Bitter conflict arose between the Education Ministry, which insisted on national sovereignty in textbook matters, and the Foreign Ministry, which is responsible for maintaining good neighborly relations.

More typical of its relations with other Asian nations since 1945, Japanese officials have given war reparations, aid, investment, and trade, and have expressed regret, sorrow, and/or apology to Asian countries for World War II. But as Japan rose in the world's power hierarchy in the 1980s, some public figures—notably in relation to the textbook controversy—showed confidence bordering on national arrogance and unabashed state support of Shinto increased. In a rare and extreme incident, Kamai Shizuka, a conservative member of Parliament, warned critical representatives of Korea that continued interference with Japan's internal textbook affairs could eventually lead to war.[77] For the indefinite future, Asian nations will remain acutely sensitive to how openly and straightforwardly textbooks and officials treat Japan's behavior during the Pacific War. The persisting concern of Ienaga and others about the implications of nationalism and restrictive bureaucratism for freedom of expression and other rights will remain timely. In the 1990s, Japan's use of vast numbers of enslaved "comfort women" for its troops became the test of honesty about wartime behavior.

CONCLUSION: FREEDOM AND COMMUNITY IN CONSTITUTIONAL CULTURES

Each constitutional democracy is a partially open, partially closed, coherent cultural whole, operating according to a sometimes subliminal consensus about what should be done for survival, success, and adherence to national values. Each constitutional culture nurtures, protects, regulates, and represses freedom of expression in ways often determined more by its own rules and customs than by law, government institution, or abstract ideal. Freedom lives or dies in the interplay between the public and private sectors. A relevant conviction—for example, a consensus that each person has inherent and equal dignity under God or Nature—may improve the status of free speech in competitive politics, defined as the degree to which ordinary people in a polity may peacefully express themselves on any subject with impunity. But the impact on actual practice of such a national principle can be exaggerated or misconstrued.[78] For example, a nonindividualist groupism is as compatible or more compatible with freedom of expression in sociolegal practice than are some types of individualism.

What is often called "Western individualism" in American discourse on rights and their foundations is a cluster of attitudes peculiar to the United States, not a characteristic of the Western world or of constitutional democracies in general.[79] In some respects, these attitudes are incompatible with the conception of human rights in human rights documents of the United Nations and other international agencies.[80]

For example, a rather extreme emphasis in America on economic liberty and on the human as a free chooser apart from his or her community context does not seem to fit easily with respect for the rights of others implied by their equal human dignity. On the other hand, as Robert Bellah and others show, the "individualism" of the United States is not univocal, but diverse and complex in meaning; so generalizations here admittedly would need qualification.[81] In some forms, the cultural imperative of U.S. individualism weakens rather than buttresses the status of rights and freedom; in other contexts, probably less common than Americans tend to think, individualism adds sociopolitical strength to freedom of expression. Analogously, under Japan's written and unwritten constitutions, groupism operates both for and against free speech, depending on the people and context involved. In general, groupism may provide a stronger basis in the social structure for a vigorous system of freedom of expression under law than some forms of individualism, because "an individual outside a group is ineffectual and generally much less competent than a well-organized group in preserving, developing, and expressing an idea for consideration by relevant publics."[82] Yet inward-looking groupism may exacerbate the problems of restrictive bureaucratism in Japan's government and myopic pursuit of group interests by some private groups.

In Japan's democratic politics and law since 1945, however, coherent groups have formed and have vigorously, freely, and peacefully pursued their ends. In comparative terms, it is not freedom itself that is usually pursued by activists in democracies —as in Burma and South Korea in 1988, in China in 1989, or in the Philippines earlier—but some concrete benefit or change of policy.[83] Japan's mass media will continue to regulate themselves and effectively protect their own prerogatives. The Japanese courts are likely to continue protection of press freedom, and they may become more at ease in the future about collective activities than they have been in decisions discussed here. In any case, irrepressible group actions involving workers, media companies, students, housewives, farmers, and other components of society seem as perennially essential to the nation's constitutional democracy as periodic elections and restraints on government power under law.

The study of democratic constitutionalism in radically different cultures makes more obvious the difficulty of clearly separating the public and private sectors, and of formulating theory or assessing national performance in such a way as to separate appropriately what is essential from what is peculiar to a particular country or group of nations. Identification of the distinctive aids and obstacles to free speech found within any given constitutional culture can provide a foundation for taking remedial steps in law, administration, and the private sector.[84]

Theory regarding freedom of expression and constitutionalism awaits adequate attention to groupism and a more careful sorting out of the different meanings of individualism for its future development. As a transculturally neutral term that may better express the ideal and empirical nature of freedom in a constitutionalist community, I would offer the encapsulating word "mutualism." "Mutualism" integrates both the individual and the social sides of freedom and other rights more organically than either "individualism" or "groupism." "Mutualism" points to the inherently reciprocal nature of individual rights, the mutual regard and respect they demand, and their existence within concrete interpersonal relationships of specific communities, not in individualist isolation, in an imaginary universalist world, or in groupist submersion. "Mutualism" also offers a perspective which is compatible with the powerful affirmation of human dignity at the foundation of Japan's constitutional democracy and human rights.[85]

NOTES

1 Mayor Motoshima was seriously wounded by an ultranationalist on January 18, 1990. Sanger, "Mayor Who Faulted Hirohito Is Shot," *N. Y. Times*, January 19, 1990, at A6, col. 4.

2 Japanese count years according to the Christian Era, but also from the first year of the incumbent emperor's reign. Hirohito's era, the (Shōwa) Bright Peace Period, began in 1926; after death, an emperor is referred to by the era name rather than his personal name, hence Emperor Shōwa. Emperor Akihito's reign is referred to as (Heisei) Achieving Peace.

3 Gibson & Bingham, "On the Conceptualization and Measurement of Political Tolerance," *76 am. pol. sci. rev.* 603 (1982); Powell, "American Voter Turnout in Comparative Perspective," 80 *Am. Pol. Sci. Rev.* 35 (1986).

4 J. Marshall, *Japan's Successor Generation: Their Values and Attitudes* (1985).

5 *See especially* 1947 Const. arts. 11–40 (ch. 3).

6 Petition Law, Law No. 13 of 1947. For a translation of this law, see L. Beer, *Freedom of Expression in Japan: A Study in Comparative Law, Politics and Society* 193–94 n.9 (1984).

7 Other provisions also affect the freedom of religious expression and the separation of religion and the state. Article 19 guarantees "freedom of thought and conscience," and Article 89 prohibits the use of public resources for a religion or for any nonprofit institution "not under the control of public authority."

8 Article 82 allows other types of cases to "be conducted privately" if "a court unanimously determines publicity to be dangerous to public order or morals."

9 Japan v. Sugino, 4 Keishū 2012, 2014 (Sup. Ct., G.B., 1950). *See also* Beer, *supra* note 6, at 151–52 (on the public welfare). The public welfare also qualifies *specific* rights to property (Article 29) and to choice of residence and occupation (Article 22).

10 Beer, *supra* note 6, at 100–28. The precise impact of a cultural attribute on freedom in a given case is a matter for subtle interpretation of empirical data; the problems are well discussed in Ramseyer & Nakazato, "The Rational Litigant: Settlement Amounts and Verdict Rates in Japan," 18 *J. Legal Stud.* 263 (1989). *See also* Gaenslen, "Culture and Decisionmaking in China, Japan, Russia, and the United States," 39 *World Pol. 78* (1986) (comparative study).

11 This preference does not mean that Japanese disputants settle for less than they would receive as a result of a trial. *See* Ramseyer & Nakazato, *supra* note 10.

12 L. Beer, Human Rights Commissioners (Jinken Yōgo Iin) and Lay Protection of Human Rights in Japan (Occasional paper No. 31, Int'l Ombudsman Inst., 1985).

13 Historically, the institution was inspired by discussions during the Occupation between Japanese and American officials about the new Civil Rights Section of the Criminal Division of the United States Department of Justice (now the Civil Rights Division) and about civil liberties, the primary American emphasis in the human rights area.

14 Human Rights Commissioner Law, Law No. 139 of 1949.

15 *See, e.g.*, R. Mitchell, *Censorship in Imperial Japan* (1983); R. Mitchell, *Thought Control in Prewar Japan* (1976); McKean, "Equality," in *Democracy in Japan* 201 (T. Ishida & E. Krauss eds., 1989) [hereinafter Democracy]; Steinhoff, Protest and Democracy, in *Democracy* 171; Turner, "Democratic Consciousness in Japanese Unions," in *Democracy* 299.

16 Road Traffic law, Law No. 105 of 1960; *see also* Beer, *supra* note 6, at 166–68.

17 Itō v. Japan, 14 Keishū 1243 (Sup. Ct., G.B., July 20, 1960). For the text of the Tokyo Ordinance and a translation of the decision, see J. Maki, Court and Constitution in Japan 84–116 (1964).

18 Treaty of Mutual Cooperation and Security, Jan. 19, 1960, U.S.-Japan, 11 U.S.T. 1632, T.I.A.S. No. 4509. *See also* Japan v. Sakane, 23 Keishū 685 (Sup. Ct., G.B., Apr. 2, 1969) (decision on an incident arising during the Security Treaty crisis). For the texts of the treaty and the *Sakane* opinion, see H. Itoh & L. Beer, *The Constitutional Case Law of Japan* 103–30 (1978).

19 *See* Maki, *supra* note 17, at 88.

20 *Id.* at 89.

21 *Id.*

22 *Id.* at 90.

23 *Id.*
24 Japan v. Teramae, 29 Keishū 489 (Sup. Ct., G.B., September 10, 1975).
25 Katō v. Japan, 854 Hanji 52 (Tokyo H. Ct., June 7, 1977). *See also* Beer, *supra* note 6, at 187.
26 *Asahi Shimbun* (evening ed.) October 4, 1986; Japan Times, October 19, 1986, at 2, col 1.
27 A. de Tocqueville, *Democracy in America* 191 (P. Bradley ed., 1945).
28 Subversive Activities Prevention Law, Law No. 240 of 1952.
29 1947 Const. arts. 28, 21.
30 Law No. 25 of 1946.
31 *Id.* arts. 6, 12.
32 T. Hanami, *Labour Law and Industrial Relations in Japan* 182 (1979); Beer, *supra* note 6, at 216; *see also id.* at 222.
33 The general legal basis for restraints are article 102 of the National Public Employees Law, Law No. 120 of 1947, and article 26 of the Local Public Employees Law, Law No. 261 of 1950. The prohibited political acts are left to prescription in detail in the Rules of the National Personnel Authority.
34 Toyama v. Japan (The Tokyo Central Post Office Case), 20 Keishū 901 (Sup. Ct., G.B., Oct. 26, 1966); for a translation of this case, see Itoh & Beer, *supra* note 18, at 85–130.
35 20 Keishū 901; see Itoh & Beer, *supra* note 18, at 85 for translation.
36 *See* Itoh & Beer, *supra* note 18, at 91 for translation.
37 Tsuruzono v. Japan (The All-Japan Agriculture and Forestry Workers Union Case), 27 Keishū 547 (Sup. Ct., G.B., Apr. 25, 1973).
38 Japan v. Ōsawa, 28 Keishū 393 (Sup. Ct., G.B., Nov. 6, 1974), *rev'g* 514 Hanji 20 (Asahikawa Dist. Ct., Mar. 25, 1968) *and* 560 Hanji 30 (Sapporo H. Ct., June 24, 1969).
39 *See* Beer, *supra* note 6, at ch. 6, and Japanese sources cited therein.
40 Hokkaido Education Commission v. Hayashi, *Asahi Shimbun* (Sup. Ct., 1st P.B., Dec. 19, 1986).
41 *See* articles 37 and 61 of the Local Public Employees Law, *supra* note 49, as translated in Itoh & Beer, *supra* note 18, at 86–87.
42 Article 175 provides that:

> A person who distributes or sells an obscene writing, picture, or other object or who publicly displays the same, shall be punished with imprisonment at forced labor for not more than two years or a fine of not more than 5,000 yen or a minor fine. The same applies to a person who possesses the same for the purpose of sale.

Keihō (Criminal Code), Art. 175 (as translated from Ministry of Justice, Criminal Statutes I 39 (1961)).
43 Customs Standards Law, Law No. 54 of 1910 (amended 1980).
44 Matsue v. Japan, 38 Minshū 1308 (Sup. Ct., G.B., Dec. 12, 1984). *See* Beer, *supra* note 6, at 347–55 (on obscenity decisions of the Supreme Court); Ishii v. Japan, 23 Keishū 1239 (Sup. Ct., G.B., Oct 15, 1969), *translated in* Itoh & Beer, *supra* note 18, at 183–217; Koyama v. Japan, 11 Keishū 997 (Sup. Ct., G.B., Mar. 13, 1957), *translated in* Maki, *supra* note 17, at 3–37). The works at issue were Japanese translations of D.H. Lawrence's *Lady Chatterley's Lover*, and de Sade's *The Travels of Juliette*.
45 *Japan Times Weekly*, December 14, 1985. This pattern of concerns is consistent with other poll data since the late 1970s.
46 Article 710 provides that "[a] person who is liable [under art. 709] shall make compensation therefore even in respect of a non-pecuniary damage, irrespective of whether such injury was to the person, liberty or reputation of another or to his property rights." Minpō (Civil Code), art. 710.
47 Article 723 provides that "[i]f a person has injured the reputation of another, the Court may, on the application of the latter, make an order requiring the former to take suitable measures for the restoration of the latter's reputation either in lieu of or together with compensation for damages." *Id.* art 723.
48 The Criminal Code of Japan provides:

> Article 230. A person who defames another by publicly alleging facts shall, regardless of whether such facts are true or false, be punished with imprisonment at or without forced labor for not more than three years or a fine of not more than 1,000 yen. . . .
>
> Article 230–2. When the act provided for [in article 230] . . . is found to relate to matters of Public Interest [*kōkyō no rigai*] and to have been done solely [*moppara*] for the benefit of the

> public and, upon inquiry into the truth or falsity of the alleged facts, the truth is proved, punishment shall not be imposed. . . .
>
> Article 230–3. When the act provided for [in article 230] . . . is done with regard to matters concerning a public servant or a candidate for elective public office and, upon inquiry into the truth or falsity of the alleged facts, the truth is proved, punishment shall not be imposed.

Keihō, art. 230. For judicial doctrine on defamation, see Kochi v. Japan, 23 Keishū 259 (Sup. Ct., G.B., June 25, 1969) (*translated in* Itoh & Beer, *supra* note 18, at 175); *see also* Beer, *supra* note 6, at 318–25. In a much-discussed political case, in which the Japan Communist Party demanded that the *Sankei Shimbun* newspaper publish its unpaid advertisement responding to the Liberal Democratic Party's paid advertisement attacking the Japan Communist Party in December 1973, the Supreme Court denied a constitutional right to refutation under Article 21. Japan Communist Party v. Sankei Shimbun (Sup. Ct., 2d P.B., Apr. 24, 1987), Asahi Shimbun, Apr. 25, 1987, at 1.

49 Gekkan Pen v. Japan, 35 Keishū 34 (Sup. Ct., 1st P.B., Apr. 16, 1981).

50 1128 Hanji 32 (Tokyo H. Ct., July 18, 1984).

51 Ona v. Igarashi, 40 Minshü 872 (Sup. Ct., G.B., June 11, 1986) *See also* Asahi Shimbun (evening ed.), Oct. 2, 1981, at 1.

52 Arita v. Mishima, 15 Kaminshü 2317 (Tokyo Dist. Ct., Sept 28, 1964).

53 Hasegawa v. Japan, 23 Keishū 1625 (Sup. Ct., G.B., Dec. 24, 1969), *translated in* Itoh & Beer, *supra* note 18, at 178. A right to likeness as a privacy right was unsuccessfully claimed in a case challenging the constitutionality of a system automatically taking photos of speeders. 40 Keishū 48 (Sup. Ct., 2d P.B., Feb. 14, 1986). *See also* Japan Times, Jan. 12, 1987, at 2, col. 6.

54 Marshall, *supra* note 4.

55 *See* Beer, *supra* note 6, at 281–89; the Recruit scandal emerged in 1988. Japanese prosecutors contend that the information services and real estate corporate conglomerate Recruit Company and a subsidiary bought influence in government by giving cash and discounted stock to top political figures in the ruling Liberal Democratic Party, high-ranking government bureaucrats, and prominent businessmen. *See* "Ex-Recruit Chief Questioned over Objective in Share Deals," *Japan Times Weekly* (overseas ed.), January 4, 1989, at 2. *See also* Samuels, "Japan in 1989: Changing Times," 30 *Asian Survey* 46 (1990) and subsequent January issues of *Asian Survey*.

56 Kaneko v. Japan, 23 Keishū 1490 (Sup. Ct., G.B., Nov. 26, 1969), *translated in* Itoh & Beer, *supra* note 18, at 246.

57 Nishiyama v. Japan, 32 Keishū 457 (Sup. Ct. 1st P.B., May 31, 1978).

58 Sasaki v. Japan, 930 Hanji 44 (Sapporo Dist. Ct., Mar. 30, 1979).

59 Brown, "Government Secrecy and the 'People's Right to Know' in Japan: Implications of the Nishiyama Case," 10 *Law in Japan* 112, 138 (1977).

60 Ishii v. Japan, 6 Keishū 974 (Sup. Ct., G.B., Aug. 6, 1952), *translated in* Maki, *supra* note 17, at 38.

61 Articles 105 and 149 of the Code of Criminal Procedure establish as privileged professional confidences those of "a person who is, or was, a doctor, dentist, midwife, nurse, practicing attorney, patent agent, notary public or a religious functionary." Keisohō (Code of Criminal Procedure) arts. 105, 149.

62 30 Minshū 403 (Sapporo H. Ct., Aug. 31, 1979); *see also Asahi Shimbun* (evening ed.), March 8, 1980 (Sup. Ct., 3d P.B., Mar. 8, 1980).

63 Article 281 of the Code of Civil Procedure provides:

> A witness may refuse to testify in the following cases: . . . In a case where a doctor, dentist, pharmacist, druggist, midwife, lawyer, patent attorney, advocate, notary public, or an occupant of a post connected with religion or worship or a person who was once in such profession is questioned regarding [professional secrets].

Minsohō (Code of Civil Procedure) art. 281, *translated in* EHS L. Bull. Series, Vol. III, No. 2300, La-54 (1963).

64 Repeta v. Japan, 43 Minshū 89 (Sup. Ct., G.B., Mar. 8, 1989), *rev'g* 1222 Hanji 28 (Tokyo Dist. Ct., Feb. 12, 1987) *and* 1262 Hanji 30 (Tokyo H. Ct., Dec. 25, 1987); *Asahi Shimbun*, March 9, 1989, at 2; 936 Jurisuto 17–44 (June 15, 1989).

65 Article 71 provides:

> The presiding judge or a single judge who has opened a court shall maintain order in the court.
>
> . . . .

> The presiding judge or a judge who has opened a court may order any person who interferes with the exercise of functions of the court or who behaves himself improperly, to leave the court, and may issue such other orders or take such measures as are necessary for the maintenance of order in the court.

Court Organization Law, Law No. 59 of 1947, *translated in* EHS L. Bull. Series, vol. II-AA, 23 (1966).

66 For example, the restrictive policy may have arisen in reaction to trials arising from mass political activity during May Day observances in 1952, during the Security Treaty crisis in 1960, and during the University crisis in 1969. Beer, "Japan, 1969: 'My Homeism' and Political Struggle," 10 *Asian Surv.* 43 (1970).

67 The United Nations' declaration provides that "[e]veryone has the right to freedom of opinion and expression; this right includes freedom to hold opinions without interference and to seek, receive and impart information and ideas through any media and regardless of frontiers." United Nations Universal Declaration of Human Rights, General Assembly Resolution 217 A(III) of Dec. 10, 1948, art. 19. The International Covenant reads:

> 1 Everyone shall have the right to hold opinions without interference.
> 2 Everyone shall have the right to freedom of expression; this right shall include freedom to seek, receive and impart information and ideas of all kinds, regardless of frontiers, either orally, in writing or in print, in the form of art, or through any other media of his choice.
> 3 The exercise of the rights provided for in paragraph 2 of this article carries with it special duties and responsibilities. It may therefore be subject to certain restrictions, but these shall only be such as are provided by law and are necessary: (a) For respect of the rights or reputations of others; (b) For the protection of national security or of public order (*ordre public*), or of public health or morals.

International Covenant on Civil and Political Rights, UNGA Res. 2200 A(XII) of December 16, 1966, (entered into force on March 26, 1976; ratified by Japan June 1979). The full texts of these and other documents, along with excellent analyses, can be found in D. Forsythe, *Human Rights and World Politics* (2nd ed., 1989).

68 "Except for those rights with special characteristics indicating they have only Japanese citizens as their subject, the fundamental human rights guaranteed under Chapter III of the Constitution extend equally to foreigners residing in our country." McLean v. Japan, 32 Minshū 1223 (Sup. Ct., G.B., Oct. 4, 1978), *cited in Repeta*, 1299 Hanji 43–44 as claiming equal rights for foreigners. *See also*, Beer, *supra* note 6, at 363–64. In the 1980s, progress was made in Japanese statutory law and policy toward equal treatment of foreigners residing in Japan.

69 Beer, *supra* note 6, at 303; Masaaki, "Mass Media in Japan," *The Japan Foundation Newsletter* (1983); Yamamoto, "The Press Clubs of Japan," 15 *J. Japanese Stud.* 371 (1989).

70 *Japan Times Weekly*, September 21, 1985.

71 *Id.*

72 Ienaga v. Minister of Education, Japan, 604 Hanji 35 (Tokyo Dist. Ct., July 17, 1970); Ministry of Education v. Ienaga, 800 Hanji 19 (Tokyo H. Ct., Dec. 20, 1975); 1040 Hanji 3 (Sup. Ct., 1st P.B., Apr. 8, 1982); Ienaga v. Minister of Education, 751 Hanji 50 (Tokyo Dist. Ct., July 16, 1976); 1188 Hanji 1 (Tokyo H. Ct., Mar. 19, 1986).

73 The term "State Shinto" is used here because in the past fifteen years a pattern of judicial decisions and other acts of government may in effect have given uniquely privileged status to Shinto. Shinto is not a religion in the sense of a universal religion or religion as understood in the West. It became infected with statism under the Meiji Constitution, and the trend noted seems more a mode of expressing neonationalism than of uniting religion and the state. *See especially* Takizawa, "Religion and the State in Japan," *J. Church & St.* 89 (Winter 1988); *see also* Beer, *supra* note 6 at 248–54; H. Hardacre, *Shinto and the State*, 1868–1988 (1989); Higuchi, When Society Is Itself the Tyrant, 35 *Japan Q.* 350 (1988); "Shōchō Tennōsei," *Jurisuto* (May 5, 1989).

74 The context is explained in Beer, *supra* note 6, at 252–64.

75 *See* 1947 Const. arts. 19, 23, 26.

76 Ienaga v. Minister of Education, *Asahi Shimbun* (evening ed.), October 3, 1989; *Japan Times*, October 4, 1989. The 1987 suit was held moot by the Tokyo High Court in 1989 due to changes in the government's curricular guidelines. Minister of Education, Japan v. Ienaga, 1317 Hanji 36 (Tokyo H. Ct., June 27, 1989).

77 *Japan Times*, October 31, 1986, at 3, col. 3.

78 K. Greenawalt, *Speech, Crime, and the Uses of Language* (1989) (fusion of such theory with detailed analysis of context and empirical data seems the necessarily laborious way of gaining wisdom when assessing a nation's free-speech record). Greenawalt, "Free Speech Justifications," 89 *Colum. L. Rev.* 119 (1989) (free-speech theory that includes attention to the significance of urging, requesting, encouraging, threatening, and other communicative acts which vary importantly in manner with culture).

79 McKay, "Why is There a European Political Science," 21 *Pol. Sci. & Pol.* 1051–54 (1988). The relatively narrow "liberal individualism" (of the left, the right, and the center) underlying American social science contrasts sharply with the diversity of intellectual and political views in Europe, reflecting perhaps the narrow spectrum of political parties that the constitutional culture of the United States finds tolerable.

80 Legal positivism and economic liberalism seem to militate against establishment in American law and policy of socioeconomic rights taken for granted in many constitutional democracies, and to weaken attention to equality of criminal justice rights. Regarding socioeconomic rights, see International Covenant on Economic, Social and Cultural Rights, UNGA Res. 2200A(xxi) of Dec. 16, 1966, which, with the Universal Declaration of Human Rights, *supra* note 67, and the International Covenant on Civil and Political Rights, *supra* note 67, is referred to as the "International Bill of Rights." On U.S. and international rights, see J. Auerbach, *Unequal Justice: Lawyers and Social Change in Modern America* (1976); P. Sighart, *The Lawful Rights of Mankind: An Introduction to the International Legal Code of Human Rights* (1985); *Human Rights Sourcebook* (A. Blaustein ed., 1987); *International Human Rights Instruments of the United Nations*, 1948–1982 (UNIFO ed., 1983).

81 *See* R. Bellah et al., *Habits of the Heart: Individualism and Commitment in American Life* (1985).

82 Beer, *supra* note 6, at 398.

83 *See* W. Spinrad, *Civil Liberties* (1970), and the synopsis of his sociology of free speech in Beer, *supra* note 6, at 403–4.

84 Examples of remedial constitutionalism are the provisions in the 1987 Constitution of the Philippines against appointing relatives to government office, in reaction against the nepotism of the past. The Constitutions of both the Philippines and South Korea limit presidents to one term in office (six years and five years respectively), to counter the tendency of leaders in those countries to perpetuate themselves in power. Article 9 of the Japanese Constitution may also be seen in this light as a remedy for extreme militarization of government and politics before the end of World War II. *See* L. Beer, *Constitutional Systems in Late Twentieth Century Asia* (1992).

85 The primary governmental purpose of freedom of expression does not seem to be to assure through debate and voting the determination and implementation of the majority will on any subject ("democracy"), but rather to assure the persistent pursuit of fundamental human rights for all citizens and to regularize limitations on government power ("constitutional democracy"). The dilemma is not between majority rule and minority rights, whether the minority be privileged or severely deprived. Instead, the problem is adding to the notions of majority rule and majority rights those of equal protection and promotion of the basic human rights of *all*. Human rights do not reside in the individual apart from others; rather, they are enjoyed or violated within interpersonal relationships, whether the right in question is to food or to reputation.

■ First published in L.W. Beer & H. Itoh, *The Constitutional Case Law of Japan, 1970 through 1990*, Seattle, University of Washington Press, 1996, pp. 3-29, 54-66.

11

Japan's Constitutional Law, 1945-1990

⌘

1 JAPAN'S CONSTITUTIONALISM SINCE 1945

The barbarism of the Second World War ended with Emperor Hirohito's announcement of surrender on August 15, 1945; Japan has fought in no war since, despite the Cold War environment and the wars of Asian geopolitics. That is part of the remarkable story of constitutional transformation which began under the United States-led Occupation (September 2, 1945–April 28, 1952) and continues on today.[1] Peacefulness has replaced myopic nationalism and militarism at home and abroad; capricious authoritarianism in the name of the emperor is gone; and a revolution for human rights, more democratic choice of leaders, and a responsible government of limited and divided powers has been institutionalized.

The Constitution of Japan was drafted, debated, approved by parliament, and promulgated by the emperor between February and November, 1946, in the form of a revision of the 1889 Constitution of the Empire of Japan (the so-called "Meiji Constitution");[2] it came into effect on May 3, 1947.[3] However, radical systemic changes began in the fall of 1945 when personnel working in the General Headquarters (GHQ) of "SCAP" (Supreme Commander for the Allied Powers), General Douglas MacArthur, disassembled the old order and served as the catalyst for the new democratic order required by Japan's acceptance of the Potsdam Declaration.[4] Unlike Germany and southern Korea, Japan was not ruled directly by the Allied Powers, but indirectly by means of directives called "SCAPIN" ("IN" referred to the index number of a directive) to Japan's government.[5] SCAPIN were converted by the government into laws, ordinances, or new policies, or led to the abolition of repressive laws and agencies. For example, freedom of expression swept through Japan with the issuance of SCAPIN 66 (September 27) and 93 (October 4). The government had attempted to censor publication of a photograph of the diminutive Emperor Hirohito alongside the imposing MacArthur, and met with a quick and decisive SCAPIN response overruling the censorship.[6] Another example is the new House of Representatives Election Law of December 1945 which gave women the right to vote for the first time and lowered the voting age from twenty-five to twenty.[7]

Although some still speak of the 1947 fundamental law as the "New Constitution," by comparative standards the Constitution of Japan is one of the world's venerable basic legal documents. Of roughly 180 single-document national constitutions in effect in 1994, Japan's is one of about twenty whose ratification dates back before 1950.[8] Its longevity is particularly striking when viewed against the kaleidoscopic backdrop of constitutional changes occurring around the world since 1945.

World patterns in constitutional development

For perspective, a few historic patterns. Most non-Western states of today became independent after 1945; their acquisition of independent nation-statehood represents the most fundamental constitutional revolution in the world's collective political system in the past fifty years. Diverse forms of colonialism and United Nations trusteeship have ended, for Japan in eastern Asia, for the United States in the Philippines, Cuba, Panama, and South Pacific island territories, for the United Kingdom, France, Portugal and other European countries in Africa, Asia, the Middle East, and the Caribbean, and more recently for the Union of Soviet Socialist Republics (USSR) in its constituent Republics, Mongolia, and East Europe.[9]

A second pattern in the second half of the twentieth century is unprecedented creative experimentation around the world in forms of government and law under written constitutions, as each nation-state has sought stability and appropriate definition of its constitutional identity, by writing, rewriting, amending, or re-interpreting its constitution, or by a combination of the above. As an example of the latter, the United States began revolutionary redefinition of its constitutionalism to fully legitimize racial equality for the first time during the 1950s and 1960s, by law, amendment, judicial interpretation, and a mass movement driven by African-American and liberal elites and religious conviction. France freed itself from its colonialism in "Indochina" (Vietnam, Cambodia, Laos) and in Algeria in the process of losing wars and regaining stability under the 1958 Constitution of the Fifth Republic.[10] Most of the pieces of the broken Soviet bloc emerged as social democracies modeled on Western European constitutional practice. And in the 1990s South Africa remade itself from within, replacing in 1994 a minority *apartheid* regime with majoritarian democracy. More generally, over 125 countries trace the ratification of their constitutions back no farther than 1970.[11] The frequency of revisions or amendments in some areas has been due to leadership changes after independence and to stages of adjustment in a process of developing stable government responsive to indigenous political realities, sociolegal culture, and economics as well as to transcultural principles of modern government such as human rights, political accountability, and predictability in legal practice.

A third phenomenon, the end of the Cold War, has given new elbow room since the late 1980s for national and subnational self-definition around the planet in countries long locked into the logic of bipolar nuclear deterrence. Although a welcome sign of long-desired collective freedom, the re-emergence of intense ethnonationalism sometimes resulted in violent conflict (for example, in the former USSR and Yugoslavia and in Africa). In the name of preserving group identity and self-determination as well as universalist principles of human rights and humane world religions (Christianity and Islam, most prominently), particularistic interests were pursued with ethnic rage and disregard for the just concerns of others.[12]

On the other hand, by the mid-1990s educated internationalist elites of whatever clime reciprocally accepted for the first time the authentic humanity of a great array of radically diverse cultures. Racism and cultural chauvinism continued to be prime motive forces in world politics and economics, and differences in leadership styles, socioeconomic conditions, social culture, and ideology still led to varying governmental emphases; but the protection and promotion of human rights by nation-states are now the most widely accepted test of quality in governance and national legal practice. In juristic circles, human rights are commonly understood not as vague philosophical abstractions, but as stipulated in the 1948 United Nations Universal Declaration of Human Rights and the UN's subsequent detailed covenants and protocols.[13] For most nations, human rights law has become treaty law, international customary law (for example, in the U.S., through the appellate holding in *Filartiga v. Pena-Irala*),[14] and/or domestic constitutional law (as in Spain's 1978 Constitution which makes UN human rights provisions the standard for interpretation).[15] At the least, human rights performance is the key status symbol at work on the world's political mind. Supported by the revolutions in the technology of communication and transportation, the current unprecedented process of clarification of world constitutional standards is a major advance in civilization. What is surprising is not so much the continued conflicts and disagreements, as the degree of clarification and acceptance of standards achieved. Insofar as any is emerging, "the new world order" of government and law *within* nation-states bases legitimacy on regimes' human right behavior.

A fifth characteristic of the constitutional situation is the acceptance by most countries of elements in Europe's civil law tradition or in Anglo-American common law as a proper part of their framework for thinking about, organizing, formulating and practicing modern law, and not simply because those traditions are now essential to world diplomatic and economic relations.[16] Non-Western leaders have found the colonial legacy of law extremely useful in some respects. Only very few other traditions of state law, such as Islamic law and Confucian legalism, are transnationally influential. The birth and near death of Communist legalism—an offshoot of the civil law tradition—in the nations formerly within the Soviet orbit illustrate the adaptability of a major legal tradition to political change. Analogously, Japan's postwar constitutional revolution shows how a country can move from repressive statism to democratic constitutionalism within the same modern legal tradition. Her constitutional history since the 1860s also illustrates how possible it is for at least some countries to selectively and successfully integrate into their government and law constitutional principles, legal processes and state organs at radical variance with earlier indigenous traditions.[17] One result of the world ascendancy of the two main Western legal traditions is a level of mutual understanding among jurists, governments, businessmen and scholars in their occupational interactions around the globe that is unprecedented and was probably unimaginable a mere century ago.

A country's capacity to participate in this world legal dialogue depends on its degree of legal development. Legal development does not imply adherence to a particular constitutional ideology, but rather an ever-more-sophisticated, detailed and effective national rule system and the capacity to implement that law. Although the gradual maturation of Japan's civil law system between 1860 and 1945 did not set the stage for an inevitable explosion into constitutional democracy after the War, it would at best have taken much longer for democracy and human rights law to take firm root in the absence of a developed modern legal system and many personnel trained in law and its implementation. (Such an absence in contemporary China would delay democratic human rights there even should her leaders opt for that ideology in the future. In that sense, China's recent herculean efforts at legal development are supportive of human rights law.)[18] That universal compulsory education, an effective bureaucracy, and modern mass media were already in place also made the tasks of sociopolitical engineering easier when emperor-centered constitutionalism suddenly yielded to people-oriented constitutionalism. Suggestions that economic development or economic liberalization lead with predictability to democracy or an enhanced human rights regime are not borne out by the data. The picture presented by such countries as China, Taiwan, Malaysia, Singapore, former components of the USSR, and other areas is too complicated to confirm a linkage between economic liberalism and civil and political rights.[19] In Japan's case the contribution of stable political democracy and law to prosperity is usually understated, while the importance of economic success to her democracy is sometimes exaggerated.

The revolutionized constitutional order

Japan's constitutional revolution since 1945 has fundamentally altered the status of the emperor (*tennō*), ordinary people and their rights, the military, the courts, and local government under the "new" constitution. By "constitutional revolution," I mean a basic change in the primary public values legitimized and served by law and constitution, values diffused throughout a nation's culture by public and private community means of education, persuasion, and coercion such as schools, religious institutions, the mass media, and administrative policies and processes.[20] At the outset of Japan's revolution between 1945 and 1948 the primacy of the emperor and his state was replaced by the primacy of popular sovereignty, the individual person, and human rights, what I would call "human rights constitutionalism." As theory, "human rights constitutionalism" grounds government and law in recognition of the equal inherent dignity of each human and thus in a comprehensive notion of human rights[21] and community responsibility to honor those rights.

In an earlier constitutional revolution, the traditionally powerless emperor institution was not modified, but transformed. The 1889 Meiji Constitution gave a suprahuman *Shintō* emperor state sovereignty, but it was exercised by generally authoritarian officials in his name. He was

> . . . above and beyond politics, and worthy of the total self-sacrifice of each of his subjects . . . all blood members of the "national family" (the State, *kokka*) could bask together in his benevolent presence, in a warm aura of security, belonging, solidarity, and mentally isolated superiority over other peoples.[22]

At least that was the ideal of "*kokutai*" (the imperial form of the Japanese state) until Japan's crushing defeat. The Japanese word "tennō" was translated "emperor" but is a particularistic term implying the person is more than an emperor or king, and is of a uniquely sacred Japanese dynasty.[23] Today, the word "king" used of other monarchs would seem preferable.

What to do with the emperor may have been the most controversial question in 1946: Arrest him as a war criminal? Replace him with his young son Akihito? Abolish the imperial institution? Leave the emperor with some, most or none of his formal prerogatives under the Meiji Constitution? Or render him virtually powerless in real as well as formal terms, but preserve the dynasty; and in return require his support for a transition to a new and demilitarized democratic order? The latter option was chosen by Occupation policy makers to optimize chances for political stability in the challenging tumult of the early Occupation years.

Now, "sovereign power" resides in the people of Japan (Preamble and Article 1); the emperor is only "a symbol" of Japan (like the flag) and "shall not have powers related to government" (Article 4).[24]

"Article 15. The people have the inalienable right to choose their public officials and to dismiss them.

2. All public officials are servants of the whole community and not of any group thereof."

The people and their representative parliament are thus constitutionally superior to the emperor and the appointive bureaucracy, although in many circumstances the small, able higher civil service is quite influential and proposes policy or law.[25] Since 1946, national and local elections have been conducted under democratic law without interruption.[26] Discrimination against a candidate based on "race, creed, sex, social status, family origin, education, property, or income" is prohibited (Article 44). In 1993, the city Assembly of Kishiwada, Osaka Prefecture voted unanimously to ask the central government to give foreign taxpayers in Japan the rights to vote and to hold public office.[27] (Might future constitutional law permit more citizens of other countries to run for national or local office in the future, in Japan and elsewhere?) Like the United States but unlike some other democracies, Japan has had serious difficulty restraining political campaign spending; but like other democracies Japanese law has assured fair, equal and limited candidate access to the mass media more effectively than U.S. law.[28]

Malapportionment of seats in the Diet (*Kokkai*; National Assembly, lit.), especially in the House of Representatives (*Shūgiin*), has been a major issue in constitutional law for decades (see, for example, Cases 22, 23, and 24 below). Until 1994 reforms under Prime Minister Morihiro Hosokawa, Japan had a very unusual single vote multi-member (two-to-six seats) constituency system without an effective requirement for periodic reapportionment to reflect the shift of population to the cities.[29] Under the new single-member, two-vote system, one vote is cast for a candidate in one's own electoral district to fill 300 Diet seats, and another is cast for a national political party. A party must gain at least two percent of the national popular vote to share in the 200 seats proportionally distributed for the 500-member House of Representatives.[30] It is widely accepted in Japan that any variance in the value of a vote between districts should be minimal and that the law should allow no more than a two-to-one difference in vote value. Half of the 252 members of the House of Councillors (*Sangiin*), the less powerful house of the Diet, are elected to six-year terms every three years (Article 46). One hundred are chosen from national party lists in proportion to the number of popular votes garnered by a party, while the remaining 152 Councillors are elected from election districts consisting of the prefectures or metropolitan areas such as Tokyo and Osaka. Regarding the House of Councillors, the Supreme Court has not held unconstitutional a 5-to-1 discrepancy between districts in vote values,[31] but to many constitutional lawyers this seems excessive.

Individual rights were not set forth in the Meiji Constitution as natural rights with pride of place among public values, but as rights of Japanese subjects bestowed by a paternal emperor and limited by laws and officials in his name.[32] Chapter 3 of the 1947 Constitution turns things around: "The people [of Japan] shall not be prevented from enjoying any of the fundamental human rights" (Article 11) of all individuals everywhere; and within the broad boundaries of the common good, these rights shall be "the supreme consideration in legislation and in other governmental affairs" (Article 13). "All of the people shall be respected as individuals" (the textual basis for privacy rights under Article 13 since the 1960s),[33] and "all . . . are equal under the laws" (Article 14). Articles 11 to 40 present a comprehensive set of specific "human rights" which are "to be held for all time inviolable" (Article 97), and "maintained by the constant endeavor of the people" (Article 12).

In contrast to the subject matter of prewar adjudication, the great majority of judicial decisions since 1947 have been concerned with defining the parameters of individual rights and freedoms.[34] On balance, Japan's human rights record compares well with those of other democracies. Among problems debated in and out of court are improper use of confessions in a generally lenient criminal justice system, restriction of public employee political activities to voting, malapportionment, a ban on door-to-door election canvassing, preferential treatment of Shinto and insensitivity to other religious sensibilities, and social equality issues involving women or one of the small minority groups. As Yasuhiro Okudaira suggests, "Japanese are equality-minded rather than liberty minded."[35] Few large countries manifest less of an income gap between the top ten percent and the bottom ten percent than Japan; over 90% consider themselves "middle class." Japan has a complex social hierarchy of individuals and small groups, but is not a class society. In its government and law, Japan also honors freedom of expression and other freedoms; restraints arise more commonly from the private sector than from the state, as to some degree in all constitutional democracies.[36]

Japan's constitutional revolution has increased the importance of local government and politics; this has been particularly noticeable since the emergence in the 1970s of citizen movements against pollution and other local problems. The premodern Tokugawa Dynasty (1603–1868) gave Japan a feudal federalism, with hundreds of colorfully diverse feudal domains held together for some legal and administrative purposes by the militarily predominant Tokugawa family and its allies. Analogous to some modern federalism, each feudal domain had its own system of government and law, which yielded to Tokugawa authority with respect to a limited number of "federal subjects" and when disputes involved more than one domain.[37] To gain independence from the unequal treaties forced upon Japan by the West in the 1850s and to win Western respect, the Meiji government (1868–1912) created a centripetal, unitary, and almost absolute monarchy; one effect was to deemphasize local government and local interests and to require central government appointment of local officials. Now, local assemblies, prefectural governors and the mayors of cities, towns and villages are "elected by direct popular vote within their several communities" (Article 93, 2). Local governments manage their own affairs (Article 94) within limits set by national law, especially the Local Autonomy Law.[38] A "special law" which applies to only one "local public entity" must be approved by the voters in that place (Article 95). These checks on national power within a unitary state have added vigor and variety to Japan's democracy.

Unique is Chapter 2, "Renunciation of War," which consists of one provision, Article 9. Article 9 renounces war, military power, and "the threat or use of force as a means of settling international disputes." The presence of military officers in the Cabinet is also prohibited (Article 66, 2); in practice, the military is totally subordinate to civilian leaders, in contrast to its privileged status in pre-1945 modern Japan. In 1928 war was outlawed by the Kellogg-Briand Pact ratified by Japan, the United States, Germany, the United Kingdom, the Soviet Union and other countries.[39] Although technically never revoked, the treaty was disregarded when the Second World War erupted in the 1930s.[40] Particularly since the mid-1950s, Japan has gradually developed a modest military capacity, but as James Auer notes, Japan "simultaneously has attempted to live up to the ideals of the Constitution to a degree that the other signatories of the Kellogg-Briand Pact never have."[41] Japan's concept and practice of quasi-pacifism are an original and valuable contribution to world understandings of constitutionalism.

Pursuant to its right of self-defense under natural and international law, Japan has "Self-Defense Forces" (SDF; *Jieitai*), land, sea and air; but they have never fought, and a number of laws and policies concretely restrict military activities and resources. For example, by policy or legal interpretation: under Article 18 conscription is considered unconstitutional as "involuntary servitude" and voluntary enlistment quotas have not been met; no legal provision is made for martial law or for dealing with acts of war such as declaration of war or conclusion of a peace; less than one percent of Japan's GNP is spent on the SDF; Japan may not manufacture, possess, or introduce nuclear weapons; Japan's participation in post-cease fire United Nations peace-monitoring operations is severely limited by law, yet still controversial;[42] offensive weapons, such as long-range bombers or missiles, are forbidden; and arms manufacture and trade are restrained, to Japan's economic loss. Moreover, in her capacity as the world's leading aid donor, Japan looks critically at arms manufacture and trade policies of potential recipient nations when making aid decisions.[43]

On the other hand, the public accepts the SDF as a legitimate part of the constitutional order, though less for defense purposes than for humanitarian relief and for technical and logistical support of United Nations operations.[44] Although its ratification in 1960 occasioned the largest mass protest movement in Japanese history, Japan's lone "Security Treaty," with the United States, is now widely accepted, and serves as the basis for history's most dense economic, cultural, diplomatic and military relationship between two great powers of radically different culture. Upon challenge the Supreme Court did not find the treaty "clearly contrary to provisions of the Constitution,"[45] such as Article 9 and the Preamble. Relatively few Japanese have perceived any serious foreign military threat for decades, and fewer yet want Japan to become a major world military power.

Japan's experience illustrates that given the right geopolitical and domestic circumstances, quasi-pacifism can be a responsible, possible, and pragmatic policy for at least some nation-states. In contrast, though defeated in 1945, earlier modern Japan had demonstrated powerfully that in that age only with heavy militarization to match that of the West could a non-Western country achieve full independence and status in world politics. In the future, many countries may well enhance their prosperity, stability, and international status without threat to their national security, precisely by restraining their military at home and abroad.

Under the revolutionary regime of popular sovereignty, anti-militarism and human rights, the nature of parliament, the executive and the courts has also been changed fundamentally. The popularly elected Diet, not the emperor and his minions (for example, the Privy Council, the House of Peers, and the Imperial Household Agency),[46] is "the highest organ of state power" and the state's "sole law-making organ" (Article 41). The "executive power shall be vested in the Cabinet" group (Article 65), not in the Prime Minister alone, nor in organs formally but not really subordinate to the emperor as under the Meiji Constitution. The Cabinet is "collectively responsible to the Diet" (Article 66, 3), not, as under the former constitution, to the emperor, that is, to no one. As usually before, the courts are independent in deciding individual cases (Article 76,3), but the judiciary is now an independent branch of government, co-equal with parliament and the Cabinet. The courts have used their considerable power of judicial review sparingly against other agencies of government.

As this book illustrates, the courts have settled a broad range of issues in tens of thousands of cases. Before focusing on the judiciary and its decisions, two distinctive features of Japan's constitutional politics deserve attention: the revision debate and political linkages between the emperor, the military, and human rights. Since 1945, conflicts involving either the emperor and Shinto, or the military and its wartime behavior, or human rights issues (for example, freedoms of religion and expression), have sometimes carried implications for the other two elements at the core of the constitutional revolution. For instance, visits of Cabinet officials (in public or "private" capacity) to or public funding of Tokyo's Yasukuni Shrine honoring the war dead have been considered by many to be unconstitutional support of a particular religion, Shinto (Articles 20 and 89), and have raised the spectre of repressive prewar State Shinto.[47] Public official mourning for the military dead is restricted and bears no political resemblance to the humane, innocent paying of respect at Arlington National Cemetery in the United States. In a case illustrating the linkage of Shinto, the military, and individual rights, official tampering during a textbook review process with a high school history text for its demythologized representation of the ancient imperial institution and Japan's military behavior during the Second World War was attacked as unconstitutional censorship.[48] Occasionally, extreme nationalists go beyond harassment and threats (as to moderate newsmen), and take dramatic but ineffectual action to challenge the constitutional order. For example, on January 19, 1990, Mayor Hitoshi Motoshima of Nagasaki was the victim of a rightist assassination attempt for suggesting that Emperor Hirohito should bear some of the responsibility for the Second World War, although Emperor Akihito at his first press conference the previous August had defended free speech, including the right to criticize his father or the imperial institution itself.[49] For his comments, Motoshima was also disowned by his own party, the ruling Liberal Democratic

Party. In January, 1989, Hirohito passed away and Akihito succeeded to the throne. Leaders of 158 countries attended the official funeral rites for Emperor Hirohito on February 24, 1989. Many must have been puzzled by the strong protests of some Japanese that the official rites had been inadequately separated for constitutional purposes from the royal family's private *Shintō* rites.[50] Similarly controversial to constitutional lawyers and politicians was the relationship in November, 1990 of Akihito's official enthronement under Article 7 of the Constitution and his traditional secret *Shintō* accession rite (*Daijōsai*).[51] Anomalies persist: upon becoming Emperor, Akihito told leaders of the three branches of government that he wished to "defend the Constitution with them," but past LDP governments had not shown similar respect for the Constitution, under which all official imperial acts, including this statement, should have been approved beforehand by the Cabinet.

The revision debate

The 1947 Constitution of Japan has never been amended or revised. Formal amendment under Article 96 requires concurrence of "two-thirds of all the members of each House" and ratification by a majority in a special referendum. From the time of its establishment the Constitution has enjoyed the support of a strong majority of the Japanese people, and the level of popular satisfaction increased over time. In fact, some survey data have suggested the Constitution is the most respected and trusted of all Japan's national institutions, with political parties being the least trusted.[52] Yet, over the decades, recurrent calls for revision arose from the ruling (1955–1993) Liberal Democratic Party (LDP) and from loud and persistent but small right-wing nationalist groups.[53] Revisionist forces have never been able to gain the necessary two-thirds majority in parliament. Reelection of some LDP Diet members was dependent on downplaying their revisionist views and on the absence of less unpopular political parties. Most constitutional lawyers have supported the "Peace Constitution" and have been wary about any tampering with its essentials, whether by amendment, law, judicial interpretation, or shift in policy direction. Constitutional debate surfaced again in the 1980s and 1990s and opposition to any possible amendment abated somewhat; a note on the history and issues of revisionism seems in order.

In early February 1946, General MacArthur asked General Courtney Whitney to have staff draw up a document for Japan's government to use as a guide in revising the Meiji Constitution along peaceful democratic lines.[54] Colonel Charles Kades of Government Section, GHQ, an attorney, was in charge of what turned out to be the momentous task of drafting in a week a great deal of what is now the Constitution of Japan. MacArthur took this action upon finding inadequate the changes proposed by the government's "Matsumoto Committee" in response to his fall, 1945 revision demand. By mid-March, 1946, most of a draft constitution had been ironed out by Kades and his colleagues in consultation with Japanese in and out of government. In April, the first postwar House of Representatives was elected. It was this House, rather than holdovers from the wartime or surrendering government, which functioned as a sort of constitutional convention, debating, modifying with very little SCAP interference (for example, adding the House of Councillors to the Diet), and approving the Constitution of Japan on August 24, 1946, by a vote of 421 to 8.[55] Other amendment procedures of the Meiji Constitution were followed and on

November 3 the emperor promulgated the Constitution; it came into effect six months later. During the Occupation and since the return to sovereign independence in 1952, a persistent minority of Japanese have advocated constitutional change.

Revisionists and others have held that the Constitution was "*imposed*,"[56] and indeed MacArthur, Kades and other SCAP personnel were among "the Founding Fathers" of the current Constitution; they were probably the necessary catalyst for Japan's decisive move toward constitutional democracy. Their views and those of the 1946 House of Representatives were not far apart and were more representative of Japan's constitutional consciousness since the Second World War than those of the "lame duck" government (late 1945-early 1946) and later revisionists. Moreover, origins are less critical to the legitimacy of a constitution than its enduring support by a nation's adult populace, as in "autonomous" Japan since 1952. The intent of SCAP framers seems to matter little now. Japanese interpretations and judgments will determine whether or not constitutional change is advisable.

A second suggested rationale for revision is the infelicity of the Japanese language in some provisions of the Constitution, due to the haste with which they were drafted and/or were translated from English to Japanese.[57] In addition, more careful editing in more leisurely and apolitical circumstances might have eliminated some vague language and anomaly. For example, the Article 66, 2 requirement that Ministers be "civilian" could be interpreted to imply the constitutional existence of military forces, though such a reading is usually rejected by scholars. However, in general, the text of the Constitution of Japan, in Japanese and in the English version, has served well as the blueprint for Japan. (No translation is official, but that from the Justice Ministry is sometimes used as if legally official.)[58] The Preamble and a few other passages are eloquent, the language is reasonably clear and in conformity with world legal usage in the 1990s, and in general terms the coverage of principles, institutions and procedures seems adequate. It is a very good constitution, arguably more suited to the times than, for example, the venerable eighteenth-century United States Constitution. However, it is generally agreed that the language and content could be better yet. The principal barriers to improvements of language and added coverage (see below) has been disagreements on principle and the deep mutual distrust between revisionists and anti-revisionists; the latter have feared revisionists would tamper with essentials in the name of tidying up the text.

A third category of issues is additions which would not weaken but arguably would strengthen the foundation of the Constitution, while bringing it more fully into conformity with judicial law (for example, a provision on privacy rights), well-debated issues (for example, freedom of information; more effective pre-indictment rights in the criminal justice process), or common world practice (for instance, provisions on environmentalism and political parties), or apparent anomalies (as that between Articles 9 and 66 mentioned above). In addition, Article 89's primary intent seems denial of state support to "any religious institution or association," based on American influence; but it goes on to extend that ban to "any charitable, educational or benevolent enterprises not under the control of public authority." This ban on public support of various good works not under government "control" has been so divorced from public policy and felt-need that Japan's government has in effect ignored it and given substantial aid to private schools, whether religiously affiliated or not. Finally, some analysts have suggested it would improve the constitutional system if, like Germany, South Korea, and other democracies, Japan were to establish a constitutional court separate from the ordinary courts to decide constitutional issues more expeditiously than now.

The fourth group of issues is most important, those affecting the core elements of the 1945 constitutional revolution: the emperor, popular sovereignty, the military and human rights. In the early 1950s the revisionist movement called for strengthening the emperor's status and weakening popular sovereignty, unequivocally sanctioning rearmament, and restoring the patriarchal extended family system (*ie*), to the detriment of the equality of women and other individual rights. When the LDP was formed in 1955, it unsuccessfully pursued such a revisionist program, but then backed off for fear of losing votes. No government since has openly called for revision of the Constitution.[59]

However, under a controversial law, the Commission on the Constitution (*Kempō Chōsakai*) conducted investigations and deliberated from 1957 to 1964 on each provision of the Constitution to determine whether or not changes should be recommended. Anti-revisionist politicians and many scholars refused to join with the Commission's efforts on grounds that its intent was to prepare for revision.[60] A parallel, private, anti-revisionist body, the Committee to Study Constitutional Issues (*Kempō Mondai Kenkyūkai*) was also established. Professor Isao Sato, principal author of the Commission's final report, was involved with both groups.

The nationwide public hearings, massive consultation of virtually all interest groups, and pursuit of expert foreign opinion abroad on issues raised might be seen as an extended, Japanese-style "constitutional convention," building group consensus through unhurried, exhaustive discussion. It may be recalled that months of enormous and passionate, yet usually peaceful, demonstrations during the 1960 "Security Treaty Crisis" (before Diet ratification of the current U.S.-Japan Security Treaty) powerfully confirmed the requirement of Japan's consultative, communal democratic culture that broad consensus be patiently pursued on critical issues.[61] Although Prime Minister Nobusuke Kishi's LDP held a large majority in parliament, the Diet's resort to the allegedly arrogant "tyranny of the majority" denied political legitimacy to the Treaty in many Japanese eyes for quite some time. Kishi was forced to resign by his own party on the public's demand, and by 1964 the "low posture" consensus politics of his successor, Prime Minister Hayato Ikeda, were in place, as Japan prepared for the Tokyo Olympics and experienced explosive economic growth.

In these circumstances and under the astute leadership of Professor Kenzo Takayanagi (1887–1967), the Commission on the Constitution submitted its required final report to the Cabinet without recommendations, and the Cabinet thought it better not to comply with the legal requirement to transmit the report to the Diet.[62] A near consensus had emerged, favoring a symbolic emperor, popular sovereignty, quasi-pacifism, and human rights, or so it seemed.

The flames of revision controversy died down in the 1960s and 1970s, but flickered at times. Revisionists and anti-revisionists generally held to their positions into the 1980s. In 1982, a report of the LDP's Constitution Commission advocated changing the emperor's duty under Article 7(8) from "*attestation* of instruments of *ratification* of treaties and other diplomatic documents" approved by the Cabinet to "ratification" of treaties and other instruments. According to Yoichi

Higuchi, this and the usual way of formulating the emperor's "attestations," of an ambassador for example, illustrate "concealed revisionism" and an intent to create the impression in foreigners and Japanese that the emperor is a head of state with some substantive powers as in prewar days.[63] Regarding Article 9, in the 1980s the LDP came to rely on flexible interpretation to legitimize expansion of the SDF and stressed technological and economic power rather than military prowess as the primary basis for "comprehensive security." No prime minister expressed an immediate desire to revise the Constitution, regardless of the revisionist desires of some LDP colleagues.[64]

Affecting both civil liberties and international relations in 1982, the Education Minister's guidelines for dealing in courses and textbooks with the ancient emperor institution and Japan's modern treatment of neighbors glossed over unpleasantries such as Japan's colonialism in Korea (1905–1945) and wartime aggression and atrocities in China and Southeast Asia.[65] This infuriated eastern Asia—as well as many Japanese, including the Foreign Minister—and drew charges of rank dishonesty and insensitivity. More typical of Japan's Asian relations since the 1950s have been her war reparations payments, aid, investment, trade, and expressions of sorrow and regret about the Second World War. Some Japanese are proud and/or nostalgic about the era which others call the "dark valley," 1930–1945. Others, with a neonationalist great power consciousness, want what they see as endless harping on the Second World War to stop. Many older Japanese see themselves as the war's victims (millions did die), but too often without a similar appreciation of the sufferings of their victims. Asian nations will likely remain indefinitely sensitive to how straightforwardly Japan's officials, politicians, and history textbooks deal with the past. In the 1990s, the test of honesty about the war became Japan's reactions to revelations about the many thousands of "comfort women," from Japan, Korea and other Asian countries, who were forced to act as sexual servants for Japan's troops in East and Southeast Asia.

From the late 1980s changes in the domestic and world contexts (some noted earlier) revived and changed the terms of the revision debate to preoccupation with Article 9 issues. The death of Emperor Hirohito and the succession of Emperor Akihito occasioned national reflection about Hirohito, the emperor institution, and the long *Shōwa* (Bright Peace) reign (1926–1989), an era highlighted by war ending in unprecedented, numbing defeat followed by radical change and a relatively quick rise to "economic superpower" status. In 1989, for the first time, the LDP lost control of the House of Councillors to a coalition of parties led by Takako Doi's Social Democratic Party of Japan (*Nihon Shakaitō*; SDPJ).[66] Elsewhere the Soviet Union came apart under Mikhail Gorbachev and Boris Yeltsin. The Cold War ended. East Asia prospered. By the early 1990s democratic regimes in Asia had increased in number (for example, South Korea, Taiwan, The Philippines, Nepal, Thailand, Mongolia), and the world reflected on the implications of the "Tienanmen Massacre" in China of June, 1989, even as "semicapitalism" was promoted.[67] But the Persian Gulf, a major source of Japan's petroleum, impacted Article 9 revision debate most. Iraq invaded Kuwait and the United States and United Nations' "Coalition Forces" responded militarily. Japan contributed $13 billion to their effort, but not one SDF troop.

How best to respond to such aggression and to other reasonable UN peacekeeping needs while honoring Article 9, its text and spirit? Given Article 9 and

Japan's new status as a world leader, what were its appropriate roles? Vigorous and unusually open debate ensued, in and outside of the Diet. Japan's dispatch of four SDF minesweepers to the Persian Gulf in 1991 after the war was her first overseas military deployment since the Second World War, with one exception in 1950 during the Korean War.[68] Japan played a major role in the UN's momentous effort to bring peace and democratic government to Cambodia, and Japanese SDF engineers and medical teams participated from October 1992, with loss of life.[69] After extended bitter debate, the Diet passed in June, 1992 the Law on Cooperation in United Nations Peacekeeping Operations ("PKO Law")[70] and the International Emergency Rescue Force Law.[71]

Public discourse on constitutional revision intensified, but issues other than Article 9 often received scant attention. For example, in 1992 the *Yomiuri Shimbun* newspaper established the Yomiuri Constitution Study Council (*Kempō Mondai Chōsakai*).[72] In December 1992, its first report dealt extensively with Article 9 questions and recommended retention of Article 9, paragraph 1, which forever renounces war "as a right of the nation and the threat or use of force as a means of settling international disputes." However, the Yomiuri group calls for revision of paragraph 2 regarding possession of "war potential" and "the right of belligerency." Human rights problems (for example, in the criminal justice system) went unmentioned in this report, but it called for extended national debate in the 1990s leading to other possible changes.

On November 3, 1994, Yomiuri issued a comprehensive proposal to revise the Constitution, including Article 9, and published "A Proposal for the Outline of a Comprehensive Security" on Constitution Day, May 3, 1995. On the same day, influential rival *Asahi Shinbun*, culminating a five-year study of related issues, published a ringing call for Japan to be an "international conscientious objector" nation, retaining Article 9 as is and generously taking on leadership responsibilities in a wide range of non-military cooperative activities with a new "International Cooperation Law" and a "Peace Support Corps" (*Heiwa Shientai*).[73] Such daily newspapers, with their multi-million national circulations and high social credibility, wield considerable opinion-making power. The Asahi and Yomiuri proposals present in detail two competing visions of Japan and its world functions in the future. The bulk of Japan's constitutional lawyers support the Asahi proposals, if not in all details. Unfortunately, as in the economic sphere, so in the realm of Japan's constitutional politics, too many American political and opinion leaders have made little effort to comprehend Japan's thought-provoking model.

In 1993, a scandal-plagued LDP government was replaced by a reformist coalition in the House of Representatives under Prime Minister Morihiro Hosokawa. An unprecedented realignment of political parties and factions was underway. The likelihood of an LDP-led constitutional revision diminished further on June 30, 1994, when a decimated LDP joined the anti-revisionist Social Democratic Party of Japan to form a new government under Socialist Prime Minister Tomiichi Murayama. No one knew from whence a revision effort might come next, but the living Constitution of Japan enjoyed incontestable legitimacy in Japan's sociopolitical culture.

In general principle, there exists a consensus that the emperor should be the powerless "symbol of the State and of the unity of the people" (Article 1), that the broad range of human rights in the Constitution and in United Nations instruments should be honored in practice, and that at least paragraph 1 of Article 9 should continue to support Japan's essentially non-military approach to international problem solving.[74] But in each area unresolved controversies remain. To this writer, it seems improbable that an extensively revised constitutional document could achieve the high legitimacy now enjoyed by the 1947 Constitution of Japan, one of the world's most revered modern national legal documents. (Analogously, the unmatchable legitimacy of the present document in the nation's constitutional culture may also be the most compelling reason not to substantially revise and up-date the Constitution of the United States.) That said, the practical question remains: In civil law theory and practice—as modified by common law inductions—should a given subject be explicitly dealt with by a change in the Constitution, or should it be left to a custom, a Code, a basic law, a statute, judicial determination, a local ordinance, or administrative regulation? By its practices since 1947, Japan has decided upon a mixed answer, but one which apparently gives decisive authority to the Supreme Court of Japan and the independent lower courts.

2 THE COURTS

Japan's postwar constitutional revolution remade the judiciary into a separate branch of government, administratively beholden only to the Supreme Court, equal in status to the Diet and the Cabinet, empowered to render final judgment on all questions of constitutionality and legality, and preeminently responsible for upholding in concrete cases the human rights of individuals. This postwar revolution marked the only basic change in the modern system of laws and courts since Japan decided to adopt the civil law tradition and theories of continental Europe over a century ago.[75]

The constitutional powers of judges are somewhat like those of their U.S. counterparts; but unlike American judges, they must comply when deciding cases with statutes and with great magisterial "Codes" (*hōten*), a hallmark of the civil law tradition, the world's most extensively used framework for modern law. The "Six Codes" (*Roppō*) provide the basic law governing public, private, criminal and commercial matters.[76] All statutes, local ordinances, and administrative rules and actions must be consistent with the Constitution of Japan, the Civil Code (*Minpō*), the Code of Civil Procedure (*Minji Soshōhō*), the Criminal Code (*Keihō*), the Code of Criminal Procedure (*Keiji Soshōhō*), and the Commercial Code (*Shōhō*). Scholars' architectonic theories of law, the codes, and the state also resemble those of Europe.[77] In addition, since 1947 judges have been guided by prior judicial decisions.[78]

Article 81 of the Constitution, with echoes of *Marbury v. Madison*,[79] makes the Supreme Court "the court of last resort with power to determine the constitutionality of any law, order, regulation or official act." The courts are given "the whole judicial power" and "no extraordinary tribunal shall be established, nor shall any organ or agency of the Executive be given final judicial power" (Article 76, paragraphs 1 and 2). This contrasts sharply with the Meiji Constitution:[80]

> Article 61. No suit at law, which relates to rights alleged to have been infringed by the illegal measures of the administrative authorities, and which

shall come within the competency of the Court of Administrative Litigation specially established by law, shall be taken cognizance of by a Court of Law.

"All judges shall be independent in the exercise of their conscience and shall be bound only by this Constitution and the laws" (Article 76, paragraph 1). Of the laws, the Codes are central to the system and, in effect, almost constitutional in nature. Under the Court Organization Law, "a conclusion in a decision of a superior court shall bind courts below in respect of the case concerned" (Article 4).[81] In most instances, precedent is honored. A principal ground for appeal under the Code of Criminal Procedure (Article 405, paragraphs 2 and 3)[82] is incompatibility with established precedent not only of the Supreme Court but also of the High Courts in certain instances. The Supreme Court has on rare occasion explicitly reversed itself; but consistency is duly honored in most cases by courts at all levels. The study and use of precedent, including foreign judicial decisions (especially of U.S. and German courts), has become a common feature of judicial life.[83] Some decisions of the pre-1945 supreme court, the Great Court of Cassation (*Daishin'in*), were reported, but under Article 4 of the 1875 *Rules for the Conduct of Judicial Affairs*,[84] court decisions were not to be treated as law or precedent for future cases. Nevertheless, the present Supreme Court has on occasion used *Daishin'in* decisions as precedent. The Supreme Court is not a "constitutional court" and decides issues of constitutionality only in the context of concrete controversies involving parties with proper standing.

Judges have developed a proud tradition of independence in deciding individual cases according to law. The landmark is the 1891 *Otsu* Case.[85] In defiance of government and popular demands that an attempted assassination of a Russian prince be punished with the death penalty, the highest tribunal followed the law and imposed instead a prison sentence, the normal punishment for attempted homicide. Under the 1889 Meiji Constitution, judges had authority over ordinary private law disputes and criminal cases, but the courts were within the emperor's executive branch as part of the Justice Ministry. Judicial authority to deal with allegations of official violation of a subject's limited rights was restricted to one Administrative Court located in Tokyo. In effect, constitutional rights were not justiciable.[86] Since 1947, no administrative court, courtmartial, or other special tribunal has been allowed by the Constitution; the ordinary courts have comprehensive jurisdiction over all types of legal disputes (Article 76). Under the 1947 Constitution, the judiciary has become the most widely trusted governmental institution.[87] Its roles in enforcing the rule of law are crucial and complex; its record in confirming human rights mixed, under a dynamic fusion of Japanese, European and American legal elements.

Court organization and jurisdiction

At the apex is the Supreme Court (*Saikō Saibansho*) with fifteen Justices, which renders final judgment on appeals from lower courts, makes court rules and appointments, administers all the nation's courts, and trains their personnel. Usually, it divides into three five-member Petty Benches (*Shōhōtei*), which decide all but the few cases transferred to the Grand Bench (*Daihōtei*) of all Justices because they involve constitutional questions or a possible change in established legal doctrine. The Supreme Court normally relies exclusively on appellate briefs and lower court records, but oral proceedings may be held when they consider an appeal possibly sustainable. The Justices are ably assisted by around thirty Research Judges (*shihō chōsakan*) drawn from the ranks of experienced lower court judges, who eliminate as without legal justification 80% of appeals in civil and criminal cases.[88] Nine constitutes a Grand Bench quorum; decisions are by majority, and each Justice not fully satisfied with the majority opinion must write her/his dissenting or concurring opinion, alone or in collaboration with one or more other Justices. The prewar Great Court of Cassation (*Daishin'in*) issued only one view.

About 2,700 judges are authorized by law. Below the Supreme Court are eight high courts (*kōtō saibansho*), located in Tokyo, Osaka, Nagoya, Hiroshima, Fukuoka, Sendai, Sapporo, and Takamatsu, with six branches elsewhere. Eight Presidents oversee about 280 high court judges. In a high court or district court, judges serve in either the criminal division or the civil division. Three-judge panels decide high court cases[89] and certain major disputes in district courts.

At the base of the judicial hierarchy are: fifty districts courts (*chihōsaibansho*) sited in the principal city of each large governmental territory (*ken*, prefectures; *Tokyo-to, Osaka-fu, Hokkaido*) with 201 branches in other cities and towns; over 300 family courts (*katei saibansho*); and 448 summary courts (*kan'i saibansho*). The latter handle minor crimes and civil disputes, involving sums up to $5,000. In all, 910 judges and about 460 assistant judges occupied the district court bench in 1991. Trials are public (Article 82). There is no jury system.[90] Most district court disputes and all family court and summary court cases are decided with a single judge presiding.

Family courts seek non-litigious settlement of domestic disputes and have jurisdiction over all crimes of minors (under twenty) and of adults adversely affecting juveniles. Usually, youth crime is treated privately with educational remedies, dismissal of the case, or probation. Only in a rare extreme case and where the juvenile is over sixteen is a minor's case referred to a criminal court.

Family court judges (some concurrently serving as district court judges) are assisted by laypeople and by 1,500 family court probation officers who prepare records and advise. A major feature of Japan's legal structure is the use in many official decisionmaking contexts of respected laypeople with knowledge and broad experience; for example, a psychiatrist, teacher or social worker may participate in the work of a family court. Such volunteers assist judges and parties to work out mutually acceptable settlements without wasteful trials or neglect of rights. Moreover, court-established conciliation (*chōtei*) committees with a judge and two lay conciliation commissioners often devise voluntary compromise plans. Rooted in premodern Tokugawa compulsory conciliation, this system continued in predemocratic modern Japan and has flowered in the past forty years under democratic conciliation law (*chōtei hō*).[91]

Under the final authority of the Justices, the General Secretariat (*Jimu Sōkyoku*) of the Supreme Court is the most important institution servicing the court system and managing personnel matters. It oversees the operation of the Training and Research Institute for Court Clerks, the Institute for Family Court Probation Officers, and the Legal Training and Research Institute (LTRI; *Shihō Kenshūsho*), which trains virtually all judges, prosecutors and attorneys as Japan's only postgraduate quasi-"law school."

The recruitment and appointment of judges

The rigorous selection process assures Japan an exceptionally able body of jurists, but may produce too few to meet needs. Any adult of any educational background may take the National Law Examination (*shihō shiken*) any number of times. This examination is not a "bar examination" on an American model, but a kind of graduate school entrance examination. Of over 20,000 aspiring (mostly, university graduates) each year, roughly 700 pass (only around 500 till 1992).[92] Almost all successful examinees have spent years in special cram schools; their average age reached thirty in 1991. Legal "apprentices" (*shūshūsei*) receive two years of training with the LTRI. Besides lectures and practice in preparing briefs, all spend four months each interning in a criminal court, a civil court, a prosecutor's office, and a law office. Each year the great majority become attorneys, over fifty become judges, and about thirty choose a prosecutor's career. Currently, around 14,000 Lawyers (*bengoshi*; more like a British barrister than an American lawyer) serve 125 million citizens. Among major reforms discussed in the 1990s were a substantial increase in the number passing the law examination and a limit on the times it may be taken. For example, Justice Sonobe has suggested the examination should be taken no more than three times and within a period of three-to-five years.

Well over half of Japan's attorneys practice in Tokyo or Osaka, where most larger corporations are based. Medium-size and small businesses and the general citizenry are underserviced, consulting a lawyer never or only after serious problems arise.

The limited number of Notary Publics (*kōshōnin*) are important in law practice because they confirm contracts in law. To some degree, the effects of a paucity of attorneys are mitigated also by family courts, conciliation procedures, unpaid Human Rights Commissioners (*Jinken Yogoiin*, lit. "human rights protectors" but commonly "Civil Liberties Commissioners"), Local Administrative Counselors (*Gyōsei Sōdan Iin*), the local police, and other avenues of rights protection and dispute resolution.[93] Moreover, Japan's many undergraduate "law faculties" (*hōgakubu*) have added very substantially to the nation's legal expertise by educating tens of thousands for law-related careers in government and business without need for LTRI credentials; so non-attorneys perform many tasks undertaken by lawyers in the United States. (Such undergraduate law faculties in civil law countries are the world's most important source of legal knowledge. The post-graduate technical "law school" is peculiar to the United States and very few other countries.) Nevertheless, the shortage of attorneys, judges, prosecutors, and legal aid seems noteworthy to many observers.

Besides LTRI training, a full judge (*hanji*) has had ten years of experience as an assistant judge (*hanjiho*), prosecutor (*kenji*) or attorney; a law professor can qualify for a judgeship after five years of teaching law in a university. (Professors are rarely LTRI-trained attorneys.) In the *Taku* decision (Case 1), the Supreme Court held that the participation of assistant judges in district court trials is legal, provides them with necessary experience, and involves no exercise of judicial power (at most, the conveyance of their opinions to full judges). Judges serve for renewable ten-year terms and retire at sixty-five. Justices and summary court judges must retire at seventy. In 1990 judges on the bench or in teaching or administrative positions numbered 1,400, assistant judges 610, and summary court judges 810.

Able laypeople, retired judges, and legal professionals with three years of experience may serve as summary court judges.

To make court rules, the annual budget and personnel assignments to specific courts, the Supreme Court constitutes itself the "Judicial Conference." Although in formal law the Cabinet appoints judges, in fact almost all recommendations of the Chief Justice and the Secretary General of the Supreme Court Secretariat are approved with little or no discussion among incumbent Justices or Cabinet members.[94] Under Article 6 of the Constitution the emperor "shall appoint the Chief Justice as designated by the Cabinet." By law, Justices must be appointed by the Cabinet from among distinguished judges, attorneys, prosecutors, scholars and (rarely) persons of other background—for example, diplomats.

The Chief Justice can play a major role in the choice of his successor. In practice, the Chief Justice, the Prime Minister and the Cabinet usually confirm choices for Justice positions autonomously made within the organizational centers of the various law professions. Thus, judge-members of the Supreme Court are selected by the Secretary General and Chief Justice; prosecutor-members by the Office of the Procurator General; and attorney-members by the largest bar associations, usually of Tokyo or Osaka, taking turns. The legal scholars are underrepresented because they have no unified representative organs(s) like the other law professions; only many learned societies each focusing on a relatively narrow subfield of legal studies (for example, a single Code). To avoid chaos in selecting the one or two scholar-Justices, by custom an eminent professor has been tapped after his compulsory retirement at age 60 from Tokyo University's Faculty of Law. Professor-Chief Justice Kotaro Tanaka was immensely influential in the early decades of the Supreme Court. Professor-Justices such as Jiro Tanaka, Shigemitsu Dando, and Masami Ito have stood out for their concern about human rights. The current scholar-Justice, Itsuo Sonobe, had prior experience both as a professor at Kyoto University and as a judge. Most other Justices have been appointed in their mid-or late sixties to allow a maximum number to enjoy this high honor before retiring at seventy. Article 79 of the Constitution requires a newly appointed Justice to be "reviewed" by the people at the next general election for the House of Representatives and each ten years thereafter; all have been approved, most with little dissent.

The Cabinet formally legitimizes choices made by others. No political tests are imposed from beyond the judiciary, but the exceptionally long regime of the Liberal Democratic Party *cum* bureaucracy made unlikely the appointment to the best judicial positions of those favoring more rigorous human rights protection (for example, in criminal cases) or an extreme rightist view. Very rarely, an aggressive Prime Minister (such as Yasuhiro Nakasone) may politically intrude on a judicial personnel decision. In 1994, Hisako Takahashi, past Director of the Labor Ministry's Women's and Minors' Bureau, became the first woman to serve on the Supreme Court of Japan, appointed by the coalition Cabinet of Prime Minister Morihiro Hosokawa.[95]

The political roles of the judiciary

The judiciary normally maintains an establishmentarian demeanor of high dignity above the hurly-burly, and keeps its internal politics to itself. Only in the late 1960s and 1970s did politicized courts come center stage. On ideological grounds, impeachments of judges by the Diet (including Chief Justice Kazuto Ishida) were demanded at both ends of the political spectrum, judicial appointments were denied, and pressures exerted on younger judges not to associate with the left-leaning Young Lawyers Association (*Seihōkyō*). A young assistant judge was denied reappointment, presumably because of his membership in this association. In addition, a judge-to-be was denied an appointment due to his disruptive behavior at the commencement ceremony in opposition to the conservative ideology of the Supreme Court and the LDP government. Furthermore, a senior judge was accused of improperly advising a junior judge who was presiding over the highly controversial Naganuma Nike Missile Site case (Cases 3, 4, 5) discussed earlier. Finally, a very conservative assistant judge attempted in vain to discredit the incumbent liberal Prime Minister Takeo Miki in relation to the criminal trial of former Prime Minister Kakuei Tanaka in the highly publicized Lockheed bribery scandal of the 1970s. However, settlement of legal issues in concrete cases, not general policy debate or dramatic action, is the main judicial mode of political participation. For example, in 1991 the Sendai High Court held local legislative funding of Shinto shrines to the war dead to be unconstitutional.[97]

On only a few occasions has the Supreme Court held law unconstitutional, for allowing: seizure of third-party evidence in a smuggling case (1962);[98] more severe punishment of patricide than ordinary murder (1973);[99] restraints on pharmacy siting near an existing pharmacy (1975);[100] denial of the right to division of jointly owned forest land (1987);[101] and malapportionment in election districts (1976, 1985).[102] Judicial decisions have also vindicated victims of industrial pollution, improper reliance on crime confessions,[103] excessive trial delays,[104] economic discrimination against women employees,[105] and interference with aspects of freedom of expression. On the other hand, it has allowed laws and practices of questionable constitutionality to stand; for example, Customs Bureau censorship of obscenity,[106] denial of reasonable attorney access in criminal justice, and a ban on election canvassing.[107]

The Supreme Court is not a constitutional court responsible for judging the constitutionality of a law during or after a legislative process, such as exist in some countries; rather a court can pass judgment on constitutional validity only in the context of settling a concrete dispute brought before it according to legally prescribed procedures. In this sense, Japan's courts, like most, are inherently passive unless case-activated. In its 1952 Suzuki decision,[108] the Court denied its capacity to pass judgment in the abstract and in the absence of a concrete legal dispute on the constitutionality of the National Police Reserve (NPR) under the Article 9 "no war clause." The 75,000 man NPR was set up for allegedly internal security reasons based on MacArthur's July 1950 order to Prime Minister Yoshida shortly after the Korean War began. Similarly in 1953, the supreme tribunal held that the courts could not determine the constitutionality of a Cabinet dissolution of the House of Representatives as an abstract question and without a concrete dispute.[109] With respect to legislative processes as well as the bounds of local autonomy the Supreme Court has usually deferred to the Diet. For example, in the 1962 *Shimizu Police Law* Case,[110] the Court declined to examine a legislative process in which the House of Councillors had not passed the Police Law until June 7, 1954, four days after the Diet session had ended and with doubts existing about whether the Speaker had legally extended the session:

> [A]s long as the said law was passed by resolution of both houses and was promulgated through lawful procedures, the court should respect the autonomy of both houses of the Diet, and should not examine and pass its judgment on the validity of facts, as argued in court, concerning the procedures followed in enacting the said law.

This decision also left to the legislative branch definition of the constitutional requirements of "local autonomy" in upholding the Diet's decision to transform existing city, town, and village police into prefectural police.

On the other hand, in 1978 the Sapporo High Court[111] found the Diet's failure to give handicapped people the right to submit absentee ballots by mail to be unconstitutional legislative inaction. Amendments in the election law had removed the absentee voting right of the handicapped in 1952 and did not restore it until 1975. The handicapped plaintiff sued for State damages, but the court could not find the intentional or negligent infliction of injury in this case to justify payment under the State Compensation Law. Most laws are sensitive to individual rights and freedoms; but lower courts and especially appellate courts have deferred rather often to the democratic government's broad legislative and administrative discretion in human rights cases, as this book demonstrates.

Although little discussed, the Cabinet Legislative Bureau deserves mention as an element in the ecology of the courts providing pre-legislative constitutional review.[112] The Bureau meticulously examines all Cabinet bills—and most important bills are Cabinet bills—before they are formally considered by the Diet to make sure their wording is not constitutionally suspect and thus open to future challenge in the courts after passage. The Bureau thus performs part of the function of constitutional courts under other systems.

Since 1947, the judiciary has been the nation's core institution for settling millions of disputes in a civilized, authoritative manner. Typically, Japan's jurists are able, honest, dedicated, and a bit bureaucratic. In their work, they are bound in law and largely in practice only by their consciences, the Constitution and the law. The courts have served as a restraining presence in the background during law-making and policy deliberations, and as a provider of standards and court case examples to guide behavior under law. In the public perception, their consistency, integrity, stability, predictability and attention to justice counterbalance the recurring disrepute of party politics, the changeability of Cabinet group leadership, the considerable discretion of executive functionaries, and the hierarchy and favoritism of social dynamics.

3 CRIMINAL JUSTICE

A key indicator of the status of human rights in constitutional law is the quality of a country's enforcement of criminal justice rights. In Japan's civil law system, Codes such as the Criminal Code and the Code of Criminal Procedure are fundamental, even quasi-constitutional in nature. This partially explains the tendency in juristic discourse to treat individual rights under a Code—for example, the rights of an accused—primarily as matters of basic statutory law and to understate or even sidestep, by Code-specific interpretive method or theoretical doctrine, core issues of constitutional law. Thus, to some, the constitutional rights of the "accused" (*hikokunin*) do not extend to a "suspect" (*higisha*). Some critics contend that such interpretations of detention and release law violate Article 9(3) of the United Nations Covenant on Civil and Political Rights, which Japan has ratified.[113] (Legal scholars commonly specialize and organize around one of the Six Codes or a narrower subfield.)

In criminal justice, Japan's constitutional system differs so strikingly from that of the United States as to dictate a brief explanation. Arguably, the quasi-judicial prosecutors (*kenji*) affect the actual status of constitutional rights in criminal justice practice more profoundly than the courts themselves. Prosecutors receive the same training as judges and attorneys at the LTRI. They are responsible for monitoring police investigations and they receive police reports and recommendations regarding criminal cases. The prosecutor decides whether or not to indict and proceed to trial in a case. Regarding about 40% of provable crimes, prosecutors tend towards leniency and do not indict; for penological reasons they "suspend prosecution" (*kiso yūyo*). (At an earlier stage, police also release a significant number of perpetrators of the law under special procedures.) Convictions bring no career advantages; the theory is that truth and justice should out, and that justice should be tempered with compassion. With good attitudes and behavior, a suspect may never be formally accused. Of those indicted, over 99% are convicted. Most are fined and/or placed on probation. The court may "delay the execution" (*shikkō yūyo*) of a sentence; if the person's behavior is satisfactory during the designated period (say, one or two years), the sentence, whether a fine or imprisonment, may never be imposed. By world standards, few are sent to prison; the incarceration rate of those convicted is one-fifth of that in the United States.[114] If parole is granted, volunteer parole officers nurture the individual towards full reintegration into the community.

To counterbalance possibly excessive leniency on the part of prosecutors, lay Prosecution Review Commissions (*kensatsu shinsakai*) review serious criminal cases not sent to trial. Each of these 207 Commissions consists of eleven local voters chosen by lot who serve for six-month terms and who function independently without external instruction. Between 1948 and January 1, 1990, Prosecution Review Commissions handled 77,922 cases, of which 5,240 were sent back to the prosecution with a recommendation of further investigation or prosecution.[115]

The judicial conviction rate of over 99% is one factor leading to advocacy of a jury system in the 1980s, and 1990s. Although judges are legally and administratively independent when sitting on the bench, a judge-turned-defense attorney typifies the sensibility of a judge as follows:

> [W]hen a judge issues an acquittal, the faces of his superiors and the displeased faces of prosecutors with whom he's become friendly will appear in his mind. Those sorts of psychological pressures exist at the subconscious level, and there's a psychological brake at work that leads judges to issue as few acquittals as possible.[116]

Some think lay jurors would be more sensitive than some judges, prosecutors and police to perennial procedural problems such as: police use of "voluntary accompaniment" in a manner which constitutes illegal arrest; over-reliance on confessions, in a culture where the readiness to confess is particularly notable; improper pressure on a suspect to confess while held in a police station holding cell ("substitute prison," *daiyō kangoku*) for as long as twenty-three days; lack of easy and frequent access to defense counsel even after indictment; and no right of discovery of the prosecution's files, even regarding potentially exculpatory evidence. Reestablishment of a jury system has been seriously advocated by many judges, scholars and attorneys.[117] (Under a limited jury system in effect from 1928 to 1943, under which a majority sufficed for conviction, 15.4% of the accused in 611 cases who used that option were acquitted.)[118] In any case, many who place more emphasis on the high quality than on the problems of criminal justice would agree with B. J. George's conclusion: "If there is any deficiency in the Japanese system, it probably lies in the unavailability of any form of claim to release during periods of arrest or custody before the institution of criminal prosecution."[119] In criminal justice processes from the first contact with police through the final judgment in sentencing practices, the law of the Constitution mandates effective limits on state prerogatives.

Among the multitude of judicial decisions not translated, those concerning the retrial (*saishin*) of inmates sentenced to death early in the era of the present Constitution merit special attention and illustrate perennial problems of constitutional justice.[120] The Criminal Code establishes thirteen capital offenses and other penal provisions cite five additional crimes punishable by death; but in practice now a death sentence is imposed only for murder. The constitutionality of the death penalty was upheld by the Supreme Court in 1948, against a claim that it violates Article 36: ". . . cruel punishments are absolutely forbidden."[121] In the *Ichikawa Hanging* Case (1961), the method for hanging the condemned, established by an 1873 Cabinet Order but by no statute then or later, was unsuccessfully challenged.[122] However, since 1975 judicial decisions as well as scholarly and political discourse have significantly altered the status of capital punishment in Japanese law and society. Execution statistics may reflect this change. From 1951 through 1960 254 prisoners were executed, but only thirteen from 1982 through 1992; none from 1990 through 1992, but at least seven in the 1993–1994 biennium.[123]

So eminent a criminal law scholar as former Justice Shigemitsu Dando has joined others in calling for an end to capital punishment in Japan.[124] Moreover, the four socalled "death penalty retrial cases" have occasioned broad-based debate on flaws in the criminal justice performance of some police, prosecutors, defense attorneys, and judges. This dialogue has often focused on the constitutional and legal pre-indictment rights of suspects and the gathering and use of evidence, especially confessions. Although generally humane, lenient and characterized by democratic professionalism and "benevolent paternalism,"[125] in a country with a low crime rate and high marks for quick clearance of criminal cases, the criminal justice system has a darker side and sometimes slow processes. In the civil law tradition of Japan, once begun a trial does not end within a relatively short, predictable period; in difficult cases, widely spaced sessions may extend over a period of years, and may be followed by appeals adding years to the life of case proceedings. The death penalty retrial cases touch on soft spots in Japan's constitutional law.

In 1975, the Supreme Court modified interpretation of the legal requirements for a judicial grant of a retrial. Prior interpretations had placed a burden of establishing innocence on the convicted petitioner; the new interpretation shifted the burden and required a showing that new and prior evidence taken together establish a reasonable doubt about the guilt of the convicted person.[126]

In the death penalty retrial cases, four young men in their teens or early twenties had been convicted of murders committed between 1948 and 1955 and had been sentenced to death. (The *Menda* Case murders took place in 1948; the *Saitakawa* Case killing in 1950; the *Shimada* Case in 1954; and the *Matsuyama* Case in 1955.) Each confessed to brutal murder under severe duress in police custody, but each had renounced his own confession before or at trial, and each had insisted upon his innocence ever since. All avoided execution by extended though unsuccessful retrial petitions and requests for clemency until the above change in judicial doctrine. All were granted retrials and all were acquitted in district court between 1983 and 1989, but only after having spent from twenty-nine to thirty-five years (collectively, over 130 years) in confinement and only after protracted trials and appeals by both prosecution and defense. The inmates had relied in their retrial petitions on Article 435 (6) of the Code of Criminal Procedure,[127] which stipulates a right to a new trial if "clear evidence is newly discovered requiring the declaration of innocence of . . . one who has been found guilty."

To summarize but the most famous case, Sakae Menda, a young farmer, was accused of committing two murders by hatchet and knife in late 1948 in a town ten miles from his home. Police did not arrest him, but asked him to "voluntarily accompany" them (January 13, 1949) to the police station, and he did so. He initially denied involvement in the murders, but within thirty minutes of their 2:30 AM (January 14) arrival at the police station, he confessed to two thefts of rice, and he was formally arrested for theft with the warrant backdated to the time he was taken into custody. On January 15 the police recommended to the public prosecutor's office that he not be indicted for larceny, and prosecution was suspended (*kiso yūyo*).[128] However, Menda was kept in custody and formally arrested on suspicion of murder; he was not allowed a real sleep until he gave a full confession after some eighty hours of virtually continuous questioning.[129] He repeated his confession to the prosecutors, and again to the court which granted the prosecution pre-trial custody. It happened that at this juncture in his life his child died and his wife divorced him. He pleaded innocent at his trial, which began on February 17, 1949, and ended with his conviction and death sentence on March 23, 1950. With the affirmation of the verdict by the high court in March 1951 and by the Supreme Court on December 25, 1951, the conviction became legally "final."

Menda subsequently filed retrial petitions six times. In 1952 and in 1953, the courts rejected his petitions on procedural grounds; the third petition succeeded at the district court level (the *Nishitsuji Ruling*)[130] August 10, 1956, but was reversed by the high court and then by the Supreme Court in December 1961. He promptly filed his fourth petition, and in this effort as well as with his 1964 and 1972 petitions, he received significant assistance from the Human Rights Protection Committee of the Japan Federation of Bar Associations (JFBA). While his sixth petition was on appeal from a district court rejection, the Supreme Court relaxed the retrial standards, and the Fukuoka High Court in 1979 reversed and ordered a retrial.[131] The prosecution's appeal to reverse the retrial order was denied in December, 1980.[132] Menda was then acquitted in a new trial by the Kumamoto District Court on July 15, 1983, and released from custody on July 29, thirty-three years after

CASELOAD OF JAPAN'S JUDICIARY

Courts	*Year*	*Civil & Administrative Cases*			*Criminal Cases*		
		Newly received	*Disposed of*	*Pending*	*Newly received*	*Disposed of*	*Pending*
Supreme court	1985	1,837	1,922	1,678	1,781	1,794	819
	1986	1,771	2,024	1,425	1,671	1,781	709
	1987	1,812	1,879	1,358	1,611	1,591	729
	1988	2,024	2,075	1,307	1,626	1,625	730
	1989	2,012	2,088	1,231	1,507	1,552	685
	1990	2,288	2,224	1,400	1,913	1,971	686
High courts	1985	21,136	21,212	13,690	8,630	8,921	2,045
	1986	21,274	21,143	13,821	8,799	8,609	2,235
	1987	21,659	21,775	13,705	8,317	8,427	2,125
	1988	22,401	22,297	13,809	7,637	7,886	1,876
	1989	22,885	23,079	13,615	7,012	6,991	1,897
	1990	23,184	22,767	14,032	6,897	6,986	6,808
District courts	1985	759,229	717,780	504,886	269,895	270,068	25,584
	1986	743,067	713,161	534,792	265,253	257,390	24,447
	1987	725,570	741,985	518,377	255,265	256,384	23,328
	1988	669,598	730,163	487,812	237,108	239,639	20,797
	1989	651,405	700,027	439,190	214,120	215,237	19,680
	1990	611,466	671,753	378,903	196,084	198,175	175,589
Summary courts	1985	1,764,930	1,789,958	121,830	2,761,460	2,760,225	31,992
	1986	1,666,729	1,685,689	102,870	2,625,529	2,629,154	28,367
	1987	1,579,705	1,584,244	98,331	1,947,961	1,958,438	17,890
	1988	1,392,053	1,410,305	80,079	1,626,273	1,627,362	16,801
	1989	1,152,409	1,164,040	72,448	1,490,901	1,493,971	13,731
	1990	1,077,434	1,081,699	68,183	1,488,840	1,492,156	10,415
Family courts	Family Relations Cases				Juvenile Cases		
	1985	403,230	403,038	48,526	686,514	686,969	122,370
	1986	403,992	401,793	50,725	671,973	674,405	119,938
	1987	389,480	388,731	51,474	574,467	597,891	96,514
	1988	382,814	379,358	54,930	538,919	538,832	96,601
	1989	350,542	349,837	55,635	505,226	503,462	98,365
	1990	342,998	340,232	58,401	483,442	494,136	87,671

his conviction.[133] In 1994 Mr. Menda remained active in the movement to abolish capital punishment in Japan.

NOTES

1 Masami Ito, Lawrence W. Beer, and Nobuyoshi Ashibe, "Japan: The United States Constitution and Japan's Constitutional Law," in Lawrence W. Beer (ed.), *Constitutional Systems in Late Twentieth Century Asia* (1992), hereafter, *Constitutional Systems*, 128–269; Lawrence W. Beer, *Freedom of Expression in Japan: A Study in Comparative Law, Politics and Society* (1984), hereafter *Freedom*, 71–85; Robert E. Ward and Sakamoto Yoshikazu (eds.), *Democratizing Japan: The Allied Occupation* (1987).

2 A translation of the text of the Meiji Constitution is presented at 16, Hideo Tanaka and Malcolm D. H. Smith (eds.), *The Japanese Legal System* (1976). The amendment provision was Article 73:

> "When it has become necessary in future to amend the provisions of the present Constitution, a project to the effect shall be submitted to the Imperial Diet by Imperial Order.
> "(2) In the above case, neither House can open the debate, unless not less than two-thirds of the whole number of Members are present, and no amendment can be passed, unless a majority of not less than two-thirds of the Members is obtained." Regarding the Meiji Constitution, see Junji Banno (trans. J. A. A. Stockwin), *The Establishment of the Japanese Constitutional System* (1992).

3 On the process of writing the 1947 Constitution of Japan, see Lawrence W. Beer, "Constitutionalism and Rights in Japan and Korea," in Louis Henkin and Albert Rosenthal (eds.), *Constitutionalism and Rights: The Influence of the United States Constitution Abroad* (1990), 230–235; and Sato Tatsuo, *Nihonkoku Kempō Seiritsushi*, Vol. 1 (1962), Vol. 2 (1964); Sato Isao and Sato Tatsuo, *Nihonkoku Kempō Seiritsushi*, Vols. 3 and 4 (1994).

4 The text of the "Potsdam Declaration: Proclamation by Heads of Governments, United States, United Kingdom, and China," July 26, 1945, is "Appendix A-3" Government Section, SCAP, in *Political Reorientation of Japan: September, 1945 to September, 1948* (n.d., 1949), at 413.

5 Beer, *Freedom*, 71–78.

6 Id., 75.

7 Law of December 17, 1945, translated as "The Law for the Election of Members of the House of Representatives," in *Political Reorientation of Japan*, 822.

8 Albert P. Blaustein, "The Blaustein Register of Latest Constitutional Revisions," June 23, 1994.

9 On Asia, see the annual country surveys, *Asian Survey*, January and February; Edward Friedman (ed.), *The Politics of Democratization* (1993); and Chakravarthi Raghavan, *Recolonization: Gatt, the Uruguay Round & the Third World* (1990).

10 Jean Blondel, in Michael Curtis (ed.), *Introduction to Comparative Government* (1993), 104–114; William Safran, *The French Polity* (1985).

11 Blaustein, 1994.

12 Walker Connor, *Ethnonationalism: A Quest for Understanding* (1994); William Safran, "Non-separatist Policies Regarding Ethnic Minorities: Positive Approaches and Ambiguous Consequences," 15 *International Political Sci. Rev.* (1) 61–80 (1994).

13 For the records of Asian countries in ratifying twenty-two United Nations human rights instruments, see Beer, *Constitutional Systems*, 41–42.

14 *Filartiga v. Pena-Irala*, 630 F. 2d 876 (2d Cir. 1980).

15 Constitution of Spain, 1978; Nishi Osamu, 20 *Japan Echo* (2) 17 (Summer 1993).

16 Beer, *Constitutional Systems*; M. L. Marasinghe and William E. Conklin (eds.), *Essays on Third World Perspectives in Jurisprudence* (1984).

17 Masami Ito, in Beer, *Constitutional Systems*, 129–174.

18 Lazlo Ladany, *Law and Legality in China: The Testimony of a China Watcher* (1992); Du Xichuan and Zhang Lingyuan, *China's Legal System: A General Survey* (1990); and translations of laws published by the Foreign Language Press, Beijing.

19 Benjamin Harris, *The Road Less Traveled: A Development Economist's Quest* (1989); Andrew Gordon (ed.), *Postwar Japan as History* (1993). Common American ideological tendencies further complicate comparative analysis of relationships between economy and human rights by excluding from rights thought the "welfare rights" taken for granted by both democratic and nondemocratic

developed economies, while adopting an absolutist tone with respect to property rights. See Mary Ann Glendon, "Rights and Responsibilities Viewed from Afar: The Case of Welfare Rights," 4 *The Responsive Community* (2) 33 (Spring 1994), and my comment, Summer 1994.

20 Lawrence W. Beer, "Constitutional Revolution in Japanese Law, Society, and Politics," 16 *Modern Asian Studies* 33–67 (1982).

21 Beer, *Constitutional Systems*, 4–20. Since I posit the protection and promotion of the human rights of the individual as the prime imperative and goal of government and law, I suggest "human rights constitutionalism" as a clear term preferable to "democracy" (majority rule, sometimes in violation of non-electoral human rights) or "constitutionalism" (predictable, regularized limitation and division of state power under law, without a necessary linkage to the primacy of human rights).

22 Hiroshi Itoh and Lawrence W. Beer, *The Constitutional Case Law of Japan: Selected Supreme Court Decisions*, 1961–70 (1978), 4.

23 Yasuhiro Okudaira, "Forty Years of the Constitution and Its Various Influences: Japanese, American and European" and Yoichi Higuchi, "The Constitution and the Emperor System: Is Revisionism Alive?," in Percy R. Luney, Jr. and Kazuyuki Takahashi (eds.), *Japanese Constitutional Law* (1993), 6, 30, and 57.

24 Article 4 is in Itoh and Beer, at p. 257.

25 John C. Campbell, "Democracy and Bureaucracy in Japan," in Takeshi Ishida and Ellis S. Krauss (eds.), *Democracy in Japan* (1989), 113.

26 Gregory W. Noble, "Japan in 1993; Humpty Dumpty Had a Great Fall," 34 *Asian Survey* 19 (January 1994); Theodore McNelly in Curtis, 278–284, Perendra C. Jain, "A New Political Era in Japan: The 1993 Election," 33 *Asian Survey* 1071 (November 1993).

27 *Japan Times Weekly International Edition*, September 20–26, 1993, and April 3–9, 1995.

28 Bingham Powell, "American Voter Turn-out in Comparative Perspective," 80 *American Political Science Review* (1) 35 (1986); Michael Oreskes and Robin Toner, "The Trouble with Politics," *The Oregonian*, March 28, 1990; Beer, *Freedom*, 372–378.

29 *Constitutional Systems*, 185–187, 210–212; and Cases 22, 23 and 24, below.

30 Under the new system, in effect since January 1, 1995, besides the 300 single-member districts, the country is divided into eleven regions and 200 seats are distributed among political parties according to their relative electoral strength. "Dual candidacy" is possible; so even if a politician loses in his own constituency, he may be placed high enough on his party's list of candidates to win one of the 200 proportionately distributed seats. Campaign financing was also reformed. All parties with a minimum of five Diet seats and two percent of the national vote in the previous national election receive a proportionate share of a public fund based on individual taxpayer contributions of ¥250 each; the initial fund was estimated at ¥30.9 billion (about $350 million). A corporation may contribute no more than $5,000 a year to a candidate, and each politician must report even modest contributions to the Home Ministry. *Japan Times Weekly*, February 7–13, 1994; Michael Blaker, "Japan in 1994: Out with the Old, In with the New?" *Asian Survey*, January 1995, 3–6.

31 Case 23, below.

32 "Chapter II. Rights and Duties of Subjects," Meiji Constitution, Tanaka and Smith, 19–20.

33 "Chapter III. Rights and Duties of the People," 1947 Constitution of Japan, Appendix 3, below.

34 Beer, *Constitutional Systems*, 189–196, 227–269; Beer, *Freedom*, 161–270, 362–378; and Luney and Takahashi, 173–318.

35 Luney and Takahashi, 12.

36 Beer, *Freedom*, 100–128, 378–404; I. Getreuer-Kargl and S. Linhart, "Three Books on Japanese Women and Work," *Journal of Japanese Studies* (2), Summer 1994, 477–486.

37 Dan Fenno Henderson, *Conciliation and Japanese Law: Tokugawa and Modern*, 2 Vols. (1977).

38 Yoshiaki Yoshida, "Authority of the National and Local Governments under the Constitution," Luney and Takahashi, 109; Terry E. MacDougall, "Democracy and Local Government in Japan," Ishida and Krauss, 139; Kurt Steiner, *Local Government in Japan* (1965); Chung-Si Ahn (ed.), *The Local Political System in Asia: A Comparative Perspective* (Seoul National University Press, 1987); Hitoshi Abe et al., *The Government and Politics of Japan* (University of Tokyo Press, 1994).

39 James E. Auer, "Article Nine: Renunciation of War," Luney and Takahashi, 69–86; Beer, *Constitutional Systems*, 187–189. See Appendix 3 for the text of Article 9, and Cases 3, 4, 5, and 6.

40 Luney and Takahashi, 70.

41 Id. In 1994, almost 80% of Japanese supported Article 9, up from 77% in 1991. *Mainichi Shimbun*, August 19, 1994.

42 United Nations Peace-keeping Cooperation Law ("PKO" Law), June, 1992; Luney and Takahashi, 79–80. See the symposium, "Japan: Redefining Its International Role," especially Aurelia George's "Japan's Participation in U.N. Peace-keeping Operations: Radical Departure or Predictable Response," at 560, 33 *Asian Survey* (June 1993); see n. 70 *infra*. The Constitution contains no provision regarding military secrets, but secrecy regarding U.S. weaponry is required under the Special Criminal Law to Implement the Agreement under Article VI of the Treaty of Mutual Cooperation and Security Between Japan and the United States of America Regarding Facilities and Areas and the Status of United States Forces in Japan (Law 138 of 1952, as amended).

43 Among factors examined when a country asks Japan for aid are its human rights record, its environmental policies, the level of democracy, and its policies on trade and production of weapons of mass destruction.

44 International Emergency Rescue Force Law, June 1992; Luney and Takahashi, 80.

45 *Japan v. Sakane et al.*, Itoh and Beer, 111.

46 Tanaka and Smith, 20–21; Kenzo Takayanagi, "A Century of Innovation: The Development of Japanese Law, 1868–1961," in Arthur Von Mehren, *Law in Japan* (1963), 5; Masami Ito, in Beer, *Constitutional Systems*, 128–174.

47 Higuchi in Luney and Takahashi, 57–67, and Koichi Yokota, "The Separation of Religion and State," id., 205–220; Takizawa, "Religion and State in Japan," *Journal of Church and State* 89 (Winter 1988); Norma Field, *In the Realm of a Dying Emperor* (1992); Cases 35, 36, and 37, below.

48 Case 36, below; Beer, *Freedom*, 248–270.

49 Beer, in Luney and Takahashi, 221–223; Stephen S. Large, *Emperor Hirohito and Showa Japan* (1992).

50 Higuchi, in Luney and Takahashi, 64–66.

51 Id., 66.

52 James Marshall, *Japan's Successor Generation: Their Values and Attitudes*, USIA Report (1985).

53 Ivan Morris, *Nationalism and the Right Wing in Japan* (1960).

54 Beer, in Henkin and Rosenthal, 230–235; Theodore McNelly, "Induced Revolution: The Policy and Process of Constitutional Reform in Occupied Japan," and Tanaka Hideo, "The Conflict between Two Legal Traditions in Making the Constitution of Japan," in Ward and Sakamoto, 76–132; Sato, *supra* n. 3.

55 Beer, *Constitutional Systems*, 176–182.

56 H. Fukui, "Twenty Years of Revisionism," in Dan Fenno Henderson (ed.), *The Constitution of Japan: Its First Twenty Years* (1968), 41–70; Higuchi, in Luney and Takahashi, 58–60; L. W. Beer, "The Founding of Constitutional Democracy, with Special Reference to Japan," a paper presented at the Seminar on Comparative Constitutionalism, Princeton University, April 21, 1995.

57 Kyoko Inoue, *MacArthur's Japanese Constitution: A Linguistic and Cultural Study of its Making* (1991); Fukui, in Henderson, 41–70.

58 Ministry of Justice of Japan, *The Constitution of Japan and Criminal Statutes* (1958).

59 Kitaoka Shin'ichi, "The Constitution: Ready for Revision?," a symposium, 20 *Japan Echo* (2) 7 (Summer 1993).

60 Fukui, 50–52; John M. Maki (trans. and ed.), *Japan's Commission on the Constitution: The Final Report* (1980); Kenzo Takayanagi, "Some Reminiscences of Japan's Commission on the Constitution," in Henderson, 71; Robert E. Ward, "The Commission on the Constitution and Prospects for Constitutional Change in Japan," 24 *Journal of Asian Studies* 401 (1965).

61 George R. Packard III, *Protest in Tokyo: The Security Treaty Crisis of 1960* (1966).

62 Maki, *Japan's Commission on the Constitution*, 8.

63 Higuchi, in Luney and Takahashi, 58–63.

64 Auer, id., 74–78.

65 Executive Committee International Public Hearing, *War Victimization: International Public Hearing Report* (1993); Beer, in Luney and Takahashi, 243–245. Building on Yoshiaki Yoshimi's work, "Documenting the Truth: The Japanese Government and the 'Comfort Women' Issue," three panels at the 1994 Annual Meeting of the Association for Asian Studies (Boston, March 25–27, 1994) discussed related issues: "The Militarization of Sex: War in Asia and the Allied Occupation of Japan" (Marlene Mayo, Chair), and "Colonialism, War and Sex," Parts I and II (Norma Field and Chungmoo Choi, Chairs). Haruko Cook and Theodore Cook, *Japan at War: An Oral History* (1992). Prime Minister Tomiichi Murayama and other Japanese leaders are now straightforwardly repentent about wartime behavior as on August 15, 1995, at the annual remembrance of the war dead and

surrender. *Japan Times Weekly Int'l Edition*, August 22–28, 1994, and *Asahi Shimbun*, August 15–17, 1995.

Six South Korean women representing many coerced into sexual slavery as "comfort women" during the Pacific War filed a complaint with the Tokyo Public Prosecutor's Office against military officials and civilians engaged in that practice; the complaint was rejected on the legal grounds that the complainants failed to specify individuals. *Japan Times Weekly Int'l Edition*, February 21–27, 1994. However, Japan's government pursued the alternative of compensating former comfort women indirectly through support of related private groups.

66 Kent E. Calder, "Japan in 1990: Limits to Change," 30 *Asian Survey* 21 (January 1991).

67 In 1989, events in China and elsewhere in Asia, see 29 *Asian Survey* (January and February 1990).

68 Rather few "Japanese know that SCAP ordered the sending of over ten times more Japanese minesweepers to Korea in 1950 to sweep mines for U.S. Forces serving as UN Forces . . . (They) served extremely well in combat operations (two minesweepers were sunk and one Japanese sailor was killed and eight were injured)." Auer, in Luney and Takahashi, 79.

69 In October 1992, Japan sent 600 SDF members, 75 police, and 40 election monitors for one year to support the UN's Cambodia operation. Two were killed there. Forty-eight SDF personnel were in Mozambique in 1994; *Japan Times Weekly Int'l Edition*, June 20–26, 1994, 7.

70 The PKO Law, which must be reviewed in three years, allows the overseas dispatch of up to 2,000 SDF personnel; each dispatch must be approved by the Diet, except when the purpose is humanitarian disaster relief.

The SDF troops may participate in UN peacekeeping operations "but not peace-enforcing operations, on the ground that Japan should demonstrate its willingness to support UN peace efforts but that Article 9 prohibits Japan to resort to the 'threat or use of force.' " SDF troops may not go to trouble spots where a ceasefire agreement is pending and must not take part in armed conflicts. They cannot enter combat zones and must withdraw immediately from any area in which hostilities break out." Auer, in Luney and Takahashi, 79–80. Under the PKO Law, Japan's policy on participation in UN peace-keeping operations sets five conditions: (1) a cease-fire agreement must be in effect; (2) the parties in conflict must approve of Japan's peace-keeping mission; (3) the peace-keeping operation must be neutral; (4) Japan's units will withdraw if any of the above conditions is not met; (5) the Japanese use of weapons must be limited to the minimum required to prevent injury or death.

On July 12, 1994, the German Constitutional Court first ruled that with parliamentary approval German troops may legally act as "peace forces" with the "task of securing peace (as) part of the United Nations system of collective security," Rick Atkinson, *The Washington Post*, July 13, 1994. The SDF's more limited participation must also be approved by the Diet.

71 Debate on implementing this law continued; *Japan Times Weekly Int'l. Edition*, May 30–June 5, 1994, 4.

72 See Yomiuri Constitution Study Council, "An Initial Proposal on Japan's Constitution," December 9, 1992, translated in 20 *Japan Echo* (2) 23 (Summer 1993).

73 Id., 29. The *Yomiuri Shinbun*, "A Proposal for the Revision of the Text of the Constitution of Japan," Tokyo, November 3, 1994, and "A Proposal for the Outline of a Comprehensive Security," Tokyo, May 3, 1995. Asahi Shinbun Editorial Office, *Kokusai Kyoryoku to Kenpō*, Tokyo, Asahi News Shop, June 30, 1995. On the Western, especially Anglo-American problem of comprehending the Japanese or East Asian model of nationalist "thinking capitalism," see David Williams, *Japan: Beyond the End of History* (1994).

74 Noble, "Japan in 1993." On the resignation of Hosokawa and the short-lived minority government of Tsutomu Hata, see *Asahi Shimbun*, April 1–July 5, 1994. During Diet questioning on July 20, 1994, about his government's stance on Article 9, Socialist Prime Minister Tomiichi Murayama made a historic response, changing his party's long-held position, but expressing the view most widely held in Japan: "Please listen very carefully. It is constitutional to possess the minimum defensive power to defend the nation." Quoted in Peter Landers, Associated Press, July 21, 1994.

75 Takayanagi in Von Mehren, 5; M. Ito in Beer, *Constitutional Systems*, 128.

76 The *Roppō Zensho (Compendium of the Six Codes)* is annually updated by law publishers.

77 Hiroshi Itoh, *The Japanese Supreme Court: Constitutional Policies* (1989), especially chapters 2 and 6; Beer, *Freedom*, 393–396; David Beatty, "Protecting Constitutional Rights in Japan and Canada,"41 *Am. J. Comp. L.* 535 (1993); John Henry Merryman, *The Civil Law Tradition*, 2nd ed. (1984).

78 On the effects of court decisions, see Itoh, 106–110.

79 1 Cranch 37 (1803).

80 John O. Haley, "Japanese Administrative Law: An Introduction," in John O. Haley (ed.), *Law and Society in Contemporary Japan: American Perspectives* (1988), 37–39; Beer, *Freedom*, 66.
81 Law 59 of April 16, 1947.
82 Law 131 of 1948.
83 On the uses of cases, see Lawrence W. Beer and Hidenori Tomatsu, *A Guide to the Study of Japanese Law, Occasional Papers/Reprint Series in Contemporary Asian Studies*, No. 7 (1978), at 29–52; and Tanaka and Smith, 833.
84 Council of State Order No. 103, June 8, 1875.
85 Takayanagi, in Tanaka and Smith, 626–627. John O. Haley, "Judicial Independence in Japan Revisited" and Daniel H. Foote, "Resolution of Traffic Accident Disputes and Judicial Activism in Japan," 25 *Law in Japan*.
86 Hideo Wada, "The Administrative Court under the Meiji Constitution," 10 *Law in Japan* 1 (1977).
87 Marshall.
88 Statistics on page 242 regarding civil and family relations cases show the number of defendants and juveniles. Courtesy of Justice Itsuo Sonobe and the General Secretariat, Supreme Court of Japan, August 1994.
89 The exception is that a five-judge panel decides insurrection cases.
90 Ito, in Beer, *Constitutional Systems*, 172, n. 61; Okudaira, in Luney and Takahashi, 11–12; Daniel H. Foote, "From Japan's Death Row to Freedom," *Pacific Rim Law & Policy Journal* (1) (81–84 Winter 1992); text infra at n. 118.
91 Henderson, *Conciliation and Japanese Law*, Vol. 2. Under separate laws, there are three conciliation systems: for labor relations, for domestic affairs (*kaji chōtei*), and for other disputes in civil affairs (*minji chōtei*). See also Kazuo Sugeno (trans. Leo Kanowitz), *Japanese Labor Law* (1992), and Tanaka and Smith, 492–505.
92 Data provided by Justice Itsuo Sonobe, Supreme Court of Japan, 1991 and 1994. By 1992 the number admitted to the LTRI had risen to 594; 632 were accepted in 1993 and 703 in 1994.
93 Lawrence W. Beer, "Human Rights Commissioners (*Jinken Yogo Iin*) and Lay Protection of Human Rights in Japan," Occasional Paper No. 31, International Ombudsman Institute (October, 1985); Joel Rosch, "Institutionalizing Mediation: The Evolution of the Civil Liberties Bureau in Japan," 21 *Law and Society Rev.* (2) 243 (1987).
94 Discussions with Justices Masami Ito and Itsuo Sonobe, 1991.
95 January 25, 1994. *Japan Times Weekly Int'l. Edition*, January 24–30 and February 7–13, 1994. In February 1994, Rueko Sakurai (58) became the first woman to head a Japanese police station (Mita, Minato-ku, Tokyo). In 1993, a record 144 women were among those who passed the National Law Examination, and Douglas Kenji Freeman became the first American citizen to pass these written and oral tests; *Japan Times Weekly Int'l. Edition*, November 15–21, 1993.
96 Itoh and Beer, 16–18.
97 1370 *Hanrei Jihō* 3 (Sendai High Court, January 10, 1991).
98 *Nakamura et al. v. Japan* (1962), translated in Itoh and Beer, 58.
99 *Aizawa v. Japan* (1973), Case 7, below.
100 *Sumiyoshi, Inc. v. Governor, Aichi Prefecture et al.* (1971), Case 11, below.
101 *Hiraguchi v. Hiraguchi* (1987), Case 20, below.
102 *Kurokawa v. Chiba Prefecture Election Commission* (1976) and *Kanao et al. v. Hiroshima Election Commission* (1985), Cases 22 and 24, below.
103 For example, Isamu Yoshida (66) was acquitted March 22, 1994, of a 1946 murder for which he was convicted based on a friend's (an alleged accomplice) confession. He was released on an amnesty in 1955, and asked for a retrial in 1990 of the Takamatsu High Court. *Japan Times Weekly Int'l. Edition*, April 4–10, 1994. See supra, n. 90.
104 *Park et al. v. Japan* (1972), Case 28, below.
105 *Nissan Motors, Inc. v. Nakamoto* (1981), Case 9, below.
106 *Matsue v. Hakodate Customs Director et al.* (1984), Case 31, below.
107 Beer, *Freedom*, 372–378.
108 *Suzuki v. Japan*, Sup. Ct., G.B., October 8, 1952; 6 *Minshiū* 9 at 783; translated in Maki, *Court and Constitution in Japan*, 382.
109 *Tomabechi v. Japan*, Sup. Ct., G.B. April 15, 1953; 7 *Minshiū* at 305; translated in Maki, 366.
110 *Shimizu v. Governor, Osaka Metropolis* (1962); Itoh and Beer, 41.
111 *Japan v. Sato* (1980), Case 2, below.

112 Okudaira, in Luney and Takahashi, 29–30.

113 B. J. George, "Rights of the Criminally Accused," in Luney and Takahashi, 289, and "Discretionary Authority of Public Prosecutors in Japan," in John Haley (ed.), *Law and Society in Contemporary Japan* 263 (1988), at 94. See also 23 *Law in Japan* (1990); David H. Bayley, *Forces of Order: Police Behavior in Japan and the United States* (1976) and *Forces of Order: Policing Modern Japan* (1991); Foote, "Death Row," "The Benevolent Paternalism of Japanese Criminal Justice," 80 *Calif. L. Rev.* 317 (1992), hereafter "Benevolent Paternalism" and "Confessions and the Right to Silence in Japan," 21 GA. *Journal of Int & Comp L* (3) 415 (1991); John Braithwaite, *Crime, Shame and Reintegration* (1989), and John O. Haley, *Authority Without Power* (1991).

114 Bayley, *Forces of Order* (1991), 132–136.

115 General Secretariat, Supreme Court of Japan, *Justice in Japan* 41 (1990).

116 Hidenori Aoki, as quoted in Foote, "Death Row," 81–82.

117 Foote, id. 79, 83–85; Richard Lempert, "A Jury for Japan?," 40 *Am. J. Comp. L.* 37 (1992). A comprehensive survey of the issues and the case law is William B. Cleary, *The Law of Criminal Procedure in Contemporary Japan*, doctoral dissertation, Faculty of Law, Hokkaido University, Sapporo, 1989.

118 Foote, id.; sources *supra* n. 90 and n. 113. The jury system was established by Law 50 of 1928 and was suspended by Law 88 of 1943, and never revived. The system was quite different from the U.S. jury system and from those proposed in Japan in the 1980s and 1990s. Article 3(3) of the Court Organization Law (Law 59 of April 16, 1947) states that nothing in that Law precludes establishment of a jury system by another law. On the other hand, one influential view has been that jury verdicts binding on judges would violate Article 76 of the Constitution, under which judges have the "whole judicial power" and are "bound only by this Constitution and the laws" in exercising "their conscience."

119 George, in Luney and Takahashi, 303.

120 Foote, "Death Row;" Japan Civil Liberties Union, *1993 Report concerning the Present Status of Human Rights in Japan* (May 1993).

121 Maki, *Court and Constitution in Japan* (1964), 156; *Murakami v. Japan*, Sup. Ct., G.B., March 12, 1948; 2 *Keishū* 3 at 191.

122 *Ichikawa et al. v. Japan*, Sup. Ct., G. B., July 19, 1961; 15 *Keishū* 7 at at 1106; translated in Itoh and Beer, at 161.

123 Supreme Court data, courtesy of Justice Itsuo Sonobe, July 1994. For Japan's annual execution record from 1875 to 1987, see Beer, *Constitutional Systems*, 218; Foote, "Death Row," 103.

124 Shigemitsu Dando (B. J. George trans.), *The Japanese Law of Criminal Procedure* (1965) and *Shikei Haishiron*, 4th ed. (1994). Kenichi Nakayama, "*Shikei seido*," 154 *Hōgaku Kyōshitsu* (1993).

125 Foote, "Benevolent Paternalism," 80.

126 The *Shiratori Ruling, Murakami v. Japan*, Sup. Ct., First P. B., May 20, 1975; 29 Keishū 177 (1975). Foote, "Death Row," 68.

127 Law 131 of 1948. For a 1994 acquittal on retrial for a 1946 murder, see *supra*, n. 103.

128 Foote, "Benevolent Paternalism," 15. n. 12.

129 Id., 17.

130 *Menda v. Japan*, Kumamoto Dist. Ct., August 10, 1956; Study Group on the Criminal Retrial System, *Chomei Saishin Jiken Mikōkan Saibanreishū Daiisshū* 12 (1979).

131 *Menda v. Japan*, Fukuoka High Ct., September 27, 1979; 939 *Hanrei Jihō* 13.

132 *Japan v. Menda*, Sup. Ct., First P.B., December 11, 1980; 34 *Keishū* 562.

133 *Japan v. Menda*, Kumamoto Dist. Ct., July 15, 1983; 1090 *Hanrei Jihō* 21.

■ First published in S. Coliver et al. (eds.), *Secrecy and Liberty: National Security, Freedom of Expression and Access to Information*, The Hague, Kluwer Law International, 1999, pp. 349–360.

12

National Security and Freedom of Expression in Japan

⌘

I Introduction

In 1997, in the aftermath of the Cold War, colonialism and the break-up of blocs, many are trying to reframe questions and answers regarding national security and freedom of expression in law and policy throughout the world. In this endeavor, it may help to lay bare even the most obvious of the long-dominant assumptions about national security needs, and then to see whether these assumptions should not be modified, if not for all countries, at least for many. I make no claim to expertise in national security studies; I have a long-term interest in freedom of expression and constitutionalism in Japan.[1] With important results, Japan's operative assumptions regarding national security for five decades have deviated from what most scholars and nation-state leaders would consider normal. Under its "Peace Constitution," Japan has renounced, in theory, law and practice, war and the threat or use of force to settle international disputes. For decades, Japan has almost always limited its defense expenditures to less than 1% of its GNP. Japan (without U.S. assistance) is not militarily competitive with other East Asian nations; but without the unique restraints of Article 9 of the Constitution, Japan would likely be one of the few great military (and, arguably, nuclear) powers, with considerably less concern for freedom of expression than now.

To create a setting for explaining the nature and possible usefulness to other countries of aspects of Japan's model for thinking about freedom and national security, I would begin by setting forth my understanding of the current world context and common security assumptions.

II The Current World Context and Common Security Assumptions

I take the present world context as defined by such factors as the end of the Cold War, the USSR and colonialism; the rearrangement of ethnic relationships in a number of areas (sometimes peacefully, often with violence); historic continuing growth in mutual understanding among authentic representatives of the major world religions (e.g. Islam, Buddhism, Christianity) and their converging support of universal human rights; the destructive power of nuclear, chemical and biological weapons; multinational needs for sustainable development, employment and environmental protection; explosive growth in communication and transportation technology; the economic might of Japan, other Asian nations, and the G-7 countries; the capacity of predatory capitalism to obstruct the evolution of world peace under law; the unmatched barbarism of twentieth-century warring; the flimsy linkages between national security law and protection of freedom of expression; and the unprecedented worldwide attention to constitutional government and human rights. It is a significant advance in world civilization that 181 of 186 nation states now have single-document national constitutions, some 130 of which have been adopted since 1970. Most constitutions contain human rights provisions reflecting what is now broadly respectable around the world. However, imperfect human rights enforcement is seen in all nations; the revolutionary assumption that the inherent dignity and value of each human being demands socio-legal respect is now commonplace. Accordingly, it is a particularly propitious time for thinking to center on "the right to live in peace, free from fear and want," as stated in the Preamble of the Constitution of Japan.[2]

Following are several of the most common assumptions regarding freedom and security in many countries:

1. Leaders of many, if not most, countries consider their countries to be under serious threat of attack. They believe that one or more external and/or internal political enemies *threaten* the existence of the territory of their political and/or economic system (and/or those who currently hold power). For leaders to *motivate* their people to accept the credibility of their national security assessments and the legitimacy of their military policies, it is helpful for them to be able to create the impression that the threat is to the very *existence* of the state, culture or regime, and not simply to a limited national interest such as short-term economic benefit or a temporary wound to national pride. Unfortunately, there is at times a grand canyon between reality and leaders' definitions of threat, as in the unjustified acts of President George Bush against the helpless small state of Panama to get General Manuel Noriega.
2. Maintenance of the ability to respond to such threats with adequate deterrent force – military and/or police – should be the highest priority of the state.
3. To assure effective military and/or police response to threats, special laws, policies and regulations limiting civil rights and expanding government prerogatives are necessary, because freedom of expression may add to the threat and because secrecy of state information may be necessary to respond to the threat.
4. With respect to government budgetary priorities and policy preoccupations, no other public interest should be allowed to challenge effectively military and/or police ascendancy, whether the primary perceived threat be internal or external or both, and whether or not the threat actually exists.
5. With historical logic, great power status should be defined in modern times primarily in terms of great military power, including destructive capacity superior to that of other nations. It is inevitable that other civilizational values be radically subordinate to military security, although economic and technological power

are beginning to compete with military capacity as the primary foundation of national security.

The above seem to have been the dominant assumptions up to now, and the world has as yet no adequate peace enforcement mechanism under the United Nations. In some states these assumptions exist in tension with democracy, human rights, constitutionalism and/or some other system of belief and thought. On all continents, in politico-legal systems ranging from those allegedly most democratic to those bluntly dictatorial, freedom of the press and other mass media, freedom of social, political and economic speech, the freedoms of assembly and association, and free access to government information about official acts and about oneself have been needlessly suppressed under these assumptions by both official and informal means.

III Expression and National Security in Japan

A Japan's arc: from isolationist to militaristic to non-military superpower

Before September 1945, Japan was masterfully repressive in operating under the above assumptions. How did the prewar system develop? In the 1850s, Western military power forced Japan to open diplomatic and trade relations under unequal treaties. The Tokugawa family regime (1600–1868) rigorously enforced isolation from the outside world for over 200 years as the foundation for Japan's national security. To achieve full independence from the imposed treaties and a place of pride in the world, Japan adopted Western military thought and technology, and engaged in broad-ranging legal, social and economic changes. By 1905 when she defeated Russia in war, Japan had achieved her goals and was a world power.

Critical to Japan's modernizing efforts was the development of a completely new legal and constitutional system.[3] In 1868, Japan's oligarchs transformed the Emperor (*Tenno*), a virtually powerless institution for roughly 1,000 years, into the central legitimizing symbol for a unitary state and the formal repository of sovereign power in the state. Others made decisions in the Emperor's name as hundreds of feudal domains were replaced by a centralized state under a near absolute monarchy. Over many decades, modern means of universal education, indoctrination, and control created an effective police state enforcing reverence and absolute obedience to the sacred Emperor's government.[4] Well-educated Special High Police (*Tokko*, "thought police") and the dreaded military police (*Kempeitai*) systematically fomented extreme nationalism and personal self-abnegation. From the 1850s until 1945 Japan was for substantial periods in the equivalent of a state of national emergency.

Aggressive militarism, suppression of freedom and other individual rights, and reverence for the Emperor-centered state (*kokutai*) utterly failed with Japan's defeat in the Second World War in 1945. The low point in Japan's long history was 1930 to 1945, what the Japanese call "the dark valley period."[5] The wartime constitutional system was rejected and replaced, with catalytic input from the U.S.-dominated Occupation,[6] by the 1947 Constitution of Japan (*Nihonkoku Kempo*) which renounced war as a national right, established popular sovereignty in place of the Emperor's sacral sovereignty, and protected and promoted rather than denied fundamental human rights. To understand Japanese constitutionalism with respect to national security, it is essential to keep in mind this modern history and the revolution of freedom which began in 1945 and continues today.

In Japan's constitutional culture, the three core elements in the constitutional system have been seen as intimately related: popular sovereignty and a truly powerless Emperor under the Preamble and Article I, renunciation of war under the Preamble and Article 9, and a guarantee of a range of rights under Articles 11 to 40, 44, and 97. In Japan's recurring vigorous debates about the Constitution, tampering with the Article 9 "no war clause" has often been seen as implying a danger to individual freedoms and a portent of a restoration of the Emperor to his status as the center of an authoritarian state. Inadequate attention to human rights has been interpreted as a harbinger of militarism and imperial control. Any show of special respect for the imperial family or *Shinto* ceremonies, as was displayed after the death of Emperor Hirohito (1989) and at the accession of Emperor Akihito, or in judicial decisions, raises in some minds the specter of repression under a mythologized Emperor.[7] Put simply, any hint of militarism or even apparently modest emphasis on the needs of the Self Defense Forces (SDF, *Jieitai*) or a sniff of Emperor-*Shinto* nationalism has tended to provoke a vigorous response from civil liberties advocates. Of course, in analogous forms, unbalanced nationalism or ethnocism and excessive pre-occupation with military needs rather than other priorities bode ill for freedom of expression in many countries. The strength of Japan's system of protecting and promoting freedom is undoubtedly due in part to the clarity of her renunciation of militarism.

The Constitution of Japan was "imposed" upon a lame-duck Cabinet in 1946, but not on Japan's people. The most representative body in Japan's history to that time was elected in April 1946, with suffrage extended to all men and women of age twenty or above. This House of Representatives thoroughly debated the draft constitution co-authored by Japanese and Occupation personnel, and approved the document with only a few dissenting votes. The Constitution has been welcomed by most Japanese ever since as an appropriate expression of their political ideals and social values.[8] Awareness of the popular consensus of respect and support for the Constitution has constrained the small but powerful political minority which chafes under one or more aspects of the Constitution or the security relationship with the United States.

In short, the Japan of 1997 has broken the old mold of assumptions as a quasi-pacifist, democratic superpower, and her experience over the past fifty years deserves wider study.[9] (The term "superpower" now seems inappropriate in light of the collective and limited nature of the emerging world leadership.) Japan's fifty year record of peace with freedom is impressive and is as much a cause as a result of her prosperity. In long range terms, militarism tends to have anti-development effects. Of crucial importance and contrary to internationally common assumptions, most Japanese have not felt militarily threatened by any country near or far; so Japan has not felt a pressing need for a military establishment that is competitive with even her smaller neighbors (the two Koreas and Taiwan), let alone commensurate with her considerable economic and technological power since the 1960s. The only major question marks in Eastern Asian security are the intentions of North Korea and China; the preponderant view among Japanese is that no country has now or is likely to have in the foreseeable future, any persuasive reason to attack Japan. The economic dependence of China and other nations on Japan is a strong deterrent; the U.S.-Japan Mutual Security Treaty is another factor diminishing any sense of international danger. On the other hand, recurring perceptions by Asian neighbors of Japanese insensitivity to its wartime aggression still trigger vehement responses and alleged fear of reemergent militarism, at home and abroad. This pattern has served the purpose of discouraging militarist nationalism in Japan's politics and society. Only the United Nations and the United States are Japan's security allies, and the U.S. sense of security threat in Asia is much stronger than Japan's. Japan's current SDF are technologically advanced and costly for their numbers, but are geopolitically modest. More important to the present discussion, the SDF are not presumed to be the highest budget priority and they are significantly limited by the Constitution of Japan, by law and policy, and by the quasi-pacifist attitudes of the great majority of Japanese.

B Japan's constitutional principles

The key provisions are the following:[10]

> *The Preamble.* We, the Japanese people [are] resolved that never again shall we be visited with the horrors of war through the action of government . . . We . . . desire peace for all time . . . and an honored place in an international society striving for the preservation of peace . . . free from fear and want.
>
> *Article 9.* 1. Aspiring sincerely to an international peace based on justice and order, the Japanese people forever renounce war as a sovereign right of the nation and the threat or use of force as a means of settling international disputes.
>
> 2. In order to accomplish the aim of the preceding paragraph, land, sea and air forces, as well as other war potential, will never be maintained. The right of belligerency of the State will not be recognized.

The SDF have never been used to fight. Japan stopped shooting in August 1945, and has never begun shooting again. In what other ways has the intent of these provisions been manifested in legal and political practice? What has not been done is as instructive as what has been done. Japan has no national security law system under which freedom of expression may be subjected to special restraints in times of crisis or war. The Constitution of Japan contains no provisions relating to acts of war, such as declaring war or concluding peace; no article touches on martial law declarations or preservation of military secrets. Article 76(2) precludes military courts: "No extraordinary tribunal shall be established, nor shall any organ or agency of the Executive be given final judicial power."

The Supreme Court has held that under Article 9 Japan retains the natural law right to self-defense, that the Treaty of Mutual Cooperation and Security between the United States of America and Japan (the Mutual Security Treaty, 1960) is not on its face unconstitutional, and that, although generally the Court must take into account the political nature of such issues, the Court retains the right to determine whether a law or other government action is clearly and obviously in violation of Article 9.[11] The Supreme Court has not directly decided whether the SDF are unconstitutional. The great majority of Japan's constitutional lawyers continue to consider the SDF unconstitutional, as did the 1973 Sapporo District Court in its

Naganuma Nike Missile Site decision (overturned on appeal on technical grounds).[12] The public, however, accepts the SDF as constitutional as long as they do not fight abroad and are kept to a modest level.

Military interests are not presumed to be a high priority. For example, a Tokyo High Court decision, which was let stand, denied that in peacetime Defense Agency activities involve a higher public interest than those of civilian airports or other government agencies. Noise pollution is a general concern affecting "the public welfare"; the noise of military aircraft violated the personal rights of citizens (Articles 12, 13 and 29 of the Constitution).[13] Even less might one assume that civil liberties and other "rights and freedoms of the spirit" (*seishinteki jiyuken*)[14] may be subordinated to military interests.

C Relevant laws

No law provides for special restraints on the rights and freedoms of ordinary citizens for reasons of national emergency or national security; but civil servants and military personnel operating under virtually identical provisions in the National Public Employees Law, the Local Public Employees Law, or the Self-Defense Forces Law must not divulge secrets which have come to their knowledge in the course of performing their duties, whether they are on active duty or retired. In its 1978 *Nishiyama* decisions, the Supreme Court convicted a journalist for inducing a Foreign Ministry employee to give him a cable which suggested the government had lied about financial arrangements attendant to the reversion of Okinawa to Japanese sovereignty in 1972.[15] Japan has no general espionage law or state secrets law; but special legislation implementing Article VI of the U.S.-Japan Mutual Security Treaty protects secrets regarding U.S. military forces in Japan and weapons supplied to Japan by the United States.[16] In the 1980s, the government sought passage in the Diet (Japan's parliament) of "State Secrets Bills," but strong opposition from minority parties, the mass media, the legal community, and citizen groups doomed them to failure. The bills were not well crafted and aroused technical objections as well as alleged fears of authoritarian secretiveness. In 1997 Japan was expected to pass a Freedom of Information Law; forty-three of forty-seven prefectures already have freedom of information and privacy ordinances. Some Diet members contend the Defense Agency has not always been as forthcoming with information to the Diet as is called for by civilian control. Nevertheless, that control is assisted by the prohibition on military persons serving in the Cabinet (Article 66.2 of the Constitution).

D Limits on military and emergency powers

Due to the wartime abuses of their authoritarian governments, the postwar democratic constitutions of Germany, Japan and Italy carried no provisions on emergencies. This situation continues in Japan, but not in Europe:

> Despite a lot of resistance [emergency rules] were introduced into the German Constitution in 1968. Both the newly established democracies in Spain, Portugal, and Greece in the 1970s and in Central and Eastern Europe in the 1990s have included emergency provisions in their Constitutions.[17]

The Prime Minister represents the Cabinet and has jurisdiction over the SDF under Article 7 of the SDF Law. There is no independent military command structure as under the prewar system. Article 71 of the Police Law gives the Prime Minister, upon the recommendation of the civilian National Public Safety Commission, the authority to declare a state of "national emergency" and to assume direct control over Japan's police. "National emergency" is understood to cover such events as foreign invasions, a large-scale natural disaster, or internal disturbances. However, in the "Great Hanshin Earthquake Disaster" (Kobe) of 1995, which took 6,300 lives, the central and local governments were criticized for their slow mobilization of the SDF in the absence of an adequate pre-existing system for rapid response. The actual primary function of the SDF since the 1950s has been disaster relief.

The House of Representatives must approve actions taken pursuant to a declaration of emergency. If that House is not in session at the time of the Emergency, the Cabinet may call an emergency session of the House of Councillors, but actions then taken are "provisional and . . . null and void unless agreed to by the House of Representatives" within ten days of the opening of the next Diet session, pursuant to Article 54.2 and 54.3 of the Constitution.[18] It is not clear what measures affecting freedom of expression might be taken provisionally in an emergency.

Article 18 bans "bondage of any kind. Involuntary servitude, except as punishment for crime, is prohibited" also.[19] This is interpreted in the spirit of Article 9 to mean that military conscription would be unconstitutional as "involuntary servitude." The export of weapons is prohibited, to Japan's considerable economic loss; but under 1980s agreements Japan supplies the U.S. with its superior "dual-use" (i.e. civilian and military) technology. Some advocate a formal legal ban on both the import and the export of weapons.[20]

The vigor of freedom of political speech in Japan has allowed the tolerant co-existence of radically diverse views and has also given the time necessary in a factionalized but consensus-oriented society for agreements with strong majority support to emerge which creatively concretize implementation of Article 9. For example, prior to the restoration of Japan's sovereignty over Okinawa in 1972, the Japanese assumed that the United States maintained dreaded nuclear weapons on that island. Representing a multi-party consensus, the Diet established the "three no-nuclear principles" in November 1971, although political parties and factions within the ruling Liberal Democratic Party (LDP) differed among themselves on other security issues. These principles ban Japan's manufacture or possession, or the introduction into Japan, of nuclear weapons even if potentially hostile neighboring countries should develop nuclear weapons (e.g. China, Russia, North Korea), and even though Japan's nuclear power technology is of the highest order. Anti-militarist sentiment is strengthened each year by substantial media and social commemoration of the Hiroshima (August 6, 1945) and Nagasaki (August 9, 1945) atom bombings. The popular consensus is that all nuclear weapons testing should cease and that all nuclear weapons should be destroyed.

Japan has almost always limited its defense expenditures to a maximum of 1% of its GNP. Japan (without U.S. assistance) is not militarily competitive with other nations in the region. Its forces in the 1990s rank twenty-sixth in the world in size. In the absence of Article 9, Japan would have likely become one of the few great military (and arguably nuclear) powers. Most important in the present context, it is improbable that a militarized Japan would consider freedom of expression compatible with national security. Militaries tend to exaggerate threats; their business is to foresee and prepare to fight threats, not to engage in peaceful democratic governance. Japan's earlier militarist nationalism was contemptuous of other peoples and of human rights in general. Now, Japanese are much more internationalist and respectful of rights, and assume freedom as part of the natural order of things in Japan. Japan illustrates the possibility of a nation state changing from a thoroughly militarist and repressive government to a country that is free and peaceful, unthreatened and unthreatening.

Japan does not define national security primarily in terms of internal order or military security, but as a "comprehensive security."[21] By this is meant not only national security (secured with the help of the United States and the United Nations), but also security with respect to long-term social and economic needs, protection of human rights and democracy under the Constitution of Japan, and attention to regional and world developmental and ecological concerns. Japan supports the United Nations generously and unequivocally, and continues to place hope idealistically in the further development of its institutions for peace and freedom. In addition, Japan leads the world in non-military development aid to less fortunate countries, under ODA (Official Development Assistance) formulas of the OECD (Organization for Economic Cooperation and Development). On the other hand, even modest SDF participation in UN peace-keeping operations is rigorously limited by law under Article 9 of the Constitution, and roughly 80% of Japanese oppose overseas SDF military action even under UN auspices.[22]

The anti-militarist "Peace Constitution" undergirds Japan's system of national security and freedom of expression, and allows for paradoxes. For example, for decades a series of highly controverted court cases (the *Ienaga Textbook* Trials)[23] has revolved around the high school history textbook coverage of modern Japanese militarism and aggression against Asian neighbors before 1945. Some politicians and Ministry of Education officials have wanted to downplay Japanese aggression and atrocities while others have favored repentant honesty and openness. The continuing equivocal stance regarding war responsibility of some politicians and bureaucrats infuriates other Asian countries and many Japanese. Yet, the young have been conditioned to a quasi-pacifism through the education system. A foreigner teaching at a Japanese university may be stunned to find students puzzled at the inability of many foreigners to comprehend Japan's undeviating rejection of war and preference for peaceful means of settling international disputes. After all, war is horror, peace is pleasant and humane. Such students can understand when cadets of Japan's multi-service national academy, the Defense University (*Boei Daiqaku*) quit upon graduation because the SDF might be becoming more "3D" (dirty, difficult, dangerous) with participation in United Nations peace-keeping. Under Articles 9 and 18 of the Constitution, they cannot be forced to serve. Although Japan's social system, like those of all democracies, restricts free speech in certain contexts, law and politics enforce a high degree of tolerance for the expression of diverse ideas, from pacifism to militarism, from Communism to radical economic liberalism, and many views in between.

IV CONCLUSION

Japan's (near) absolute renunciation of war and the use of force in international relations, along the lines of the 1928 Kellogg-Briand Pact signed by so many nations, coexists with a refusal to find other countries very threatening. The past fifty years of Japan's international experience show their assumptions to have been quite realistic for Japan, not mindlessly or irresponsibly Utopian. In that same period, trigger-happy leaders in nations large and small have caused untold suffering to many millions, not least in Asia. While Japan's constitutional stance may seem to have been impossibly Utopian for many countries in other geopolitical settings of the past decades, we now live in a new post-colonialist and post-Cold War era when rethinking of assumptions is in order. Whatever the past justifications for restraint of freedom of expression based on perceived threats, internal or external, the number of countries in which military security can be credibly adduced as grounds for limiting free speech seems to have substantially decreased in the past ten years.

As the foundation for national security, Japan's reliance under Article 9 on unequivocal renunciation of war and dependence on peaceful means of dispute resolution and on the United Nations, a strong system of freedom of expression, increased reliance on economic and technological indispensability to other countries, and heavy investment in cultural interlocking (as through the Japan Foundation and the Japan-U.S. Center for Global Partnership) presents a thought-provoking and useful new model. Leaders of militarized political cultures like that of the United States might well look hard at the geopolitical example of Japan while redefining military roles in the emerging era. Japan illustrates how a country can get over authoritarianism, militarism, and war. Primary dependence for national security on an integrated government-military-industrial complex is needlessly costly and harmful. For many countries, the assumption that foreign nations generally represent a threat necessitating preparation for military response is not empirically credible, nor is the frequently attendant suspicion regarding freedom of expression. Japan's peaceful constitutionalism is not now Utopian, but a major contribution to the world's constitutionalist traditions: military influence on political decisions should be nil; military budgets should not be given privileged consideration in the absence of clear, credible national danger; military action is usually unacceptably barbaric; no special legislation restricting freedom of expression in the name of national security is justified, and legal restraints in times of genuine national emergency should be minimal and subject to review; as basic to international law as the national right to self-defense should be the duty not to resort to arms to settle international disputes. This seems the vision emanating from Japan's law, policy and experience since 1945.

NOTES

1 Lawrence W. Beer, *Freedom of Expression in Japan: A Study in Comparative Law, Politics and Society* (1984); and "Freedom of Expression in Japan: The Continuing Revolution," in P. Luney & K. Takahashi eds., *Japanese Constitutional Law* 221 (1993).

2 For the text of the 1947 Constitution of Japan, see Lawrence W. Beer & Hiroshi Itoh, *The Constitutional Case Law of Japan, 1970 through 1990* at 653–65 (1996).

3 Masami Ito, "The Modern Development of Law and Constitution in Japan," in L. W. Beer ed., *Constitutional Systems in Late Twentieth Century Asia* 129–44 (1992); Junji Banno (trans. J.A.A. Stockwin), *The Establishment of the Japanese Constitutional System* (1992).

4 Beer, *supra* note 1 at 45–71; Gregory J. Kasza, *The State and the Mass Media in Japan, 1918–1945* (1988); Richard H. Mitchell, *Thought Control in Prewar Japan* (1976).

5 *Id.*

6 Beer, *supra* note 3 at 175–82; and "Constitutionalism and Rights in Japan and Korea," in L. Henkin and A. Rosenthal eds., *Constitutionalism and Rights: The Influence of the United States Constitution Abroad* 225–59 (1990).

7 Lawrence W. Beer, "Constitutional Revolution in Japanese Law, Society and Politics," 16 *Modern Asian Studies* 33–67 (1982). Related judicial decisions have focused on public funding of *Shinto* shrines to the war dead. The Supreme Court first held such local government support unconstitutional in 1997. *Nikkei Weekly*, April 17, 1997. See David M. O'Brien, *To Dream of Dreams: Religious Freedom and Constitutional Politics in Postwar Japan* (1996).

8 Sato Tatsuo, assisted by Sato Isao, *Nihonkoku Kempo Seiritsushi* (The History of the Establishment of the Constitution of Japan), 4 volumes (1994); James S, Marshall, *Japan's Successor Generation* (1985); Beer, *supra* note 6.

9 On Japan's security thought and system, see Peter J. Katzenstein, *Cultural Norms and National Security: Police and Military in Postwar Japan* (1996); Richard J. Samuels, *Rich Nation, Strong Army: National Security and the Technological Transformation of Japan* (1996); Henry Shue, *Basic Rights* (2d ed. 1996); and, on Japanese public opinion, Office of Research, U.S.I.A., *"Global Partnership": Views of the Japanese Public* (1992).

10 Beer and Itoh, *supra* note 2 at 653–55.

11 For translations of the Supreme Court decisions, see John M. Maki, *Court and Constitution in Japan: Selected Supreme Court Decisions, 1948–1960*, 198 (1964); Hiroshi Itoh & Lawrence H. Beer, *The Constitutional Case Law of Japan: Selected Supreme Court Decisions, 1961–70*, 103 (1978).

12 Beer & Itoh, *supra* note 2 at 83 (Cases 3, 4, and 5).

13 13 Tokyo High Court, *Asahi Shimbun*, July 15, 1987.

14 Scholars refer to the following cluster of freedoms in the Constitution as "rights and freedoms of the spirit": the right of petition (Article 16); freedom of thought and conscience (Article 19); freedom of religion (Article 20); "freedom of assembly and association as well as speech, press and all other forms of expression" (Article 21); academic freedom (Article 23).

15 Beer, *supra* note 1 at 304–305; Beer & Itoh, *supra* note 2 at 543 (Case 38). Since the 1995 rape of a twelve-year-old school girl by U.S. military personnel, U.S. facilities on Okinawa, comprising 18% of the land area and 75% of U.S. forces in Japan, have received the political attention long denied them by both the U.S. and Japanese Governments. The inequity of burdens on Okinawans, the post-Cold War base needs, and a stronger Japanese government voice in determining U.S. force levels were among pressing issues in Japan's domestic politics as well as in Japan-U.S. relations in mid-1997. *Christian Science Monitor*, April 10, 1997. See the symposium on Okinawa issues *in 23(3) Japan Echo*, 32–55 (Autum, 1996).

16 Headquarters, United States Forces *Status of Forces Agreement with Related Documents* (1960); Special Criminal Law to Implement the Agreement under Article VI of the Treaty of Mutual Cooperation and Security between the United States of America Regarding Facilities and Areas and the Status of United States Forces in Japan, Law 138 of 1952, as amended. For a translation of the law, see The Japan Newspaper Publishers & Editors Association *Press Laws in Japan* 10–11 (1993).

17 "Conference Report: Human Rights and the Functioning of Democratic Institutions in Emergency Situations," *The Japan Foundation Newsletter*, Vol. 24, No. 5, at 7 (Jan. 1997).

18 James Auer, "Article Nine: Renunciation of War," in Luney & Takahashi, *supra* note 1 at 69–86; Osamu Nishi, *The Constitution and the National Defense Law System in Japan* (1987).

19 Beer & Itoh, *supra* note 2 at 656.

20 See *supra* note 9.

21 *Id.*

22 Japan may participate in overseas peace-keeping operations only if: (1) they are under United Nations auspices; (2) Japan's participation is welcomed by the parties to ceasefire arrangements as a neutral party; (3) Japanese SDF only use small arms and only to prevent injury or death; and (4) it is understood that Japan will withdraw from monitoring the ceasefire if it is broken. Of the many opinion polls on defense issues, see, e.g. *Tokyo Shimbun*, July 23, 1994, reporting on the view of 13,723 respondents.

23 Beer, *supra* note 1 at 248–80; Beer & Itoh, *supra* note 2 at 516 (Case 36).

■ Delivered to the Mid-Atlantic Region Association for Asian Studies at the George Washington University, Washington D.C., October 26, 2003, and first published in *Vital Speeches of the Day*, January 1, 2004, pp. 175-178.

13

Rejection of War: Japan's Constitutional Discourse and Performance

⌘

Of all the great-power signatories of the Paris Peace Pact of 1928, Japan since 1945 has pursued most impressively its peaceful spirit in law and policy. For over fifty years commitments to international peace, human rights, and popular sovereignty, not so much the Emperor system, have been central to Japan's constitutionalism. Article 9's rejection of war and of force to settle international disputes continues in effect. The individual Japanese enjoys a wide spectrum of rights and freedoms under Chapter 3, Articles 11–40 and Article 97 of the Constitution of Japan. "All of the people shall be respected as individuals" and generally these rights and freedoms are to be "The supreme consideration in legislation and in other governmental affairs" (Article 11). Over time, social and political rights have enjoyed increased protection and promotion under law. In some areas of performance, such as democratic stability, pre-collegiate education, and health care delivery, Japan has become a world leader.

All but a few of the 191 nation-states in the United Nations in 2003 have a single document national constitution; over 135 have been ratified since 1970. The exceptions are the United Kingdom, New Zealand, Israel, and three states which use the Qran as their basic document, Saudi Arabia, Libya and Oman. The 1947 Constitution of Japan is one of the world's oldest and most effectively implemented basic laws, but as in all constitutional democracies, political culture generates imperfect compliance with constitutional demands.

Since 1946 Japan has enjoyed an unbroken succession of national and local elections under democratic law. All men and women over twenty have had the right to vote, and exercise that right more than Americans do. Since the 1990s, an on-going legal reform process has attacked stubborn problems of malapportionment and excesses in political fund-raising which have reduced occasional corruption, but campaign finance is less of a problem for democracy than in the United States. Much creative improvement has been achieved in Japan; problems remain.

In recent years, far-reaching administrative reforms have been proposed to strengthen the Prime Minister, the Cabinet and the Diet in their relations with the formally subordinate but powerful bureaucracy, and to enhance the position of local governments *vis-à-vis* the central government. The goal is a more democratic leadership structure. Noteworthy reforms in the judiciary and in legal education are also afoot early in the 21st century to better integrate reform policies with the daily lives of the self-governing people.

Under Article 96, amendment of the Constitution of Japan requires approval by a two-thirds majority of all members of each House of the Diet, followed by approval by a majority of those voting in a special or regular election. For half a century the possibility of amendment has been much discussed, but no amendment has been passed. From 1958 until 1964, a Commission on the Constitution (Kempo Chosakai) conducted an exhaustive study and unearthed no flaws, omission or needed corrections regarding basic principles of the document. In 1999 the Diet approved the establishment of two "Committees to Investigate the Constitution" (Kempo Chosakai). The House of Representatives committee has fifty members and the House of Councillors committee forty-five. (The House of Representatives is the larger and more powerful of the parliamentary assemblies.) Their mission is to conduct a "broad and comprehensive" study and to submit separate reports with recommendations to the Speaker of each House. Each Speaker will then submit the report to the full House for debate and possible action. What the results of this multi-year study will be is not yet clear, but the issue of amendment itself is no longer as incendiary as in the decades following World War II. Among possible changes are clarification of the right of self-defense under Article 9, easing the rigor of the amendment process, and the establishment in the basic document of constitutional rights to privacy and a clean environment.

Since World War II, more has been written in Japan about Article 9 pacifism than about any other topic of Japanese legal discourse. The remainder of this talk will focus on that provision of the Constitution. Article 9 reads as follows:

> "Aspiring sincerely to an international peace based on justice and order, the Japanese people forever renounce war as a sovereign right of the nation and the threat or use of force as a means of settling international disputes.
>
> "2. In order to accomplish the aim of the preceding paragraph, land, sea and air forces, as well as other war potential, will never be maintained. The right of belligerency of the state will not be recognized."

Article 9 is in the spirit of the Preamble:

> "We, the Japanese people, . . . determined that we shall secure for ourselves and our posterity the fruits of peaceful cooperation with all nations and the blessings of liberty throughout this land, and resolved that never again shall we be visited with the horrors of war through the action of government . . .
>
> "We, the Japanese people, desire peace for all time and are deeply conscious of the high ideals controlling human relationship, and we have determined to preserve our security and existence, trusting in the justice and faith of the peace-loving peoples of the world. We desire to occupy an honored place in an international society striving for the preservation of peace . . . We recognize that all the peoples of the world have the right to live in peace, free from fear and want."

Theoretically consistent philosophical or religious pacifism rules out violent response to individual or collective violence. Genuine pacifism requires, in all circumstances, that a person (or a community) turn the other cheek and refrain from hostile reaction, based on faith in human goodness and disciplined conviction in the face of provocation, or on a belief that, on balance, violent response is counter-productive by some other cost-benefit analysis. Only peaceful resistance to evil violence is permissible. That does not describe the official or popular pacifism of Japan, although some Japanese continue to believe that Japan should not respond militarily even to an invasion, so horrible is war.

Japan's Article 9 is supported at home and is now drawing increased respectful attention abroad, rather than cynical dismissal as absurdly idealistic or dangerous to a nation's security. Political parties and opinion leaders in Japan seem close to a consensus in favor of paragraph 1 of Article 9, but not on the proper interpretation of paragraph 2 on "war potential."

Like all governments, Japan's recognizes in practice a natural-law right of self-defense and the legitimacy of police violence in response to some crimes; so Japan's pacifism is a qualified, "quasi-pacifism." On the other hand, Japan denies the legitimacy of taking violent initiatives to settle international disputes (for example, to contest territorial claims). It would not necessarily be more "normal" for Japan to seek maximum military power as some claim. Like the peoples of most other countries, a large majority of Japanese opposed the 2003 preemptive war of the United States against Iraq; but Prime Minister Junichiro Koizumi quietly supported the U.S. action, but within a framework of United Nations sponsorship. A thousand or so Ground, Air and Sea Self-Defense Forces were envisioned in back-up services for Iraqi reconstruction, such as supplying fuel, purifying water, relocating people, and hauling vehicles and relief supplies.

The government takes the term "war potential" in paragraph 2 of Article 9 to mean any military capacity beyond the minimum "land, sea and air forces" needed for self-defense, avoiding use of the term "military forces." In the 21st century, debate often centers on whether a particular deployment policy, weapon system, or logistical support system (for example, long-distance tanker aircraft) is essential for defense and in compliance with Article 9. Although the SDF has usually accounted for less than 1% of GNP since 1976, Japan's economy is the world's second largest, so the defense budget is one of the largest. According to authoritative James Auer, however, the Self-Defense Forces (SDF) would be insufficient for Japan's defense (for example, against North Korea) without the U.S. supplement in heavily militarized Northeast Asia. The likelihood of North Korea using nuclear weapons seems less than many Americans suggest. Use of nuclear weapons by North Korea would almost certainly result in a kind of self-genocide.

A substantial majority of Japan's constitutional lawyers criticize some government policies as violating the letter and/or spirit of Article 9. They contend the SDF are unconstitutional, not because of a mindless idealism, but because they believe the text of the 1947 Constitution does not lend itself to a less rigorous interpretation.

They generally support Japan's mode of constitutional pacifism. Rarely indeed do foreign mass media accurately convey the nature of Japan's constitutional discourse.

Opposition political parties have modified long-held positions regarding Article 9 in recent years. For example, in the 1990s under Prime Minister Tomiichi Murayama the Social Democratic Party first recognized the constitutionality of the SDF. In 2000 the Japan Communist Party changed a policy established in 1958 and approved the use of the *de facto* military, the SDF, in "emergencies" while continuing to claim the SDF are unconstitutional. The largest parliamentary opposition party, the Democratic Party of Japan, reversed its policy and now supports the use of the SDF in United Nations peace-keeping operations.

Japan has long been a leading provider of non-military ODA (Official Development Assistance) under OECD (Organization for Economic Cooperation and Development) policies and a most generous supporter of the United Nations. Since the hotly contested passage of the 1992 UN Peace-Keeping Operations Cooperation Law ("PKO Law"), Japan has expanded considerably its overseas involvements, but without participating in hostilities (for example, in Cambodia, East Timor, Africa, Afghanistan, and the Indian Ocean). In October, 2001 (due in part to America's "9/11" tragedy), Japan first allowed under new law SDF personnel to use small arms abroad not only to defend themselves but also to protect those "under their care," such as refugees and wounded troops of other countries.

The general public considers the SDF constitutionally acceptable as long as they do not fight abroad and are of relatively modest capability. When asked in 2000 to name up to two primary fiinctions of the SDF in the 21st century, about 70% felt the primary function was disaster relief, while about 41% cited military deterrence and 36% chose international peace-keeping and emergency aid abroad as most important. Only 10.7% supported an increase in the size of the SDF, while 13.9% called for cut-backs and 61.7% thought current levels appropriate.

Japan's implementation of Article 9 in the spirit of the Preamble in international relations has been premised for decades on a realistic popular and governmental perception that Japan is not likely to be militarily threatened by a foreign state. Other countries have been similarly blessed by the absence of a credible threat on their borders for various geopolitical reasons, though this reality is rarely given the attention it deserves in security analysis. Japan may also see itself as too useful to other nations' economies and technologies to make foreign attack a rational option. Many in the highly militarized political cultures of the United States and other countries which see themselves as persistently (permanently?) threatened have found Japan's approach hard to understand. Under its comprehensive security policy, Japan has felt no need for military power commensurate with its economic and technological prowess. Elites and others have also been leery of military influence on domestic politics, such as led to disaster in World War II.

To illustrate a practical consequence, the recent development of Japan's NEC Earth Simulator, which works at a speed of 35,000 gigallops (a gigallop is a billion mathematical operations per second), was driven by a desire to understand climate change, global warming, and earthquake patterns. In contrast, the policy priority served by U.S. supercomputers, which in combination have less capacity than the NEC Earth Simulator, is simulation of weaponry. Like Japan's dual-use technology (for example, in optics), the Simulator may benefit the U.S. military among other uses.

The Japan-United States Treaty of Mutual Cooperation and Security (1960) has served Japan's legitimate geopolitical needs. And Japan's operative priorities have been served by Article 9 pacifism. The Supreme Court of Japan has never directly decided whether the Self-Defense Forces founded in 1954 are unconstitutional. The 1959 Supreme Court's Sunagawa Decision refrained from finding the Japan-U.S.

Security Treaty unconstitutional, in an Article 9 case contesting the extension of a runway at the Tachikawa Air Base of the U.S.

In the famous Naganuma Nike Missile Site Case, the Sapporo District Court (1973) found the SDF unconstitutional, but the high court (1976) and the Supreme Court (1982) reversed on technical grounds, avoiding the constitutional issue. Farmers in Naganuma in northern Japan had challenged a government decision to establish a Nike anti-aircraft missile site in a forest reserve, alleging that the base illegally interfered with their water supply and flood control system and also violated their Article 9 right to peace. The appellate courts decided that the farmers had lost their standing to sue when the government eliminated their water problems.

A 1987 Tokyo High Court decision, let stand by the government, denied that in time of peace Defense Agency activities involve a higher public interest than those of civilian airports or other government agencies. In the spirit of Article 9, noise pollution was seen as a legitimate public concern and noise from military aircraft as a violation of the personal rights of citizens. In other cases the courts have ordered the government to compensate local residents for noise from U.S. and SDF aircraft.

On March 6, 2002, the Kanazawa District Court ordered the government to pay Y810 million to compensate 1,729 (of 1,776) plaintiffs for SDF aircraft noise around the Komatsu Air SDF base exceeding the tolerable level under the international environmental standard, 75 WECPNL (Weighted Equivalent Continuous Perceived Noise Level). For the first time in such noise-pollution cases, the plaintiffs claimed the SDF are unconstitutional. The court declined to judge the issue of constitutionality or to require the SDF to limit its flights and make future compensation payments.

What Japan has not done under Article 9 is as instructive as what it has done. Japan's government interprets Article 9 to mean that Japan may not come to the assistance of another state (principally, the United States) under a collective self-defense arrangement, because Article 9 does not permit the use of force to settle international disputes, whether alone or with another nation. Japan has no independent military command structure. By policy, Japan is sworn not to develop, possess, introduce or use nuclear weapons. Unlike some European democracies, Japan has no national security law under which freedom of expression might be restricted during times of emergency. Neither the Constitution nor other laws until 2003 have had provisions related to acts of war, such as declaring war or concluding peace treaties. No article refers to martial law or military courts. Until a controversial amendment of November, 2001, the SDF Law mandated no "defense secrets" (except under the Japan-U.S. Security Treaty).

In 2003, however, for the first time since 1945, Japan adopted laws which ease efficient governmental and SDF response to "military attack situations," while reaffirming its rigorously defense-oriented foreign policy under Article 9 and "utmost" protection of fundamental human rights. A supplementary Diet resolution requires other laws within a year to assure the safety and rights of citizens during emergencies, not to increase possible restraints on national security grounds. Military emergencies remain unlikely to occur. The new laws enable SDF forces establishing frontline battlefield positions, for example, to use or expropriate privately owned land, houses and trees. The SDF also became exempt in wartime from a number of peacetime legal procedures affecting, for example, road traffic, hospital activities, building standards, medical use of narcotics, and protection of national parks.

Under the 1954 SDF law, the primary duty of the SDF is the defense of Japan. If Japan is attacked or in imminent danger of attack, under 2003 law the government is required to draft a plan of action which must be approved by the Cabinet and the Diet. If the situation is extremely urgent, the government may mobilize the SDF without a plan of action, but the Diet has authority to halt by resolution measures taken by the government in response to military attack.

Among the "auxiliary duties" of the SDF are United Nations-sponsored peace-keeping activities, civil engineering projects (for example, the 690 personnel in East Timor in 2003), transport of state guests, and response to natural disasters and acts of terrorism. The new laws and attendant policy changes look toward a regime with an emergency management agency which deals with both military and other emergencies, an expanded national Security Council under the Prime Minister, prime ministerial power to issue orders to local government officials in time of war, and enhanced status for international peace-keeping activities. Peace-keeping activities have become a "primary duty" of the SDF, leading to new SDF equipment and organizational needs. In place of past *ad hoc* and allegedly ineffective response to emergency situations (for example, after the Kobe Earthquake of 1995, which cost 6,000 lives), the SDF will have specialized stand-by units for quick dispatch at home and abroad. Conscription is considered unconstitutional not only in the spirit of Article 9, but also under Article 18 which bans "bondage of any kind" and "involuntary servitude" except as punishment for crime.

Civil servants in general are forbidden by law from revealing secrets learned in the course of their work. The courts retain for themselves the power to determine whether a secret is a legitimate state secret or a political secret. All efforts to establish a state secrets law have been effectively opposed. The government's information disclosure responsibilities have been increased under the recent Information Disclosure Law (2001), the crowning achievement of the national Freedom of Information Movement. The Movement was led by prefectures and municipalities which passed many local freedom of information ordinances one by one over decades long before the national government acted in this issue area.

It is not clear in 2003 whether Article 9 should be or will be amended to clarify Japan's right of self-defense. As many as 74% of Japanese have in recent years opposed amending the wording of Article 9. Should there come a time for amendment, Japan might seriously consider adding a third paragraph to Article 9, forever renouncing the development, manufacture, possession or use of nuclear, chemical, biological, or other (for example, electronic) weapons of mass destruction. It would enhance Japan's "honored place in an international society striving for the preservation of peace." Given its unique experience of disastrous militarism, atomic warfare and quasi-pacifism, might not Japan then quite appropriately urge others to do likewise? Any progress toward including such a commitment in constitutions would be a victory for humankind.

PART III

THE FUTURE

■ First published in Lawrence W. Beer (ed.), *Constitutional Systems in Late Twentieth Century Asia*, Seattle, University of Washington Press, 1992, pp. 707-718.

14

Conclusion: Towards Human Rights Constitutionalism in Asia and the United States?

⌘

The most significant development in institutions of politics and law during the twentieth century may have been the human rights revolution, a global explosion of awareness that humans of whatever size and shape, race and religion, sex and ethnic identity are all equally endowed from the womb with an inherent dignity requiring respectful response from governments and societies. The status of human rights has depended less on the instruments of force than on the elements of nobility and shame at exposure of barbarism in the human character. Human rights counterbalance unprecedented power to destroy peoples and environments, and give coherence and meaning to bewildering advances in knowledge, science, and technology, and to their worldwide diffusion.

Millennia of yearning and groping in all inhabited points on the planet for humane standards of just governance gradually issued in diverse political wisdoms, some recorded in writing, others refined and passed on by communal ritual, art, story-telling and unwritten law. Coerced world dialogue on the foundations of statehood during the recent centuries of Western colonialism and imperialism brought global attention to Western conceptions of constitutionalism, rights and law. This discourse gradually undercut the legitimacy of Western dominance with universalist doctrines calling for the freedom and equal treatment of all peoples and for democratic processes under law. These ideas also undermined in whole or in part a multitude of non-Western understandings of just rule and community life.

Efforts to institutionalize *human* rights under international law based on recognition of each human's inherent dignity began in nineteenth-century Europe's attention to the treatment of war victims and prisoners,[1] and meshed with the earlier spread of documentary constitutionalism after the revolutions of the United States and France. Comprehensive formulations of human rights did not gain serious worldwide consideration until the International Bill of Human Rights developed after 1945 in the United Nations, following the long agonies of world wars, colonialism, and regional and civil conflicts. Majoritarian democracy has failed as a sufficient basis for human rights enforcement, but until recent decades, human rights were not commonly discussed as *the* appropriate defining foundation for constitutionalist government everywhere. In public discourse and academic analysis on Asia, as on other continents, economic development, military conflict, leadership problems, and political culture preoccupied scholars and publicists, to the neglect of law and constitutions as elements of a successful civilization.[2] Yet "constitutionalizing" a right is often important for its legitimizing and institutionalization.

By 1991, 168 of 173 states had a single-document national constitution with substantial provisions about human rights, and shared for the first time in history a common understanding of a few alternative modern models of government and law. Of course, understanding among the world's opinion-makers implies precision about disagreements rather than agreement and tells us nothing about the views of a general citizenry. Discourse was still dominated by Western categories without adequate attention to non-Western varieties of constitutionalism. Old terminology—words like "liberalism," "conservatism," "communism," "socialism," "modernization," "development," "free enterprise," "individualism," and "collectivism"—does not enliven transcultural analysis of the foundations of constitutional government and human rights.[3] Usage may be particularly brittle in America's public parlance, because rhetoric and human rights realities have in many respects parted company here. In Asia and elsewhere, ethnic tribalism and religious faith often replaced secular ideology as dominant public forces, along with economic factors. But politico-legal traditions in many countries retained their relevance for the future insofar as they could accommodate the intellectual power and moral authority behind human rights imperatives. Human rights arguments gained widening acceptance as an effective response to exaggerated collectivism or individualism and amoral legal positivism,[4] and as the basis for a life with dignity in a free community.

"Mutualism" was offered in chapter 1 as a better word than "individualism" or "collectivism" to capture the ideals of human rights constitutionalism. Unlike some terms, mutualism would not posit as fact or norm a weak community composed of solipsistic selves, but rather the possibility of strong awareness of reciprocity as inherent in interpersonal relations and government-citizen relations, and the inseparability of rights and responsibilities under democratic law. Mutualism does not recognize a war of all against all in economic life; nor does it legitimize hierarchical strata determinative of unequal rights in society. Institutionalization of human rights law began in the modern West, but much more noteworthy than their geographical and historical origins, human rights have become the most widely accepted universalist, secular basis for government and law in the world.[5]

In the analytical terms used in chapter 1, human rights constitutionalism has become the most commonly shared constitutional ideal in Asia. Within the ruling and politically active elites of many countries, even in some "nonconstitutionalist" authoritarian states, an increasingly firm agreement was emerging that the primary purpose of government and law is precisely to protect and promote human rights, not for example, property rights, state rights, or military interests. Respect for individual human rights in criminal and civil justice, socio-economic rights, rights of political participation, and other civil liberties were commonly perceived to be essential to a national claim of honoring human rights in law and policy. In recent years, the practical issue for human rights constitutionalism was not simply how to limit as suspect the power of government, in general or in deference to a particular economic or social interest group, but how to channel under law as much power as possible on behalf of human rights, whether to restrain police or mobs or to gain pragmatic cooperation between the public and private sectors on economic problems. Constitutionalist government requires that power be divided and that it be limited in some contexts (for example, in regulating business and press freedom); but it is just as essential for human rights to restrict private power (for example, in giantist mass media companies, global corporations, and exploitive landholdings), to enhance a government's capacity to effectively deliver services, and to monopolize means of coercion to protect personal security rights. In the economically less prosperous countries of Asia, insufficient government resources and the limited reach of official authority beyond major cities have sometimes meshed with private denial of rights, even where government policy strongly favored rights. Government priorities and public values rather than inadequate resources seemed to explain America's major performance deficiencies in criminal and social justice.

What of trends in Asia's constitutional systems? In 1991 five themes stood out in Asia's constitutional politics: leadership succession problems; corruption based on family or patron-client favoritism; the military's diminishing role in governance; the salience of religion as a positive or negative force in constitutionalism; and human rights issues.

In the 1980s and 1990, leadership changed hands in many Asian countries, not just in the sense of one leader succeeding another—after election, assassination, natural death, popular upheaval, coup d'état, or oligarchic selection—but in the deeper sense of a generation passing away and established modes of governance beginning to change direction. By 1991, the incidence and legitimacy of militarized and military-dominant regimes appeared to be receding in importance and civilian constitutionalism advancing. It was at least being challenged, except perhaps in Indonesia and Burma. Human rights concerns found fresh emphasis on the world scene with the diplomacy of President Jimmy Carter (1977–1981), with the spreading acceptance of United Nations and regional human rights documents, and with the growth of human rights studies and advocacy. At the fortieth anniversary of the United Nations' Declaration of Universal Human Rights on December 10, 1988, on balance, the increased rhetorical prominence of individual rights in Asia seemed to be matched by more government and private effort than in the past to institutionalize constitutional rights in law.

Religion—most widely, Islam and Buddhism—occupied a central place in the increasingly firm sense of constitutional identity that emerged in many Asian nations and subnational groupings. Christianity played a major role in the democracy revolutions of the Philippines and South Korea, and buttressed other supports for human rights in Japan, Taiwan, Indonesia and elsewhere. Religions were accorded a modicum of tolerance in China and Vietnam, while religio-ethnic intolerance was a factor in communal tensions within India, Sri Lanka, Malaysia, China, Indonesia, and other countries. Nevertheless, religion as a powerful motive force either for democratic development and tolerance or for hypernationalism and intolerance was still neglected in constitutional studies. The distinguished commentator on religious affairs, Martin Marty, explains:[6]

> Everybody, 15, 25 years ago, and for the past 200 years, was predicting that the world's future would be secular, rational, serene. The religions that would survive would be rational, tolerant, cool, ecumenical, interactive.

> To everybody's surprise, therefore, we have to cope with the fact that every hot spot in the world . . . is nationalist and is tribal, and usually religious, and when it's religious, it's fundamentalist or fundamentalist-like. . . .
>
> Americans get much madder over the Pledge of Allegiance and burning the flag than they do about equality, justice and freedom.

A further trend was a generational change of leadership, linked in many cases with shifts in the status of military politics and human rights. One symbol of such transitions was the passing on January 7, 1989, of Emperor Hirohito of Japan. Although postwar Japan has been marked by peaceful democracy, Hirohito had continued to remind some, at home and abroad, of the aggressive militarist government which ended in September 1945. Emperor Akihito and Empress Michiko were both educated more to peaceful internationalism and awareness of human rights than to Shinto nationalism. During U.N.-sanctioned actions against Iraq to liberate Kuwait and oil flow in 1990–91, the strong opposition in Japan to sending military aid to the U.S.-dominated "coalition forces" confirmed dramatically the seriousness of Japan's constitutional renunciation of war (Article 9); in addition, many criticized as "unconstitutional" Japan's generous financial support of the United Nations effort. A major issue for constitutional and political debate is the shape which Japan's non-military world leadership will take in the 1990s.[7]

Nepotistic succession in India's Congress Party occurred when Rajeev Gandhi followed Indira Gandhi as Prime Minister in 1984, but ended with his own tragic assassination in 1991. The sons of North Korea's Kim Il-sung and Singapore's Lee Kuan Yew also rose. A son or daughter of a national leader may have excellent credentials, as in the case of Chiang Ching-kuo (1910–1988) of Taiwan and apparently in the case of Benazir Bhutto of Pakistan, the first woman prime minister of a major Islamic country, removed prematurely by the military in 1990. Or legitimate doubts may exist about the stature of a leader's offspring, as in the case of Kim Jong-Il. The problem may be especially sensitive if, as in Thailand, the monarch (King Bhumibol Adulyadej) is of great constitutional importance and the heir apparent excites considerably less respect than the incumbent.

Restraint of abuses of family power remained a seminal constitutional problem in a number of Asian systems, due to the clash between public duties under law and ingrained tendencies toward family favoritism and patron-client loyalty. However, efforts against familistic corruption in the Philippines, South Korea and India were sometimes impressive; in most Asian countries, such corruption was not fatalistically accepted as the norm or inevitably normal behavior. For example, the Philippine Constitution bans presidential appointment of relatives to high office.[8]

Cambodia was ravaged by Pol Pot's massacre of his own people after the Vietnam War, and then by a protracted civil-international war involving Vietnam. The great exodus of refugees from Indochina (Laos, Vietnam, Cambodia) and Afghanistan after 1975 raised the world's awareness of human rights during the 1980s. Despite continuing multi-lateral efforts, peace, a viable constitutional order, and the stability essential for human rights have eluded Cambodia, a country with no experience of democratic leadership succession. For China and its Communist Party, the historic period of group leadership which began in 1935 entered its final phase when Mao Zedong and Chou Enlai died around 1975, but will not end until Deng Xiaoping passes away. Modern China has no precedent for such a generational succession, and Deng's efforts to put new leaders—most notably, Hu Yaobang and Zhao Ziyang—into place in the 1980s proved abortive. In June 1989, Premier Li Peng, his colleagues, and the People's Liberation Army, lost public trust and rendered the future even more problematic when they crushed the democracy movement in Tiananmen Square, Beijing. Semi-capitalism combined with harsh repression. Other Asian popular movements called, some successfully, for more freedom and more democratic governance in Bangladesh, Burma, Nepal, Pakistan, the Philippines, South Korea and Taiwan. More local autonomy was fought for in Tibet and Sri Lanka (Tamils). The Philippines and South Korea have shared in the past a major constitutional problem affecting human rights: the unwillingness of an incumbent to relinquish power after a legally set period in office, and the lack of a stable, routinized system in law and politics for passing from one leader or group of leaders to the next. Since 1961, South Korea's presidents have been former generals first chosen by their military colleagues rather than by popular vote and open processes. At the end of Roh Tae Woo's five-year term in 1993, will the military allow transition to a president of civilian background? In 1990, Burma's General Newin allowed elections, then suppressed the democratic victors. Will the pattern of military political involvement change in China, Pakistan, the Philippines, and Taiwan? If not, as in Thailand in February, 1991, will the military respect or dismiss the need for quick return to democratic civilian government? Which general will succeed President Soeharto in the 1990s?

Since the 1940s, some of Asia's military-dominated governments have had noteworthy peacetime accomplishments, and one-party civilian governments obviously can be as inimical to constitutionalism and human rights as military leaders. These points are clear from the repressive record of Asia's communist and other non-constitutionalist states, and from instances elsewhere of military leaders yielding to civilian democracy. Nevertheless, a military is an irregular center of government power accountable only to itself and prone to martial suspension of ordinary constitutionalist law. In general, military primacy in a government is as reliable an indicator of weak constitutionalism as are deficient systemic provisions for democratic leadership succession, freedom of expression, or criminal justice rights.

In sum, prescinding from their wildly varying and in some cases irrelevant levels of economic development, the accomplishments of many Asian countries since 1945 in overcoming formidable obstacles and building law, constitutionalism and human rights commitments into their state systems and policies have been impressive. Where human rights constitutionalism is not accepted, more peoples have grounds for hope (if not optimism) than have reasons for pessimism about the likelihood of humane change.

A NEW AMERICAN CONSTITUTIONALISM?

A comparative study of constitutional systems in Asia at the Bicentennial of the United States Constitution and Bill of Rights can sharpen perspective on the state of American constitutionalism. The U.S. Constitution is of course important, but public policy choices and deficient leadership, not lack of resources, explain more than the operative constitution about the appalling quality of life and criminal justice endured by tens of millions of Americans and passively accepted by a majority in government, politics and society. That acknowledged, nevertheless, as an instrument for modern and democratic governance, the U.S. Constitution, with all its amendments and judicial interpretations to date, seems defective. For example, it does not include a clear statement of human rights or American constitutional goals and values. Formal revision of the near-sacred text may not be on the near political horizon, but seems needed. More modestly, may not a constitutional consensus exist or be achievable on one or more of the following issues explicitly dealt with in one or more Asian constitutional systems discussed in this volume?

a *A new Preamble*—A simple, eloquent formulation of what American constitutionalism and democracy stand for, drawing upon historically honored sources such as the Declaration of Independence, the U.S. Constitution, and Abraham Lincoln's major addresses. The Preamble might end with elucidation of a few key policy commitments, spelled out as "Directive Principles of State Policy."

b *Judicial review*—Formal recognition in the U.S. Constitution of the power of federal courts to determine issues of constitutionality and legality.

c *Restraints on militarization and possession of arms*—A constitutional renunciation of the use of force as a means of settling international disputes apart from carefully delimited exceptions, and a stated commitment to the development of reliance upon United Nations peace-keeping capacities. Unnecessary and excessive American use of armed forces in Grenada, Nicaragua, Panama, and the Persian Gulf region in recent years have manifested a highly militarized political culture and a sometimes lawless lack of restraint which are at odds with U.S. claims to respect peace, life, law, and constitutional government. Finally, the current serious abuse of "the right to bear arms" clause could be remedied by an amendment removing the provision and instituting restraints on the private possession and use of firearms.

d *Socioeconomic rights*—Explicit constitutional provision for:

1 The right of each person to minimum levels of food, clothing and shelter in keeping with human dignity. A mandate for remedial action on behalf of the endemically disadvantaged. (A world standard for local determination of a survival wage is needed.)

2 The centrality of the family and parental-filial responsibilities in the nurturing and education of children.

3 The right to roughly equal public education, rather than radically unequal opportunities as at present, based on tax revenue differentials among school districts.

4 The right of all to a modest level of publicly assured health care, but not to all expensive medical procedures; a mixed (public + private) health care delivery system, as in a number of democracies.

5 Employee rights to organize unions, to bargain collectively, to strike with impunity, to work under labor conditions as safe and humane as those of management, and to freely report employer wrongdoing to authorities without fear of reprisal. (The latter, because in the U.S., private employers now commonly have a legal right to dismiss an employee "at will," that is, for any reason, even for reporting a company's crimes. Public employees are also punished for "whistleblowing".)[9]

e *Equality rights*—The right to equal treatment under public and private law. A ban on both negative discrimination based on race, gender, religion or ethnic identity, and positive discrimination (for example, in criminal justice practices) based on wealth or social position.

f *Political participation rights*—

1 The right to vote under radically simplified voter registration requirements at all levels of government, in place of the current restrictive and disparate requirements.

2 The right of each political party to publicly funded, limited air time on TV and radio. A ban on TV and radio political advertisements during election campaigns, because abuse has proven to be serious and unavoidable.

3 The right of each candidate for major national office to public campaign funds, and a restraint on the amount that may be spent on any campaign for national office (i.e. Congress, Senate, Presidency).

4 A limitation of the President to one six-year term.

5 Exclusion from federal appointive posts of close relatives of elective or appointive high officials.

g "*First Amendment rights*"—This constitutional provision seems appropriately unchangeable, but not in its interpretation (as suggested under d) and f), for example). More in keeping with constitutional practice elsewhere would be an approach to the separation of religion and the state that, while not establishing a specific religion, is not secularist but appreciative of the general public value of religion. While U.S. law bans a few minutes of content-neutral silent meditation in public schools, many democratic states support opportunities for education in the religions of choice in a spirit of tolerance. With respect to freedom of expression, as yet only a narrow spectrum of views seems to enjoy effective sociopolitical tolerance.

Documentary changes are obviously less critical to a living constitution than the intent of the political and legal professions to honor human rights. Using again the terms in chapter 1, the United States seems more in favor of majoritarian democracy than human rights constitutionalism, with only limited constitutionalist constraints on private wealth and private power. Asians who lavishly praise American democracy are often uninformed or less interested in human rights within the United States than in discrete politeness or aid emanating from the U.S. Unless they are refugees from one of Asia's repressive regimes who have happily tasted freedom and local community kindness and have avoided urban and rural poverty pockets, the positive imagery Asians may have of America seems exaggerated. American public rhetoric about rights sometimes overstates U.S. accomplishments and rarely reflects knowledge of comparative data. In fact, the U.S. is an unusually dangerous country to live in and, from a human rights perspective, governmentally harsh.[10] One is rarely electable to public office on a strong human rights platform. The economic system is less humane to the less fortunate than other prosperous democracies and some authoritarian states, and since 1981 has fostered a widening division between the majority and a very large, endemically deprived minority. Compared to most other democracies, the U.S. plutocratically favors the extraordinary wealth of a relative few.

The American President has been elected by a small plurality of voting-age Americans; indeed, only a bare majority participated in the constitutional system's most important election in 1988. The school system has no plan to remedy the national pattern of political apathy or "disconnectedness." Many of Asia's democratic electoral systems have much more impressive records. In addition, the results of U.S. voting in some recent elections have been more affected by unrestrained spending and the manipulation of TV images in negative campaigning and deceptive use of flag symbolism than by the candidates' accomplishments or positions on issues. In this constitutionally crucial mode of corruption and in campaign spending per national candidate, perhaps no Asian (or other?) democracy rivals the United States.[11] In some respects at least, the influence of American constitutionalism abroad is more in its afterglow and abstract ideals than in its current substantive performance.

Besides slavery and its enduring aftermath, non-white immigrants—most notably Asians—were "ineligible to citizenship" from 1790 to 1952.[12] The greatness of America's living constitutionalism has not been in the country's human rights performance or its commitment to tolerance of diverse beliefs and ideas. Many have surpassed the U.S. on both scores, without the pretentious claims of superiority all too common among Americans. Some of these nations have reinforced human rights in the world by ratifying the International Bill of Human Rights, while our government has declined to ratify the major Covenants with a dismissive claim to be honoring rights more effectively than countries which do ratify.[13] With meanness of spirit, the U.S. absented itself from UNESCO, a major world forum for human rights dialogue. Domestically, only two relatively similar political parties are viable in American political culture, the Democratic Party and the Republican Party, each with interchangeable parts; while other democracies accommodate a more vibrant diversity of viewpoints in organized parties.

Rather than in the above performance categories, if there is greatness in American constitutionalism, it may be in its halting and sometimes weakly sustained, yet historically impressive effort to *welcome* to citizenship and community life *all* ethnic and religious groupings and eventually all races as *equally human*, subject to only a few conditions: a willingness to honor the constitutional system which lends a measure of coherence to American culture, a willingness to speak the English language, and a willingness to assert one's subcultural and other interests in a manner minimally respectful of good manners, fairness, and constitutional conventions. That, at least, seems the operative ideal more in keeping with the Declaration of Independence than with the 18th century constitution, as we try to leave racism behind. While sometimes caught up in arrogant imaginings that "We are the world," as the song would have it, Americans at their authentic best do, in a very large country, try to live out a dream that is appropriate in part for the whole world, a dream of respect for diverse peoples within a democratic community. That element of broad, universalist idealism about *the possibility of tolerance and respect* for each human as human is admirable. It is not indigenous to at least some Asian constitutional cultures. Tolerance of each person is more critical to human rights than tolerance of all ideas, not an American trait. Human rights constitutionalism requires both tolerance and assurance to all of basic needs and services, the goals of many Asian constitutional systems in the late twentieth century.

NOTES

1 On the Red Cross movement, and the evolution of human rights treaty law, see David Forsythe, *Human Rights and World Politics*, Lincoln, University of Nebraska Press, 1989, 7–23.

2 Vernon Bogdanor, ed., *Constitutions in Democratic Politics*, Aldershot, U.K., Gower Publishing Co., 1988, 1–13, 380–386.

3 On the theoretical importance of regional and local economic variations, on which analogies can be made regarding constitutionalism, see Benjamin Harris, *The Road Less Traveled: A Development Economist's Quest*, Canberra, National Centre for Development Studies, 1989; and Kazuko Tsurumi and Tadashi Kawata, eds., *Naihatsuteki Hatten Ron* (The Theory of Endogenous Development), Tokyo, Tokyo University Press, 1989, and the review by Ronni Alexander in *Journal of International Studies*, Sophia University, Tokyo, July, 1989, 79–83.

4 On the distinctive relativism of American legal positivism, see Mary Ann Glendon, *Abortion and Divorce in Western Law: American Failures, European Challenges*, Cambridge, Harvard University Press, 1987, 114–125.

5 Jack Donnelly, *Universal Human Rights in Theory and Practice*, Ithaca, Cornell University Press, 1989; Robert F. Drinan, *Cry of the Oppressed: History and Hope in the Human Rights Revolution*, New York, Harper & Row, 1988.

6 In 1990, Martin Marty and a multinational group were engaged in a comparative study of fundamentalism in the world; interviewed by Carol M. Ostrom, "A Study of Fundamentalism," *The Seattle Times*, March 24, 1990. On religion and public life in the U.S., see *First Things*, a monthly. On problems attendant to foreign perceptions of Islam, see Akbar S. Ahmed, "Postmodernist Perceptions of Islam: Observing the Observer," *Asian Survey*, March, 1991, 213–231.

7 See Courtney Purrington and A.K., "Tokyo's Policy Responses During the Gulf Crisis," *Asian Survey*, April, 1991, 307.

8 See *Supra*, Chapter 8, Article 7, Sec. 13, Philippine Constitution.

9 On the limited effects of whistleblowing, see R.A. Johnson and M.K. Kraft, "Bureaucratic Whistleblowing and Policy Change," *The Western Political Quarterly*, Vol. 43, No. 4, December, 1990, 849.

10 See David Ellwood, *Poor Support: Poverty in the American Family*, New York, Basic Books, 1988; Michael B. Katz, *The Undeserving Poor: From the War on Poverty to the War on Welfare*, New York, Pantheon Books, 1989 (1990 figures continued this trend); *The Forgotten Half: Non-College Youth in America*, Washington, D.C. William T. Grant Foundation Commission on Work, Family, and Citizenship, January, 1988. The proportion of jobs that are low paying will continue to increase rapidly in the years ahead.

Another indicator of U.S. harshness is its leadership of the world in number of citizens in jail, 426 per 100,000, well above the next two in this unenviable ranking, South Africa (333) and the Soviet Union (268). Black Americans are incarcerated at four times the rate of black imprisonment in South Africa, 3,109 to 729 per 100,000. On the Sentencing Project, see *The Christian Science Monitor*, March 8, 1991.

See also Frances Moore Lappe', *Rediscovering America's Values* (New York: Ballantine Books, 1990), and the U.S. Census Bureau Report to the House Committee on Children, Youth, and Families, Washington, D.C., March, 1990.

11 See Bingham Powell, "American Voter Turnout in Comparative Perspective," *American Political Science Review*, Vol. 80, No. 1, 1986, 35; and David Scott, *Christian Science Monitor*, May 22, 1990.

12 On the historic experience of Asian immigrants and the racist views of some of America's Founding Fathers, see Ronald Takaki, *Strangers from a Different Shore: A History of Asian Americans*, New York, Penguin Books, 1990, especially at 11–18.

13 For instances of American opposition to international human rights, see David P. Forsythe, "Human Rights in U.S. Foreign Policy," *Political Science Quarterly*, Vol. 105, No. 3, 1990, 435; and R. Brody, P. Parker, and D. Weissbrodt, "Major Developments in 1990 at the U.N. Commission on Human Rights," *Human Rights Quarterly*, Vol. 12, 1990, 559.

15

Afterword: Asian Constitutionalism in the Twenty-first Century

⌘

The twentieth century saw the most barbaric of wars, but also the beginning of a revolution in thinking about constitutions and human rights law. This continuing revolution emerged in the West out of horror at war and outrage at the widespread inhumane treatment of the individual by laws and governments, and a tradition of constitutional reflection. It was "globalized" by a combination of colonialism, imperialism, and the free choice of many non-Western peoples who gained independence after the great wars. With over half the world's population Asia was profoundly affected by Western constitutional thought but dominated by Europe, the United States and Japan. By the 1930s Japan was the only fully independent Asian state.

During the Second World War, U.S. President Franklin D. Roosevelt spoke of human rights in terms of "Four Freedoms" for which the Allies were fighting: Freedom of Speech, the Press, and Expression; Freedom of Religion and Worship; Freedom from Want and Poverty; and Freedom from Fear. Later, his wife Eleanor would play an important role, along with other representatives of diverse cultures, in the formulation of a more expansive view of individual rights and freedoms in the United Nations Universal Declaration of Human Rights approved by the United Nations General Assembly on December 10, 1948.

That Declaration gradually took on the color of international humane customary law in the decades which followed. It has been supplemented by numerous refinements in related international legal instruments. It has placed human rights at the center of constitutional discourse around the world, however imperfectly implemented by many countries. Human rights have become the subject of a global movement sustained by still limited coordination and an infrastructure of non-governmental and governmental entities promoting and protecting a few or all enunciated human rights. The movement is an enterprise based on hope of ever more respectful treatment of each person.

Most of the 192 UN member states have made human rights a core element in their national constitutionalism, along with nation-state sovereignty, limitation and division of state power, and the principles of rule of law and popular sovereignty. The term "human rights constitutionalism" seems preferable to "democratic constitutionalism" which commonly overemphasizes the will of the majority and property rights to the neglect of socioeconomic and criminal justice rights.

Discussions of the slogan "globalization" early in the 21st century centered more often on problems of economic and technological development and national security than on the status of human rights in diverse cultures. But the global collective conscience has ached in response to tragic massive slaughters and unaccountable governments; human rights are now at the political margin less frequently than in the past.

In 2005 UN Secretary General Kofi Anan described human rights as the third pillar of the UN's architecture along with development and security. The International Council on Human Rights Policy finds human rights increasingly salient:[1]

> International law has also extended its range enormously since the 1960s. Not only are the core treaties much more widely recognized; many new standards have been created, and international human rights law has reached out beyond states to encompass private actors. Far more governments and many other organizations—from nongovernmental organizations (NGOs) to business and trade unions—have integrated human rights explicitly in their policies (or at least their rhetoric), and a host of non-governmental and civil society organizations now refer to human rights in their work. Human rights have also become academically respectable: numerous universities have created human rights centers and offer courses.

Three factors in the background of constitutional discourse in Asia and elsewhere deserve special attention: 1) governmental transparency and freedom of information flow regarding climate change and other effects of environmental pollution as a likely condition for human survival; 2) a world haunted by the presence of a number of nuclear weapons and other weapons of mass destruction (e.g. chemical, biological, electronic and space weaponry) that is excessive in light of national security needs, a further threat to human civilization; and 3) deeply institutionalized ignorance and intolerance of foundational beliefs different from one's own on the part of governmental and other cultural elites, sometimes linked with ethnic bias. Such intolerance has served as an excuse for indiscriminate mass killings, in radical denial of human rights.

TOLERANCE OF HUMAN RIGHTS

The walls of intolerance and ignorance are thick, but high level cross-cultural discourse is increasing. In Asia, Islam, Christianity, Buddhism, Confucianism, Hinduism, and political and legal canons from the West provide cultural resources useful in discussing constitutionalism and nurturing tolerance of human rights. In academe, thousands of scholars in the Association for Asian Studies and other learned societies continue to build an infrastructure of reliable studies facilitating development of informed policy options. More by the undramatic accumulation over decades of increasingly precise and perceptive studies of elements within diverse cultural systems than by theories rooted in abstractions (Asian and non-

Asian), Asianists have picked away at the task of revealing Asians as humans to those of other regions. Knowledgeable Asian constitutional lawyers interact with each other and foreign counterparts in such forums as the International Association of Constitutional Law and the Fulbright exchange programs.[2]

A great majority of Muslims live in Southern Asia and a large majority of these are moderate. In this era of warring in the Middle East journalistic coverage of events often conveys the impression that Muslims are generally extreme and intolerant in their views.[3] Hundreds of millions of Muslims are in Bangladesh, Pakistan, Afghanistan, Indonesia, India, Malaysia, and elsewhere in Asia as noteworthy minorities. Their constitutional systems and discourse commonly meld Islamic law (Sharia) with indigenous, culture-specific legalisms and secular legal forms in varying degrees affected by the European civil law tradition. Sadly, relatively few graduate from university in the West with even elemental knowledge of Islam, or the other major traditions of Buddhism (for example, in Sri Lanka, Thailand, Japan, and Korea) and Confucianism.

Given this background, "A Common Word between Us and You," a lengthy, substantive letter of 138 Muslim scholars, religious leaders and intellectuals of forty-two countries sent to all other "peoples of the Scripture" (i.e. Christians and Jews) on October 13, 2007, is historically momentous. The document rests on a major achievement of consensus among quite diverse Muslims and calls for peace, dialogue and tolerance based on a shared foundation in the love of God, love for one's neighbor, religious freedom, and rejection of violence on religious grounds. The project was sponsored by the Royal Aal al-Bays Institute for Islamic Thought in Jordan (www.ACommonWord.com) and received far too little coverage from the mainstream mass media. In response, many more leading Muslims have endorsed the letter. Yale Divinity School coordinated a response of hundreds of diverse Western religious figures (carried as a full-page ad. in *The New York Times*). Pope Benedict XVI invited a delegation of Muslim representative to Rome to begin major dialogue there in the spring of 2008.[4] The agenda will focus on the dignity of each person, interreligious dialogue based on reciprocal understanding, and an urgent call for instruction of the young in tolerance.

Any long-term solution to global terrorism and intercultural hostility will require institutionalized tolerance and consideration of human rights constitutionalism. The adequate foundation for human rights is attribution of transcendant public value to each person. Agreement on general and specific rights issues based on varying religious or philosophical views may be difficult or impossible to achieve over time; but human rights constitutionalism, as a kind of "secular religion," may provide a promising framework for global constitutional and legal discourse.

But why attribute such value to humans? How best motivate government leaders and their countrymen to comply with human rights law when it is inconvenient? Many human rights activists find motivation and justification for their work in religious and philosophical convictions that make it a duty to care for others, even strangers, even apparent enemies. Others simply feel good about human rights, even when they see no intellectual basis for claiming humans have significant value, and even when the work is hard.

Another problem affecting perspectives on Asia is illustrated by the experience of ASEAN (Association of Southeast Asian Nations), in contrast to that of Europe. ASEAN is a loose federation of nation states composed of Brunei Darussalam, Cambodia, Laos, Malaysia, Indonesia, The Philippines, Thailand, Vietnam, Singapore, and Myanmar. It was formalized as a political consultative forum in 1967 to combat colonialism and communism, to prevent escalation of regional tensions, and to facilitate the establishment of sovereign independent nation states and trade. Some members are constitutional democracies, others are not; but non-democratic countries agree that democratic peace is something all member states should aspire to. All subscribe to the "principle of non-interference in the internal affairs" of member states, even in the face of serious violations of human rights, as in Myanmar. Unlike the European Union, ASEAN did not arise out of a historic regional consensus on basic constitutional values legitimizing coercive collective response to member state violations of human rights. ASEAN, now with a Committee of Permanent Representatives in Jakarta, continues to be a useful institution for nation building, peaceful international relations, and free trade.

Regarding issues of cultural diversity, human rights principles transcend any one culture in Asia or elsewhere, but that does not preclude the need for sensitivity to important national and local norms and practices. All cultures honor human rights imperfectly. There is no right to cultural privacy, no legitimate claim to immunity from scrutiny under international human rights law. No adequate comprehensive standard exists for determining whether a particular policy or community practice is or is not compatible with human rights constitutionalism. In many cases of barbarism, such as torture, the violation of human rights is obvious. As a guideline for appropriately taking into account both human rights principles and cultural particulars when making a sophisticated judgement in a complex case, it is useful to ask what an indigenous human rights advocate familiar with local context would decide. In other words, is the claim that a given behavior (expressive or silent) is respectful of, compatible with human rights principles, intersubjectively persuasive to indigenous, authoritative human rights advocates?

In Asia (as elsewhere), great emphasis is placed on the family and fictive kinship systems when assessing the human rights record of a national government.[5] Families and communities try to pass on cultural values and customs to their young. The challenge comes in also teaching the young to welcome the existence in the world of many civilizationally legitimate alternatives to one's own culture.

Just as a hospitable family welcomes a guest and just as a good guest honors the host family's sensibilities on matters of importance, so should diverse ideas be welcomed courteously into the household and the community. Tolerance is grounded in respect for the person as such, not in high regard for the beauty or truth-value of the opinions, beliefs or convictions of other individuals or communities, which may have much or little transcultural, intersubjectively persuasive value. Mutualist tolerance should govern. While taking pride in their own identities and heritages, families and nations should welcome the expression of new ideas and diverse cultures as they would welcome a visitor with hospitable treatment. Diversity should delight. With this perspective, admittedly demanding, human rights can be newly appreciated in the great human traditions of courtesy, hospitality, and respect for honor.

Climate Change and Freedom of Information

In 2008, global warming and other effects of environmental pollution are already a clear and present danger to global ecology and human survival. The science is clear and not credibly questioned. This situation makes the constitutional freedom of information and the citizen's right to know about the environment among the paramount human rights considerations in Asia as elsewhere. Carbon emissions from China, India and the United States are leading sources of climate change. Vastly improved communication technology facilitates the processing and sharing of data for transparent global discourse on environmental policy and law, with strong support from the worldwide freedom of information movement (http://www.freedominfo.org). While many leaders in the world community, such as the G-8 group and oil interests, express serious concern, their response continues to be inadequate in light of the immediacy of the crisis. Governments and business interests, whether democratic or authoritarian, do not have the luxury of withholding accurate information on the environment. Political censorship or falsification of scientific reports on climate change, as in the White House of President George W. Bush, is not helpful.[6]

The Kyoto agreement, which the U.S. did not endorse, set targets for thirty-seven industrial countries to reduce emissions from 1990 levels, to be attained between 2008 and 2012 (for example, Japan 6%, European Union 8%); but it covered only 30% of the world's carbon emissions. The European Union set a post-2013 carbon emissions reduction goal, commiting itself to cuts of 20% to 30% below 1990 levels by 2020. At the UN Bali conference on climate change in December 2007, the European Union and developing countries went further, calling for reductions of between 25% and 40% by 2020. Japan was expected to call for a post-Kyoto Protocol framework involving all major polluters. Japan was also considering a major aid package for around forty developing countries, some of it targeted for emission reduction projects.[7]

In Asia, Japan is likely to continue for some time to be the leading country with resources useful to other nations in developing environmental law and communication systems and encouraging freedom of information.[8] Symbolic of Japan's position in Asia, a recent survey of the world's sixty most influential cities based on fourteen criteria finds Tokyo, by a very large margin, the most influential city in Asia, and fourth most important in the world (behind London, New York, and Paris). Among the criteria were such factors as economic and cultural strengths.[9]

Freedom of information and a right to a healthy and clean environment are major topics in Japan's constitutional discourse, along with the quasi-pacifism of Article 9. Japan's freedom of information system began with a small group of visionary professors and lawyers such as Hideo Shimizu, Takashi Ebayashi, Miko Akiyama, and Mamoru Kitaoka,[10] and developed over time into an effective national movement, culminating in Diet passage of the Information Disclosure Law.

Public demands for greater access to government information on the impact on health of pesticides, food additives, and drugs first surfaced in 1961 when Japan's Ministry of Health and Welfare delayed the release of information about thalidomide-related birth defects until ten months after the information became public in the West.

Freedom of information under law was first recognized in the Japanese courts on November 26, 1969, in a unanimous decision of the fifteen-member Supreme Court. The Justices held that Article 21 of the Constitution of Japan guarantees not only freedom of expression but also the freedom to gather news and report facts in service to the people's "right to know."[11] "Article 21. Freedom of assembly and association as well as speech, press and all other forms of expression are guaranteed." The occasion was the Hakata Station Film Case, in which the court confirmed the freedom of information but decided also that a judicial order to mass media companies to present evidenciary film to the court was constitutional as an exception to the rule when other credible evidence is not available.

In the 1970s, the importance of public access to government information was dramatically illustrated by the Lockheed Scandal.[12] It was first revealed in the U.S. Senate that popular Prime Minister Kakuei Tanaka had taken a bribe from the aircraft giant in exchange for his assistance in gaining lucrative contracts for Lockheed products. Tanaka was convicted.

In a 1978 case, the Supreme Court affirmed freedom of information and reserved to itself the power to decide whether government information is a legitimate state secret or merely political information, but upheld the conviction (and probation) of Takichi Nishiyama, a newspaper reporter. He had induced a Foreign Ministry secretary to give him secret information on funds involved in the reversion of Okinawa to Japanese sovereignty in 1972. Nishiyama claimed press freedom to expose Prime Minister Eisaku Sato's political lies, to no avail. Since 2000, however, reliable documentation revealed in the U.S. and Japan has confirmed Nishiyama's claim; he has sued the Japanese government for damaging his career.[13]

The freedom of information movement called upon local governments across the country to establish local information disclosure ordinances. The first public call for a disclosure law came in November 1976 from the Japan Consumers Federation, driven by product safety concerns (for example, the effects of dioxin and thalidomide). In September 1979, the Japan Civil Liberties Union issued an influential "Information Disclosure Guideline" to serve as a basis for discussion of proposals to establish local ordinances and a national freedom of information statute.

In 1981, the Citizens Movement for an Information Disclosure Law issued a Declaration of the Right of Public Access to Information, beginning with a quote from the Preamble of the Constitution of Japan and elucidating eight principles:[14]

> Government is a sacred trust of the people, the authority for which is derived from the people, the powers of which are exercised by the representatives of the people, and the benefits of which are enjoyed by the people.
>
> 1 As a general principle, all written documents and other information in the possession of the national government, local governments and other public entities shall be disclosed to the citizens and residents of Japan.
>
> 2 All citizens and residents of Japan shall be granted the right to request that the national government, local governments and other public entities disclose information and in the event that this request is denied, the requesting party shall have the right of appeal to an independent administrative committee or court of law and to receive a substantive decision on the merits of his request.
>
> 3 In the event that it is decided that, as an exception, certain information need not be disclosed, such information shall be limited to the necessary minimum, it shall be required that the conditions of such exceptional cases shall be clearly provided in the relevant law or ordinance, and the national government, local governments or other public entity shall bear the burden to prove the fulfillment of such conditions.
>
> 4 Information relating to matters affecting the life, health and security of mind and body of the people and other matters having a substantive effect

on the daily life of the people, as well as the records of deliberative councils, committees, and similar entities concerned with such matters shall be absolutely subject to disclosure, and disclosure thereof may not be denied for any reason.

5 Information relating to the determination of operational plans of monopolistic industries affecting the public welfare (electricity, gas supply, and similar industries) and other such information that exerts a substantial impact on the daily lives of the people shall be absolutely subject to disclosure . . .

6 Information relating to individuals must be disclosed to the individual concerned upon request. Unless otherwise provided by law, information relating to individuals shall not otherwise be disclosed. Provided, however, that the foregoing shall not apply to information concerning government employees or the employees of public entities.

7 The national government, local governments and other public entities shall bear the duties to record their activities, to preserve written documents and other forms of information, and to prepare indexes to such information.

8 Oversight committees in which citizens and residents may participate shall be established to monitor the assembly, disposition, use and disclosure of information. Further, it is recognized that laws concerning open meetings, privacy protection, and assets disclosure and like information of special public employees must be established in an Information Disclosure Law.

During the 1980s, minority political parties joined with private efforts to refine models, legislative drafts, and local ordinances dealing with government information disclosure. In July 1994, the Japan Federation of Bar Associations produced an outline for a law with strong guarantees of the people's right to know. By mid-1997 all parties agreed in principle on the desirability of information disclosure legislation and a law was passed in May 1999.[15] Grass-roots ordinances led to a national statute.

The first related local ordinance was passed in 1982 at Kanayama Village in Yamagata Prefecture.[16] Kanagawa Prefecture (Yokohama area) passed the second information disclosure ordinance on October 7, 1982. Other prefectures and cities followed suit. By 1998, all forty-seven prefectures had such ordinances. In 2000 the citizens movement published a compilation of 100 cases dealt with under information disclosure ordinances (*Joho Kokai no Jirei*), and this served as a precedential guide for other local government units in the process of establishing and interpreting ordinances around the country. On April 1, 2001, the Information Disclosure Law came into effect, calling for all local government units to have disclosure ordinances. By April 2004, virtually all 3,170 local governments units had established such ordinances. While in detail local disclosure systems differ, their provisions are very similar in basic requirements for openness and in setting up local citizen review committees to deal with allegations of improper government failure to provide requested information.

Each year thousands of requests are made by citizens and residents under such ordinances and under the Information Disclosure Law, and all but a few result in compliance with the request. If a request is turned down, in whole or in part, an appeal can be made to an independent local Disclosure Review Board composed of local community leaders such as lawyers, professors, retired officials and businessmen, and mass media professionals. Such boards are typically respected for their fairness and pro-disclosure preference. The national Information Disclosure Review Board (*Joho Kokai Shinsakai*) also enjoys prestige and trust under the statutory law.

Once the goal of a freedom of information law had been achieved, the citizens movement rethought its purposes and activities in service to the people's right to know. The "Information Clearing House Japan" (the English title for "*Joho Kokai Kuriaringuhausu*") was established as a non-profit, non-partisan, non-governmental institution in December 1999.[17] The Clearing House assists individuals and organizations seeking information held by a local agency or the national government. The Clearing House publishes the "*Joho Kokai Digest*" (*Information Disclosure Digest*), disseminates information on a web site, holds symposia and workshops for citizens, local governments and elected officials, and carries out contract projects. The Secretariat has lobbying expertise and conducts research on freedom of information issues. Also important, Clearing House specialists provide procedural guidance in preparing Information Request Forms. Appeals against an unfavorable agency decision can be filed in Tokyo or at one of fifty-one "information disclosure windows" at the local offices of national government agencies.

In the first months of activity under the new Law, April 1–December 31, 2001, 37,942 requests for information were lodged. In 31,137 cases the decision was for full or partial disclosure (87%), and for non-disclosure in 4,477 instances (13%). Administrative appeals against non-disclosure decisions numbered 1,136, while only eleven cases were appealed to a court.

The Law requires government agencies to respond to information requests within thirty days, and this norm is generally honored. In the first six years under the law, 86.7% of information requests received a response within that time limit, with one exception, the Ministry of Foreign Affairs (MoFa). Article 11 of the Law allows agencies to extend the statutory time for a "reasonable period." On December 26, 2007, the Tokyo District Court held that MoFa showed an unlawful pattern of delaying responses at variance with the sovereign people's right to receive prompt response to requests for information. Some 300 people had lodged a request in April 2006 for 30,000 or more documents concerning the 1965 normalization talks between Japan and the Republic of Korea. The documents concern compensation for injuries suffered during Japan's rule, 1910 to 1945. The court did not decide whether some or all of the documents should be released but established a precedent strengthening the right to know. In fiscal 2006, government agencies failed to meet Article 11 time limits in 186 cases; 182 concerned requests to MoFa.

Six categories of information may not be released under the Law:

1 Private information about an individual unless that information has already been made public.
2 Information about a corporate or individual business legal person, the disclosure of which would cause loss of legitimate profit or would violate a promise of occupational secrecy.
3 Information affecting a legitimate national security interest which would harm trust relations in negotiation with another country.
4 Information whose disclosure would interfere with a criminal investigation and the maintenance of public safety and public order.

5 Information whose disclosure during a process of decision-making would negatively affect the quality of the resultant decision.
6 Reports about the internal operations of an administrative agency which would interfere with its pursuit of proper administration.

The freedom of information movement receives further support from the Information Disclosure Citizens Center in Tokyo and the Citizen Ombudsman Movement (COM). The latter drew national attention in 1995 when investigating corrupt official entertainment expenses, by filing requests for food and beverage records of officials in all forty-seven prefectures and in national government offices in Tokyo, all on the same day. Since that time, requests for such information have been common and, in general, officials have been responsive.

The COM is a network of private prefectural groups of attorneys and other concerned citizens who monitor the compliance of officials with information disclosure legislation. They help people gain access to government documents in such areas as construction contracts, environmental issues, official entertainment expenditures, drug and pesticide safety, and military procurement funding.

Each year they hold a "National Liaison Conference of Citizen Ombudsmen" at which they announce their ranking under a point system of all prefectures and major cities in terms of their openness and responsiveness to citizen requests for information.[18] Supporting materials are gathered in fifty files at a national Secretariat in Nagoya.

Japan's freedom of information movement is now deeply embedded in laws and in sociopolitical and administrative practices.[19] Its drive towards transparency is now part of a global effort to hold leaders accountable and to improve democratic governance by expanding citizen access to officially held information. Perhaps some aspect of Japan's system may be usefully suggestive to others in Asia and beyond. In Asia, South Korea and Thailand preceded Japan in passing a freedom of information statute.

Sixty-eight countries guarantee their citizens the legal right to know what their governments are up to.[20] The first annual "International Right to Know Day" was celebrated on September 28, 2003, established by the Freedom of Information Advocates Network.[21] Material on the freedom of information internet site is edited by a multinational volunteer Editorial Board hosted and staffed by the National Security Archives (http://www.nsarchive.org) at George Washington University in Washington DC, the leading non-profit user of the U.S. Freedom of Information Act (http://www.freedominfo.org).

After many years of overemphasis on secrecy in U.S. government processes, in 2009 President Barack Obama brought on a resurgence of government transparency and information disclosure in America. The United States rejoined the global freedom of information movement.

A RIGHT TO PEACE

A third cluster of issues calling for extended constitutional discourse in Asia includes weaponry, war and the human right to peace. In 2008, many Asian nations are heavily militarized even in the absence of any credible external threat. Under varied constitutions, governance has been strongly influenced by military establishments in such countries as Myanmar (Burma), Pakistan, Indonesia, Philippines, South Korea, and Thailand. China, India, Pakistan and North Korea have nuclear weapon capability.

The United States military is subordinate to the civilian government, but plays a defining role in the nation's political culture and economic system. Its military budget dwarfs the budgets of most other nations combined. According to the independent Weapons of Mass Destruction Commission, the U.S. has an "alarmingly high" number of nuclear weapons, roughly 27,000, of which some 12,000 are deployed for quick use. Many call for declarations of nuclear-weapon-free zones (e.g. in the Arctic and Antartic), continuous radical reductions in the world's arsenal of nuclear weapons, and effective bans on chemical, biological, electronic and space weaponry. There is no solid basis for assuming humankind will continue to avoid self-destruction indefinitely.

War is more about destructive action than about constructive thinking, but an outbreak of war should be an occasion for the leaders and the led, and their media interlocutors in a constitutional democracy, to critically reexamine their presuppositions about the legitimacy of waging war. The United States has a special need to reconsider its long-term relations with the Asian world, in light of its wars since 1941 involving Japan, Korea, Vietnam, Iraq and Afghanistan, and with attention to the contours of constitutionalism in Asia.

However barbaric its war history, the West has also developed an honorable tradition of sober theoretical discourse on war, both just and unjust. Much of such theorizing about war has entered elite political discourse in many Western and Asian nations. Questions asked are sometimes very basic.

For example, should a human right to peace be taken into account by war policy-makers? Does war require justification? Or is war a morally neutral phenomenon that requires no justification, like an earthquake, a typhoon, a volcanic eruption, or a tidal wave (tsunami)? In the practice of war, that ethically detached view may resemble the perspective of a pilot engaged in a high-altitude bombing mission which results in countless civilian deaths.

If the national or international community requires some justification for starting a war, is it sufficient that the leaders of a government desire war for raison d'état, a reason of state, whatever the sovereign wants, in effect, for whatever real reasons? This view would seem compatible with Hermann Goering's testimony at the Nuremberg Trials:[22]

> Of course people don't want war. But, after all, it's the leaders of the country who determine the policy, and it's always a simple matter to drag the people along whether it's a democracy, a fascist dictator, or a parliament, or a communist dictatorship. Voice or no voice, the people can always be brought around to the bidding of the leaders. That is easy. All you have to do is tell them they are being attacked, and denounce the pacifists for lack of patriotism, and (for) exposing the country to greater dangers.

In Western civilization, a strong presupposition against going to war has been recognized for centuries, along with bloody wars. As Hugo Grotius put it, "War has no place among the useful arts." Much of the development of international law and institutions has been driven by this healthy belief that peace is almost always more honorable and reasonable than war, that war is a suspect option in almost all cases, and that leaders who choose war usually underestimate grossly the costs of war, cultural, human, economic and political.

A just war is one undertaken as a last resort, in response to empirically verifiable threat, with approval from the international community, with good prospects for success, with minimum necessary use of force by conventional weapons, with benefits proportionate to losses, and with respect for human rights under international law and international morality. Whether a particular war is just or not, war brings with it deep sorrow for countless people. War represents singular failure on many levels. As Evan Wright said, "War should be undertaken with a very heavy heart," not with mindless patriotism or an amoral triumphalist rejection of appeals for diplomacy and restraint.[23]

In Asia, Japan's experience for over sixty years has demonstrated the possibility of an alternative to conventional perspectives on war, peace and weaponry, in Article 9 of the "Peace Constitution" and in its implementation in policies and laws. In 1945 Japan was a pariah state in Asia due to the failure of its colonialism and militarism; ever since, Japan has followed a path of human rights constitutionalism and peaceful international relations. Few nations have so unequivocally rejected the use of force to settle international disputes (discussed elsewhere in this volume). Japan continues to limit its Self-Defense Force to logistical, infrastructural, and humanitarian activities sanctioned by the United Nations, adhering to the spirit set forth in the Preamble and Article 9 of the 1947 Constitution:[24]

> "We, the Japanese people . . . (are) resolved that never again shall we be visited with the horrors of war through the action of government. . . . We desire peace for all time . . . We desire to occupy an honored place in an international society striving for the preservation of peace. . . . We recognize that all the peoples of the world have the right to live in peace, free from fear and want. . . ."
>
> "Article 9. Aspiring sincerely to an international peace based on justice and order, the Japanese people forever renounce war as a sovereign right of the nation and the threat or use of forces as a means of settling international disputes.
>
> "2. In order to accomplish the aim of the preceding paragraph, land, sea and air forces, as well as other war potential, will never be maintained. The right of belligerency of the state will not be recognized."

At the least, Japan's constitutionalism invites study and a measure of emulation.

NOTES

1 International Council on Human Rights Policy, "Catching the Wind: Human Rights", Geneva, Switzerland, December 10, 2007.

2 The headquarters of the International Association of Constitutional Law is c/o SAIFAC, P.O. Box 84666, Greenside 2034 Johannesburg, South Africa. E-mail: info@saifac.org.za Internet: www.iacl-aidc.org.

3 F.E. Peters, *The Voice, the Word, the Books: The Sacred Scriptures of the Jews, Christians and Muslims*, Princeton, Princeton University Press, 2007.

4 Nicole Winfield, "Historic", Associated Press, January 5, 2008; Rita Ferrone, "Uncommon Opportunity: When Islamic Moderates Speak: Who Listens?", *Commonweal*, January 18, 2008.

5 Lucian W. Pye, *Asian Power and Politics: The Cultural Dimensions of Authority*, Cambridge, Harvard

University Press, 1985; Wm. Theodore deBary, *Asian Values and Human Rights*, Cambridge, Harvard University Press, 1998, and *Nobility and Civility*, Cambridge, Harvard University Press, 2004.

6 For current reports on all Asian nations, see the annual *Asia Yearbook*, published by the *Far Eastern Economic Review*, and *Asia Week*.

7 "60 Minutes", CBS-TV, January 20, 2008. On the U.S. experience, see A. Fung, M. Grahan, and D. Weil, *Full Disclosure: The Perils and Promise of Transparency*, New York, Cambridge University Press, 2007.

8 *The Japan Times*, January 14 and 21, 2008.

9 *The Japan Times*, Januaary 22, 2008.

10 *The Japan Times*, January 4, 2008. Beijing, Seoul, Hong Kong, Shanghai and Singapore also made the list.

11 Yukiko Miki, "Information Disclosure System in Japan: Development, Implementation, and the Role of Civil Society," International Conference on the Guarantee of Public Access to Information to Realize Open and Democratic Government, Jakarta, April 22, 2002.

12 23 *Keishu* 11, p.1490; H. Itoh and L. W. Beer, *The Constitutional Case Law of Japan: Selected Supreme Court Decisions, 1961–70*, Seattle, University of Washington Press, 1978, p.246. Richard H. Mitchell, *Political Bribery in Japan*, Honolulu, University of Hawaii Press, 1996.

13 Law 42 of May 14, 1999. Lawrence Repeta, "Japan: Tokyo Court: Foreign Ministry's Failure to Provide Documents on 1965 Japan-Korea Normalization Pact Illegal," http://www.freedominfo.org/features. *The Japan Times*, February 9, 2006, and March 22 and 28, 2007.

14 Lawrence Repeta, "Japan: Tokyo Court: Foreign Ministry's Failure to Provide Documents in 1965 Japan–Korea Normalization Pact Illegal," http://www.freedominfo.org/features

15 Law 42 of May, 1999.

16 Lawrence Repeta, *Local Government Disclosure Systems in Japan*, Seattle, National Bureau of Asian Research, 1999, and "The Birth of the Freedom Information Act in Japan: Kanagawa 1982", MIT Japan Program Working Paper 03–01, September, 2003.

17 Materials provided by Yukiko Miki of the Clearinghouse. E-mail yukiko.Miki@nifty.com

18 "*Dai 8 kai Zenkoku Joho Kokaido Rankingu*" (The *Eighth* National Ranking (of government units) by Degree of Openness), March, 2004; *Asahi Shimbun*, June 5, 2004.

19 F.J. Schwartz and S.J. Pharr (eds.), *The State of Civil Society in Japan*, New York, Cambridge University Press, 2004.

20 Survey of freedom of information law in many countries by David Banesar, http://www.freedominfo.org. At the inception of his presidency, President Barack Obama issued a "Memorandum on the Freedom of Information Act," an executive order rejecting executive denial of access to information under the Presidential Records Act, and a "Memorandum on Transparency and Open Government". All three actions established the ideas that state and society are not enemies and that openness, accountability and collaboradion benefit all. (http://www.freedominfo.org/news/20090123289

21 Material on the internet site is edited by a multinational volunteer Editorial Board which is hosted and staffed by the National Security Archives (http://www.nsarchive.org) at George Washington University in Washington DC, the leading non-profit user of the U.S. Freedom of Information Act.

22 G.M. Gilbert, *Nuremberg Diaries*.

23 Evan Wright, *Generation Kill*, New York, G.P. Putnam's Sons, 2004; Thomas E. Ricks, *Fiasco: The American Military Adventure in Iraq*, New York, Penguin Press, 2006; Anonymous, *Imperial Hubris: Why the West Is Losing the War on Terrorism*, New York, Potomac Books, 2004; Thomas Graham, Jr., *Common Sense on Weapons of Mass Destruction*, Seattle, University of Washington Press, 2005.

24 For example, Kaho Shimizu, "Nations Swap Papers Limiting MSDF Fuel Use," *The Japan Times*, February 6, 2008.

■ Acceptance Speech, Distinguished Asianist Award, Mid-Atlantic Region Association for Asian Studies, George Washington University, October 25, 2003

Appendix

Adventures with Asia: Studying Human Rights Constitutionalism Here and There

⌘

Thank you for the Distinguished Asianist Award. I was surprised and humbled. The Mid-Atlantic Region Association for Asian Studies is a unique and valuable community of educators, civil servants, and other friends of Asia. Our associations have been a privilege and a pleasure for me. And thank you for the enlightened challenges presented by this year's MAR/AAS program. Not since the 1940s perhaps has the United States been so in need of rethinking its place in Asia and the world.

I have been invited to combine memoir with comment on human rights at present. My adventures with Asia began in 1957, when I taught English as a foreign language and Philosophy at Sophia University in Tokyo. I would like to start my story by referring to a few improbable events that took place many years later and then trying to suggest how they came about. I was quite sure until the age of thirty that law was the one subject I would never waste my time on, but most of my writings are about law. Whatever coherence my career has had is based on a preoccupation with Asia and human rights law.

IMPROBABLE HIGH POINTS

In April 1976, I found myself at the United States Supreme Court in the Chambers of Chief Justice Warren Burger, as a temporaary State Department Escort taking care of some eminent Asians scholars and Supreme Court Justices. This visit was part of a program honoring the Declaration of Independence in which Asian jurists traveled around the United States giving their views of American influence on Asian constitutionalism. At the time, neither the American Bar Association nor the Association of American Law Schools gave substantive attention to Asia, but legal scholars and practitioners on the Committee on Asian Law of the Association for Asian Studies(which I chaired) planned and carried out an elaborate, month-long bicentennial program. We had no money; all the bills were paid by supporters in the public and private sectors.

As in other disciplinary contexts, the AAS provided an essential point of contact between Asia and the United States. Another example close to home: when Donald MacDonald was President of MAR/AAS, we cooperated with the State Department in welcoming North Korean scholars to participate for the first time in an American conference, the Annual Meeting of MAR/AAS.

The bicentennial program in 1976 involved quite an adventure with much sensitive protocol and occasional drama. During the commemorative panel introduced by President Marius Jansen at the AAS Annual Meeting, demonstrators protested loudly but peacefully against the regime of Ferdinand Marcos. In India, Prime Minister Indira Gandhi blocked Professor P.K. Tripathi's departure from the country at the airport. His paper was smuggled out and was read at public forums by a Committee specialist in Indian law, Marc Galanter. During the editing of my first book on Asian constitutionalism (*Constitutionalism in Asia: Asian Views of the American Influence*, 1979, 1988), one country attempted unsuccessfully to censor content.

A second improbable event took place in 1987; May 3 is a national holiday in Japan, Constitution Day. On May 3, 1987, at the 40th anniversary celebration of the Constitution in Yomiuri Hall, downtown Tokyo, the two main speakers were the eminent Professor Nobuyoshi Ashibe of the University of Tokyo and a little-known American scholar, myself. Only one other foreigner was present in the crowded hall. Because my speech, among other themes, was critical of the remnant of excessive nationalism in Japan, a few colleagues feared a violent rightist response, but none occurred. However, on the same day, an *Asahi Shimbun* journalist was assassinated, presumably by extreme nationalists; the crime remains unsolved and unrepeated. Threats are occasional.

A third unlikely occasion: in the fall of 1989, the progressive Governor Kazuji Nagasu of Kanagawa Prefecture and the International Association of Constitutional Law sponsored in Yokohama the first in a series of International Symposia on Asian Constitutions, drawing scholars from East, Southeast, and South Asia. I was the only non-Asian invited to make a presentation.

Finally, in 1997 the Japan Federation of Bar Associations (*Nichibenren*) opened a new national headquarters building. As the inaugural public event, they asked me to present reflections on Japan's fifty years under the 1947 Constitution. These and other adventures with Asia were not sought and still seem highly improbable.

Why did law leaders of Japan and other Asian countries become interested in the views of such a foreign scholar? They were open-minded and curious about the thinking of this weird Westerner who took their countries seriously. How did he get that way? A little biography to clarify my path toward understanding human rights law and constitutionalism in Asia. My attitudes were formed gradually, one set of human rights at a time.

A BIOGRAPHICAL NOTE

I was born in Portland, Oregon in 1932. My father exported the rare decorative woods of the Pacific Northwest to Japan and Europe. He taught me that foreign businessmen are fascinating and friendly, not strange, and not hostile except during wartime. He also passed on to me *Colloquial Japanese*, a language book he had received from a Japanese ship captain. My first study of the Japanese language was a search in this book for impolite expressions with which to regale uncouth teen-age friends.

My mother was a managing secretary for a large lumber company and a founder of the Lumber Jills, the professional association of women in the lumber industry. She suffered significantly from gender discrimination, a fact that sensitized me to women's rights in the marketplace well before the feminist revolution.

I attended public and parochial schools in Portland. Teen-age experiences, for good and ill, can have disproportionate importance in shaping one's mind. Playing football and basketball kindled my appreciation of friendly competition, unselfish cooperation, and the joy of group achievements. I later found the Japanese emphasis on groupism more often than not compatible with an American team-approach to tasks. My loathing of religious and anti-religious bigotry was nurtured when the parents of Protestant girl friends broke up promising relationships solely because I was a Roman Catholic.

My first Asian friend was a Japanese college student in Tokyo with whom I exchanged letters and photos from 1949. We first met in Nagoya in 1970. He wrote about the harsh realities of postwar Japan. Like millions then, he had tuberculosis and was more concerned about food than thought. But he made me aware of the deep ideological conflicts between liberal and social democracy, militant nationalism, Christianity, communism, capitalism, nihilism, existentialism and other Japanese and European views competing for the allegiance of young and old in the cultural wreckage of Japan in the 1940s and 1950s. Which path to the future Japan would take was not at all clear to anyone. In the midst of this complex uncertainty, the 1947 Constitution of Japan (*Nihonkoku Kempo*) was a stabilizing and clarifying force. It has remained so.

My support for workers' human rights and unions was influenced by three high school summers as a "gandy dancer" servicing railroad track for the Spokane, Portland and Seattle Railroad, working alongside immigrant workers from Greece, Italy and Yugoslavia. I shared their excitement when the United States moved from a six-day work week toward a five-day schedule, a historic advance in U.S. labor relations.

From 1950 until mid-1961 I was a student Jesuit, a member of a global Christian religious organization heavily committed to education. This provided a long experience of community-living with people of many countries and made me more comfortable with the stress of many Asian cultures on social interdependence than with an at times exaggerated American emphasis on self-reliance, individualism, and irresponsible capitalism.

From 1950 to 1957 I studied the Classics, liberal arts and sciences at Gonzaga University in Spokane. In 1950 I met John O. Hopkins, the first African American student body president of a white high school in the U.S., charismatic debater (with teammate Tom Foley), and the first Black to earn a doctorate at Columbia University in his field. He taught me about America's apartheid and inspired my involvement with the civil rights movement in the 1950s and 1960s.

There I also learned in informal conversations with an economics graduate student about the great value of credit unions in combating poverty in the U.S. and around the world. Credit unions are democratic, non-profit credit cooperatives that provide small loans at very low interest rates and with consumer-friendly repayment conditions. The primary security for a loan is the honesty of the borrower. Of all lending institutions credit unions have the best loan-repayment record. With the help of the Credit Union National Association in Madison, Wisconsin, I later promoted the credit union movement in Japan and other Asian countries, on behalf of such poor as the ragpickers (*bataya-san*) in Adachi Ward, Tokyo. That experience and a year as a training director for the California Credit Union League (1961–1962) confirmed my appreciation of informal conversation as a research tool and my belief that socioeconomic rights are human rights deserving inclusion in every country's constitution. This credit union interest also resulted in my first book (with Colin Chilton), *Credit Union Family Financial Counseling* (1962).

From 1957 to 1961 I studied Japan's language and culture in Japan, and taught at Sophia University. Perhaps 1960 was the pivotal year for democratic constitutionalism and foreign policy in Japan's 20th century, and for my own appreciation of constitutional law and politics. Until 1959 I had little interest in law or politics due to an exaggerated cynicism about both. I saw around the globe the tragic human propensity for lethal political violence within and between countries. Even relatively small-scale public conflicts commonly resulted in deaths. Japan's so-called "Security Treaty Crisis" in 1959 and 1960 was not a crisis but a confirmation of democracy, and it seemed to present a contrapuntal empirical datum. Week after week, I saw a mass movement of a size, length, freedom and passion unprecedented in Japan's history. And yet, only one person died, and that by accident. This led me to write my dissertation about freedom of assembly in Japan and to appreciate the possibility of societies which impose rather effective limits on violence.

In 1961 I married Keiko Harada. Interracial marriage was still illegal in a good many American States, but not in Federal law, and not in Japanese law. Family on both sides of the Pacific warmly welcomed a foreign relative. Half my relatives are Asian.

The main house of the samurai Harada family has been in the Nagano mountains since AD 1585, when they lost out in the feudal wars. Innumerable interactions with Japanese relatives and friends for over forty years have made my perspectives on Japan's law and constitution less abstract than they would otherwise be. Steeped in the ordinary humanness of Japanese and other Asians, little about them seems to me esoteric. Much seems highly civilized. As in America, a few characteristics elude quick explanation.

From 1962 to 1966 I studied East Asia and Japanese constitutional law and politics in the Asian Law Program, the Political Science Department, and what is now the Henry M. Jackson School of International Studies at the University of Washington. I then taught at the University of Colorado for sixteen years, and at Lafayette College for fifteen years, retiring to Boulder, Colorado in 1997.

Dan Fenno Henderson and John M. Maki, leading scholars of Japan's law, suggested I make a career of studying Japan's constitutional law, combining my interests in anthropology, theory, politics and law. I was the first American doctoral student in the field. No course on the subject was offered in the Western world, but I could read the works of Japan's leading scholars, such as Toshiyoshi Miyazawa, in the University of Washington's superb Asian Law Collection.

Serious books in English on Asia were still few in those days; the only advantage over today's situation was that one could keep up with the literature on Asia beyond one's narrow specialty. It was easier to avoid becoming a one-country, one-discipline

Asianist. Besides the works of my mentors, I appreciated especially the books of Robert and Edwin Reischauer and Sir George Sansom.

Henderson and Maki understood the great value for scholars of foreign and comparative law of translations of authoritative Japanese judicial decisions as seminal scholarship. John Maki published *Court and Constitution in Japan: Selected Supreme Court Decisions, 1948–60* (1964). Hiroshi Itoh and I have followed that volume with two of our own containing decisions handed down from 1960 through 1990 (1978, 1996).

STUDYING ASIAN LAW

From the beginning my studies have been guided by an epistemologically simple, perhaps too obvious, rule: learn from those who know the most about your subject (for me, civil liberties law), from Japanese scholars, judges, civil servants, journalists, NGOs, and attorneys. The first of my many distinguished Japanese teachers was Isao Sato, who helped Professor Maki and me plan my dissertation when he visited Seattle to solicit opinions for Japan's Commission on the Constitution (1958–1964). Professor Sato was present at the birth of Japan's basic law in 1946 and was the principal author of the Commission's final report in 1964 after its exhaustive study of Japan's constitutional health.

Another of my principal teachers was Masami Ito, Dean of the Faculty of Law, University of Tokyo, Justice of Japan's Supreme Court (1970–1980), and recipient of his country's highest honor for his many public services. Six times I have been hosted and helped by Professor Ito and his colleagues at the University of Tokyo.

A third master teacher has been Hideo Shimizu, the mass media law specialist who heads "BRO" (Broadcast and Human Rights/Other Related Rights Organization), a prestigious independent group which considers citizen complaints against the mass media for rights violations. Other teachers, too numerous to mention, have been exceptional in their generosity and help.

My circle of distinguished teachers expanded gradually over decades through a succession of *introductions*, not at my initiative, but at the initiative of Japanese experts who thought I should meet some additional specialist or who provided access to valuable unpublished materials. There have been many helpful *conversations* (a term that I prefer to "interviews"). Listening and relying on others has been critically important to my research; as has avoidance of an assertive demeanor.

I have been the only American member of the Public Law Association of Japan (*Koho Gakkai*). I have been exposed to further Asian teachers through involvements with the Law Association for Asia and the Pacific (which for some years excluded U.S. attorneys due to their alleged arrogance), the Public Law Association of Japan (*Koho Gakkai*), the International Association of Constitutional Law (a European creation), and the World Jurists Association (World Peace through Law Center, here in Washington, DC), particularly as Co-Chair of the World Association of Law Professors (1985–1987).

The pool of instructors grew as I worked on *Constitutional Systems in Late 20th Century Asia* (1992), a book commemorating the bicentennials of the U.S Constitution (signed September 17, 1787) and the Bill of Rights (ratified December 15, 1791). (That book was written at the urging of Professor Albert P. Blaustein of Rutgers University who had read the earlier book on Asian constitutionalism.)

Including a few translators, about twenty-five authors wrote its thirteen country studies; most were distinguished indigenous scholars. For considerations of academic freedom in China, North Korea and Vietnam at the time, chapters on those countries were contributed by American specialists.

ASIAN VIEWS

What were the views of the Asian jurists about the United States? They uniformly expressed deep respect for the Declaration of Independence and Abraham Lincoln's Gettysburg Address, and their relevance to their own nations' constitutionalisms. Like all but a few of the world's 191 countries, they accepted as a necessary and useful institution a single-document national constitution, which is an American invention. The Bill of Rights was also generally honored. However, many found its conception of human rights incomplete by the modern standards expressed in United Nations documents and in constitutions throughout the world. They thought the American institution of judicial review—the courts' power to decide whether something is or is not constitutional or legal—very significant and in some form applicable to at least some of their systems (for example, India, the Philippines, Japan and South Korea)

Common views of human rights here in the United States and there in Asia differ for a number of reasons. Some reasons are obvious, based on differences in cultural and legal history; but some are less widely known in the United States. For example, a majority of Asian and other States have modern legal systems heavily influenced by the European civil law tradition, not the Anglo-American common law tradition. Moreover, few in America know how the Islamic legal traditions of Asia fit in. And many American leaders and other elites continue to nurture a unique national discomfort with, even a fear of "socialism," even socialism of the most democratic kind. In this, the U.S. differs not only from most democratically inclined Asian nations, but also from most similar states around the globe.

In addition, U.S. understandings of "democracy" and "constitutionalism" seem to stop at majority rule, limited legal equality, civil liberties, property rights, and procedural rights. Some would call it plutocracy, with the democratic world's greatest gap between the haves and have nots. Some Americans also mistakenly believe that free-market capitalism somehow easily blends with democracy. In fact, capitalism just as easily co-exists with an authoritarian State, given the monopolistic tendencies and autocratic structure of many corporations. Moreover, history tells us that democratic election rights do not inevitably lead to enforcement of other important rights. On the other hand, a system may lack democratic elections but have a good record of protecting other human rights.

The human rights movement is concerned with more than civil liberties and more than legal equality. A clumsy term "human rights constitutionalism" may help in distinguishing between majoritarian democratic constitutionalism and a constitutionalism based on commitment to human rights more comprehensively understood. With the term "human rights" I am referring to all the rights set forth in the United Nations Universal Declaration of Human Rights (December 10, 1948) and later Covenants (1966) and other refinements. Obviously, the level of implementation of some rights depends as much or more on a nation's human and other resources as on policy, but in response to the inherent dignity of each person, the individual has a legitimate claim to enforceable rights not only to democratic governance, civil liberties, property rights, equality under the law, and procedural rights, but also worker rights and rights to education, health care, food, shelter, a healthy environment, and adequately regulated capitalism. These rights, influenced by U.S. thought as of 1948, have been recognized by many as international humanitarian customary law.

(I would describe a "constitution" as, written and unwritten, the principles, institutions and processes for organizing, exercising, and limiting governmental and community power on behalf of a country's primary public values in a promulgated and reasonably predictable manner. Examples of primary values are liberty and individual wealth in the U.S., socioeconomic equality and rejection of war in Japan.)

In the United States the lack of constitutional status given some human rights seems to militate against policies and laws which guarantee the social rights, neatly summarized under Article 25 of Japan's Constitution, "the right to maintain the minimum standards of wholesome and cultured living." America's narrow conception of human rights in international law may also explain in part the widespread acceptance by U.S. business of woefully inadequate wages and working conditions for "offshore" employees in Asia and elsewhere. Any persuasive view of globalization includes commitment to sustainable development and world labor standards, such as safe working conditions, a five-(or six-)day work week, an eight- or nine-hour work day, a right to unionize, and the development of global and regional formulas for calculating a living wage in differing economies.

The key development in world politics and law during the 20th century may have been the emergence of a coherent human rights movement, not rational choice theory or the coming and going of politically powerful ideologies. In the 21st century, nations and thinkers will continue to disagree on specific issues and on the philosophical or religious foundations which intellectually justify human rights globalization, but perhaps a consensus can be approached in most countries at the level of behavioral standards, such as the abolition of torture and establishment of minimal labor standards, making the guidelines of international customary law, in effect, the world's "secular religion."

At the beginning of my talk I suggested that the United States may now be more in need of rethinking its role in Asia and elsewhere than at any time since the 1940s. Since 9/11, the United States has seemed to many, if not most nations unwisely unilateral and disdainful of the United Nations and of its own major allies. Some American leaders have also forgotten international traditions of courtesy in diplomacy.

In the United States, we do not require of university graduates even minimal acquaintance with even one Asian country or Islam. Students are missing a lot. The world's Asianists, in our on-going conversations with each other and with Asians, have enjoyed the great traditions, the courtesy and the hospitality of Asia. Collectively, we can provide the human rights movement with an accurate account of the context of each issue in each Asian country. We find liberating adventure in discovering and teaching about Asia's exciting human diversity.

In my own life with Asia, I have found thought-provoking a 20th century short story by Kunikida Doppo ("Meat and Potatoes"). In the story a group of university graduates gathers for a reunion at one of their favorite watering holes. They decide that each of them should tell the others what he most wants out of life, and each tells of his predictable hopes. There is much drink and good-humored mutual ridicule.

Except for one, the last to speak, who has been sitting quietly as the others loudly told their stories. I will close with his words (approximate wording):

> I want to be surprised. I want to be surprised by each day when I wake up. I want to be surprised by each season, by each person I meet. I want to be surprised by the immensity of the universe and the mystery of life. Most of all I want to have always THE CAPACITY TO BE SURPRISED.

Asia is full of surprises. May all your surprises with Asia be pleasant.

Bibliography

⌘

The following is a list of published books, articles, chapters and reviews by Lawrence W. Beer in order of the oldest first, classified as A=Books, B=Articles and Chapters, C=Publications in Japanese, D=Publications in Korean, E=Book reviews.

A. Books

Co-editor & co-author, with Colin Chilton, *Credit Union Family Financial Counseling*, California Credit Union League, Oakland & Pomona, 1962, and Credit Union National Association, Madison, Wisconsin, 1963.

With Hiroshi Itoh, *The Constitutional Case Law of Japan: Selected Supreme Court Decisions, 1961–1970*, Seattle, University of Washington Press, 1978, xix & 283 pp.

Editor and co-author, *Constitutionalism in Asia: Asian Views of the American Influence*, Berkeley & Los Angeles, University of California Press, 1979. Reprinted, with a new Introduction, in *Occasional Papers/Reprint Series in Contemporary Asian Studies*, School of Law, University of Maryland, 1988, xi & 210 pp.

Editor & co-author (Isao Sato, Supervising Translator), *Ajia no kempo seido*, Tokyo, Gakuyo Shobo Publishing Co., 1981, xiv & 259 pp. A translation of *Constitutionalism in Asia.*

Freedom of Expression in Japan: A Study in Comparative Law, Politics and Society, Tokyo & New York, Kodansha International, 1984, 415 pp.

Editor & co-author, *Constitutional Systems in Late Twentieth-Century Asia*, Seattle, University of Washington Press, 1992, ix & 752 pp.

With Hiroshi Itoh, *The Constitutional Case Law of Japan, 1970 through 1990*, Seattle, University of Washington Press, 1996, 702 pp.

With John M. Maki, *From Imperial Myth to Democracy: Japan's Two Constitutions, 1889–2002*, Boulder, University Press of Colorado, 2002. Published in Japanese as *Tenno Shinwa kara Minshushugi e: Nihon no Futatsu no Kempo, 1889–2004* (Asanuma Kiyoshi), Tokyo, Shinzansha Publishing Co., 2005.

B. ARTICLES AND CHAPTERS

"The Public Welfare Standard and Freedom of Expression in Japan," in Dan F. Henderson (ed.), *The Constitution of Japan: Its First Twenty Years, 1947–1967*, Seattle, University of Washington Press, 1969, pp. 205–238; reprinted from 43 *Washington Law Review* 1095 (1968).

"Some Dimensions of Japan's Present and Potential Relations with Communist China," *Asian Survey*, University of California Press, March 1969, pp. 163–177. Reprinted in K.C. Chen (ed.), *The Foreign Policy of China*, Roseland, New Jersey, East-West Who/ Seton Hall University Press, 1972, pp. 424–442.

"Japan, 1969: 'My Homeism' and Political Struggle," *Asian Survey*, January 1970, pp. 43–55. Reprinted in Stephen S. Large (ed.), *Showa Japan*, London, Routledge, 1998.

"Japan Turning the Corner," *Asian Survey*, January 1971, pp. 74–85

"Freedom of Information and the Evidentiary Use of Film in Japan: Law and Sociopolitics in an East Asian Democracy," *The American Political Science Review*, Vol. 65, No. 4, December 1971, pp. 1119–1134.

"Life and Society," "Constitutionalism in Japan," "Japan's Political Problems," and "Japan's Economy," in John M. Maki, *We the Japanese*, New York, Praeger Publishers, 1972, pp. 15–60. Translations from the Japanese of T. Nishioka (*Atarashii Shakai*) and N. Ukai (*Seiji-Keizai*).

"Defamation, Privacy, and Freedom of Expression in Japan," *Law in Japan: An Annual*, Vol. 5, 1972, pp. 192–208.

"American Approaches to East Asia: Education, Images, and National Interest," *Vital Speeches of the Day*, Vol. 39, No. 15, May 15, 1973, pp. 458–465. Revised version, *Colorado Quarterly*, University of Colorado, Vol. 22, No. 1, 1973, pp. 5–25.

With Hidenori Tomatsu, "A Guide to the Study of Japanese Law," *The American Journal of Comparative Law*, Vol. 23, No. 2, Spring, 1975, pp. 284–324. Expanded edition is *Occasional Papers/Reprint Series in Contemporary Asian Studies*, No. 7, 1978, 52 pp.

"Education, Politics and Freedom of Expression in Japan: The Ienaga Textbook Review Cases," *Law in Japan: An Annual*, Vol. 8, 1975, pp. 67–90.

"Constitutionality of Restricting the Freedom of Expression of Public Employees," *Law in Japan: An Annual*, Vol. 8, 1975, pp. 206–208.

"Freedom of Expression in Japan with Comparative Reference to the United States," in Richard P. Claude (ed.), *Comparative Human Rights*, Baltimore, Johns Hopkins University Press, 1976, pp. 99–126.

"*La Libertad de Expression en Japan Comparada con Estados Unidos*," in Richard P. Claude (ed.) and Carlos Moreno & Diana Montes (trans.), *Derechos Humanos Comparado*, Montevideo, Uruguay, Ediciones Centenario, December, 1979, pp. 107–128. A translation of the previous entry.

"The AAS Committee on Asian Law: Some Whats and Whys," *Asian Law Forum*, Committee on Asian Law, Association for Asian Studies, Vol. 1, 1976, pp. 1–4.

Editor, "Asian Perspectives on the American Constitutional Influence," *The Asian Student*, The Asia Foundation, April 24, 1976, pp. 6–8. Reprinted in *Asian Law Forum*, Vol. 2, 1977, pp. 12–27.

With Clarence Dias et al., "Asian Legal Studies in the United States: A Survey Report," *Journal of Legal Education*, Association of American Law Schools, Vol. 29, No. 4, 1978, pp. 501–567.

With C. G. Weeramantry, "Human Rights in Japan: Some Protections and Problems," *Universal Human Rights* (renamed *Human Rights Quarterly*), Vol. 1, No. 3, 1979, pp. 1–33.

"Some Reflections on Japan and America's National Interest," *Vital Speeches of the Day*, Vol. 46, No. 14, May 1, 1980, pp. 443–448.
"Group Rights and Individual Rights in Japan," *Asian Survey*, Vol. 21, No. 4, April, 1981, pp. 437–453.
"Constitutional Revolution in Japanese Law, Society and Politics," *Modern Asian Studies*, Cambridge University Press, Vol. 16, No. 1, 1982, pp. 33–67. Reprinted in *Occasional Papers/Reprint Series in Contemporary Asian Studies*, No. 5, 1982, 35 pp.
"Constitutionalism in Japan, Past and Present," *Proceedings of the Ohira Commemorative Series*, University of British Columbia, Vancouver, Canada, 1983, 12 pp.
"Japan's Constitutional System and Its Judicial Interpretation," *Law in Japan: An Annual*, Vol. 17, 1984, pp. 7–41. Revised version in John O. Haley (ed.), *Law and Society in Contemporary Japan: American Perspectives*, Dubuque, Kendall-Hunt, 1988, pp. 7–35.
Articles in *Kodansha Encyclopedia of Japan*, Tokyo & New York, Kodansha International, 1983:
"Law in Contemporary Japan," Vol. 4, pp. 379–380
"*Lady Chatterley's Lover* case," Vol. 4, p. 362
"De Sade case," Vol. 2, pp. 87–88
"*After the Banquet* case," Vol. 1, p. 20
"Obscenity," Vol. 6, pp. 49–50
"Privacy, right to," Vol. 6, pp. 249–250
"Public Welfare," Vol. 6, p. 267.
"Postwar Law on Civil Liberties in Japan," *Pacific Basin Law Journal*, UCLA Law School, Vol. 2, Nos. 1 & 2, 1983, pp. 98–115.
"The Interplay of Legal Traditions: Europe and Non-Western Legal Education," Proceedings, Berlin Conference on the Law of the World, World Peace through Law Center, Washington, DC, 1985, 11 pp.
Human Rights Commissioners (Jinken Yogoiin) and Lay Protection of Human Rights in Japan, Occasional Paper No. 31, International Ombudsman Institute, October, 1985, 21 pp.
"Freedom of Expression in Japan and Asia: Some Comparative Perspectives," in Nobuyoshi Ashibe et al. (eds.), *Nihonkoku Kempo no Riron* (Theories on the Constitution of Japan), Tokyo, Yuhikaku Publishing Co., 1985, pp. 701–730.
"Domestic Constraints on Japanese Security Policies," in Ronald A. Morse (ed.), *Option 2000: Politics and High Technology in Japan's Defense and Strategic Future*, Washington, DC, Woodrow Wilson International Center for Scholars, Smithsonian Institution, 1987, pp. 5–14.
"Japan," in Jack Donnelly & Rhoda Howard (eds.), *International Handbook of Human Rights*, Westport, Connecticut, Greenwood Press, 1987, pp. 209–226.
"The Constitution of Japan in the Age of Internationalization," a translation of the editorial in *Asahi Shimbun*, May 3, 1988, in *The MAR Asian Messenger*, Vol. 10, No. 2, 1989, pp. 5, 8, 9. Reprinted in *Public Culture*, University of Pennsylvania, Vol. 2, No. 2, 1990, pp. 139–142.
"The Influence of United States Constitutionalism in Asia," *Korean Public Law Review*, Seoul, Public Law Association of Korea, Vol. 15, 1987, pp. 217–235.
"Civil Liberties in Japan: The Freedom Revolution," *Vital Speeches of the Day*, Vol. 56, No. 19, July 15, 1990, pp. 596–601. Reprinted in *Current*, No. 328, December 1990, pp. 22–28.
"The Legacy of William S. Clark to Japan's Future: Vision, Motivation, and Practicality," in Tadakazu Fukase (ed.), *William Smith Clark: In Commemoration of the Centennial*

of His Death, Sapporo, Japan, Sapporo Peace Studies Association, 1988, pp. 11–15, 22–26.

"Japan (1947): Forty Years of the Postwar Constitution," in Vernon Bogdanor (ed.), *Constitutions in Democratic Politics*, Aldershot, United Kingdom, Gower Publishing Co., 1988, pp. 173–205.

"Law and Liberty," in Takeshi Ishida & Ellis S. Krauss (eds.), *Democracy in Japan*, Pittsburgh, University of Pittsburgh Press, 1989, pp. 67–87. Reprinted in Meryll Dean, *Japanese Legal System: Text and Materials*, London, Cavendish Publishing, 1997.

"Constitutionalism and Rights in Japan and Korea," in Louis Henkin & Albert Rosenthal (eds.), *Constitutionalism and Rights: The Influence of the United States Constitution Abroad*, New York, Columbia University Press, 1990, pp. 225–259.

"The United States-Japan Partnership: The Wave of the Present," *Vital Speeches of the Day*, January 1, 1989, pp. 167–170. Reprinted in Robert E. Long (ed.), *Japan and the United States*, New York, H.W. Wilson, 1990, pp. 107–117.

"Epilog: Comparative Perspectives on Human Rights in Korea," in William Shaw (ed.), *Human Rights in Korea: Historical and Policy Perspectives*, Cambridge, Council on East Asian Studies Publications/East Asian Legal Studies Program, Harvard University, 1991, pp. 265–282, 333–335.

"The Influence of American Constitutionalism in Asia," in George A. Billias (ed.), *American Constitutionalism Abroad*, Westport, Connecticut, Greenwood Press, 1990, pp. 113–141.

"Freedom of Expression: The Continuing Revolution," *Law and Contemporary Problems*, School of Law, Duke University, Vol. 53, No. 2, 1990, pp. 39–69. Reprinted as *Freedom of Expression: Continuing Revolution in Japan's Legal Culture, Occasional Papers/Reprint Series in Contemporary Asian Studies*, No. 2, 1991.

With John Wahlke et al., "Political Science," *Reports from the Fields: Liberal Learning and the Arts and Sciences Major*, Washington, DC, Association of American Colleges, 1990, pp. 131–149. Another version is "Liberal Learning and the Political Science Major," *PS: Political Science and Politics*, American Political Science Association, March 1991, pp. 48–60.

"Constitutionalism in Late 20th-Century Asia: Guidelines and Trends," in Yoichi Higuchi et al. (eds.), *Kempogaku no Tembo: Kobayashi Naoki Sensei Koki Shukuga* (*An Overview of Constitutional Studies, in Celebration of Professor Naoki Kobayashi's Seventieth Birthday*), Tokyo, Yuhikaku Publishing Col., 1991, pp. 824–846.

"Response to the 'Forum on Universalism and Relativism in Asian Studies'," *Journal of Asian Studies*, Vol. 50, No. 4, 1991, pp. 874–876, invited article on "Law as Relational."

"Introduction: Constitutionalism in Asia and the United States" (pp. 1–52), "Japan's Constitutional System" (pp. 175–223), and "Conclusion: Towards Human Rights Constitutionalism in Asia and the United States?" (pp. 707–718) in Lawrence W. Beer (ed.), *Constitutional Systems in Late Twentieth-Century Asia*, 1992. (See Books.)

"Legal System", *Japan: An Illustrated Encyclopedia*, Tokyo & New York, Kodansha Publishers, 1993, Vol. 1, p. 884, and related topics in both volumes.

"Freedom of Expression: The Continuing Revolution," in Percy R. Luney & Kazuyuki Takahashi (eds.), *Japanese Constitutional Law*, Tokyo, University of Tokyo Press, 1993, pp. 221–254. Reprinted in Kenneth L. Port (ed.), *Comparative Law: Law and Legal Process in Japan*, Durham, Carolina Academic Press, 1996, pp. 212–227.

"Japan" entries in Article 19 (ed.), *The Article 19 Freedom of Expression Manual: International and Comparative Law, Standards and Procedures*, London, Article 19 International Centre against Censorship, 1993, pp. 38. 73, 136–137, 159–160, 166–167, 185, 210–211.

"Censorship (*ken-etsu*) and Nationalism in Japan," in James Huffman & F. Kawashima (eds.), *Modern Japan: An Encyclopedia of History, Culture, and Nationalism*, New York, Garland Press, 1998, pp. 26–29.

"The Judiciary," in Richard Bowring & Peter Kornicki (eds.), *The Cambridge Encyclopedia of Japan*, Cambridge, United Kingdom, Cambridge University Press, 1993, pp. 293–298.

"Current Human Rights Issues in Asia," *Vital Speeches of the Day*, June 1, 1995, pp. 506–509. Revised version, *Occasional Paper No. 1*, Center for Democracy and Social Change, Lehigh University, 1996, 17 pp.

With Sandra Coliver et al., *The Johannesburg Principles on National Security, Freedom of Expression and Access to Information*, Article 19, the International Centre against Censorship, October, 1996.

"Cecilia Munoz Palma" and "Margaret A. Somerville," in Rebecca Mae Salokar & Mary L. Volcansek (eds.), *Women in Law: A Bio-Bibliographical Sourcebook*, Westport, Connecticut, Greenwood Press, 1996, pp. 231–236, 292–298.

"The Constitution of Japan, at the Founding and 50 Years Later," *1996 Yearbook of the New Zealand Association of Comparative Law/Victoria University Law Review*, Wellington, New Zealand, 1997, pp. 15–24. Reprinted, with a summation in French, in 3 *Revue Juridique Polynessienne*, Banque Socrado, 1997, pp. 1–12.

"Human Rights Theory and 'Freedom Culture' in Eastern Asia," in Antony Anghie & Garry Sturgess (eds.), *Legal Visions of the 21st Century: Essays in Honour of Judge Christopher Weeramantry*, The Hague, Netherlands, Kluwer Law International, 1998, pp. 145–165.

"Peace in Theory and Practice under Article 9 of Japan's Constitution," *Marquette Law Review*, Law School, Marquette University, Vol. 81, 1998, pp. 815–830.

"National Security and Freedom of Expression in Japan," in Sandra Coliver et al. (eds.), *Secrecy and Liberty: National Security, Freedom of Expression and Access to Information*, The Hague, Netherlands, Martinus Nijhoff Publishers, 1999, pp. 349–360.

"Rejection of War: Japan's Constitutional Discourse and Performance," *Vital Speeches of the Day*, January 1, 2004, pp. 175–178.

"The Constitution of Japan in 2004: "Pacifism" and Mass Media Freedom," in Daniel Foote (ed.), *Law in Japan: A Turning Point*, Seattle, University of Washington Press, 2007, pp. 257–275.

"National Security and Mass Media Freedom," in Hiroshi Itoh (ed.), *The Impact of Globalization on Japan's Public Policy*, Lewiston, NY, The Edwin Mellen Press, 2008, pp. 193–208.

C. PUBLICATIONS IN JAPANESE (JAPANESE NAMES ARE GIVEN IN THE JAPANESE NAME ORDER, SURNAME FIRST)

With Ito Masami et al., "*Keiji shiho to hodo no jiyu*" (Criminal Justice and Freedom of Information), *Jurisuto* (The Jurist), Tokyo, Yuhikaku Publishing Co., No. 439, December 1969, pp. 15–24.

With Kobayashi Naoki et al., "*Shimin no naka no saibankan*" (The Judges and the Public), *Hogaku Seminah* (Law Seminar), Nihon Hyoronsha Publishing Co., February, 1971, pp. 169–181.

"*Nihon ni okeru masu komi to hyogen no jiyu*" (Mass Communications and Freedom of Expression in Japan), *Amerika Ho* (Law in America), Japan Branch, Japanese American Society for Legal Studies, University of Tokyo Press, No. 2, 1970, pp. 173–186.

"*Watakushi to Nihonkoku Kempo*" (The Constitution of Japan and I), *Jurisuto*, No. 600, November 1975, pp. 45–46.

"*Miyazawa Toshiyoshi sensei no koto o omou ichishosei*" (One Student's Remembrance of Professor Miyazawa Toshiyoshi), *Jurisuto*, No. 684, February 16, 1979, pp. 11–12; trans., Tomatsu Hidenori.

"*Nihon no saibankan*" (The Judges of Japan), *Jurisuto*, No. 700, September 15, 1979, pp. 306–316; trans. Takahashi I.

"*Hikaku kempo kenkyu no mondaiten*" (Some Problems in the Comparative Study of Constitutional Law), *Gakujutsu Kokusai Koryu Sanko Shiryoshu* (Reference Materials for International Scholarly Exchange), Tokyo, Meiji University, No. 51, August, 1979, 24 pp.

"*Ho no moto no jiyu ni kansuru hikaku kenkyu: hitotsu no chobunkateki shiron*" (Comparative Study of Freedom under Law: A Transcultural Approach), in Tanaka Hideo (ed.), *Eibeiho no Shoso*, University of Tokyo Press, 1980, pp. 147–190; trans. Tajima Yutaka.

"*Kanryo, kirisutokyo to hyogen no jiyu*" (Tolerance, Christianity, and Freedom of Expression), in Uchikawa Yoshimi & Moriizumi Akira (eds.), *Ho to Janarizumu* (Law and Journalism), Tokyo, Gakuyo Shobo Publishing Co., 1983, pp. 283–293.

"*Nichibei ryokoku ni okeru hyogen no jiyu to ho: saikin no jirei o chushin ni*" (Freedom of Expression in Japan and the United States: Some Recent Issues), *Jurisuto*, No. 881, April 1, 1987, pp. 102–108; trans. Shimizu Hideo & Oishi T.

"*Nihonkoku kempo oyobi kempogaku: Amerika no kenkyusha ni yoru kosatsu*" (Constitutional Studies and the Constitution of Japan: Reflections of an American Colleague), *Jurisuto*, a Symposium on the 40th Anniversary of the Constitution, No. 884, May 3, 1987, pp. 59–70; trans. Endo H.

"*Nihonkoku Kempo to tomo ni 40nen: rekishi no omosa to shorai no yume*" (Forty Years with the Constitution of Japan: The Weight of History and Dreams for the Future), *Hogaku Seminah* (Law Seminar), Vol. 32, No. 7, July, 1987, pp. 14–18; trans. Shimizu Hideo, Oishi T., Sonobe Itsuo, & Keiko Beer.

With others, "*Gaikokujin ga mita Sapporo, Hokkaido*" (Sapporo and Hokkaido in Foreign Eyes), *Gekkan Dan* (The Dan Monthly), Sapporo, Hokkaido Shimbunsha, January 1987, pp. 34–39.

"*Futatsu no bunka: futatsu no kempo*" (Two Cultures, Two Constitutions: Japan and the U.S.), *Sophia*, Tokyo, Sophia University, Vol. 36, No. 4, Winter 1987, pp. 74–88.

"*Ajia ni okeru Gasshukoku rikkenshugi no eikyo*" (The Influence of United States Constitutionalism in Asia), *Trends*, Tokyo, U.S.I.S., December 1987, 73–77.

"*Shai no hyomei: Nihonho ni kansuru hogaku korekushyon kizo ni atatte*" (An Essay of Thanks to Japan's Jurists for the Japanese Law Collection), *Jurisuto*, No. 996, March 1, 1992, pp. 2–3.

"*Nihonkoku Kempo no 50nen*" (Fifty Years with the Constitution of Japan), *Jiyu to Seigi* (Freedom and Justice), Tokyo, Japan Federation of Bar Associations, Vol. 47, No. 5, May 1996, pp. 14–25.

"*Nihon no kokusai kyoryoku to kempo*" (Japan's International Cooperation and the Constitution of Japan), *Shakai Seigi* (Social Justice), Tokyo, Sophia University, Vol. 17, 1998, pp. 23–34. Reprinted in Yamada Keizo et al. (eds.), *Kokusai Kyoryoku to Nihonkoku Kempo: 21 Seiki e no Nihon no Sentaku* (International Cooperation and the Constitution of Japan: Choices for Japan in the 21st Century), Tokyo, Institute for the Study of Social Justice, Sophia University & Social Science Research Institute, International Christian University, 1998, pp. 3–20.

D. PUBLICATIONS IN KOREAN

"Constitutionalism and the American Influence in Asia," *Jukan Chosun* (The Korea Weekly), Seoul, South Korea, No. 708, September 12, 1982, pp. 5–10. A speech presented at the Korean Legal Center.

With Dae-Kwon Choi, "Constitutional Politics in China and Asia," *Shin Dong A* (New East Asia), Seoul, October 1982, pp. 240–247.

E. BOOK REVIEWS

The American Journal of Comparative Law, The American Political Science Review, The Journal of Asian History, The Journal of Asian Studies, The Journal of Politics, Monumenta Nipponica, Pacific Affairs, Human Rights Quarterly.

Index

⌘

Where no specific country appears in an index entry, Japan should be assumed.

www.ingramcontent.com/pod-product-compliance
Lightning Source LLC
LaVergne TN
LVHW052251200926
848481LV00002B/332